GERMANY AND THE SOVIET UNION
1939—1941

STUDIEN ZUR GESCHICHTE OSTEUROPAS
STUDIES IN EAST EUROPEAN HISTORY
ÉTUDES D'HISTOIRE DE L'EUROPE ORIENTALE

HERAUSGEGEBEN VON / EDITED BY / ÉDITÉ PAR

W. PHILIPP
Freie Universität Berlin

P. SCHEIBERT
Universität Köln

UNTER MITARBEIT VON / IN COLLABORATION WITH / AVEC LE CONCOURS DE

A. M. AMMANN S.J.
Pontificio Istituto Orientale
Roma

F. T. EPSTEIN
Library of Congress
Washington, D.C.

M. KARPOVICH
Harvard University
Cambridge, Mass.

Redaktionssekretär / Secretary of the Editorial Board / Secrétaire de la Rédaction
Dr. P. SCHEIBERT, Bad Godesberg, Viktoria Strasse 38

I

GERHARD L. WEINBERG
GERMANY AND THE SOVIET UNION 1939–1941

LEIDEN
E. J. BRILL
1972

GERMANY
AND THE SOVIET UNION
1939-1941

BY

GERHARD L. WEINBERG

LEIDEN
E. J. BRILL
1972

The quotations herein from the Diary of General Franz Halder are made with the permission of the Attorney General of the United States under License JA-1645.

The quotation from *The Gathering Storm*, by Winston Churchill, is reprinted with permission of the Houghton Mifflin Co.

The quotations from *Soviet Russia's Foreign Policy 1939-1942*, by David Dallin, are reprinted with the permission of the Yale University Press.

First edition 1954
Reprinted 1972

PREFACE TO THE FIRST PRINTING

An attempt is made in this study to bring together material on one of the most interesting, important, and controversial episodes of recent history—the period of the Soviet-German Non-Aggression Pact of 1939. An examination of recently published materials and the large collections of documents gathered by the prosecution and defense for the Nuremberg trials has produced such an amount of evidence concerning German-Soviet relations in the period from 1939 to 1941 as to warrant a presentation of the course of events in that period in the form of a chronological survey.

It should be noted that in the account of the events leading up to the signing of the Pact, generally available evidence and episodes previously analyzed by several competent historians have not been treated at such length as has the later period for which much of the relevant documentation has hitherto remained unknown.

The free and complete access accorded the writer by the Law School of the University of Chicago to its vast collection of documents, transcripts, and other materials from Nuremberg has made this work possible. The large number of unpublished documents cited throughout the text indicates that the search through these mountains of paper, though tedious, is rewarding. The Divisions of Manuscripts and Aeronautics of the Library of Congress have kindly permitted access to some interesting German documents in their custody.

Many thanks are due to Dr. Hans Rothfels under whose guidance most of the research was done, to Dr. George B. Carson and Dr. S. William Halperin who followed the writing of the text with the greatest care, and to Dr. Fritz T. Epstein whose detailed examination led to many improvements.

GERHARD L. WEINBERG

Washington, D.C.
January, 1953.

PREFACE TO THE SECOND PRINTING

During the nearly two decades since the appearance of the first printing, a number of important new sources for the period covered by this book have become available. The continued publication of the collections of German and Italian foreign office documents; the appearance of an analogous Hungarian series; the opening of German, American, British, and Japanese archives; and the steady stream of articles and monographs have all enriched our knowledge of those years. Various re-evaluations of the past within the Soviet Union have brought to light some documents, important memoirs, and a considerable serious secondary literature, much of it dealing with the exceedingly controversial subject of Soviet preparation and readiness — or lack of both — for the German invasion of June, 1941.[1])

If this book still has any usefulness in the fase of such developments, two factors may be responsible. First, the new sources have in many cases provided added detail rather than substantial alteration. Even where corrections are needed, these affect minor matters while leaving the main theses unaffected. Thus the appearance of Volume VI of Series D of the *Documents on German Foreign Policy* makes possible a correction in the date of a crucial meeting between the German and Soviet trade negotiators, Karl Schnurre and Eugene Babarin, from July 22, 1939, as deduced in this book (p. 37) on the basis of an erroneous translation in the Tokyo War Crimes Trial collection, to July 18, 1939. As for the basic policy issue, however, this correction only gives added support to the assertion (p. 38) "that the Soviet decision to resume formal economic negotiations must have been made before the news of the Hudson-Wohlthat talks were published on July 22, and in all probability before the talks took place on July 20." The more accurate dating now possible should finally demolish the thesis that the Hudson-Wohlthat episode led the Soviet government to move toward Germany.

A second factor to be noted is the development of the secondary literature on the subject of this book. The thesis that Hitler made his decision to attack the Soviet Union in the summer of 1940 produced a scholarly controversy,[2]) but the serious scholar involved in that exchange, Andreas Hillgruber, largely abandoned his earlier position and moved toward the one argued in this book in his own more recent thoughtful study of Hitler's policy.[3]) Neither of the books published since 1954 on the subject of this work is particularly pursuasive. Phillip W. Fabry's book, published in 1962, is too full of errors and distortions.[4]) Characteristic of his scholarship, to cite an example

---

[1]) The author summarized the then current state of the scholarly discussion of the subject in "Deutsch-sowjetischer Nichtangriffspakt," *Sowjetsystem und demokratische Gesellschaft, Eine vergleichende Enzyklopädie* (Freiburg: Herder, 1966), cc. 1177-87, which also contains a bibliography.

[2]) See *Vierteljahrshefte für Zeitgeschichte*, I (1953), 301-18; II (1954), 240-54.

[3]) *Hitlers Strategie; Politik und Kriegführung, 1940-41* (Frankfurt/M: Bernard & Graefe, 1965).

[4]) *Der Hitler-Stalin-Pakt, 1939-1941, Ein Beitrag zur Methode sowjetischer Aussenpolitik* (Darmstadt: Fundus-Verlag, 1962). There is a detailed review by the author in *Jahrbücher für Geschichte Osteuropas*, XII (1964), 132-35, and a comparison of Fabry's book with the author's by Fritz T. Epstein in *Neue Politische Literatur*, VIII (1963), 337-42. Fabry's subsequent treatment of the subject, *Die Sowjetunion und das Dritte Reich, Eine dokumentierte Geschichte der deutsch-sowjetischen Beziehungen von 1933 bis 1941* (Stuttgart: Seewald, 1971), has not profited greatly from the criticism of his earlier work.

related to the controversy just mentioned, is his use of a letter by General Walter Warlimont as evidence against a decision by Hitler in the summer of 1940 and in support of a decision after the Molotov visit of November, 1940, when that letter in fact contains a full page of arguments which led Warlimont "to the conclusion that Hitler made his firm decision to attack Russia in the second half of July 1940."[5] The second volume of James E. McSherry's work on German and Soviet diplomacy is more useful because of its summarization of the published documents, but leaves much to be desired in analysis and interpretation.[6] A comprehensive new study of the relationship between Germany and the Soviet Union before and during their temporary alignment with each other would be welcome indeed, but remains to be written.

If one were to recast major aspects of this book in the light of new material, it might be in terms of broad perspectives rather than specific detail. Our understanding of the ideological preconceptions governing Hitler's foreign policy, assisted by the discovery of his second book,[7] would suggest greater stress on Hitler's predisposition to launch a war on the Soviet Union, in the face of which the decision of July, 1940, assumes a somewhat different appearance. On the other hand, the willingness of Stalin to come to an agreement with Hitler in previous years and the failure of those hopes because of the latter's disinterest at the time — now more clearly documented than in the earlier literature — places the ability of the two dictators to reach an accomodation in 1939 in a different light also.[8] Within its self-defined limits as a chronological survey, however, the account now reprinted may still be useful to those interested in one of the more fascinating episodes in the history of this century.

October, 1971

---

[5] Walter Warlimont to Andreas Hillgruber, October 12, 1954; copy in Institut für Zeitgeschichte, Munich, under Z.S. 312.

[6] *Stalin, Hitler, and Europe*, Vol. II, *The Imbalance of Power, 1939-1941* (Cleveland: World Publ. Co., 1970).

[7] Gerhard L. Weinberg (ed.), *Hitlers zweites Buch, Ein Dokument aus dem Jahr 1928* (Stuttgart: Deutsche Verlags-Anstalt, 1961).

[8] The author has dealt with this in *The Foreign Policy of Hitler's Germany, Diplomatic Revolution in Europe, 1933-1936* (Chicago: University of Chicago Press, 1970), esp. pp. 220-23, 310-12.

INHALT — CONTENTS — SOMMAIRE

Preface to the First Printing v
Preface to the Second Printing v
Introduction 1
   I. From Munich to the March on Prague 4
  II. March 15,—May 31, 1939 14
 III. June 1,—August 13, 1939: the Basis for the Pact . . 33
 IV. August 14,—September 28, 1939: the German-Soviet
     Agreements 41
  V. From the Peace Offensive to the Attack in the West . 62
     A. The Peace Offensive 62
     B. Economic Cooperation 65
     C. Naval Cooperation 75
     D. The Soviet-Finnish War 85
     E. German-Soviet Cooperation and the Axis . . . 91
  VI. From the Attack on Norway to July 19, 1940 . . . 97
 VII. July 20,—August 27, 1940 106
VIII. Finland, Rumania, and the Danube 125
  IX. From the Tripartite Pact to the End of 1940 . . . 135
   X. From the Bulgarian Crisis to the Yugoslav Coup . . 148
  XI. From the Soviet-Japanese Pact to the German Attack
     on Russia 159
Conclusions 169
Appendixes
   I. Germany and the Soviet Blockade of Finland . . . 174
  II. The Abwehr Order of September 6, 1940 176
 III. Concealment of German Intentions 178
 IV. The attack on Soviet-Russia and the Invasion of Crete . 180
Bibliography 183
Abbreviations and Technical terms 209
Index 211

INTRODUCTION

The relations between Germany and Soviet Russia in the years 1939
to 1941 were of great significance within the changing world picture
of that period. They are related here largely on the basis of German
sources. There are, of course, the foreign policy speeches of Stalin and
Molotov, the communiqués and notes published in the Soviet press,
and the Soviet notes and memoranda given to the Germans. There
are also the actions of the Soviets themselves; but these, as well as
the talks of Soviet diplomats with German officials, come to us
mainly through the accounts of others.

On the other hand, the available documentation from the German
side is very extensive. Many very important documents were published
in 1948 by the United States Department of State[1]). Others are
to be found in the published record of the main trial at Nuremberg[2]).
A very large number of relevant documents were included among
those collected by the prosecution and defense for the main trial and
the subsequent proceedings at Nuremberg. These include many military and economic documents as well as those of a strictly diplomatic
nature. The former are often more reliable than the latter as they
generally deal with very practical issues like trade transactions and
troop movements—matters which need to be recorded accurately. In
order that the citations to these documents can be understood, a list
of the technical terms and abbreviations has been appended to this
work.

An important source of information has been the testimony of
witnesses and defendants at the war crimes trials. This material must,
of course, be used with even greater caution than the documents. In
the case of trial testimony, there is no substitute for a separate evalu-
ation of every single statement made. When only the testimony of a
defendant or witness is cited for some point, a careful check on the

---

[1]) United States, Department of State, *Nazi-Soviet Relations, 1939-1941* (Washington, D.C., 1948) (cited hereafter as *NSR*). Die Beziehungen zwischen dem
nationalsozialistischen Deutschland und der Sowjetunion (Washington, D.C.). (Cited
hereafter as *B.D.S.*).

[2]) International Military Tribunal, *Trial of the Major War Criminals* (42 vols.;
Nuremberg: 1947-49) (cited hereafter as *TMWC*). Der Prozess gegen die Hauptkrieg-
verbrecher vor dem Internationalen Militärgerichtshof. Nürnberg 1947-49 (cited
hereafter as *PHKV*). The volumes including the documents are identical, so that the
citation of the English edition covers the German as well.

reliability of the testimony offered has been made. Where testimony is cited along with other material, this is done for purposes of elucidation and comparison; sometimes the testimony clarifies a document, sometimes it is clearly contradicted by the documents, sometimes conflicting testimony by several men provides some insight into the events described.

Throughout the text there are discussions of the reliability of some of the evidence, gaps in the publications, and other aspects of the sources used. It might be said by way of summary that the available German material taken as a whole contains sufficient reliable evidence so that a coherent account can be pieced together.

This leaves the problem of the presentation of relations between two countries based primarily on sources from one of them. This unfortunate disadvantage is not, in this case, very likely to be remedied for some time. The choice is between the fullest use of German material and avoidance of the subject altogether. The adoption of the first alternative is considerably eased by the fact that during the period from 1939 to 1941 the dynamic element in German-Soviet relations is provided by Germany, while Soviet policy is essentially a reactive one which attempts to make the best of opportunities offered and avert the worst of the threatening dangers. Though this does not affect the difficulty of an understanding of the long-term aims and principles of Soviet policy, it does provide a useful opportunity for study of the short-term workings of Russian diplomacy. As long as the documentation comes from only one country, it is at least fortunate that it comes from the one which was, so to speak, setting the pace.

It must not be assumed, however, that there are not large gaps even in the German material. At various places significant omissions from the State Department's publication will be noted. The files of some of the German consulates in the Soviet Union might be helpful. There are as yet vast gaps in the documentation on the extremely important field of economic relations between Germany and Russia. Little has come to light about the activities of the German Communist party in this period. The continued systematic publication of the German and English foreign office documents will be of considerable help[3]). It is to be hoped that the captured German diplomatic, economic, and military files will be opened to scholars in the not too distant future. Perhaps some day at least a few of the Soviet documents will be released.

---

[3]) For a critique of the relevant chapter in the first volume of German documents for the period 1939-41, see the author's note "The Chapter on Russo-German Relations in Volume IV of *Documents on German Foreign Policy, 1918-1945*," *Journal of Central European Affairs*, XII (1952), 70-74.

Finally, it should be pointed out that an effort has been made in this work to restrict the narrative to a straightforward account of German-Soviet relations; larger issues have generally been avoided. While this may have the disadvantage of lessening the perspective, it does result in heavier emphasis on the specific events which the reader must then interpret for himself.[4]

---

[4]) The second volume of the study of American diplomacy in the world crisis by William L. Langer and S. Everett Gleason, *The Undeclared War, 1940-1941*, appeared too late for consideration in this study. While some additional details are contained in the second volume, no substantive changes in the account presented here appear to be required.

CHAPTER ONE

FROM MUNICH TO THE MARCH ON PRAGUE

The Munich agreement opened a new period in European diplomacy. The action of the Western Powers at Munich and the alleged willingness and ability of the Russians to help Czechoslovakia will not be examined here. Whatever the causes and character of the Munich agreement, its results are fairly clear, and it is these which must be examined.

It might be said that the immediate effect of Munich on Europe was a general disruption of the existing order. The claims of Hungary and Poland on Czechoslovakia, the complicated maneuvers concerning the Carpatho-Ukraine, the collapse of the Little Entente, the failure of the French system of alliances, the obvious openings for further German advances—all these were signs of disruption.

What were to be the policies of the major powers under these circumstances? The following is a brief survey which may serve to indicate the general trends of the period.

Britain and France continued to steer fitfully along the path of appeasement for several months. This can be most readily understood from a reading of the recently published record of the Anglo-French conversations in Paris on November 24, 1938[1]). In spite of some objections from French Prime Minister Daladier, to say nothing of the clear meaning of the promises made to the Czechs, the British insisted that no guarantee be given to Czechoslovakia which might involve Britain and France in a war in defense of that country were Germany to attack it[2]). Then as always, French Foreign Minister Bonnet was the great advocate of concessions to Germany. By the time British Prime Minister Chamberlain and Foreign Secretary Halifax were in Paris on January 10, 1939, on their way to Rome, the French had come to agree to the British position on the guarantee[3]). To some extent the British attitude had stiffened by

---

[1]) E. L. Woodward and Rohan Butler (eds.), *Documents on British Foreign Policy, 1919-1939*, third series (hereafter cited as *BD*): Vol. III, *1938-39* (London, 1950), pp. 285-311.

[2]) *Ibid.*, pp. 302-05.

[3]) Memorandum of Phipps, 10 January 1939, *ibid.*, p. 515.

then as evidenced by the warnings to Mussolini concerning the possible effects of further German aggression eastwards[4]).

This stiffening of British policy becomes very clear with the rumors of German designs on Holland. By February 7, 1939, the British government had decided, after detailed consultation with France, that they would go to war if Holland or Switzerland were attacked by Germany[5]). The seriousness of the international situation was becoming more fully appreciated in England; a fact which must be kept in mind if the British actions after March 15 are to be understood[6]).

The policy of Germany was characterized by three main themes. The first concerned Czechoslovakia. Hitler had planned to annex *all* of Czechoslovakia from the very beginning and had merely been using the Sudeten question as a useful means toward the complete annexation of Czechoslovakia, whose population problem he viewed not as one of detaching areas populated by Germans, but as one of expelling millions of Czechs from their homeland. Munich had thwarted this aim, robbed him of his pretext, and left him looking around angrily for another approach[7]). Hitler therefore decided to take over the rest of Czechoslovakia at the earliest opportunity and arranged for a variety of schemes to be worked out inside that country which should provide the necessary pretexts at the appropriate moment[8]). No action on the part of the Czechs could stave off annexation; a

---

[4]) Chamberlain-Mussolini Conversation, 12 January 1939, *ibid.,* p. 525; cf. Memorandum of Chamberlain, 13 January 1939, *ibid.,* p. 529. It is interesting to note that the information on these talks received by the Soviets was interpreted by them to show that the English were trying to promote German expansion eastwards. Mario Toscano, *L'Italia e gli accordi Tedesco-Sovietici dell'Agosto 1939* (Florence, 1952), pp. 8, 13-21.

[5]) Halifax to Mallet, 7 February 1939, *BD,* IV, 83; see also *ibid.,* pp. 16-83, *passim.*

[6]) The invitation to Polish Foreign Minister Beck to come to England dates from this period. See also the statement that the British government had received reports "pointing to the possibility of a military occupation of Czecho-Slovakia (Halifax to Lindsay, 27 February 1939, *ibid.,* p. 160)."

[7]) This summary of German policy toward Czechoslovakia may seem rather sweeping in its implications but is fully substantiated by the documents. Memorandum of Hossbach, 10 November 1937, 386 - PS, *TMWC,* XXV, 410; Hitler-Henlein Conversation, 28 March 1938, United States, Department of State, *Akten zur Deutschen Auswärtigen Politik, 1918-1945,* Series D, Vol. II, *Deutschland und die Tschechoslovakei, 1937-1938* (Baden-Baden, 1950), p. 158; Erich Kordt, *Wahn und Wirklichkeit* (Stuttgart, 1948), pp. 135, 137.

[8]) Keitel to Schmundt, 11 October 1938, 388-PS, *TMWC,* XXV, 520; Germany, Oberste Befehlshaber der Wehrmacht, OKW, L, Ia, "236/38," 21 October 1938, C-136, *TMWC,* XXXIV, 477-81; Germany, OKW, WFA, L, Ia, "248/38," 17 December 1938, C - 138, *TMWC,* XXXXIV, 483-84; for an account of the German machinations inside Czechoslovakia, see Walther Hagen (pseud. for Wilhelm Höttl), *Die geheime Front* (Linz, 1950), pp. 166-78, 180-86.

secret Czech attempt to settle all outstanding issues by giving in all along the line and even inviting a representative of the German Government to sit on their cabinet failed when the Germans refused even to see the Czech emissary[9]).

The second line of policy concerned Poland. That country was now at the top of the list. The next in Hitler's series of "final demands" was served on the Polish Ambassador on October 24, 1938, and was repeated and elaborated in the usual manner until the outbreak of war[10]). In this case also the presence of Germans inside Poland was to be used as a pretext for demands leading to the destruction of that country.

The third line of policy was the attempt to secure a three power military alliance including Germany, Italy, and Japan. This project had first been discussed in the summer of 1938; it seemed to be making great strides, particularly when the strongly pro-German Japanese Military Attaché Hiroshi Oshima became ambassador in October, 1938[11]). This aspect will be considered further in the next chapter.

These three themes of German foreign policy, and especially the first two, provide the dynamic elements in the world situation of 1939. The repercussions from Germany's pursuit of the first two, and the failure of the third, were to contribute largely to the changed German attitude toward the Soviet Union.

For Soviet Russia, Munich marked the final collapse of the policy pursued by Foreign Commissar Litvinov of securing a common front of Russia with the Western Powers against Germany. Whatever the motives and sincerity of that policy, after Munich it could hardly continue to play any substantial role in Soviet eyes. After Litvinov saw Bonnet on October 1, the latter described him to the British ambassador as "highly incensed at recent events"[12]). On Litvinov's return to Moscow, there were undoubtedly long discussions of what the Soviet Union should do next in the field of foreign policy. The

---

[9]) Memorandum of Altenburg, 1 March 1939, United States Department of State, *Documents on German Foreign Policy 1918-1945*, Series D, (Washington, 1948-) (hereafter cited as *GD*), IV, 221-24 (see also notes 1 and 6 to this document); Memorandum of Weizsäcker, 3 March 1939, *ibid.*, p. 225; Memorandum of Altenburg, 9 March 1939, *ibid.*, p. 232; for additional details see Hagen, pp. 166-69.

[10]) Lipski to Beck, 25 October 1938, Poland, *Weissbuch der Polnischen Regierung* (Basel, 1939), pp. 62-63; Memorandum of Hewel, 24 October 1938, Germany, Auswärtiges Amt, *Dokumente zur Vorgeschichte des Krieges (Weissbuch 2)* (Basel, 1940), pp. 217-19 (the complete text is given as No. 81 in *GD* V). See also Jean Szembek, *Journal 1933-1939* (Paris, 1952), p. 366.

[11]) See Herbert Feis, *The Road to Pearl Harbor* (Princeton, 1950), pp. 27-28.

[12]) Phipps to Halifax, 1 October 1938, *BD*, III, 67.

scope of these discussions probably included Litvinov's position as well as his policy[13]).

In the Soviet view of Europe, one problem clearly required some action. The Soviet attitude toward Poland's conduct in the Czech crisis had brought about great strain in Russo-Polish relations. As the Czech affair was over, the Russians probably believed that the continuance of the tension could only have the effect of pushing Poland into the arms of Germany. A restoration of the previous condition of suspicion and dislike, as contrasted with one of bitter tension, seemed desirable, and was accomplished by the joint Soviet-Polish communiqué of November 26 which was followed by a trade agreement in February of 1939.[14])

The more serious problem facing the Soviets was that of working out an over-all policy to secure and advance their interests in the new, post-Munich, Europe. The foreign policy of Soviet Russia in this period is most easily understood if it is viewed as one of looking over all possible foundations for a new approach to the new conditions. Such a process could certainly include a reexamination of the relations between Russia and Germany.[14a]) In this regard, the Russians may also have been thinking of interfering with the negotiations for the three power alliance which was certain to be directed against them.[15])

A further factor in the reorientation of Russian policy is a strong isolationist note. Whatever the real intentions of the Soviet Union might have been in the period before Munich, the explicit classification of the new war, which the Soviets believed would soon break out, as the Second Imperialist War — and as such one in which Russia might take no active part—signified a change from the earlier policy of stressing the willingness of the Soviet Union to aid those prepared to unite against Germany. This new attitude, expressed by Stalin and Molotov at the anniversary of the Bolshevik Revolution in November, 1938, was noted with care by British and German diplomats.[16])

---

[13]) See the very interesting discussion of Litvinov's position under the new circumstances after Munich in Chilston to Halifax, 18 October 1938, *BD*, III, 192-93. For the German speculations on the same subject, see Tippelskirch to Schliep, 3 October 1938, *GD*, IV, 603; Tippelskirch to Schliep, 10 October 1938, *ibid.*, p. 605.

[14]) Poland, pp. 234, 235; cf. Kennard to Halifax, 23 September 1938, *BD*, III, 24; Kennard to Halifax, 27 November 1938, *ibid.*, p. 364-65; Kennard to Halifax, 9 December 1938, *ibid.*, p. 419; Halifax to Kennard, 14 December 1938, *ibid.*, p. 430; Kennard to Cadogan, 22 April 1939, *BD*, V, 283. See also Nos. 105, 106, 108 in *GD, V*.

[14a]) Italy, Ministero degli Affari Esteri, "U.R.S.S., Situazione politica nel 1938," p. 7 (U.S. National Archives, Italian Documents, Reel 1291).

[15]) For Russian knowledge of the negotiations see Chilston to Halifax, 19 November 1938, *BD*, III, 280.

[16]) Schulenburg to Ribbentrop, 18 November 1938, *GD*, IV, 609-10 (another

The materials for the study of Russo-German relations in the period from Munich to March 15, 1939, are still fragmentary. The problem of the Carpatho-Ukraine, which attracted great publicity at the time and is dealt with at length in the British and German documents, will not be gone into here as its complications require a separate and special study. The real significance of the question of the Carpatho-Ukraine in Soviet-German relations is still unclear; in any case, its importance seems to have been overestimated[17]). The hints of an understanding between Germany and Russia coming out of the Balkans at that time must not be overemphasized in terms of later developments[18]). There is, however, enough material for the presentation of a survey with indications of the gaps still to be filled. Such a survey will now be attempted.

The main topic of Russo-German negotiations in the period from October, 1938, to March, 1939, was their future economic relations. Early in 1938 there had been negotiations between the two countries for a large credit agreement, but this did not materialize.[19]) There had been only a trade and payments agreement, which was signed on March 1, 1938. It extended until the end of 1938 the economic agreement signed by Reichsbank President Schacht and Soviet Trade Delegate Kandelaki on December 24, 1936.[20]) At the beginning of October, 1938, the German Embassy in Moscow began to urge that the possibly more favorable attitude toward Germany on the part of the Soviet Union at that time be used to work out a "new and wider" economic agreement.[21])

---

important German report on the celebration has been omitted by the editors, see *ibid.*, p. 609, n. 1); British Embassy Moscow to the Foreign Office, 20 February 1939, *BD*, IV, 611-12.

[17]) For an excellent survey of the matter, see Vereker to Halifax, 10 January 1939, *BD*, III, 575-79.

[18]) For a hint from Rumania on November 30, 1938, see Cordell Hull, *The Memoirs of Cordell Hull* (New York, 1948), I, 655-56. For a hint from Bulgaria on December 16, 1938, see Ristelhueber to Bonnet, 16 December 1938, France, Ministère des affaires étrangères, *The French Yellow Book* (New York, 1940), pp. 45-46. See also Biddle to Hull, 26 November 1938, cited in William L. Langer and S. Everett Gleason, *The Challenge to Isolation, 1937-1940* (New York, 1952), p. 59 and n. 19; Kennedy to Hull, 17 February 1939, cited in Langer and Gleason, p. 60 and n. 23. Possibly supporting a different interpretation is the evidence in Robert Coulondre, *Von Moskau nach Berlin, 1936-1939*, trans. S. L. Sigwart (Bonn, 1950), pp. 238-50; Toscano, p. 11.

[19]) Memorandum of Wiehl, 4 November 1938, *GD*, IV, 608.

[20]) The text of the agreement of March 1, 1938, was omitted by the editors of Volume I of the *Documents on German Foreign Policy, 1918-1945*. A copy of the summary, sent by Schnurre of the German Foreign Office to the German missions abroad, can be found in the files of the German Embassy in China, now in the Manuscripts Division of the Library of Congress, in file "DW 2, Deutsch-Russische Verträge." A summary of the 1936 agreement (W IV, 11/37) is in the same file.

[21]) Tippelskirch to Schliep, 3 October 1938, *GD*, IV, 603-04; see also the letter

In a memorandum of October 26, 1938, the German Ambassador in Moscow, Count Werner von der Schulenburg, outlined his plan to use the impending negotiations for the extension of the trade and payments agreement through 1939 for "an attempt to reach a settlement of the questions disturbing German-Soviet relations." [22]) The first point in this settlement was to be a new credit agreement with the Soviet Union. Other points were of a minor character.[23]) Early in November, the Director of the Economic Policy Department of the German Foreign Ministry endorsed the suggestion of the Moscow Embassy in a memorandum for Ribbentrop.[24]) The German Foreign Minister must have given his approval; for a series of inter-ministerial conferences was held in Berlin, culminating in one of December 1, 1938, at which it was agreed "that on the occasion of these talks on the extension of the economic agreement [of March 1, 1938] we should sound out the Russians about a new credit on goods."[25])

These matters, internal to the German government, have been recounted in such detail since they show that in the economic negotiations of the winter 1938-39 the initiative came from the German side. It was the Germans who decided to go beyond a simple extension of the trade and payments agreement to a substantially expanded economic treaty. One must not overemphasize the importance of this fact, however, for the motivation of the Germans seems to have had an economic rather than a political character.[26])

In the middle of December, 1938, there must have been discussions between German and Russian economic negotiators in Berlin, as on December 19, 1938, an agreement was signed extending the trade and payments agreements through 1939.[27]) In these conversations the Germans presumably indicated their desire for further economic

---

of Tippelskirch to Schliep of October 10 (*ibid.*, p. 607), in which Tippelskirch states that the German Ambassador supports this view.

[22]) Memorandum of Schulenburg, 26 October 1938, *ibid.*, p. 607.

[23]) According to Erich Kordt, then chief of the office of the German foreign minister (Büro RAM), an agreement was reached in Moscow, in October, which provided that the German and Russian press would restrain their attacks on the leaders of the other country (Kordt, p. 157, n. 2). On this agreement, see also Gustav Hilger and Alfred Meyer, *The Incompatible Allies, German Soviet Relations 1918-1941* (New York, 1953), pp. 288-89.

[24]) Memorandum of Wiehl, 4 November 1938, *GD*, IV, 608-09.

[25]) Memorandum of Schnurre, 1 December 1938, *ibid.*, p. 614.

[26]) See especially Memorandum of Wiehl, 4 November 1938, *ibid.*, p. 608, and compare Memorandum of Kamphoevener, 10 December 1938, *ibid.*, p. 349; Woermann to Mackensen, 15 December 1938, *ibid.*, p. 350.

[27]) Germany, Auswärtiges Amt, *Vertrags-Verzeichnis seit 1920. Stand Oktober 1941* [Berlin, 1941(?)] (hereafter cited as *Vertrags-Verzeichnis*), Item 1792, p. 601. The renewal of the agreement and all negotiations concerning it were ignored by the editors of the *Documents on German Foreign Policy, 1918-1945*.

negotiations, for on December 22, 1938, a conference of Russian and German trade delegates was held in Berlin.[28]) At this conference the Germans broached their new proposals to Skossyrev, the Russian representative, who showed himself quite receptive. Of interest, in view of the events which followed, is the clearly expressed understanding on the part of the Soviet delegate that the negotiations would be held in Berlin.[29]) The Soviet Government's agreement in principle to the resumption of the credit negotiations broken off in March, 1938, was conveyed to Wiehl, the Director of the Economic Policy Department of the German Foreign Office, on January 11, 1939, by Merekalov, the Soviet Ambassador in Berlin.[30]) The Russians insisted, however, in spite of Wiehl's arguments to the contrary, that the negotiations this time be conducted in Moscow. Wiehl proposed to the Foreign Minister that in view of Germany's need for raw materials some concession to the Soviet request on this point would be necessary, and suggested that Schnurre, the chairman of the German economic delegation be sent to Moscow.[31]) Ribbentrop agreed, and on January 20, Wiehl informed Merekalov that while the credit talks would have to be concluded in Berlin, the Germans were willing to send Schnurre to Moscow for about ten days at the end of a stay in Warsaw. Schnurre would pave the way for the actual signing of the agreement in Berlin.[32]) Merekalov was pleased by the German concession and said that he would recommend agreement by the Soviet Union to this proposal.

In view of subsequent events, the Soviet government must have approved the plan. In the last days of January, 1939, Ribbentrop himself was in Warsaw to confer with Polish Foreign Minister Beck; while Schnurre, who was conducting some economic negotiations with the Poles, was there also, and was planning to accompany the German Ambassador Schulenburg on to Moscow on January 30.

While Schnurre and Ribbentrop were in Warsaw, the latter was surprised by exaggerated statements concerning Schnurre's proposed visit to Moscow which appeared in the French press, and therefore cancelled that trip.[33]) The German Embassy in Moscow was in-

---

[28]) Memorandum of Hilger, 23 December 1938, *GD*, IV, 615-18.

[29]) *Ibid.*, p. 617.

[30]) Memorandum of Wiehl, 11 January 1939, *ibid.*, pp. 618-20. The date of November 1 given in the memorandum (p. 618) is clearly a mistake; the correct date is derived from Wiehl's memorandum of 12 January 1939 (*Ibid.*, p. 620).

[31]) Memorandum of Wiehl, 12 January 1939, *ibid.*, p. 621.

[32]) Memorandum of Wiehl, 20 January 1939, *ibid.*, pp. 621-22.

[33]) This incident remains unclear in spite of the evidence now available: Wiehl to Schulenburg, 28 January 1939, *ibid.*, p. 622; Schulenburg to Weizsäcker, 6 February 1939, *ibid.*, p. 623; Memorandum of Wiehl, 6 February 1939, *ibid.*, pp. 625-26; Weizsäcker to Schulenburg, 15 February 1939, *ibid.*, p. 627 (not a single document

structed to conduct the negotiations with Soviet Commissar for Foreign Trade Mikoyan without Schnurre.[34]) These negotiations started on February 10, 1939 and continued for some time thereafter.[35]) The progress of the conversations was once again set back at the beginning of March by what was practically a reversal of the German attitude; the difficulty of delivering the goods desired by Russia being the cause of the reversal.[36]) The negotiations seem to have expired in February or March, 1939, without any agreement being reached.[37])

Two repercussions of these negotiations must be noted: one on England, and one on Soviet-German relations. The British government had been informed beforehand about Schnurre's intended journey to Moscow by the German,[38]) Polish,[39]) and Soviet [40]) governments. The British thus knew of the Soviet-German economic negotiations and followed their development with great interest.[41]) Bringing the fact of these economic negotiations together with the absence of any attack on the Soviet Union in Hitler's speech of January 30, 1939,

---

on this subject from Ribbentrop or his official staff then in Warsaw has been published). See also the account in Peter Kleist, *Zwischen Hitler und Stalin, 1939-1945* (Bonn, 1950) pp. 20-21 (the reference to the London *Daily Mail* in this account is not correct); and Testimony of Schnurre, United States Military Tribunal IV, "United States v. Ernst von Weizsäcker *et alii*, "Transcript of Proceedings" (Nuremberg, 1947-49) (hereafter cited as U.S. v. Weizsäcker), German Transcript Page (hereafter cited as G.T.) 19154.

[34]) Schulenburg to Weizsäcker, 6 February 1939, *G.D.*, IV, p. 623; Memorandum of Wiehl, 6 February 1939, *ibid.*, p. 625. The new instructions are not printed; they were presumably contained in Berlin No. 12 of 4 February 1939 which has not been found (Note 1 to Schulenburg to Ribbentrop, 10 February 1939, *ibid.*, p. 626).

[35]) Schulenburg to Ribbentrop, 10 February 1939, *ibid.*, p. 626; Schulenburg to Schnurre, 11 February 1939, *ibid.*, pp. 626-27; Schulenburg to Wiehl, 1 March 1939, *ibid.*, p. 628. The published documentation on this is singularly fragmentary.

[36]) Wiehl to Schulenburg, 8 March 1939, *ibid.*, p. 630; Memorandum of Wiehl, 11 March 1939, *ibid.*, pp. 630-31.

[37]) Memorandum of Schnurre, 5 May 1939, *NSR*, p. 3; *BDS*, p. 3; Memorandum of Hilger, 17 June 1939, *ibid.*, p. 23; *BDS*, pp. 25-26; Schulenburg to Ribbentrop, 27 June 1939, *ibid.*, p. 25; *BDS*, pp. 27f.

A document of great interest which cannot be clearly fitted into the picture is a memorandum of Wiehl of 6 February 1939, entitled: "The Economic Consequences of a Rupture of Relations with the Soviet Union (*GD*, IV, 624-25)." The document was probably written in connection with the Hungarian request that Germany recall her ambassador from Moscow because the Soviet Union had broken off diplomatic relations after Hungary adhered to the Anti-Comintern Pact (see *GD*, V, No. 283 and notes).

[38]) Seeds to Halifax, 27 January 1939, BD, IV, 33-34; Ogilvie-Forbes to Halifax, 27 January 1939, *ibid.*, p. 34.

[39]) Kennard to Halifax, 26 January 1939, *ibid.*, p. 15.

[40]) Seeds to Halifax, 26 January 1939, *ibid.*, p. 14; Halifax to Seeds, 27 January 1939, *ibid.*, p. 35.

[41]) Seeds to Halifax, 30 January 1939, *ibid.*, p. 54; Kennard to Halifax, 1 February 1939, *ibid.*, p. 67; Kennard to Halifax, 6 February 1939, *ibid.*, p. 82; Seeds to Halifax, 17 February 1939, *ibid.*, p. 115; Henderson to Halifax, 22 February 1939, *ibid.*, p. 134.

and with the German proposal to convert the Anti-Comintern Pact into a military alliance of a general—not specifically anti-Soviet—nature, the British government carefully reassessed the possibility of a Soviet-German rapprochement and its probable impact on the world situation.[42]

Of more direct relevance to this study is the effect of the failure of the economic negotiations on Soviet-German relations. Aside from the obvious repercussions on Soviet-German trade, the really important outcome was the reaction of the Russians. Not unreasonably, they felt that Germany had not been fair with them in the management of the negotiations, and had perhaps not been serious in the first place —with the result that, when the question of economic negotiations came up again, the Russians were even more suspicious of Germany than usual.[43]

In spite of the outcome of the economic negotiations, the possibility of a reorientation of Soviet policy was left open by Stalin in his speech to the Eighteenth Congress of the Communist Party on March 10, 1939.[44] He denounced the Western Powers for their attempt to "incense the Soviet Union against Germany, to poison the atmosphere and to provoke a conflict with Germany without any visible grounds." The conclusion contained two particularly important points: that the Soviet Union would "continue the policy of peace and strengthening business relations with all countries," and that Russia should "be cautious and not... be drawn into conflicts by war-mongers who are accustomed to have others pull the chestnuts out of the fire for them." This last statement is a rather interesting comment on the policy of collective security. As for the first, there being no "visible grounds" for a conflict with Germany, and Russia being prepared to strengthen its business relations with "all countries," Germany, too, might obtain improved relations with the Soviet Union.

To deduce from this speech, as Angelo Rossi does in his work on Soviet-German relations,[45] that Stalin had decided to sign with Germany by March 10, 1939, is certainly not correct; or, at least, it cannot yet be substantiated by adequate evidence. What this

---

[42] Memorandum of Cadogan, 1 February 1939, *ibid.*, p. 71; British Embassy Moscow to the Foreign Office, 20 February 1939, *ibid.*, pp. 611-14; cf. Troutbeck to Halifax and enclosure, 31 January 1939, *ibid.*, p. 64.

[43] See especially Memorandum of Schulenburg, 20 May 1939, *NSR*, p. 6; *BDS*, p. 7; Memorandum of Weizsäcker, 30 May 1939, *ibid.*, pp. 12-13; *BDS*, pp. 15-17; cf. Kleist, p. 21.

[44] Full text in Joseph V. Stalin, *Leninism* (New York, 1940), pp. 619-70; the most important relevant sections are given in Max Beloff, *The Foreign Policy of Soviet Russia, 1929-1941*, Vol. II (London, 1949), pp. 221-23.

[45] Angelo Rossi, *Deux ans d'alliance Germano-Soviétique* (Paris, 1949), p. 217.

speech does represent is a hint that the possibility of an agreement with Germany existed and might be followed up if Germany were willing and offered the Soviet Union an opportunity to stay out of the coming war. Ribbentrop seems to have looked at the speech in this manner, and told Hitler about it.[46] Later, in the policy discussions in Germany in the last week of May, he was to refer to it as a sign of a new Soviet orientation.[47] This will be considered again in the next chapter. In any case, it would appear that before the march on Prague, the Russians were beginning to examine seriously the possibility of agreement with Germany as the basis of their policy in the new, post-Munich, Europe.[48]

A few days after the Stalin speech of March 10, the Germans took a step—the occupation of the remainder of Czechoslovakia—the effects of which, together with other events of March, 1939, were to lead Germany to begin looking in new directions also. As will be seen, in Soviet-German relations, as in the whole history of the modern world, March 15, 1939, represents a landmark. As an explosive event in a tense Europe, it is most clearly illuminated in all its implications for the study of German foreign policy by that portion of a survey of the situation in Czechoslovakia, prepared by the German Legation in Prague, which deals with the treatment of the Germans in Czechoslovakia. The German *press* was playing up various atrocity stories as justification for drastic action by Germany. The *report* reads:

> Representative of the German *Volksgruppe* (national group) deplores the perfectly correct, even accomodating, attitude of the Czechs everywhere.[49]

---

[46] Testimony of Ribbentrop, *TMWC*, X, 267; *PHKV* X, 303; cf. Ribbentrop to German Missions in Europe, 12 April 1939, Germany, Auswärtiges Amt, *Weissbuch 2*, p. 342.

[47] Memorandum of Ribbentrop, 26 May 1939, cited in Rossi, p. 20 and n. 2.

[48] For the interpretations of Stalin's speech made by the representatives of Britain, Germany, Italy, and the United States, respectively, see Seeds to Halifax, 20 March 1939, *BD*. IV, 411-19; Schulenburg to Ribbentrop, 13 March 1939, *GD*, IV, 632; Rosso to Ciano, 12 March 1939, quoted in Toscano, pp. 8-10; Kirk to Hull, 30 March 1939, United States, Department of State, *Papers relating to the Foreign Relations of the United States: The Soviet Union, 1933 -1939* (Washington, 1952) (hereafter cited as *The Soviet Union, 1933-1939*), pp. 747-50.

[49] Toussaint and Hencke to the Foreign Ministry, 11 March 1939, *GD*, IV, 235.

CHAPTER TWO

MARCH 15,—MAY 31, 1939

We have seen how by March 15, 1939, the leaders of the Soviet Union had apparently begun to consider at least the possibility of a rapprochement with Germany. In the period from March 15 to May 31 this attitude seems to have crystallized while the thinking of the German government began to lean seriously in the same direction.

The following account of this period, as well as the two chapters covering the period to September 28, 1939, is not designed to be a complete synthesis of the available material. Rather, it is a summary based on already published accounts as supplemented by hitherto less well-known documents. Good accounts of the various negotiations may be found in Namier's two books on the subject,[1]) and also in the works of Beloff,[2]) Gafencu,[3]) Rossi,[4]) and Dallin[5]). These and others are based largely on published documentary sources and a number of memoirs. Most of these works will be cited as well as some unpublished materials.

The German march into Prague set off a series of extremely important developments. The British government now came to the conclusion that no German promises could be trusted and no further German aggression tolerated. Just as after the *Anschluss* of Austria attention had quickly shifted to Czechoslovakia, so now after the final destruction of Czechoslovakia world attention was focused on Poland. Since Poland was obviously the next victim in line for German aggression, she was to be covered by a British guarantee. Under this guarantee Britain and France agreed to come to the defense of Poland against aggression. England planned to reinforce this guarantee militarily by conscription and diplomatically by an agreement with the Soviet Union. Here the prophecy of the Polish Ambassador to London,

---

[1]) L. B. Namier, *Diplomatic Prelude* (London, 1948) and *Europe in Decay* (London, 1950), pp. 58-77, 238-272.

[2]) Beloff, II, 224-85.

[3]) Grigore Gafencu, *Last Days of Europe*, trans. E. Fletcher-Allen (New Haven, 1948), and *Vorspiel zum Krieg im Osten* (Zürich, 1944), pp. 1-69, 287-364.

[4]) Rossi, pp. 1-85.

[5]) David J. Dallin, *Soviet Russia's Foreign Policy, 1939-1942* (New Haven, 1942), pp. 1-80, 422.

Edward Raczyński, about the implications of the introduction of conscription in England is worth quoting. Reporting to Polish Foreign Minister Beck on December 16, 1938, Raczyński had written,

> Premier Chamberlain has to this day not abandoned the platform of voluntary military service.... The Premier's restraint may be explained by his well-known tendency to conciliate the militaristic Axis powers. On the other hand, in view of the approaching elections, he has to reckon with the unpopularity of conscription.... Its introduction, which could take place if at all only after the elections, would be the most eloquent proof that Britain is passing from an attitude of mild conciliation to increased "firmness."[6])

The diplomatic negotiations between England and Russia which began with discussions between British Foreign Secretary Halifax and Soviet Ambassador Maisky immediately after March 15 looked toward some sort of common front against German aggression. They were long and tortuous. Their course has been traced most clearly in the works of Namier and Gafencu already referred to.[7]) The most important developments of that time, however, seem to have taken place in the minds of the leaders of Germany and the Soviet Union; and though it is most difficult to picture these, an attempt will be made.

It was clear that Germany was turning East. It soon became clear that Poland would probably not give in to Hitler's demands and that she seemed to have the support of the Western Powers. In viewing this situation, the Soviet leaders may well have reasoned approximately as follows. If Germany attacks Poland, Britain will either back out and leave Poland to her fate or declare war on Germany. If Britain failed to keep her promise, and Munich led the Russians to suspect that she probably would, then Soviet Russia might easily find herself fighting Germany alone. If Britain did fight, then why not let the Germans and the Western Powers fight it out? [8]) In either case, if agreement with Germany were possible, such an agreement would enable Russia to profit substantially from the overthrow of what was left of the European order.

The foregoing analysis is wrong if it is assumed that the Soviet Union was interested at the time in the maintenance of the *status quo*,

---

[6]) Russia, Ministry of Foreign Affairs of the U.S.S.R., *Documents and Materials relating to the Eve of the Second World War*, Vol. I, *November 1937-1938* (Moscow, 1948), p. 302.

[7]) Additional details are to be found in the diplomatic correspondence published in the fourth, fifth and sixth volumes of the third series of the *Documents on British Foreign Policy, 1919-1939.*

[8]) On this point, see Seeds to Halifax, 13 April 1939, *BD*, V, 104; Halifax to Seeds, 14 April 1939, *ibid.*, p. 205.

in particular in the continued unimpinged independence of Finland, the Baltic States, Poland, and Rumania; states largely created out of the former Russian empire. There is no evidence to indicate that she was especially interested in this—nor has her subsequent conduct afforded any such evidence.

If, on the other hand, this analysis is right, then the more determined England became and the more certain the entrance of the Western Powers into a European war seemed, the greater the concessions which might be obtained from Germany. Of course, this attitude did not preclude the possibility of agreement with the Western Powers—if the latter were willing to sacrifice the necessary areas; but this seemed unlikely.

It is the opinion of this writer that the Soviet Government had not made its decision on these matters before the end of May. The latter part of March, and all of April and May were spent in negotiations on various fronts simultaneously. There were the talks with the Western Powers. There were, as will be related presently, the early negotiations with Germany; and there was the trip of Potemkin. This last episode is still shrouded in some mystery; the known facts will be related first, and then an attempt will be made to assess its meaning and significance.

Vladimir P. Potemkin, Soviet Deputy Commissar for Foreign Affairs, made a trip through the Balkans and to Warsaw in April and May of 1939. During April, the Soviet Union was beginning to sound out the German government.[9] Near the end of April, a Soviet-Turkish conference on the international situation was scheduled to take place at Batum.[10] This plan was changed, and by the 22d of April it had been decided that, instead, Potemkin would go to Ankara.[11] Stopping briefly in Bulgaria on the way,[12] Potemkin arrived in Ankara on April 29 to stay until May 5.[13]

The conversations between Potamkin and Turkish Foreign Minister Sükrü Saracoglu, which were long and detailed, concerned two main points. One was the possibility of arranging a Russo-Turkish pact of mutual assistance within the framework of the common front

[9] See below, and Memorandum of Weizsäcker, 17 April 1939, United States, Department of State, *Nazi-Soviet Relations, 1939-1941*, eds. R. J. Sontag and J. S. Beddie (Washington, 1948) (hereafter cited as *NSR*), pp. 1-2; the German edition,, eds. E. M. Carroll and F. T. Epstein (hereafter cited as *BDS*), seems to the writer to have been more carefully edited.

[10] Knatchbull-Hugessen to Halifax, 20 April 1939, *BD*, V, 259.

[11] Seeds to Halifax, 22 April 1939, *ibid.*, p. 282; cf. Knatchbull-Hugessen to Halifax, 23 April 1939, *ibid.*, p. 287.

[12] Rendel to Halifax, 26 April 1939, *ibid.*, pp. 341-42.

[13] Beloff, II, 240.

against Axis agression, and the other, the ways and means of strengthening the Balkan Entente.[14]) Saracoglu explained to Potemkin Turkey's planned policy of cooperation with England and France—a cooperation which would be rounded out by agreements between England, France, and Russia on the one hand and Turkey and Russia on the other. Although an official communiqué on these talks was issued at Ankara and Moscow on May 7,[15]) the conversations appear to have been quite inconclusive.[16]) Saracoglu was to return the visit by going to Moscow in September, 1939, but by that time much had changed—the conclusion of a Soviet-Turkish agreement had to await a later swing in the tide.[17])

From Turkey, Potemkin went to Bulgaria where he conferred with the Prime Minister and King Boris. There the leanings of the government toward the Axis alarmed him. Presumably he urged the Bulgarian government to steer a course more friendly to the Balkan Entente.[18])

Potemkin's next stop was in Bucharest. In long conversations with the Rumanian Foreign Minister, Grigore Gafencu, on May 8, 1939, the problems of collective security in the Balkans were canvassed. The possibilities of strengthening the Balkan Entente were discussed; and, since this was being considered at the time, Potemkin advised against territorial concessions to Bulgaria to wean her away from her pro-German policies, until Bulgaria had affirmed and proven her solidarity with the other Balkan nations.

The Deputy Commissar was most interested in the terms of the Polish-Rumanian alliance; he was told that while the military convention attached to it contemplated only defense against attack by the Soviet Union, the Rumanian government was prepared to extend it to all contingencies—meaning of course attack by Germany.

To reassure the Rumanian Foreign Minister, who was disturbed

---

[14]) Gafencu, *Last Days of Europe*, p. 184; Gafencu, *Vorspiel zum Krieg im Osten*, pp. 77, 321, 346; Hughe M. Knatchbull-Hugessen, British Ambassador to Turkey, *Diplomat in Peace and War* (London, 1949), p. 154.

[15]) Quoted in Beloff, II, 240, n. 4; cf. Seeds to Halifax, 7 May 1939, *BD*, V, 460.

[16]) The following documents on Potemkin's stay in Ankara, published in Volume V of the *Documents on British Foreign Policy, 1919-1939*, Third Series, are of interest: Knatchbull-Hugessen to Halifax, 30 April 1939 (p. 380), reporting a conversation between Potemkin and the French Ambassador to Turkey; Knatchbull-Hugessen to Halifax, 2 May 1939 (p. 389), Knatchbull-Hugessen to Halifax, 3 May 1939 (pp. 399-400), and Knatchbull-Hugessen to Halifax, 5 May 1939 (pp. 433-35), on talks between Potemkin and the Turkish authorities; Knatchbull-Hugessen to Halifax, 4 May 1939 (pp. 411-12) on a meeting between Potemkin and Knatchbull-Hugessen.

[17]) Gafencu, *Vorspiel zum Krieg im Osten*, p. 350.

[18]) *Ibid.*, p. 322; Gafencu, *Last Days of Europe*, p. 184; cf. Halifax to Rendel, 11 May 1939, *BD*, V, 530.

by the dismissal of Litvinov a few days before, Potemkin stated that no change in policy was contemplated and that Molotov would pursue the same policy as his predecessor. He specifically clarified the position of Russia in regard to Germany, having perhaps been informed of the German leaks which will be discussed later.

> The totalitarian powers are spreading the deceiving rumor that the Soviet Union is ready to come to an understanding with Germany and Italy. This tactic is being used, particularly in Berlin, to prevent an agreement between London, Paris, and Moscow. Hitler himself is using this tactic as he would like to make it appear that he could at any convenient moment bring about a rapprochement between Germany and the Soviet Union either by means of trade negotiations or through the mediation of the German general staff. Even the Italians are making efforts to maintain official relations with Moscow in spite of the tone of their official pronouncements which its hostile to the Soviet Union. But all of this will never alter the policy of the Soviet Union which, rather than bending to the demands of opportunism, pursues the goal of general peace by pacific means.[19]

These words have certainly been given an ironic connotation by subsequent events; whether Potemkin knew at the time that this would be, is unknown.

From Bucharest Potemkin went to Warsaw where he spent May 9 and 10 conferring with Colonel Beck. Surprisingly enough, the conversation was rather friendly in spite of Beck's refusal to extend the Polish-Rumanian military convention to other contingencies. On the other hand, Beck made it quite clear that Poland would not join any combination with Germany against the Soviet Union. When Beck gave his important foreign policy speech on May 5, 1939, he had alluded to German offers of a joint front against Russia in a part of the speech answering German charges about Poland's un-cooperative attitude in the negotiations:

> But, Gentlemen, in these discussions (with Germany) another matter, going far outside the frame of the questions under dis-cussions, was alluded to. I reserve the right to come back to this point if necessary.[20]

---

[19] Gafencu, *Vorspiel zum Krieg im Osten*, p. 323, n. 1. The foregoing account of the Potemkin-Gafencu meeting is based on *ibid.*, pp. 321-24, and Gafencu, *Last Days of Europe*, pp. 184-87; cf. "Extract from Record of Conversation between the Secretary of State and M. Cretzianu at Geneva on May 23, 1939," *BD*, V, 657.

[20] Poland, p. 117; see also Coulondre to Bonnet, 7 May 1939, France, pp. 154-55; Leon Noël, *L'agression allemande contre la Pologne* (Paris, 1946), p. 359; Dallin, p. 16 and p. 431, n. 2; Kennard to Halifax, 23 April 1939, *BD*, V, 289-90; Minute by Mr. Strang, 1 May 1939, *BD*, V, 384; Foreign Office Memorandum, 4 May 1939, *BD*, V,

A general understanding seems to have been reached between Beck and Potemkin to the effect that while Poland would not commit herself to Soviet Russia, she would defend herself against German attack and seek aid from Russia; Russia, on the other hand, would observe a benevolent neutrality.[21]

At the time that Potemkin was in Warsaw, the British government had publicly clarified its position on the problem of Anglo-Soviet cooperation against aggression.[22] In the House of Commons on May 10 Prime Minister Neville Chamberlain pointed out that the British government had

> ...made it plain that it was no part of their intention that the Soviet Government should commit themselves to intervene [in case of aggression by Germany], irrespective of whether Great Britain and France had already, in discharge of their obligations, done so. His Majesty's Government added that, if the Soviet Government wished to make their own intervention contingent on that of Great Britain and France, His Majesty's Government for their part would have no objection.[23]

On the same day the British government began its fight in Parliament for a conscription bill. The bill, obviously designed to strengthen the front against German aggression, was attacked by William Gallagher, a Communist M.P., as a "swindle"[24] which should "be withdrawn".[25]

It had been expected originally that from Warsaw Potemkin would go to Geneva for the meeting of the Council of the League of Nations on May 15 and that this would provide an opportunity for Potemkin to confer with the British Foreign Secretary, Lord Halifax. At the request of the Soviet government, the Council meeting was post-

---

415-20; Kennard to Halifax, 5 May 1939, *BD*, V, 441; Henderson to Halifax, 6 May 1939, *BD*, V, 455. The relevant German documents, which were tendentiously cut to fit the propagandistic purposes of the Second German White Book, are now available in full in *GD*, V, Ch. 1.

[21] Beck to Raczyński, 13 May 1939, Poland, p. 236; Final Report of Grzybowski, 6 November 1939, *ibid.*, p. 268; Gafencu, *Last Days of Europe, pp.* 187-88; Namier *Diplomatic Prelude,* p. 133; Kennard to Halifax, 9 May 1939, *BD*, V, 476; Kennard to Halifax, 10 May 1939, *BD*, V, 500; Seeds to Halifax, 18 May 1939, *BD*, V, 589-90; "Extract from Record of Conversation between the Secretary of State and M. Cretzianu at Geneva on May 23, 1939," *BD.* V, 657.

[22] The British position referred to had been formulated and communicated to the Soviet Government in the course of the Anglo-Russian negotiations. Halifax to Phipps, 21 April 1939, *BD*, V, 267; Halifax to Phipps, 28 April 1939, *ibid.*, p. 359; Halifax to Seeds, 29 April 1939, *ibid.*, p. 373; Halifax to Seeds, 6 May 1939, *ibid.*, pp. 448-49; Seeds to Halifax, 9 May 1939, *ibid.*, p. 485.

[23] Hansard, *Parliamentary Debates* (5th series), CCCXLVII (1939), c. 454.

[24] Ibid., c. 522.

[25] Ibid., c. 524. The decision to introduce conscription had been announced on April 26 (*ibid.,* CCCXLVI [1939], cc. 1150-54).

poned to May 21 so that Potemkin could return to Moscow and report on his trip before going on to Geneva. However, when Potemkin had returned to Moscow, the Soviet government announced on May 16 that Potemkin would not go to Geneva at all; the U.S.S.R. would be represented by her Ambassador in London.[26]) The expected meeting between the British Foreign Minister and the Soviet Deputy Commissar for Foreign Affairs, therefore, did not materialize, to the regret of the British government.[27])

What was the meaning of Potemkin's trip and the subsequent failure of a Halifax-Potemkin meeting to take place? [28]) The following seems the most likely explanation. When Potemkin's trip was planned and at the time that he left Moscow, the Soviet Union wanted to explore alternative courses of action to meet the European crisis. If Litvinov was actually in control of foreign relations to the time of his dismissal, and there is no reason to suspect that he was not, the bias as between joining with the West and coming to an arrangement with Hitler was clearly on the side of the West. This balance, as we shall soon see, had already begun to waver before Litvinov's dismissal. Moreover, the conversations in Berlin which took place immediately after the dismissal of Litvinov[29]) indicated that the possibility of agreement with Germany was a real one. Therefore, further immediate commitments to Britain would be undesirable since they might settle the choice before Russia was willing to make it. Potemkin, therefore, stayed in Moscow after returning from Warsaw; thus providing the Soviet government an opportunity for further exploration of the possibilities and avoidance of a premature commitment to either side.[30]) Before continuing with the policy of the Soviets, one must turn to an examination of the German side.

After taking the remainder of Czechoslovakia on March 15, 1939, Germany turned on Poland. The demands on Poland referred to in

---

[26]) Namier, *Diplomatic Prelude*, p. 163; Dallin, p. 33; cf. Seeds to Halifax, 16 May 1939, *BD*, V, 568.

[27]) Hansard, *Parliamentary Debates* (5th series), CCCXLVII (1939), c. 1839.

[28]) It should be noted that there is *no* mention of Potemkin's trip in his own book *Politika umirotvorenia agressorov i boŕba Sovetskogo Soyuza za mir* [The policy of Appeasement and the Struggle of the Soviet Union for Peace] (Moscow 1943), nor in the third volume of the *Histoire de la Diplomatie*, trans. I. Levin, J. Tarr, B. Metzel (Paris, 1945), which Potemkin edited.

[29]) Memorandum of Schnurre, 5 May 1939, *NSR*, p. 3; *BDS*, p. 3; Memorandum of von Stumm, 9 May 1939, *NSR*, pp. 3-4; *BDS*, p. 4.

[30]) It was at this same time that the negotiations between the British and Russians were maintained in an inconclusive stage by Molotov's probably deliberate failure to comprehend the import of an important part of the British reply to Russia's proposal for a treaty of mutual assistance. (Halifax to Seeds, 9 May 1939, *BD*, V, 479; Seeds to Halifax, 9 May 1939, *ibid.*, pp. 491-92; Seeds to Halifax, 11 May 1939,

Chapter I were raised again by Germany on March 21.[31]) The Germans seem to have expected a favorable reply,[32]) but the Poles refused to agree to the German demands as stated.[33]) Hitler decided to resort to force. An order to prepare the attack on Poland was issued on April 3, a few days after the announcement of the British guarantee. This order, a covering note by Wilhelm Keitel, Chief of the High Command of the Armed Forces (OKW), to the forthcoming general revision of orders for "Fall Weiss" (the attack on Poland), states:

> The Führer has ordered the following to be added to (the order) "Fall Weiss":
>
> 1) The preparations are to be made in such a manner that execution [of the plan] will be possible at any time from September 1, 1939 onwards.
>
> 2) The OKW is ordered to set up an exact timetable for "Fall Weiss" and to clarify by consultations synchronization among the three branches of the armed forces.
>
> 3) The intentions of the branches of the armed forces and the basic materials for the timetable are to be delivered to the OKW by the 1st of May 1939.[34])

The detailed order for the attack on Poland was issued to the German armed forces on April 11, 1939.[35])

The military problems involved in an attack on Poland had to be studied by the German high command, and thus the possible attitude of the Soviet Union naturally came under consideration. There is some evidence to indicate that references to a possible agreement with Russia came up in discussions between Hitler and the highest German military leaders around this time.[36]) In any case, the last

---

ibid., pp. 520-21; Halifax to Seeds, 11 May 1939, *ibid.,* pp. 528-29.) The British policy statement of May 10 referred to above was occasioned by this misunderstanding. (Minute by Mr. Strang, 10 May 1939, *BD,* V, 506-07.)

[31]) Memorandum of Ribbentrop, 21 March 1939, Germany, Auswärtiges Amt, *Weissbuch* 2, p. 231.

[32]) Siewert, "Unterrichtung des Herrn Ob.d.H. durch den Führer am 25.3.39.," R - 100, *TMWC,* XXXVIII, 274.

[33]) Memorandum of the Polish Government, 26 March 1939, Germany, Auswärtiges Amt, *Weissbuch 2,* pp. 235-38.

[34]) Germany, OKW, WFA, LI (Keitel), "Weisung für die Wehrmacht 1939/1940," 3 April 1939, C-120, *TMWC,* XXXIV, 381; all documents cited by a Nuremberg trial document number, e.g. C -, PS -, NG -, have been translated by the writer unless otherwise indicated.

[35]) Germany, Oberste Befehlshaber der Wehrmacht, OKW, WFA L I (Hitler), "Weisung für die einheitliche Kriegsvorbereitung der Wehrmacht für 1939/40; II, 'Fall Weiss'," 11 April 1939, C - 120, *ibid.,* pp. 381, 388; cf. Affidavit of Brauchitsch, 7 November 1945, PS - 3705, *ibid.,* XXXII, 465-66.

[36]) Kordt, *Wahn und Wirklichkeit,* p. 157; Erich Kordt, *Nicht aus den Akten* (Stuttgart, 1950), p. 306.

specifically anti-Soviet act of the German government was to push
for publication of Spain's adhesion to the Anti-Comintern Pact on
April 6, 1939.[37])

During April the Germans also began to worry about the Anglo-
French-Soviet negotiations; the possibilities for holding off a new
Triple Entente had to be explored. A lessening of the tensions between
Germany and Russia seemed one avenue of approach.[38]) A further
factor which was bound to incline Germany more and more to an
agreement with the Soviet Union was the lagging of the negotiations
for a military alliance with Japan. Such an alliance would, of course,
have had a considerable restraining influence on the Western Powers
with their great interests in Asia. To have this effect, the alliance
would have to provide for all possibilities; but the Japanese government, or at least influential forces within it, was opposed to an alliance
which was not restricted in its application to the Soviet Union—the
Japanese did not want to be embroiled with the Western Powers at
that time. The negotiations between Berlin and Rome on the one
hand and Tokyo on the other were endless, involved, and inconclusive.[39]) The details of these negotiations, fascinating though they
are, will not be gone into here.[40]) The important point is that by the
last half of April, 1939, it was becoming apparent that the pact desired
by Germany—namely a pact with universal application—would almost
certainly not materialize within the time desired by Hitler.[41])

The evidences of a German-Soviet rapprochement in April are slight
but significant nevertheless. On April 7 Dr. Peter Kleist, specialist on
the Soviet Union of the *Dienststelle Ribbentrop*,[42]) was ordered by
Ribbentrop to improve his personal relations with the members of

---

[37]) Ribbentrop to Stohrer, 3 April 1939, *GD*, III, 888-89; Stohrer to Ribbentrop,
4 April 1939, *ibid.*, pp. 889-90; Weizsäcker to Stohrer, 4 April 1939, *ibid.*, p. 890;
Stohrer to Ribbentrop, 4 April 1939, *ibid.*, pp. 891-92; Woermann to Stohrer, 5 April
1939, *ibid.*, p. 892; Stohrer to Ribbentrop, 6 April 1939, cited in ibid., p. 892, n. 1.

[38])Testimony of Weizsäcker, U.S. v. Weizsäcker, English Transcript page (hereafter cited as E.T.), 7743.

[39]) The tangled mess has been rendered fairly understandable by Herbert Feis
in his excellent work on the developments leading to war between Japan and the
United States. Herbert Feis, *The Road to Pearl Harbor* (Princeton, New Jersey,
1950), pp. 19, 20, 27-32. See also, International Tribunal for the Far East, *Judgement of the International Tribunal for the Far East* (1948), Part B, Chapter IV,
pp. 362-97.

[40]) For a fairly good summary from the German side (based probably on a draft
by Gaus, head of the Legal Department), see Ribbentrop to Ott, 17 June 1939,
1827-PS (photostat, 6 pp.).

[41]) Ribbentrop to Ott, 26 April 1939, cited in Feis, p. 30 and n. 13.

[42]) The Dienststelle Ribbentrop was a personal office on foreign policy used by
Ribbentrop both before and after his appointment as foreign minister.

the Soviet Embassy in Berlin.[43]) A few days later, the exact date is not known, Kleist had a conversation with the Soviet chargé, Astakhov, in which the latter urged a German-Soviet agreement in unmistakable terms. Ribbentrop, however, was apparently interested only in finding out what diplomatic possibilities might exist and ordered Kleist not to pursue the matter further.[44]) Early in April there was a similar conversation between Schnurre and Astakhov;[45]) more such soundings may come to light in the future.

The conversation between German State Secretary Weizsäcker and Soviet Ambassador Merekalov on April 17, 1939, has attained a perhaps unwarranted fame since it is the subject of the first document published in the State Department's publication on German-Soviet relations.[46]) It is, however, interesting to note that the general themes discussed in this conversation were those which have been elaborated in this chapter—the desire of Russia to isolate herself from a possible European war, and the anxiety of Germany over the possibility of a new Triple Entente which would make an attack on Poland extremely hazardous. Since Merekalov returned to Moscow a few days after this interview—his only one with Weizsäcker during his ten months in Berlin—his report on it may have had some influence on the decisions made there. This was just before Potemkin started on his Balkan trip.

Of considerable importance in this regard was Hitler's speech on April 28. Denouncing the 1934 Pact with Poland and the Anglo-German Naval Treaty of 1935, Hitler clearly laid down the lines of the coming conflict. At the same time, he omitted the usual tirade against the Soviets. In connection with this one might consider the German press. While the orders to the German press to exercise restraint toward Russia would appear to have been issued after the dismissal of Litvinov at the beginning of May,[47]) a change of some kind can be observed a little earlier. The *Schwarze Korps*, the official paper of the Nazi Elite Guard (SS), can be expected to follow the party line with considerable faithfulness. The last of its weekly directly anti-Soviet cartoons appeared on April 6, 1939.[48]) There is a bitter cartoon on Anglo-Russian friendship on April 27,[49]) and after that it is the British who are made fools of with the Russians treated in a respectful manner.

---

[43]) Kleist, pp. 26-27.

[44]) Ibid., pp. 27-30.

[45]) Kurt Assmann, *Deutsche Schicksalsjahre* (Wiesbaden, 1950), pp. 93-94.

[46]) Memorandum of Weizsäcker, 17 April 1939, NSR, pp. 1-2; BDS, pp. 1-2; cf. Coulondre to Bonnet, 9 May 1939, France, pp. 157-58.

[47]) Testimony of Brammer, U.S. v. Weizsäcker, E.T., 1468.

[48]) *Schwarze Korps*, 6 April 1939, p. 1.

[49]) *Ibid.*, 27 April 1939, p. 1.

The event which divides the period from March 15 to May 31 into two distinct phases is the dismissal of Litvinov on May 3. Unless the trip of Deputy Commissar Potemkin was a fraud from start to finish, and there is as yet no substantial evidence to indicate that it was,[50] the decision to replace Litvinov had probably not been made before Potemkin left Moscow on April 22 or 23. It would seem, therefore, that the decision to make Molotov Commissar for Foreign Affairs was reached only shortly before the change actually occurred. The reasons for the dismissal of Litvinov can only be guessed at. The most important would appear to have been his symbolical and personal identification with the policy of collective security, the joint front against aggression. Litvinov had been against the so-called Rapallo policy of co-operation with Germany developed by his predecessor, Chicherin. He had been the spokesman for collective security at Geneva. He had tried to push the negotiations with the West in March and April of 1939, though perhaps already under restraint from higher up. His policy had received a shattering blow at Munich. He was not the man to pursue the new Soviet policy of playing both sides of Europe's uneasy balance and he was Jewish.

It is important not to identify Molotov with a pro-German policy too strongly retrospectively. When he replaced Litvinov, a swing away from the West was certainly indicated, but toward a neutral—bargaining—position, rather than a pro-German one. This last was to come as a result of the German reaction to Litvinov's dismissal, rather than from Molotov's initiative. Molotov's only direct step after becoming Foreign Commissar was to cancel Potemkin's trip to Geneva as discussed already, thus leaving all avenues open for Soviet bargaining.[51]

In Germany the reaction to Litvinov's dismissal was immediate. A change in the tone of the German press was ordered, and this was quickly noted by the Russians.[52] On May 6 Hitler asked to be briefed on the political, military, and economic position of the Soviet

---

[50] The information on the trip obtained by Schulenburg would not contradict this, even if true; see Schulenburg to Weizsäcker, 5 June, 1939, *NSR*, p. 20, *BDS*, p. 22.

[51] This view of Litvinov's dismissal is, on the whole, confirmed by the relevant documents recently published by Great Britain: Seeds to Halifax, 3 May 1939, *BD*, V, 400; Seeds to Halifax, 4 May 1939, *ibid.*, p. 410; Seeds to Halifax, 4 May 1939, *ibid.*, pp. 412-13; Loraine to Halifax, 5 May 1939, *ibid.*, p. 429; Halifax to Loraine, 6 May 1939, *ibid.*, p. 451; Seeds to Halifax, 7 May 1939, *ibid.*, p. 460; Seeds to Halifax, 12 May 1939, *ibid.*, pp. 542-46; Seeds to Halifax, 16 May 1939, *ibid.*, pp. 571-72.

[52] Memorandum of Stumm, 9 May 1939, *NSR*, p. 4; *BDS*, p. 4; Memorandum of Schnurre, 17 May 1939, *NSR*, p. 5; *BDS*, p. 5; cf. Toscano, pp. 32-27; Henderson to Halifax, 8 May 1939, *BD*, V, 463; Henderson to Cadogan, 18 May 1939, *BD*, V, 594.

Union.[53]) On the same day Ribbentrop talked to Italian Foreign Minister Count Ciano about the need and possibilities for a *détente* in German-Soviet relations.[54]) General Bodenschatz, Göring's liaison officer to Hitler, at Göring's orders leaked the possibility of a Russo-German rapprochement to the French Embassy in Berlin on May 7 [55]) and to the Polish Embassy on May 29.[56]) All sorts of rumors about Russo-German negotiations grew out of this and were reported to the various foreign offices at that time and during the following weeks.[57]) It is difficult to say whether this leak was an attempt to blackmail Poland into yielding to German demands or perhaps an attempt by Göring to frustrate Ribbentrop's foreign policy. In any case, it is clear that immediately following the dismissal of Litvinov, Berlin began to consider the possibility of agreement with the Soviet Union, both as a way of forestalling a Triple Entente and as a means of obtaining a free hand in much of Europe, as a serious possibility rather than as pure speculation.

The first steps taken by the Germans were in the economic field. The Soviet request, made at the Weizsäcker-Merekalov conversation of April 17, for the fulfillment of certain armaments contracts at the Skoda works was granted.[58]) Acquiescence to another request in the

---

[53]) Kordt, *Wahn und Wirklichkeit,* p. 158; Kleist, pp. 37-38. A detailed account of the briefing, which was given by Gustav Hilger of the Moscow embassy staff, is in Hilger and Meyer, pp. 293-97.

[54]) Memorandum of Ciano, 7 May 1939, Galeazzo Ciano, *Ciano's Diplomatic Papers,* ed. M. Muggeridge; trans. S. Hood (London, 1948), p. 286.

[55]) Coulondre to Bonnet, 7 May 1939, France, pp. 145-49; Coulondre, pp. 396-99.

[56]) Namier, *Europe in Decay,* p. 263.

[57]) Henderson to Halifax, 5 May 1939, *BD,* V, 433; Henderson to Halifax, 8 May 1939, *ibid.,* p. 463; Henderson to Cadogan, 18 May 1939, *ibid.,* pp. 594-95; Henderson to Halifax, 20 May 1939, *ibid.,* p. 620; Cadogan to United Kingdom Delegation at Geneva, 21 May 1939, *ibid.,* p. 622; United Kingdom Delegation at Geneva to Cadogan, 21 May 1939, *ibid.,* p. 625; Seeds to Halifax, 22 May 1939, *ibid.,* p. 634; Henderson to Halifax, 8 June 1939, *BD,* VI, 14; Mack to Halifax, 9 June 1939, *ibid.,* p. 17; Jacques Davignon, *Berlin, 1936-1940, souvenirs d'une mission* (Paris, 1951), p. 234.

Dr. Carl Friedrich Goerdeler, one of the leaders of the German opposition to Hitler, also warned the British Foreign Office about Russo-German negotiations on May 6, 1939. See note 2 to: Henderson to Halifax, 5 May 1939, *BD,* V, 433.

[58]) Memorandum of Schnurre, 5 May 1939, *NSR,* p. 3; *BDS,* p. 3; cf. Skoda-werke, "Protokoll No. 8 über die am 7. Juli 1939 bei der Aktiengesellschaft vormals Skodawerke stattgefundene Besprechung," 17 July 1939, NID-9395 (photostat, 5pp.), pp. 2-3. Note that while Germany promised continuance of arms deliveries from Skoda to Russia, all armaments exports to Poland were stopped on May 12, 1939 (Directive of OKW, Wi Rü Amt, cited in Reichsgruppe Industrie, Geschäftsführung, "Reichsgruppe Industrie an die Mitgliedsfirmen der A.G.K. und Meldestellen der A.G.K.; Betreff: Kriegsgeräteausfuhr nach Polen," 17 May 1939, NIK-11619 [mimeo, 2pp.]).

economic field was indicated.[59]) A more significant step was the attempt to reopen general economic negotiations. These had expired in February. In the conversation between Schnurre and the Soviet chargé, Astakhov, on May 5, the latter had asked about the possibility of resuming the negotiations.[60]) This question must have been considered in Berlin immediately after the Schnurre-Astakhov meeting of May 17.[61]) It was decided that a formal approach to the Soviet Government should be made by the German Ambassador to Moscow. The Ambassador, Count von der Schulenburg, had been in Teheran to attend the wedding of the heir to the throne. He was instructed to return to Moscow, not directly as he had planned, but via Berlin, so that he might receive special instructions.[62]) These instructions were, according to the available evidence, written by Ribbentrop himself and stipulated that Schulenburg was to raise only the question of resuming economic negotiations, while remaining reticent about all else.[63])

On May 20, 1939, Schulenburg had an interview with Molotov. Only one sentence of his report on the interview is available.[64]) Several other documents on the conversation are available, however, and from them its contents can easily be reconstructed.[65]) Molotov was evidently most cautious and stated to Schulenburg that he believed the construction of political bases essential before economic negotiations could be resumed. He did not specify how these political bases were to be produced; neither did Potemkin whom Schulenburg saw immediately afterwards.

The first reaction in Germany was negative; Schulenburg was told to keep still for a while and await the next Soviet move.[66]) The

[59]) Memorandum of Schnurre, 17 May 1939, *NSR*, p. 5; *BDS*, p. 5.

[60]) Memorandum of Schnurre, 5 May 1939, *NSR*, p. 3; *BDS*, p. 3.

[61]) See Coulondre to Bonnet, 22 May 1939, France, pp. 162-64; cf. Minute by Mr. Kirkpatrick, 30 May 1939, *BD*, V, 724.

[62]) Rosso to Ciano, 24 May 1939 (No. 1964/833), Italy, Ministry of Foreign Affairs, *I Documenti Diplomatici Italiani;* Eighth Series; 1935-1939, ed. by Mario Toscano (Rome, 1952-) (hereafter cited as *ID*), Vol. XII (23 May - 11 August 1939), p. 11.

[63]) Kordt, *Wahn und Wirklichkeit,* p. 158; Kleist, pp. 38-39; Schulenburg to Weizsäcker, 22 May 1939, *NSR*, p. 8; *BDS*, p. 8. The instructions, themselves, are not printed in *NSR*.

[64]) This was Moscow No. 73 of May 20, 1939; the sentence summarizing the interview is given in Rossi, pp. 28-29, and 29, n. 1.

[65]) Memorandum of Schulenburg, 20 May 1939, *NSR*, pp. 5-7; *BDS*, pp. 6-8; Weizsäcker to Schulenburg, 21 May 1939, *NSR*, p. 7; *BDS*, p. 8; Schulenburg to Weizsäcker, 22 May 1939, *NSR*, pp. 8-9; *BDS*, p. 10; Schulenburg to Weizsäcker, 5 June 1939, *NSR*, pp. 18-19; *BDS*, pp. 20-22. It is important that some of the details did not reach Berlin for several days. On this conversation, see also Rosso to Ciano, 24 May 1939 (No. 60), in Toscano, pp. 31-32.

[66]) Weizsäcker to Schulenburg, 21 May 1939, *NSR*, p. 7; *BDS*, p. 8. Rossi's state-

documentary evidence for the crucial period between the "wait and see" instruction of May 21 and the preparations for the Weizsäcker-Astakhov conference of May 30—preparations which seem to have started on May 29—is incomplete. However, with the help of unpublished German and recently published Italian material, it is now possible to trace the discussion and development of German policy.

Molotov's position that political bases were needed for negotiations was understood in Germany. In the secret meeting of German military leaders on May 23, 1939, at which Hitler announced his determination to attack Poland, Hitler said, "Economic relations with Russia are possible only if the political relations have improved." He added, "In press statements a careful position is appearing. It is not out of the question that Russia might show itself disinterested in the destruction of Poland." [67]

On the following day, May 24, Prime Minister Chamberlain announced in the House of Commons that an understanding with Russia had been reached on most important points and that an agreement would probably be signed soon.[68] This seems to have had an effect on the German government. Erich Kordt, who was at that time chief of Ribbentrop's office, states that a new instruction was sent to Schulenburg on the same day.[69] Very probably this instruction is actually the telegram to Schulenburg of May 26, 1939, referred to, but not printed, in *Nazi-Soviet Relations, 1939-1941*.[70] Before this instruction was sent, if it was sent at all,[71] some very serious thinking appears to have been done in the German Foreign Office on the whole question of German-Russian relations. On or about May 25, Ribbentrop prepared new instructions, or a basis for new instructions, for Schulenburg which were submitted to Hitler on May 26. In this document Ribbentrop pointed out that "a certain change" seemed to have appeared "in the Russian point of view" on foreign policy,

ment that "A Berlin on enregistre avec une vive satisfaction cette 'condition' posée par Moscou," (p. 29) ignores the instruction just cited. German policy seems to have vacillated for some days, as will be made clear in the text; unfortunately *NSR* contains *no* documents originating in Berlin during the crucial period of May 21-27. (It should also be noted that Weizsäcker's letter of May 27 [*NSR*, pp. 9-10; *BDS*, pp. 10-11] reached Moscow on June 2 [*BDS*, p 11, n. 1]).

[67] Schmundt, "Account of a Discussion between Hitler and Commanders of the Armed Forces on 23 May 1939," 079 - L, *TMWC*, XXXVII, 550.

[68] Hansard, *Parliamentary Debates* (5th series), CCCXLVII, c. 2267.

[69] Kordt, *Wahn und Wirklichkeit*, p. 159.

[70] Weizsäcker to Schulenburg, 27 May 1939, *NSR*, p. 9 and n. 6; *BDS*, p. 10; cf. Rossi, p. 20, n. 2.

[71] It is possible that this instruction was not sent; Rossi, p. 20; n. 2; Namier, *Europe in Decay*, p. 264; Weizsäcker to Schulenburg, 27 May 1939, ("a very different sort of instruction"), *NSR*, p. 9; *BDS*, p. 10.

and that one could "discern in the speech of Stalin of March [10, 1939] certains signs of a new orientation." [72]) Ribbentrop recalled that in the Molotov-Schulenburg interview of May 20 Molotov had made an improvement of economic relations dependent upon a clarification of the political relations between Germany and Russia, and that "the Russian chargé d'affaires in Berlin [Astakhov] had expressed himself to the same effect on various occasions." He therefore stated, and this would presumably be a statement for Schulenburg to pass on to Molotov, that the German government could see no objection to a "frank examination" of this subject between Berlin and Moscow.[73]) Coming to the issue immediately pressing, Ribbentrop wrote,

> Should, contrary to our wishes, hostilities with Poland occur, it is our firm conviction that this would not necessarily lead to a conflict of interests with Soviet Russia. So much we can say even today, that in a solution of the German-Polish problem— whatever the means might be—the greatest possible regard would be paid to Russian interests.

He wrote further that he could not see why Russia should want to associate itself with England as England was in no condition to offer "any *quid pro quo* really worth the trouble."[74])

The possible German approaches to the Soviet Union were also weighed by State Secretary Weizsäcker who wrote the following memorandum for Ribbentrop on May 25, 1939:

> 1) The Anglo-Russian negotiations appear to be coming to a conclusion according to which England and Russia compromise their disagreements, England on the geographical question, Russia on the material one, i. e. England seems no longer to wish to limit the *geographical application* of the Pact while Russia would yield (the demand for) complete support. Thus solidarity, not necessarily with military support, would result in case of attack by a Third Power.
>
> If these speculations are correct, the question still remains open to what extent the Russian government is really prepared to allow itself to be involved in a European conflict. A rather wide area for negotiation would, furthermore, appear to remain in Russo-German relations.[75]) Our aim must be to prevent the Russian-English-French relations from acquiring a yet more binding character and from becoming still closer.

---

[72]) Quoted in Rossi, p. 20.

[73]) Taken from Rossi, p. 29.

[74]) Quoted in Rossi, p. 25; these quotations have been translated into English from a French translation of the original German; the wording, therefore, cannot be very exact.

[75]) This sentence was incorporated into Weizsäcker's letter to Schulenburg of May 27, 1939 (*NSR*, p. 9; *BDS*, p. 10).

3) A German step in Moscow at this moment would be of value only if it is taken seriously by the Russians; otherwise it would be worthless or even dangerous. Moscow would otherwise use it against us in Tokyo among other places.

Accordingly, one might consider

a) a conversation by Hilger [German economic counselor in Moscow] in the Russian foreign office in continuation of his customary conversations there. Hilger could then refer to preparatory economic discussions which he attended in Berlin in recent weeks and which were aimed toward an increase in Russo-German trade. There would be no reason to oppose Hilger's saying casually on his own accord in this connection that he did not want to get into the political field, but that he believed that *all* possibilities in the [relations] between Germany and Russia remain open.

b) A request to the Italian Ambassador in Moscow, Mr. Rosso, to indicate clearly German readiness for Russo-German contacts (einem deutsch-russischen Kontakt); Rosso could refer in this to new reports concerning the visit of Ciano to Berlin.

The groundwork for the appropriate request to Rosso through Count Schulenburg would, of course, have to be laid by an instruction to Rosso from Rome.

c) A conversation of the Reich [Foreign] Minister with the Russian Ambassador Merekalov, concerning whose return schedule inquiries have been made in Moscow. An answer to this is still awaited.[76])

This document reveals to some extent the thinking of a group in the German Foreign Ministry around State Secretary Weizsäcker. They hoped to prevent an Anglo-Soviet agreement and to lessen Soviet-German tensions.[77]) The reference to regard for Soviet interests in the Polish question, which occurs in the Ribbentrop memorandum, seems to contain the germ of a far bigger idea—the fourth partition of Poland.

Indecision in Germany continued for a few days. This is clear not only from Weizsäcker's letter to Schulenburg of May 27, a letter which was not mailed until May 30 or 31,[78]) but can also be seen in two letters of Weizsäcker of May 31. These are letters to the German Ambassadors in Warsaw and Rome[79]) in which Weizsäcker

---

[76]) St.S. Nr. 451, (Weizsäcker) to Ribbentrop, 25 May 1939, NG - 5365 (mimeo, 2pp.).

[77]) On this point, see also Testimony of Weizsäcker, U.S. v. Weizsäcker, E.T. 9013-17, 9024-30, 9428-29, 9432.

[78]) *NSR*, pp. 9-10; *BDS*, pp. 10-11.

[79]) Weizsäcker to Moltke, 31 May 1939, NG - 5366 (mimeo, 1 p.) and Weizsäcker to Mackensen, 31 May 1939, NG - 5366 (mimeo, 1 p.); both of these were

wrote that "the question of whether and how one might try to put a spoke in the wheel of Anglo-Russian negotiations has been argued back and forth in the last few days."[80])

A decision was made in the following manner. On May 26, Ribbentrop saw the Japanese Ambassador, Oshima, and broached to him the possibility of a Soviet-German and a Soviet-Japanese rapprochement, only to receive a strongly negative reply.[81]) This seems to have made Ribbentrop somewhat reticent about taking any further steps, but on reconsidering the problem he decided to try one of the suggestions advocated in Weizsäcker's memorandum. On May 29 he telephoned Bernardo Attolico, the Italian Ambassador in Berlin, to ask whether it would be possible to have Ciano instruct the Italian Ambassador in Moscow to seek an interview with Potemkin. At such a meeting, the Italian Ambassador, Augusto Rosso, could drop a hint that it was a pity that Russia should seem to be tying herself definitely to England just at the moment when there were signs of a "natural evolution of the situation in Berlin." Ribbentrop further asked Attolico to see him immediately so that they might discuss the matter personally.

On the same day, there was thus a meeting between Ribbentrop, together with State Secretary Weizsäcker and Friedrich Gaus, Head of the Legal Department, and Italian Ambassador Attolico. Ribbentrop gave Attolico a detailed account of the Molotov-Schulenburg conversation of May 20, stressing the difficulty of interpreting Molotov's statement that "political bases" were a prerequisite to the resumption of economic negotiations. As Attolico then phrased the alternatives, was this a way of turning down the German suggestion, or was it an invitation to advance proposals of a political nature? Whichever it might be, it was the opinion of Attolico that no timid German diplomatic feeler, direct or indirect, would have any practical results at a time when an Anglo-Soviet treaty seemed only a few days distant. Ribbentrop and Weizsäcker acknowledged the force of this argument. The German Foreign Minister accordingly developed the idea that Weizsäcker should call the Soviet Chargé to a meeting and, referring to the latter's question about the Soviet commercial agency in Prague, would let it be understood that some further clarification

---

personal letters sent as covering notes to the account of the Weizsäcker-Astakhov conversation of May 30.

[80]) This wording is from the letter to Mackensen; the translation is from a somewhat colloquial German — "Die Frage, ob und wie man versuchen könnte, in die englisch-russischen Besprechungen noch etwas Sand zu streuen, ist in den letzten Tagen hin und her gegangen."

[81]) Attolico to Ciano, 27 May 1939, *ID*, XII, 32-34; cf. Weizsäcker to Schulenburg, 27 May 1939; *NSR*, p. 9; *BDS*, p. 10.

of Molotov's views on the subject of resuming economic negotiations seemed relevant and desirable. Weizsäcker would then allude to Astakhov's past mention of the possibility of "normalizing" Russo-German relations. In connection with this subject, Weizsäcker would develop the theme that although Germany saw no insurmountable obstacle to such a possibility, the real intentions of the Soviet government would have to be clarified in view of the negotiations which the Soviets were conducting with Great Britain. Ribbentrop went on to indicate that he would await the results of such a conversation and the reactions it might produce in the Kremlin.

The German Foreign Minister asked Attolico to consider this discussion as entirely unofficial as he had had no opportunity either to scrutinize the proposed action himself or to submit it to Hitler.[82]

The suggested approach to the Soviets outlined above was submitted to Hitler on the same day and received his approval.[83] Notes embodying the foregoing points were, therefore, drawn up for the Weizsäcker-Astakhov conversation which was to take place on May 30.[84] It is clear that this conversation marks a most significant step in the Russo-German rapprochement.[85] On the same day, instructions were sent to Moscow for Hilger to resume negotiations in the economic field.[86] The ground for negotiations had thus been laid by the German side.

The Soviets also seem to have been reexamining the possible alternatives in the last week of May. It appears that the Soviet government wanted to stretch out the negotiations with the Western Powers. The new proposal of England and France was submitted in Moscow on May 27.[87] It was turned down by Molotov, again with what

---

[82] Attolico to Ciano, 29 May, *ID*, XII, 44-45.

[83] Kordt, *Wahn und Wirklichkeit*, p. 159.

[84] The State Department publication contains two German Foreign Ministry memoranda which the editors of the American edition think "are apparently a series of proposals submitted by Ribbentrop to Hitler" (*NSR*, p. 10, n. 7). The editors of the German edition offer no suggestion for the author of the first and Wiehl as the possible author of the second one (*BDS*, p. 13, n. 2) In this writer's opinion, the first memorandum was written by Ribbentrop as the instruction—in the form of an almost verbatim text—which Weizsäcker was to follow in his talk. The second memorandum was probably written either by Wiehl or Gaus and approved by Ribbentrop, who gave it also to Weizsäcker to follow, as Weizsäcker's marginal notations would indicate (*BDS*, p. 13, n. 1; not given in the American edition).

[85] For the course of the conversation, see Memorandum of Weizsäcker, 30 May 1939, *NSR*, pp. 12-15; *BDS*, pp. 14-17; Weizsäcker to Schulenburg, 30 May 1939, *NSR*, pp. 15-17; *BDS*, pp. 18-19.

[86] Weizsäcker to Schulenburg, 30 May 1939, *NSR*, pp. 17-18; *BDS*, p. 20; Kordt, *Wahn und Wirklichkeit*, pp. 159-60.

[87] For details of the proposal, see Halifax to Seeds, 24 May 1939 (No. 117), *BD*, V, 668-69; Halifax to Seeds, 25 May 1939 (No 118), *ibid.*, p. 678; Seeds to

seems to be an almost deliberate misunderstanding of the proposal's meaning.[88]) Two days later, that is on May 29, Tass, the official Soviet news agency, published a communiqué denying a story which had appeared in an English publication that a German commercial delegation had been obliged to return to Germany because the Soviet government had rejected its proposals for Russo-German trade. The point made in denying the story was that no German trade delegation had arrived in Moscow.[89]) Perhaps this communiqué was designed to be a hint to the Germans that further proposals on their part might be given favorable consideration.

In any case, the German action of May 30 brought a prompt response from Moscow. On May 31, 1939, Molotov addressed the Third Session of the Supreme Soviet. In his speech he included the following passage:

> While conducting negotiations with Great Britain and France, we by no means consider it necessary to renounce business relations with countries like Germany and Italy.... At the beginning of 1939 the People's Commissariat of Foreign Trade was informed that a special German representative, Herr Schnurre, was leaving for Moscow for the purpose of these negotiations. Subsequently, the negotiations were entrusted to Herr Schulenburg... but they were discontinued on account of disagreement. To judge by certain signs, it is not precluded that the negotiations may be resumed.[90])

The period of soundings and feelers ends at this time. At the end of May, both countries were ready to enter concrete negotiations.

Halifax, 25 May 1939 (No. 100), *ibid.*, p. 678; Halifax to Seeds, 25 May 1939 (No. 119), *ibid.*, pp. 679-80; Halifax to Seeds, 25 May 1939 (No. 120), *ibid.*, pp. 680-81.

[88]) Seeds to Halifax, 27 May 1939, *ibid.*, pp. 701-01; Seeds to Halifax, 28 May 1939, *ibid.*, pp. 710-12; cf. Halifax to Seeds, 29 May 1939, *ibid.*, pp. 719-20.

[89]) Text in Rosso to Ciano, 29 May 1939, *ID,* XII, 46.

[90]) Vyacheslav M. Molotov, *The International Situation and Soviet Foreign Policy* (Moscow, 1939), pp. 10-11.

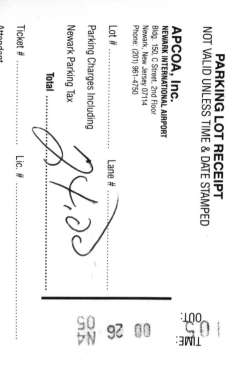

R THREE

JGUST 13, 1939
OR THE PACT

versation of May 30 and Molotov's groundwork for the resumption of wing weeks were, however, not a negotiations. Apparently neither the villing to commit themselves finally tiations which began in June may be stage in which Germany and the Soviet Union attempted to discover, in the discussion of a concrete and familiar subject, whether the other country was really seriously inclined toward a rapprochement.

The exact course of events from the beginning of June to the announcement of the resumption of economic negotiations by the Soviet radio on July 21 is most difficult to trace. Only a few of the German documents for this period have been published, and not all of the gaps can be filled from other sources. German-Soviet relations during this crucial period can, therefore, be traced only in outline.

On May 30, the day of Weizsäcker's conversation with Astakhov, the German Foreign Ministry sent instructions to Moscow authorizing Hilger to "get in touch" with the Soviet Commissar for Foreign Trade. Hilger was to reassure the Russians that Germany was indeed serious in wanting an economic agreement, but was to avoid political discussion.[1]) A few days later, Hilger had a meeting with Mikoyan in which he tried to remove any doubts about German intentions. Mikoyan asked for guarantees that this time an agreement would really be concluded, and Hilger, though unable to give such a guarantee, indicated that Germany expected the negotiations to succeed. To Mikoyan's reiteration of the statement that political bases were a prerequisite for an economic agreement, Hilger answered that while this matter was outside of his competence, he would like to

---

1) Weizsäcker to Schulenburg, 30 May 1939, *NSR*, pp. 17-18; *BDS*, p. 20.

know just what was meant. Mikoyan promised to think the matter over carefully; he did not reject the German approach.[2])

At another meeting between Hilger and Mikoyan, on June 8, a dead-lock was reached on the Soviet demand that, since the Soviet government was now willing to enter into economic discussions, Germany should make an offer based on the proposals last advanced by the Soviets in February. Mikoyan also requested the immediate dispatch of Schnurre to Moscow. Hilger, thereupon, returned to Berlin for consultations.[3]) Since Mikoyan had again raised the issue of "political bases" at this meeting, the German Ambassador also decided to return to Berlin for new instructions. He hoped to persuade the German government to give some satisfaction to the Soviets in the political field, including a declaration that Germany had no aggressive intentions against the Soviet Union, as well as other political arrangements. In return, the Soviet government would be expected to renounce the conclusion of a pact with England and France.[4])

Hilger returned to Moscow on June 17 and immediately met again with Mikoyan.[5]) Although Hilger now offered to accept the Soviet proposal of February, 1939, as the basis for discussions between Mikoyan and Schnurre (who would be sent from Berlin as a special emissary), no real progress was made in the Hilger-Mikoyan conversation of June 17.[6]) While the economic discussions continued inconclusively in Moscow, the Soviets attempted to sound out the political situation in Berlin.

The Soviet Chargé d'Affaires in Berlin, Astakhov, on June 14 called on the Bulgarian Minister. He outlined to the latter, presumably for transmission to the German government, the three possibilities which the Soviet government had under consideration—to sign with England and France, to delay the pact negotiations further, or to come to an agreement with Germany. Astakhov stated that the Soviet Union preferred the last of these, and that a declaration by Germany that she would not attack the Soviet Union or that she

---

[2]) Rosso to Ciano, 4 June 1939 (Nos. 66), Toscano, pp. 44-45; Rosso to Ciano 4 June 1939 (No. 2085/871), *ID, XII,* 88-90. For other documents on the economic negotiations in June, see Rosso to Ciano, 11 June 1939 (No. 69) Toscano, p. 47; Rosso to Ciano, 12 June 1939 (No. 70), *ibid.*; Rosso to Ciano, 12 June 1939 (No. 71), *ibid.*

[3]) Memorandum of Hilger, 17 June 1939, *NSR,* p. 23; *BDS,* pp. 25-26; Rosso to Ciano, 12 June 1939 (No. 2198/913), *ID,* XII, 175-76.

[4]) Rosso to Ciano, 12 June 1939 (No. 2198/913), *ID,* XII, 176; see also Seeds to Halifax, 10 June 1939, *BD,* VI, 22.

[5]) Memorandum of Hilger, 17 June 1939, *NSR,* p. 23; *BDS,* p. 24.

[6]) Tippelskirch to Ribbentrop, 18 June 1939 (with enclosures), *NSR,* pp. 21-25; *BDS,* pp. 24-25; Schulenburg to Ribbentrop, 27 June 1939, *NSR,* pp. 24-25; *BDS,* pp. 27-28.

would sign a non-aggression pact would probably induce Russia to refrain from signing a treaty with England. The Bulgarian Minister gave an account of this conversation to the head of the Political Section of the German Foreign Ministry on the following day.[7]

The reaction of the German government to the feeler put out by Astakhov is not yet quite clear. There is no doubt that in June there was considerable anxiety in Berlin about the possibly imminent signing of an alliance between England, France, and the Soviet Union.[8] Nevertheless, there was still considerable hesitation and suspicion in Germany.[9]

Schulenburg returned to Moscow from Berlin on June 26. He told his Italian colleague, Rosso, that Ribbentrop had been rather sceptical about the possibility of impeding an Anglo-French-Soviet agreement and was still worried about the repercussions of a German-Soviet rapprochement on Japan. Ribbentrop had, however, decided to continue the negotiations in progress by both official and unofficial means. He instructed Schulenburg to speak openly to Astakhov, the Soviet Chargé in Berlin, and more guardedly to Molotov. Before leaving Berlin, Schulenburg met Astakhov and assured him that the U.S.S.R. had no reason to fear a German attack on herself or on the Scandinavian countries. He stressed that Berlin wanted to collaborate with the Soviet Union, though a Russian agreement with England and France would be interpreted as a hostile act and make collaboration almost impossible. Schulenburg suggested that if "political bases" were to be constructed, the Soviet government would have to abandon its attitude of reserve and speak more clearly.[10]

Schulenburg's instructions for his talk with Molotov were more limited. He was authorized to assure Molotov that Germany had no hostile intentions toward the U.S.S.R. and to point out that a Soviet agreement with Britain and France would make an improvement in Russo-German relations most difficult. Any political suggestions Molotov might raise were to be referred to Berlin. In the economic field, Schulenburg was to secure agreement on a common basis for

---

[7]) Memorandum of Woermann, 15 June 1939, *NSR*, pp. 20-21; *BDS*, p. 23.

[8]) Coulondre to Bonnet, 1 June 1939, France, pp. 170-72; cf. note 1 to Schulenburg to Weizsäcker, 5 June 1939, *BDS*, p. 22.

[9]) Hewel to Weizsäcker, 29 June 1939, *NSR*, 25-26; *BDS*, p. 29; Tippelskirch to Schulenburg, 12 July 1939, *NSR*, p. 32; *BDS*, pp. 34-35. Note, however, Rossi's statement, based on a later and un-published document, that on June 15 Ribbentrop told Shiratori, the Japanese Ambassador to Italy, that Germany would sign a non-aggression pact with Russia (Rossi, p. 31 and n. 1). Ribbentrop may have been trying to spur the pro-Axis Shiratori on to greater efforts on behalf of a German-Italian-Japanese alliance.

[10]) Rosso to Ciano, 27 June 1939, *ID*, XII, 297-98; Rosso to Ciano, 28 June 1939, *ibid.*, p. 303.

negotiations. If such a basis were assured, Germany would send an economic delegation to Moscow.[11])

On June 28 Schulenburg saw Molotov. In the question of economic negotiations, Molotov referred to recent talks between Mikoyan and Hilger in which the former had requested certain information from the Germans. Molotov said that upon settlement of this issue, a trip of Schnurre to Moscow might be profitable. In political matters, Molotov listened to Schulenburg's statements with great interest but answered with considerable reserve. The first report Schulenburg sent to Berlin on this conversation emphasized the reticent attitude of Molotov and resulted in a directive by Ribbentrop that political and economic talks be temporarily interrupted.[12]) A second, and more detailed, report seems to have encouraged Ribbentrop in his thoughts about a possible German-Soviet agreement.[13]) New instructions for Schulenburg were, therefore, worked on in Germany.[14])

In the meantime, the Italian Ambassador in Moscow, acting under instructions from Ciano and in concert with his German colleague, told Potemkin, the Deputy Commissar for Foreign Affairs, on July 4, that he knew through communications from Rome that the German government was sincere in its attempts to improve relations with the Soviet Union. Potemkin replied that good relations between Germany and the Soviet Union would undoubtedly constitute one safeguard of peace.[15])

After approval by Hitler, the new German instructions were sent to the German Embassy in Moscow around July 8. They provided for further concessions in the economic sphere—presumably compliance with Mikoyan's request for certain information—but authorized no further steps in the political field.[16]) On July 10, Hilger met Mikoyan and submitted the new proposals sent by Berlin as Germany's last concession and as a token of German good faith in the negotiations.

---

[11]) Rosso to Ciano, 27 June 1939, *ibid.*, pp. 297-98; Attolico to Ciano, 27 June 1939, *ibid.*, p. 298; Rosso to Ciano, 28 June 1939, *ibid.*, p. 303; Kleist, pp. 43-44.

[12]) Schulenburg to Ribbentrop, 29 June 1939, *NSR*, pp. 26-27; *BDS*, pp. 29-30; Weizsäcker to Schulenburg, 30 June 1939, *ibid.*, pp. 27-28; *BDS*, p. 31; cf. Rosso to Ciano, 30 June 1939, *ID*, XII, 317.

[13]) Schulenburg to Ribbentrop, 3 July 1939, *NSR*, pp. 28-30; *BDS*, pp. 31-33; Attolico to Ciano, 7 July 1939, *ID*, XII, 379.

[14]) See Tippelskirch to Schulenburg, 12 July 1939, *NSR*, p. 31; *BDS*, p. 34.

[15]) Ciano to Rosso, 23 June 1939, *ID*, XII, 259; Rosso to Ciano, 25 June 1939, *ibid.*, pp. 273-74; Rosso to Ciano, 28 June 1939, *ibid.*, p. 303; Rosso to Ciano, 4 July 1939, *ibid.*, p. 344; Rosso to Ciano, 5 July 1939, *ibid.*, p. 364; cf. Toscano, pp. 56-60.

[16]) The text of this instruction is not yet available. Information on it can be found in Tippelskirch to Schulenburg, 12 July 1939, *NSR*, pp. 30-31; *BDS*, p. 34; Attolico to Ciano, 7 July 1939, *ID*, XII, 379; Rosso to Ciano, 11 July 1939, *ibid.*, p. 403.

Mikoyan reserved the right to discuss these proposals at the next meeting, presumably intending to refer the whole question of economic negotations to the Kremlin for a decision.[17]

The Soviet answer was delayed for almost two weeks. During this period the Soviet government must have decided that the German government's intentions were serious and that the "political bases" for the formal resumption of economic negotiations had been provided. This question of "political bases" was not raised again when, on July 21, 1939, Schulenburg was asked by the Soviet government to inform Berlin that Babarin, the Soviet trade delegate, would call on Schnurre on the next day to announce that he was authorized to negotiate an economic treaty.[18] Babarin, accordingly visited Schnurre on July 22, whereupon Berlin told Schulenburg that all negotiations with the Soviet Union could now proceed, Germany being "ready for outspoken concessions."[19] The resumption of formal economic negotiations between Germany and the Soviet Union was announced in the Moscow newspapers on the same day.[20]

Before going into the details of the Russo-German discussions from July 22 to August 13, which prepared the way for the actual pact negotiations, it seems desirable to turn briefly to the famous Hudson —Wohlthat conversations which aroused considerable comment at the time. It has been suggested that the leaks of these secret talks, supposedly indicating a revival of British efforts to appease Germany, produced the Soviet announcement of the resumption of trade negotiations. [21] This is most unlikely. The Hudson—Wohlthat talk which was to leak out took place on the afternoon of July 20.[22] The rather fanciful stories about these talks came out on the morning of July 22.[23] The Soviet announcement on the trade negotiations,

17) Rosso to Ciano, 11 July 1939, *ID*, XII, 403.

18) Schulenburg to Ribbentrop (Moscow No. 132), cited in Weizsäcker to Schulenburg, 22 July 1939, International Military Tribunal for the Far East, Defense Document 1633 (Exhibit 2724) (mimeo, 2pp.), p. 1; Rosso to Ciano, 25 July 1939, *ID*, XII, p. 509.

19) Weizsäcker to Schulenburg, 22 July 1939, International Military Tribunal for the Far East, Defense Document 1633 (Exhibit 2724) (mimeo, 2pp.); see also Kordt, *Wahn und Wirklichkeit*, p. 161.

20) Schulenburg to Ribbentrop, 22 July 1939, *NSR*, p. 32; *BDS*, p. 36.

21) Frederick Schuman, *Soviet Politics at Home and Abroad* (New York, 1946), p. 369. Little use has been made of Schuman's books in this work because of the difficulty of finding the facts among the fairy tales. Much of this kind of work has had to be done in the primary sources; there is no need to add to this labor when other, far more reliable, secondary sources are available.

22) Memorandum of Dirksen, 21 July 1939, Russia, Ministry of Foreign Affairs of the U.S.S.R., *Documents and Materials Relating to the Eve of the Second World War*, Vol. II, *Dirksen Papers (1938-1939)* (Moscow, 1948), p. 67.

23) *New Yorks Times*, July 23, 1939, p. 25; July 24, p. 1; cf. Potemkin III, 710.

however, had been broadcast over the Moscow radio on the evening of July 21 and was rebroadcast on the German radio the same night.[24]) From this, and from the previous notification of Schulenburg already mentioned, it is clear that the Soviet decision to resume formal economic negotiations must have been made before the news of the Hudson-Wohlthat talks were published, and in all probablity before the talks took place.[25])

On or about July 25 Ribbentrop, at Hitler's orders, personally drew up instructions to Schnurre for an informal talk with Astakhov covering a large number of topics.[26]) On the evening of July 26, Schnurre went over the whole field of German-Soviet relations with Astakhov and Babarin, the Soviet trade negotiator, as he had been instructed.[27]) Schnurre outlined the possibilities for a political agreement with the Soviet Union by way of an adjustment of interests after Astakhov had indicated that this was the course the Soviets most wanted to follow. Schnurre also indicated that this was the way Soviet Russia could stay neutral in a European conflict—clearly a major aim of German policy.[28]) At the end the Russians asked whether the statements made by Schnurre would be maintained by prominent German representatives; Schnurre answered that they would.[29])

Weizsäcker sent a copy of Schnurre's memorandum on this conversation to Schulenburg and instructed the latter to seek an interview with Molotov to find out whether Molotov held views similar to those expressed by Astakhov. Weizsäcker also authorized Schulenburg to become more specific if Molotov abandoned his reserve. The instruction states:

> In every development of the Polish question, be it in a peaceful manner as we wish or be it in another manner forced

---

[24]) Associated Press dispatches of July 21, *New York Times,* July 22, 1939, p. 3.

[25]) The details of the Hudson-Wohlthat and related conversations in July and August of 1939 are not directly relevant to this study. See Russia, *Dirksen Papers,* pp. 67-131 and 182-91 *passim;* cf. Dirksen, "Englisch-Deutsche Verhandlungen Sommer 1939" in *Die Neue Woche,* Nov. 27, 1948, p. 5; Minute by Mr. Ashton-Gwatkin, 7 June 1939, *BD,* V, 791-93. A large number of additional documents has now been published in the sixth volume of the British documents.

[26]) The text of the instruction is not available. See Memorandum of Schnurre, 27 July 1939, *NSR,* p. 32; *BDS,* p. 36; Kordt, *Wahn und Wirklichkeit,* p. 161; Testimony of Schnurre, U.S. v. Weizsäcker, G.T. 19169-70.

[27]) Memorandum of Schnurre, 27 July 1939, *NSR,* pp. 32-36; *BDS,* pp. 86-40

[28]) *Ibid.,* p. 34; *BDS,* pp. 37-38; Schnurre tried to deny this point when on the witness stand in the Weizsäcker trial but retracted his denial upon having his own memorandum read back to him by the prosecutor (U.S. v. Weizsäcker, G.T. 19134-42).

[29]) Weizsäcker to Schulenburg, 29 July 1939, *NSR,* p. 36; *BDS,* pp. 40-41.

upon us, we would be prepared to safeguard all Soviet interests and to come to an understanding with their government.[30])

This is almost verbatim the same allusion to a fourth partition of Poland that was contained in Ribbentrop's memorandum of May 25. Obviously the terms of a German-Soviet agreement were now being drawn up.[31])

On August 2 Ribbentrop conducted a conversation with Astakhov in which they went over the ground covered in the Schnurre-Astakhov conversation of July 27 in an even more definite form. Ribbentrop thus confirmed the offer of Schnurre and in turn requested Astakhov to get confirmation from Moscow.[32]) Further instructions for his forthcoming conversation with Molotov were sent to Schulenburg on August 3.[33]) These instructions have not been published, but in a supplement to them Schulenburg was informed that another conversation between Schnurre and Astakhov was planned for August 3, even before the scheduled Schulenburg-Molotov conversation—an obvious sign of Germany's anxiety for speed.[34]) At this meeting Schnurre, after discussing some aspects of the Danzig situation with Astakhov, asked about the progress of the negotiations and, in accordance with his instructions, urged speed in the economic sphere so that a political agreement could follow quickly.[35])

---

[30]) Weizsäcker to Schulenburg, 29 July 1939, *BDS*, p. 41; the American editors' translation is not quite satisfactory—the possibility of a military solution is not made as definite as the original indicates. This may have been the special instruction sent to Schulenburg at Hitler's order on July 30 according to Kordt (*Wahn und Wirklichkeit, pp.* 162-63); on the other hand, there is mention of another telegraphic directive of July 31 in Schulenburg to Ribbentrop, 4 August 1939, *NSR*, p. 39; *BDS*, p. 44.

[31]) It may be of significance that during this period — the end of July and the beginning of August—the Soviet government invited Germany and Italy to send missions to an agricultural congress in Moscow. Both Axis powers accepted the invitations. Ciano to Attolico, 26 July 1939, *ID*, XII, 516-17; Attolico to Ciano, 27 July 1939, *ibid.*, p. 531; Attolico to Ciano, 29 July 1939, *ibid.*, pp. 540-41; Ciano to Rossoni, 3 August 1939, *ibid.*, p. 573; Memorandum of Schnurre, 21 July 1939, *NSR*, p. 33; *BDS*, p. 37; Schulenburg to Schliep, 7 August 1939, *NSR*, p. 44; *BDS*, p. 49; Memorandum of Schnurre, 10 August 1939, *NSR*, p. 44; *BDS*, pp. 44-50.

[32]) Ribbentrop to Schulenburg, 3 August 1939, *NSR*, pp. 37-39; *BDS*, pp. 42-43

[33]) Berlin No. 165 of August 3; the statement in the American edition of *NSR* that the instruction is Berlin No. 166 (p. 37, n. 21) is erroneous—No. 166 is not an instruction but rather an account by Ribbentrop of his talk with Astakhov, sent to Schulenburg for his information. The German edition, identifying the instruction as No. 165 which left Berlin at 12:58 PM, August 3, before either No. 164 or No. 166, is correct (p. 41, n. 1). For a telegram from Schnurre to Schulenburg on 2 August 1939, see Langer and Gleason, p. 170.

[34]) Weiszäcker to Schulenburg, 3 August 1939, *NSR*, p. 37; *BDS*, pp. 42-43.

[35]) Testimony of Schnurre, U.S. v. Weizsäcker, G.T. 19143-44; Testimony of Kessel, *ibid.*, E.T. 9478-80. For the story that on or about August 4 Hitler made his final decision to sign with Russia, see Rossi, p. 38 and n. 1; Namier, *Diplomatic Prelude*, p. 284.

On the evening of August 3, 1939, Schulenburg had his conversation with Molotov.[36]) He again detailed the German proposals, but Molotov, no doubt combining distrust of Germany with a realization of the capital to be made out of her desire for speed, remained non-committal, though more friendly than before. The reaction of the Soviet government to the German proposals came a few days later on August 7 when Astakhov was sent new instructions as Ribbentrop had requested on August 2.[37]) These, however, seem not to have been very definite except that Astakhov was again to declare the desire of the Soviet government for improved relations with Germany. Astakhov carried out these instructions in a talk with Schnurre on the morning of August 10.[38]) Schnurre took this opportunity to define the outstanding questions in need of discussion more precisely.[39]) Astakhov received more definite instructions from Moscow on one of the following days and called on Schnurre again on August 12.[40]) He told Schnurre that the Soviet government was prepared to take up the questions raised in the informal discussions in formal political negotiations to take place in Moscow.[41]) Astakhov was informed that the German government was in agreement with this procedure.[42]) The time had come to send Schulenburg detailed instructions for the treaty negotiations. The basis for the political negotiations had been firmly laid.[43])

---

[36]) Beloff (II, 261) mistakenly places the talk on August 4. Schulenburg's report is dated August 3; it left Moscow at 12:20 AM on August 4 (*NSR*, p. 39).

[37]) Schulenburg to Ribbentrop, 7 August 1939, Moscow No. 162, not published; see Kordt, *Wahn und Wirklichkeit*, p. 163 and n. 2.

[38]) Memorandum of Schnurre, 10 August 1939, *NSR*, pp. 44-46 *BDS*, pp. 49-52.

[39]) *Ibid.;* cf. Testimony of Schnurre, U.S. v. Weizsäcker, G.T. 19145-53, *passim.*

[40]) Schnurre to Schulenburg, 14 August 1939, *NSR*, pp. 48-49; *BDS*, p. 54; the "Saturday" referred to must have been August 12.

[41]) See also Kordt, *Wahn und Wirklichkeit*, p. 163. The news of this step was sent to Berchtesgaden and created the famous interruption in the Hitler-Ciano-Ribbentrop conversations (Kordt, p. 163 and n. 3; 1871 - PS, *TMWC*, XXIX; 52; Ciano, *Ciano's Diplomatic Papers*, pp. 298 and 302). Namier has been confused by the evidence and mistakenly calls the whole business a "concoction" (*Diplomatic Prelude*, pp. 267-68; 283-84); cf. Beloff, II, 264.

[42]) Kordt, *Wahn und Wirklichkeit*, pp. 163-64.

[43]) This turning of the Russo-German negotiations into the political field led the anti-Nazi opposition within the German government to warn Great Britain of the possibility of a German-Soviet agreement. Erich Kordt went to London, with Weizsäcker's approval, to carry such a warning. He talked to Lord Vansittart who assured him that an Anglo-Soviet treaty would certainly be concluded. (Testimony of Erich Kordt, U.S. v. Weizsäcker, E.T. 7394-97; Testimony of Weizsäcker, *ibid.,* 7745-46, 9027, 9428-29, 9432; Kordt, *Nicht aus dem Akten*, pp. 310-16; cf. Fabian von Schlabrendorff, *They almost killed Hitler* [New York, 1947], p. 21.)

For information on the Russo-German negotiations furnished to the American government by members of the staff of the German Embassy in Moscow, and the action taken on the basis of this information by the United States, see Langer and Gleason, pp. 124-21, 160-61, 164, 185-86; Hull, I, 656-57.

CHAPTER FOUR

AUGUST 14, — SEPTEMBER 28, 1939:
THE GERMAN-SOVIET AGREEMENTS

This chapter covers the period from the beginning of the concrete negotiations for the non-aggression pact until the signing of the treaty of friendship on September 28. It appears to this writer that these negotiations must be viewed as an organic whole. An account of them, therefore, should not be divided, as some might wish, by the outbreak of the Second World War. The negotiations were conducted with a view to channeling the war into certain directions, and the actual outbreak of the war was so tied up with the agreements between Germany and the Soviet Union as to be almost a part of the negotiations. Any division of the period covered by this chapter into separate parts would distort, not clarify. For accounts written within another framework such a division might be appropriate; but in the history of German-Soviet relations this period is, as will appear from the account, essentially one unit.

On August 14 Schulenburg was sent a detailed instruction by Ribbentrop for an interview with Molotov.[1] Aside from general instructions on German-Soviet relations, this document contains an offer by Ribbentrop to go to Moscow to work out the details of an agreement swiftly and in person.

The Germans were, however, still worried about a possible agreement between England and the Soviet Union. Also on August 14 Weizsäcker, in accordance with instructions from Ribbentrop, sent Schulenburg a telegram on this subject which will be given here in full, both because it has not been published hitherto and because it sums up the issues rather clearly. The telegram is in answer to a telegram from Schulenburg of August 11 in which he must have reported information he had picked up about the arguments of the British military mission in Moscow, to the effect that while England might not be able to give Poland effective aid immediately, an eventual

---

[1] Ribbentrop to Schulenburg, 14 August 1939, *NSR*, pp. 50-52; the copy printed in the American edition is the text as used by Schulenburg in his conversation. For the original text as sent by Ribbentrop with an indication of the changes made in Moscow, see *BDS*, pp. 55-57.

Allied victory would bring with it a restoration of Poland. Weiz-säcker's telegram reads,

> I would ask you to counter most strenuously in the offices and with the leaders in Moscow the line of thinking you report as used by the British military. The development of the war sketched by the English military attaché in itself clearly points up (würde eindeutig zeigen) the value and significance of a Soviet understanding with Germany. How is England supposed to inter-vene effectively in support of Russia after Poland has been overrun? If Russia chooses the English side, she will in effect stand opposed to Germany alone as in 1914. If the Soviet Union chooses to come to an agreement with us, she will attain the security she desires [and] which we are prepared to guarantee fully. For your information I add that this line of thinking has been gone over in detail in the conversations with Astakhov here several times.
>
> Based on a telephoned
> directive of the Foreign Minister
>
> Weizsäcker.[2]

On the evening of August 15 Schulenburg saw Molotov to deliver the German message. In the conversation Molotov showed far greater friendliness than before and indicated considerable interest in the signing of a non-aggression pact. He gave his opinion, however, that considerable time would have to be taken up by careful negotiations.[3] On August 16 Ribbentrop sent Schulenburg instructions to see Molotov again, agree to each of the substantive points raised by Molotov on the 15th and urge the utmost speed on the Russians in receiving the German Foreign Minister. Ribbentrop would be prepared to come any time after August 18.[4]

With a German-Soviet agreement so imminent, the opposition in the German government again attempted to warn the Western Powers. On August 15 Weizsäcker dropped hints to both the British and French ambassadors in Berlin about the possible development of German-Russian relations in regard to Poland.[5]

---

[2] "Diplogerma Moskau No. 173 v. 14 August 1939 zu Poi. II 2858 für Botschafter auf Nr. 167 vom 11.8.", NG - 5367 (mimeo, 1p.).

[3] Schulenburg to Ribbentrop, 15 August 1939, *NSR*, pp. 52-53; *BDS*, pp. 58-59; Memorandum of Schulenburg, 16 August 1939 (sent 17 August), *NSR*, pp. 53-56; *BDS*, pp. 59-62, Schulenburg to Weizsäcker, 16 August 1939, *NSR*, p. 57; *BDS*, pp. 62-63; it should be noted that only the first of these reports reached Berlin before Ribbentrop sent his answer to the points raised by Molotov in the interview.

[4] Ribbentrop to Schulenburg, 16 August 1939, *NSR*, p. 58; *BDS*, p. 62.

[5] Henderson to Halifax, 16 August 1939, Great Britain, Foreign Office, *Documents concerning German-Polish Relations and the Outbreak of Hostilities between Great Britain and Germany* (British War Blue Book), (New York, 1939), pp. 118-19; Coulondre to Bonnet, 15 August 1939, France, pp. 268-69; Testimony of Weizsäcker, U.S. v. Weizsäcker, E.T. 7756-57.

In Moscow, Schulenburg again saw Molotov on the 17th, read to him Ribbentrop's latest instructions, and received the formal Russian answer to the German message of August 15. In this reply and through Molotov's supplementary remarks the Soviets indicated their pleasure at the developments and stated that the conclusion of an economic agreement should be followed, after a brief interval, by a political treaty accompanied by the appropriate secret protocols. These latter, which would be the subject of the German Foreign Minister's trip to Moscow, would require careful preparation and German drafts for the agreements were requested.[6] The Germans, however were impatient of any delays—the attack on Poland was scheduled for the morning of August 26. Schulenburg was therefore instructed to see Molotov again in an instruction sent on August 18 and received on August 19. Again Ribbentrop urged speed. He referred to the fact that the negotiations for the economic agreement were now concluded so that this condition of the Soviets had been met. A draft of a non-aggression treaty was included, as well as an offer to iron out all spheres of influence problems by oral discussions in Moscow.[7]

August 19, 1939, was a crucial day in many ways—not because on that day the course of events changed, but rather because so many series of events had their culmination. The economic agreement between Germany and Soviet Russia was signed in Berlin by Schnurre and Babarin. The actual text of the agreement has not been published, but a considerable amount of material on it is available. From these sources the main points of the agreement can be reconstructed; these are important, not just for the actual working out of the agreement, since the scope of subsequent arrangements was far greater, but rather as an indication of what the two countries wanted from each other, what they were willing to do for each other, and what pattern their economic relations might follow.[8] As foreshadowed by the previous negotiations, a German credit of 200 million Reichsmark at an effective rate of 4 % was granted for Soviet pur-

---

[6] Schulenburg to Ribbentrop, 17 August 1939, *NSR*, pp. 59-61; *BDS*, pp. 65-67.
[7] Ribbentrop to Schulenburg, 18 August 1939, *NSR*, pp. 61-63; *BDS*, pp. 67-69.
[8] The following are the main sources: Memorandum of Schnurre, 29 August 1939, *NSR*, pp. 83-85; *BDS*, pp. 82-84; the documents of the Friedrich Krupp A.G., Abteilung für Russland, "Neues Kreditabkommen mit der U.d.S.S.R.", 21 August 1939, NI-921 (photostat, 2pp.); "Neues deutsch-russisches Kreditabkommen," 22 August 1939, NI - 921 (photostat, 2 pp.); "Warenliste für das 200mill-RM Kreditabkommen vom 19. August 1939," 22 August 1939, NI - 921 (photostat, 1p.); "Warenliste für das 'Laufende Geschäft' gemäss dem deutsch-russischen Abkommen vom 19. August 1939," 22 August 1939, NI - 921 (photostat, 1p.); Germany, Auswärtiges Amt, *Vertrags-Verzeichnis*, Item 1392, p. 634; cf. Dallin, pp. 57, 422; Magistrati to Ciano, 16 August 1939 (No. 513), in Toscano, p. 81; Rosso to Ciano, 22 August 1939, *ID*, XIII (12 August-3 September 1939), p. 113.

chases. For the coming two years, goods to the extent of 180 million Reichsmark were covered. The goods Germany was to send were mainly machine tools, armaments, machinery, and certain special metals. The Russians obligated themselves to send Germany various raw materials, especially lumber, cotton, feed grain, petroleum, and platinum. The further development of German-Soviet trade was to grow out of this type of exchange with certain special features which will be discussed later. This first agreement was signed in great hurry and not all the details in it were fully settled. Its immediate importance was more in the political field.

As this time Germany was pushing toward a rupture with Poland —a form of pushing which parallels the persistent requests for an immediate reception of Ribbentrop by Moscow and must be considered in connection with it. The scheme of making and elaborating demands in such a fashion as to consciously preclude their being met had been carefully applied in the case of Czechoslovakia.[9]) This scheme was now to be used in the dealings with Poland. For a full understanding of Germany's policy of speeding developments in the world crisis into a war, the following should be read together with the various already published directives to Schulenburg. This is a telegram from Weizsäcker for transmission to Ribbentrop on August 19, 1939.

> Will you please forward the enclosed report of Veesenmayer [from Danzig] at once, jointly with the following addition:
>
> "Gauleiter Forster [of Danzig] urgently requested me [Veesenmayer] to ask whether the RAM [Ribbentrop] would approve increasing pressure against Poland to the limit. On account of the talks held on the 18th [of August] about the question of the customs officials it seems that Poland is prepared to yield.... Further discussions.... will start on Monday 21.
>
> Gauleiter Forster intends to extend claims.... Should the Poles yield again, it is intended to increase the claims further, in order to make accord impossible. Please submit at once to RAM and reply.
>
> Conclusion of report from Danzig.
>
> I suggest to reply to Veesenmayer as follows:
>
> I agree with your idea about how to conduct discussions about the customs officials dispute. Still, discussions will have to be conducted and pressure exerted against Poland in such a way that responsibility for failure to come to an agreement and the consequences rest with Poland.

---

[9]) Memorandum on the Hitler-Henlein Conversation, 28 March 1938, *GD*, II, 198; memorandum of Ribbentrop, 29 March 1938, *ibid.*, p. 204.

Conclusion of reply to Veesenmayer.
Weizsäcker."

(signed:) Weizsäcker [10])

Thus Germany was simultaneously pushing Europe into war and inviting Russia in to take her share of the spoils.

On August 19 Schulenburg twice saw Molotov. He was finally able to get a Soviet draft treaty and agreement to the arrival of Ribbentrop on August 26 or 27. No arguments on his part could secure an earlier date. Since Schulenburg's two interviews took place in the afternoon, his reports on them apparently did not reach Berlin until the morning of August 20.[11]) On August 20 Ribbentrop sent Schulenburg a letter from Hitler to Stalin which again urged the Russians to receive Ribbentrop without delay, on August 23 at the latest.[12])

On August 21 Schulenburg again saw Molotov twice and the second time received Stalin's reply agreeing to receive Ribbentrop on August 23.[13]) The persistent urgency of the German requests must have made it clear to the Soviets that they would have to deal with Germany quickly; after some deadline had passed—presumably the good campaign weather in Poland—Germany might no longer be interested in an agreement with the Soviet Union. On the morning of August 22 the forthcoming visit of the German Foreign Minister to Moscow for the purpose of signing a Non-Aggression Pact was announced in the Russian press.

To inform the German representatives abroad of the details of the new turn of events, a four-page long telegram was sent out by the Berlin foreign office on August 22 to all important missions except the one in Tokyo which received a special telegram.[14]) The telegram reviews the situation from the official German standpoint sufficiently clearly to deserve quoting.

The normalization of the relations between Germany and the Soviet Union has been in preparation through months of slow and steady development. The starting point was the resumed economic and credit negotiations.... Simultaneously with these

---

[10]) NG-2172, trans. United States, Office of Chief of Counsel for War Crimes (hereafter referred to as OCCWC), (mimeo, 1p.); cf. Lewis Namier, *In the Nazi Era* (London, 1952), pp. 79-80. The discussion of the Polish "hotheads" (Heissporne) in Weizsäcker's memoirs should be read with this document in mind.

[11]) Schulenburg to Ribbentrop, 19 Aug. 1939, *NSR*, pp. 63, 64-65, 65-66; *BDS*, pp. 70, 70-72, 72-73.

[12]) Ribbentrop to Schulenburg, 20 Aug. 1939, *NSR*, pp. 66-67; *BDS*, pp. 73-74.

[13]) Schulenburg to Ribbentrop, 21 Aug. 1939, *NSR*, pp. 67-68, 68, 69; *BDS*, pp. 75, 75-76, 76.

[14]) Weizsäcker to Foreign Missions, 22 Aug. 1939, NG - 5675 (mimeo, 2pp.).

negotiations political contacts were established, leading in recent weeks to a thorough exchange of views between Berlin and Moscow.... In view of the worsening of the crisis.... it was in our interests to prevent a commitment of the Soviet Union to the side of England. It was necessary to remove the Soviet Government's feeling of being threatened should a German-Polish conflict occur. The appropriate means for doing this was to make the conversations concerning a non-aggression pact progressively more specific up to the point now reached. Thus simultaneously the aim we had pursued from the beginning—to disrupt in Moscow the English-French negotiations for encirclement—was realized.

On the same day Hitler informed his generals of forth-coming events. In a then secret, but now famous, speech he announced that war was ahead and that Russia would sign with Germany.[15]

That day Hitler made out Ribbentrop's full powers. In accordance with the speed which Germany considered essential, the full powers stipulated that the treaty and other agreements worked out would enter into force as soon as they were signed.[16] Hitler still telephoned a last instruction for Ribbentrop which was forwarded to him from Berlin on August 23. Because it touches on a question which was to arise in the fall of 1940 and which will be considered in detail at a later point in this study, the message is translated in full.

> For the Foreign Minister.
> The Führer would be most pleased (würde es sehr begrüssen) if it were made clear within the framework of the present conversation that after agreement between Germany and Russia concerning the problems of Eastern Europe, these would be considered to belong exclusively to the sphere of interests of Germany and Russia.[17]

This message was delayed in transmission and reached Ribbentrop too late for consideration in the negotiations.[18] It does, however, show Hitler's attitude at the time.

In the evening of August 22 Ribbentrop and his delegation took off by plane for Moscow, spending the night in Königsberg. There last minute preparations were made for the forthcoming conver-

---

[15] Hitler speech of August 22, 1939, 798 - PS, *TMWC*, XXVI, 338-44; also Räder - 27, *TMWC*, XLI, 16-25; cf. Helmuth Greiner, *Die Oberste Wehrmachtsführung, 1939-1943,* (Wiesbaden, 1951), pp. 38-43.

[16] Full Powers, 22 Aug. 1939, *NSR*, p. 69; for German title, not in the American edition, see *BDS*, p. 76.

[17] Weizsäcker to Ribbentrop, 23 Aug. 1939 (Berlin No. 201), photographic reproduction in Rossi, p. 49.

[18] Kordt, *Wahn und Wirklichkeit*, pp. 180-81.

sations.[19]) That same evening the British Ambassador in Berlin, Sir Nevile Henderson, informed State Secretary Weizsäcker over the telephone of the contents of a letter from Chamberlain to Hitler of that date, stating clearly that Britain would fulfill her obligations to Poland regardless of what agreements the Germans might sign with the Soviet Union.[20]) Hitler did not believe the British would do anything of the sort.[21])

At 11:00 A.M. on August 23 the German delegation arrived in Moscow. They were greeted by Deputy Commissar Potemkin, erstwhile advocate of collective security.[22]) During the afternoon a three to four hour long conversation took place in which the various questions were apparently defined and some agreements reached.[23]) A question concerning Russia's interests in part of the Baltic area was cleared up by direct telephone communications between Moscow and Berlin, with Hitler agreeing to the Soviet demand.[24]) In the evening there was a second long meeting. At this time the final wording of the Non-Aggression Pact was agreed upon.[25]) The secret additional protocol was also written. It was denounced as a forgery by the Soviet Prosecutor at the main trial at Nuremberg.[26]) It is, nevertheless, unquestionably authentic. Later, at Ribbentrop's orders, special secrecy requirements concerning both its contents and existence were imposed[27]) and carried out.[28]) Its text is known and has been published.[29])

---

[19]) Paul O. Schmidt, *Statist auf diplomatischer Bühne 1923-1945* (Bonn, 1950), p. 441.

[20]) Henderson to Halifax, 23 Aug. 1939, Great Britain, *British War Blue Book*, p. 127; for the text of Chamberlain's letter see *ibid.*, pp. 125-27. On August 23 the text of the letter was communicated to the Italians (Loraine to Ciano, 23 August 1939, *ID*, XIII, 121-22).

[21]) Kordt, *Wahn und Wirklichkeit*, p. 177; Ernst von Weizsäcker, *Erinnerungen* (Munich, 1950), pp. 252-53.

[22]) Schmidt, p. 442.

[23]) Kordt, *Wahn und Wirklichkeit*, p. 178; Ribbentrop to Hitler, 23 August 1939, *NSR*, pp. 71-72; *BDS*, p. 79; Kleist, pp. 57-58.

[24]) Kordt to Ribbentrop, 23 August 1939, *NSR*, p. 72; *BDS*, p. 80.

[25]) For account of these negotiations see Kordt, *Wahn und Wirklichkeit*, pp. 178-79; Affidavit of Gaus, 15 March 1946, Hess - 16, *TMWC*, XL, 295-97; Testimony of Ribbentrop, *TMWC*, X, 269; *PHKV*, X, 305.

[26]) *TMWC*, XIV, 284; *PHKV*, XIV, 315. Apologists for Soviet foreign policy have found it convenient to overlook this protocol. See for example, D.N. Pritt, *The State Department and the Cold War* (New York, 1948), pp. 74-81.

[27]) Ribbentrop to Schulenburg, 26 August 1939 (Berlin No. 213), Alfred Seidl (ed.), *Die Beziehungen zwischen Deutschland und der Sowjetunion, 1939-1941* (Tübingen, 1949), p. 97.

[28]) Envelope in the Moscow German Embassy, 27 August 1939, cited in Rossi, p. 54 and n. 2. The discussion of this in Assmann, p. 116, n. 1, involves a confusion with the Protocol of September 28, 1939.

[29]) *NSR*, p. 78; *BDS*, pp. 86-87; cf. Testimony of Blank, *TMWC*, X, 192-93;

This secret protocol provided that Finland, Estonia, and Latvia would be in the Russian, and Lithuania in the German sphere of interests. The claim of Lithuania to the Vilna area was recognized. The border between the German and Russian spheres in Poland was to be formed by the Pissa, Narev, Vistula, and San rivers. The Pissa river, which forms the northernmost section of the line, was accidentally left out of the draft of the secret protocol; it was inserted by a special protocol signed by Schulenburg and Molotov on August 28.[30] The question of eventually leaving a small Poland of some kind was left to future negotiations between Germany and Russia.

The section of the protocol referring to the Balkans is not so clear. Russia's interests in Bessarabia were stated and recognized. Germany declared her complete *political* disinterest in the whole Balkan area. The meaning of this came under scrutiny when the Russians moved against Bessarabia in June, 1940. Ribbentrop then wrote a memorandum for Hitler concerning the language of this portion of the protocol in which he said:

> This was in accordance with the general instructions given by the Führer for Southeastern Europe and also, as I recall it, with a special directive of the Führer which I received before my departure for Moscow, in which the Führer authorized me to declare German disinterestedness in the territories of Southeastern Europe, even, if necessary, as far as Constantinople and the Straits. However, the latter were not discussed.[31]

There is no trace anywhere of instructions in line with Ribbentrop's summary. It seems quite likely that Ribbentrop has, for the purpose of excusing himself—as Foreign Minister he could easily have had the document searched for in the files—distorted the previously quoted telegram from Berlin of August 23, which arrived in Moscow too late to influence the negotiations. Unless there is important evidence on this point which is yet to be published, it would appear that this section of the protocol was purposely left rather vague, since an attempt to define German and Russian interests in the Balkans precisely would have made any sort of agreement extremely difficult, perhaps impossible.

There was more conversation concerning a large variety of topics

---

PHKV, X, p. 218-19. Testimony of Weizsäcker, *TMWC*, XIV, 285-86; *PHKV*, XIV, 316-18.

[30] Schulenburg to Ribbentrop, 28 Aug. 1939 (Moscow No. 229), Rossi, p. 54 and n. 1; Kordt, *Wahn und Wirklichkeit*, pp. 178 and 179, n. 2.

[31] Memorandum of Ribbentrop, 24 June 1940, *NSR*, p. 158; *BDS*, p. 177; this must be the document quoted by Namier in his essay on German-Russian relations (*Europe in Decay*, p. 271). He has failed, however, to point out that this explanation is of a much later date.

as well as some informal discussion at a subsequent session of toasts.[32])

The main points of interest in regard to the Non-Aggression Pact itself are two omissions. The Pact was not to enter into force when ratified, but rather as soon as signed; and second, there was no provision that it would become inoperative if one of the parties attacked a third country. Both of these provisions had been standard in previous treaties signed by the Soviets. The first was presumably omitted because of Germany's need for speed; the second since it was understood that Germany was about to attack Poland and that it was just to cover this contingency that the Pact was drawn up in the first place.[33]) Peace, the Soviets thought, was no longer indivisible.

The comment of Winston Churchill on this Pact deserves quotation:

> It is still worth while to record the terms of the Pact:
>> Both High Contracting Parties obligate themselves to desist from any act of violence, any aggressive action, and any attack on each other, either individually or jointly with other Powers.
>
> This treaty was to last ten years, and if not denounced by either side one year before the expiration of that period, would be automatically extended for another five years. There was much jubilation and many toasts around the conference table. Stalin spontaneously proposed the toast of the Fuehrer, as follows, "I know how much the German Nation loves its Fuehrer, I should therefore like to drink his health." A moral may be drawn from all this, which is of homely simplicity—"Honesty is the best policy." Several examples of this will be shown in these pages. Crafty men and statesmen will be shown misled by all their elaborate calculations. But this is the signal instance. Only twenty-two months were to pass before Stalin and the Russian nation in its scores of millions were to pay a frightful forfeit. If a government has no moral scruples, it often seems to gain great advantages and liberties of action, but "All comes out even at the end of the day, and will come out yet more even when all the days are ended."[34])

Ribbentrop arrived in Berlin from Moscow at 7:00 P.M. on August 24 and immediately reported to Hitler on his trip.[35]) Most of the exciting events of the next few days, the last days of peace, do not concern us here. Germany still hoped to separate the Western Powers from Poland, even after the signing of the Anglo-Polish

---

[32]) Memorandum of Hencke, 24 Aug. 1939, *NSR*, pp. 72-76; *BDS*, pp. 80-84.

[33]) Testimony of Ribbentrop, *TMWC*, X, 268-69; *PHKV*, X, 303-04; Affidavit of Gaus, *TMWC*, XL, 298.

[34]) Winston Churchill, *The Gathering Storm* (Boston, 1948), p. 394.

[35]) Kordt, *Wahn und Wirklichkeit*, p. 191.

alliance treaty on August 25.[36]) This treaty also had a secret protocol which was published after the war.[37]) It is interesting to note that this secret protocol, which specified Germany as the only country against which the Pact was directed,[38]) still included a provision for harmonizing the Anglo-Polish agreement with a possible Anglo-Soviet treaty of mutual assistance.[39])

During the five day period between August 26 and September 1, the extra days of peace resulting from Hitler's postponement of the attack on Poland, German attempts to isolate Poland took two general approaches. On the one hand various means were tried to befuddle the Western Powers into another Munich by a number of proposals and negotiation schemes. These have been detailed by Namier in his two works, by Kordt in his, and are to a considerable extent recorded in the various colored books. The second method, designed to strengthen the first, was to play on the fact that Soviet Russia was now in effect on the side of Germany. This theme recurs in the diplomatic documents involved in the negotiations just referred to. Attempts were apparently also made to bring in this fact or more directly by asking for Soviet pressure on Poland in Moscow. Only one of the relevant documents has been found, but there would appear to have been others. The text of this document, an instruction of Weizsäcker to Schulenburg of August 26, 1939, is as follows:

> *For the Ambassador only:*
>
> For your information: The tension in the German-Polish conflict is constantly increasing. In connection with the exchange of notes raised in Telegram 217 of the 25 August,[40]) please attempt to inquire discreetly:
>
> first: whether it is correct that the Soviet Union has pulled back its troops from the Polish border,
>
> two: whether, if this so, it could not be reversed, since every threat to Poland which appears, including [any] from the Russian side, would naturally contribute to an easing of the situation in the West, and could finally even diminish the willingness to help Poland a great deal (ausserordentlich).[41])

---

[36]) One reason for the signing of the Anglo-Polish treaty at this time was apparently the opinion of the British government that it would be better to work out the agreement with Russia first. "Extract from Record of Conversation between the Secretary of State and MM. Daladier and Bonnet in Paris on May 20, 1939," *BD*, V, 609; Halifax to Philipps, *ibid.*, p. 772.

[37]) Wacław Jędrzejewicz (ed.), *Poland in the British Parliament, 1939-1945* (New York, 1946), I, 191-92.

[38]) On the point, see also Halifax to Hoare, 8 April 1939, *BD*, V, 66.

[39]) See Section 2, C, of the protocol.

[40]) On the basis of the number this must have been a telegram from Moscow.

[41]) Berlin No. 218, NG - 2371 (mimeo, 1p.); the foregoing translation is from

What happened as a result of this message is not known; the whole area remains to be illuminated by as yet unpublished and unavailable documents.

In the last days before the war, Germany and the Soviet Union cleared up the minor difficulties left over from the previous agreements. On August 26 a secret German-Soviet protocol was signed in Berlin to settle certain technical economic problems which had been left open by the agreement of August 19.[42]) On August 28 a secret protocol was signed in Moscow, as has been pointed out already, which covered some minor oversights in the secret protocol to the Non-Aggression Pact of August 23. The first part of the German-Soviet treaty settlement of 1939 was thus completed. The second part was to follow the conclusion of the campaign against Poland.

In the meantime it had been necessary for Germany to notify her ally Italy and her prospective ally Japan of what had happened. The Italians were, or at least pretended to be, most pleased with the conclusion of the Pact.[43]) The Japanese, on the other hand, were most chagrined on hearing of the developments.[44]) They had been told on June 20 that the talks with the Soviet Union concerned only economic matters and that rumors about political talks were "fake".[45]) When the news of the Pact came out, the Hiranuma cabinet resigned. Its protest against the Pact was shown to Weizsäcker by Japanese Ambassador Oshima on August 26; he took it back at Weizsäcker's suggestion and on September 18 delivered a toned-down version of it for the Germans to lose in their archives.[46]) The Japanese certainly had a good case since the secret protocol of the Anti-Comintern Pact had provided as Article II:

the original, another English translation is in U.S. v. Weizsäcker, E.T. 603; cf. Testimony of Weizsäcker, *ibid.*, E.T. 7862. Rossi (p. 62 and n. 1) has apparently misunderstood this document completely.

[42]) Memorandum of Schnurre, 29 August 1939, *NSR*, p. 84; *BDS*, p. 93.

[43]) Schwerin-Krosigk to Ribbentrop, 23 August 1939, *NSR*, pp. 79-80; *BDS*, pp. 88-89; Mussolini to Hitler, 25 August 1939, *NSR*, pp. 82-83; *BDS*, pp. 90-91; Kordt, *Wahn und Wirklichkeit*, p. 191.

[44]) Memorandum of Weizsäcker, 22 August 1939, *NSR*, pp. 70-71; *BDS*, pp. 77-79; Franz Halder, *The Halder Diaries* (Washington, 1950), 27 August 1939, I, 30; Hull, I, 639; Saionji-Harada Memoirs, quoted in Feis, p. 34; Mackensen to Ribbentrop, 23 August 1939, International Military Tribunal for the Far East, Defense Document 1634 (Exhibit 2726), in Proceeding, English, pp. 24190-92.

[45]) Memorandum of Woerman, 20 June 1939, cited in Feis, p. 31 and n. 16 The date of this was *July* 20 according to International Military Tribunal for the Far East, Proceeding, English, pp. 24179-84.

[46]) Memorandum of Weizsäcker, 26 Aug. 1939, "German Documents on Relations with Japan", United States, *Department of State Bulletin*, XIV (1946), 1038; Memorandum of Weizsäcker, 18 Sep. 1939, *ibid.*, pp. 1038-39; Attolico to Ciano, 28 August 1939, *ID*, XIII, 238-39.

> The High Contracting Parties will not during the period of this treaty sign political agreements of any kind with the USSR which are contrary to the spirit of this agreement without mutual consent.[47])

The way was now clear for a German attack on Poland. The Western Powers might or might not come in. In any case, Soviet Russia would be neutral and Poland thus militarily isolated. Germany kept the Soviet informed on the final negotiations with England and stressed that they had insisted on Soviet participation in any settlement of the questions of Eastern Europe.[48]) As soon as fighting broke out on September 1, 1939, Schulenburg was given the necessary information and explanations to transmit to Molotov.[49])

On August 31 Molotov in a speech reviewing the international situation before the fourth special session of the Supreme Soviet of the U.S.S.R. gave a detailed analysis of recent events and the developments leading up to the signing of the pact.[50]) On the next day Hitler gave his war message to the German Reichstag and, stressing the great and lasting significance of the German-Russian treaty, stated his full agreement with Molotov's speech.[51])

German-Soviet relations from the beginning of the German invasion of Poland on September 1 to the Russian attack on Poland in the early morning of September 17 revolve around two main topics—the relations between Russia and Poland and the date of Russian intervention.

The first of these two topics seems to this writer as important as it is obscure. If a full account of the apparent vacillations in Soviet policy toward Poland from September 1-8 were available, much light would be thrown on the thinking behind Soviet policy in the crucial months of the summer and fall of 1939. Since the Russians had apparently not anticipated a German advance of the rapidity which actually occurred, the suggestions about help in the way of supplies

[47]) *Akten zur Deutschen Auswärtigen Politik, 1918-1945*, Serie D (1937-1945), Band I, *Von Neurath zu Ribbentrop* (September 1937-September 1938) (Baden-Baden, 1950), p. 600, n. 1.

[48]) Weizsäcker to Schulenburg, 29 Aug. 1939 (Berlin No. 227), NG - 2406 (mimeo, 2pp.), trans. United States, OCCWC. This note was probably sent during the night of 31 Aug. to 1 Sep. since it carries a handwritten note that the German army had started to march and that Schulenburg was to inform Molotov of this immediately; cf. U.S. v. Weizsäcker, E.T. 607.

[49]) *Ibid.;* Weizsäcker to Schulenburg, 1 Sep. 1939, NG - 4849, Staff Evidence Analysis, United States, OCCWC.

[50]) A good summary with extensive quotations is in Beloff, II, 274-76; full text in V.M. Molotov, *On the Ratification of the Soviet-German Pact of Non-Aggression* (Moscow, 1939).

[51]) 2322-PS, *TMWC*, XXX, 172-73.

made by the Russians to the Poles might indicate a desire to draw out the conflict in the East. The material already published has been carefully summarized by Dallin [52]) and Beloff.[53]) The author does not believe that any conclusions can be drawn with confidence from the available material, and since nothing of significance has turned up in his own research, he will not attempt to go into the problem other than to point out again its great importance.[54])

On the question of Soviet Russia's entry into the war on Poland, there is enough material for a fairly coherent account. The Russians were apparently neither eager nor ready to move quickly. To Ribbentrop's urgent request to move against Poland, a request sent as early as September 3, Molotov gave a formal reply indicating that the Soviets wanted to wait some time before acting. At the same time, while agreeing to the need of the German forces to cross the demarcation line in pursuit of Polish troops, the Soviet government emphasized that this must not interfere with strict adherence to the adopted line in the future,[55]) a point which Molotov had apparently made to Schulenburg as soon as he received the German message on September 4.[56]) The Germans assured the Soviets of their complete willingness to abide by the Moscow agreement but again urged the Russians to move against Poland.[57]) The Russians gave inconclusive answers to this in Moscow.[58]) In Berlin the new Soviet Ambassador, Shkvartsev, requested information concerning the positions of the remaining Polish military units.[59]) On Hitler's instructions the German High Command agreed to furnish the necessary

---

[52]) Dallin, pp. 66-67.

[53]) Beloff, II, 280-81.

[54]) The papers of the German Moscow Embassy, as well as other Embassies, for these days should contain some useful material, but almost nothing relevant to this topic has been published so far.

[55]) Ribbentrop to Schulenburg, 3 Sep. 1939, NSR, p. 86; BDS, p. 95; Schulenburg to Ribbentrop, 5 Sep. 1939, NSR, p. 87; BDS, p. 76; the Moscow telegram No. 261 of September 4 must have been a report on a Molotov-Schulenburg conversation on September 4 at which Schulenburg delivered Ribbentrop's message of the third.

[56]) This must also have been in the unpublished Moscow Telegram No. 261 see the "Reference" and first sentence of Ribbentrop to Schulenburg, 9 Sep. 1939, NSR, p. 89; BDS, p. 87.

[57]) Ribbentrop to Schulenburg, 9 Sep. 1939, NSR, pp. 89-90; BDS, pp. 98-99.

[58]) Schulenburg to Ribbentrop, 9 Sep. 1939, NSR, p. 90; BDS, p. 99 and 10 Sep. 1939, NSR, p. 91; BDS, pp. 100-01; cf. Halder II, 2. An interesting, though not wholly reliable, account of this affair can be found in Testimony of Jodl, TMWC, XV, 374-75; PHKV, XV, 410-11.

[59]) Kordt, Wahn und Wirklichkeit, p. 220.

information on September 12.[60]) Schulenburg was informed accordingly on September 13.[61])

Schulenburg's vigorous urgings on September 10 seem to have had
little effect on Molotov.[62]) In the next few days, however, the fear
that Germany and Poland would sign an armistice before the Soviets
marched in led the Russians to speed up their timetable. On the 10th
and 12th of September they raised the question of whether Germany
was about to sign an armistice and were reassured that this was not
the case.[63]) It was obvious, nevertheless, that unless the Russians
moved quickly, they might find themselves beginning hostilities after
the German-Polish conflict had ended. This they certainly did not
want to do; they would be sufficiently embarrassed by their non-
aggression treaty with Poland anyway. The Soviet preparations were
hurried up.[64]) On September 16 the Russians signed a truce which
ended the bitter and serious fighting between Soviet and Japanese
troops along the frontier of Manchuria.[65]) At 2:00 A.M. on September 17, Stalin told Schulenburg that the Russian forces would advance
at 6:00 A.M. that morning.[66]) The Germans regretted that the Russians had not attacked sooner,[67]) but were most pleased that they had
moved.[68])

Once the Soviet armies started to move, however, a variety of
minor frictions arose. There was the side issue of the content of the
communiqué announcing the Russian attack and the joint German-
Russian statement on the same subject—not very significant but
indicative of the mutual suspicions.[69]) More interesting is the great

---

[60]) Rossi, p. 65 and n. 3.

[61]) Ribbentrop to Schulenburg, 13 Sep. 1939, *NSR*, p. 92; *BDS*, p. 101.

[62]) Schulenburg to Ribbentrop, 10 Sep. 1939, *NSR*, p. 91; *BDS*, pp. 100-101.

[63]) *Ibid.;* Schulenburg to Ribbentrop, 12 Sep. 1939 (Moscow No. 334), cited
in Rossi, p. 65 and n. 2; Ribbentrop to Schulenburg, 13 Sep. 1939, *NSR*, p. 92;
BDS, p. 101.

[64]) Schulenburg to Ribbentrop, 14 Sep. 1939, *NSR*, pp. 92-93; *BDS*, p. 102.

[65]) Harriet L. Moore, *Soaviet Far Eastern Policy 1931-1945* (Princeton, New Jersey
1945), p. 113.

[66]) Schulenburg to Ribbentrop, 17 Sep. 1939, *NSR*, p. 96; *BDS*, pp. 105-106.

[67]) Ulrich von Hassell, *Vom anderen Deutschland* (Zurich, 1946), 20 Dec. 1939
(entry of 22 Dec.), pp. 110-11.

[68]) "Kriegstagebuch der Seekriegsleitung," Teil A, Heft 1, p. 95 cited in Assmann,
"Die Seekriegsleitung und die Vorgeschichte des Feldzuges gegen Russland," 17
Sep. 1939, C-170, *TMWC*, XXXIV, 678. The "Kriegstagebuch der Seekriegsleitung"
will henceforth be cited as Sk1, its parts by letter and its volumes and pages by
number so that the foregoing would read Sk1, A, 1, 95: 17 Sep. 1939. The source
of quotations from Sk1 will henceforth be given as the document number under
which it was registered at Nuremberg, C - 170 in this case.

[69]) The relevant documents will be found in *NSR*, pp. 91—100, *BDS*, pp. 100-111,
passim.

suspicion evidenced by the Soviet fear that Germany would not respect the line drawn in the secret protocol of August 23. The Soviets had, as has been pointed out, agreed that the Germans might have to cross the line for purely military reasons and had been reassured by the Germans that the line would be respected as the basis for the political settlement. On September 18, however, Stalin again raised the question of whether Germany would really abide by the secret protocol.[70] On the following afternoon, that is on September 19, Ribbentrop directed Schulenburg to inform Stalin that the agreements made at Moscow would certainly be kept.[71]

In the meantime, however, an incident had occurred which fed the suspicions of the Russians. On September 18 the Soviet Deputy Military Attaché in Berlin had gone to the High Command of the Armed Forces in Berlin for information on the line reached or about to be reached by the German army. Since Keitel and Jodl were in the East, the Soviet officer talked with General Walter Warlimont who headed the National Defense Department (Abteilung Landesverteidigung), the most important section of Jodl's Armed Forces Operations Office (Wehrmachtführungsamt). Warlimont did not know about the secret protocol; he merely indicated the German lines to the Russian on a map. The latter seems to have misunderstood what Warlimont was saying and immediately informed Molotov that the Germans intended to violate the secret protocol; since the Germans were moving well across the line, the lines drawn by Warlimont obviously did not coincide with the agreed border, particularly, it would appear, in the South.[72] Molotov on hearing of this summoned Schulenburg for an interview at 7:00 P.M. on September 19. It is not

---

[70] Schulenburg to Ribbentrop, 18 Sep. 1939, *NSR*, p. 98; *BDS*, p. 108; it is not quite clear whether the conversation between Stalin and Schulenburg here referred to took place on the 18th or was the one at 2:00 AM on the 17th. The telegram is labeled No. 385 of the 18.9. and refers to a conversation Schulenburg had had "this evening," yet it was sent off at 3:59 PM on the 18th of September. On the basis of the contents and phrasing of the report and the ones on the interview of September 17, it would appear that Schulenburg saw Stalin again during the night of 17 - 18 September.

[71] Ribbentrop to Schulenburg, 19 Sep. 1939, *NSR*, p. 101; *BDS*, pp. 111-112.

[72] This account is based on three sources - Schulenburg to Ribbentrop, 20 Sep. 1939 (Moscow No. 394), NG - 5776, trans. United States, OCCWC, (mimeo, 2pp.) p. 1 (a reproduction of page 1 of the German copy is in Rossi, p. 71); Testimony of Warlimont, United States Military Tribunal V, "United States v. Wilhelm von Leeb *et alii*, Transcript of Proceedings," (Nuremberg, 1948) (hereafter cited as U.S. v. Leeb), G.T. 6233; Affidavit of Wolfgang Junge, 15 Apr. 1948, Warlimont - 103, Warlimont Document Book V, pp. 54-5. Warlimont dates the incident to September 17 and refers to the Soviet Military Attaché - clearly slips of his memory since the contemporary evidence of the Schulenburg telegram is clear on these points.

clear whether Schulenburg had by this time received Ribbentrop's telegram of that date reaffirming the intention of the German government to respect the secret protocol.[73]) At the meeting Molotov was apparently very agitated. He declared that

> this way of drawing the boundary is at variance with the agreements which have been reached in Moscow during the visit of the Reich Foreign Minister.... The Soviet Government as well as Stalin personally are surprised at this obvious violation of the Moscow agreement.

Schulenburg emphasized that there was clearly some misunderstanding and asked for authorization from Berlin to clear up the matter as soon as possible. The following morning, that is on September 20, formal assurances were given to the Soviets by the German Military Attaché, General Köstring, and by Ribbentrop through Schulenburg.[75]) By the morning of September 20 Schulenburg must also have received the formal telegram from Ribbentrop of September 19 reassuring the Soviets on the question raised by Stalin on the 18th.[76])

Molotov's suspicions were no doubt aroused again that same day by an attempt on the part of the Germans to secure for themselves the Borisław-Drohobycz area with its important oil wells. This section of Poland, not far from Lwów, was in the part of Poland assigned to Russia by the secret protocol but had been occupied by German troops on September 17 and 18. On September 20 Ribbentrop instructed General Köstring to try to obtain a modification of the protocol line so that the Borisław-Drohobycz area would fall within the German zone.[77]) In an interview between Molotov and Schulenburg which presumably took place in the afternoon of September 20, Molotov rejected this demand as well as a suggestion by Schulenburg that the areas be occupied militarily provisionally by Germany pending a final political settlement.[78])

This matter has been examined in detail, both because of the general light it sheds on the extreme suspiciousness of the Russians at this time, and because of its close connection with the settlement of September 28. This last point is to some extent obscured by Schulen-

---

[73]) The instruction was sent from the special train in which Ribbentrop then had his office at 4:37 PM on September 19 (*NSR*, p. 101; *BDS*, p. 111). It is most unlikely that Schulenburg had a deciphered copy by 7:00 PM.

[75]) Rossi, pp. 70, 72: cf. Halder (20 September 1939), II, 10-11.

[76]) *NSR*, p. 101; *BDS*, p. 111.

[77]) Rossi, p. 75 and n. 1.

[78]) Schulenburg to Ribbentrop, 20 Sep. 1939 (Moscow No. 402), cited in Rossi. pp. 75, 76 and n. 1.

burg's practice of occasionally sending several reports on the same conversation, with each report covering a separate aspect of the meeting. When these reports are put together, new relationships often appear. This may well be the case here.

Schulenburg reported on September 19 on a conversation with Molotov that day in which Molotov had stated that he believed the time had come for their two governments to settle the Polish problem definitively. Molotov hinted that Russia no longer desired a residual Poland but preferred a complete and final partition along the four-river line. He also expressed the wish that the necessary negotiations commence at once and take place in Moscow, hinting that Stalin wished to take part in them personally.[79]) This conversation seems to have been the same one as the previously described meeting about the War-limont map incident.[80]) It is therefore entirely possible that the eagerness of the Russians for negotiations in the immediate future as well as their desire to drop the idea of a residual Poland may well have been connected with their suspicions of Germany. Similarly, it was at the meeting between Schulenburg and Molotov on September 20 about the oil region that the latter first suggested that the Suwalki region of Poland, a region on the Russian side of the protocol line, might be ceded to Germany.[81]) Perhaps this was to reconcile the Germans to the loss of the oil fields.

Ribbentrop agreed to the Soviet proposals for negotiations about Poland, as well as to the Soviet idea of a complete partition, in a telegram of September 22 which was sent to Moscow the following day. In it he also announced that he intended to come to Moscow himself.[82]) Since the Moscow negotiations thus agreed to constitute a turning point between the period of deep suspicion and that of real cooperation, it is important to record the settlement of the military problems before going into the political negotiations.

The Germans had suggested a joint Soviet-German military commission at Bialystok to iron out any problems which might arise.[83]) Stalin agreed to this on September 17 and stated that the Russian

---

[79]) Schulenburg to Ribbentrop, 19 Sep. 1939 (Moscow No. 395), *NSR*, p. 101; *BDS*, p. 111; the last hint is taken from the phrase "persons of the highest position of authority."

[80]) The telegrams reporting on these matters are numbered consecutively, Nos. 394 and 395, and were sent out at 0:45 AM and 2:23 AM on September 20 respectively. Furthermore, there is nothing to indicate another Schulenburg-Molotov meeting of September 19.

[81]) Schulenburg to Ribbentrop, 20 Sep. 1939 (Moscow No. 402), cited in Rossi, p. 76; cf. Halder (21 Sep. 1939), II, 13.

[82]) *NSR*, p. 102; *BDS*, p. 112.

[83]) Ribbentrop to Schulenburg, 15 Sep. 1939, *NSR*, p. 94; *BDS*, p. 104.

officers would arrive there on September 18 or 19.[84]) On September 22, 1939, Köstring and Voroshilov signed a military agreement in Moscow delimiting the military spheres of the two powers at the Pissa-Narev-Vistula-San line.[85]) The agreement had been preceded by complicated negotiations at Bialystok.[86]) These were concluded on September 21 when the idea of a "provisional intermediate line" had been dropped by the Germans "since the Russians attach overriding importance to reaching the demarcation line, if in any way possible, at an even earlier date."[87]) The technical agreement of Bialystok fixed the stages of the German withdrawal to be completed on October 3 (the Vistula at Warsaw), and provided for the Russians to conclude the occupation of their zone by October 4.[88]) The German troops began to withdraw to the demarcation line in the days following the signing of the two agreements.[89]) This matter was therefore in the process of settlement by the time Ribbentrop went on his second trip to Moscow.

The main purpose of Ribbentrop's second trip to Moscow was the final settlement of the Polish question. Economic questions were also to be discussed. It will be recalled that the secret protocol of August 23 provided for a partition of Poland along the line of the four rivers Pissa, Narev, Vistula, and San; and that Estonia and Latvia were to go to Russia while Lithuania—including the Vilna area of Poland —was allocated to Germany. The question of a residual Poland had been left for future discussion.

The Germans and Russians had both apparently favored a residual Poland at first. The Germans had considered a sort of rump Poland around Warsaw.[90]) A scheme for this sort of State was worked out by von Moltke, the last German Ambassador to Poland on September 25.[91]) The Soviets had originally also favored some such scheme, but by September 19 had apparently come to the conclusion that it would be best to partition Poland finally along the four-river line.[92]) Ribbentrop indicated that the idea of a border along the four-river line was in general approved by Germany.[93]) This would, it was expected, leave Germany free to do as she wished with the territories on her

[84]) Schulenburg to Ribbentrop, 17 Sep. 1939, *NSR*, p. 96; *BDS*, p. 100.

[85]) Rossi, p. 72.

[86]) Halder (20 and 21 Sep. 1939), II, 11-13.

[87]) Halder (21 Sep. 1939), II, 13.

[88]) For the details of the agreement see *ibid.*

[89]) Karl Schwarz, *Chronik des Krieges* (Berlin, 1940), I, 115-16, 118-20; cf. Halder, II, 10-16, *passim.*

[90]) Halder (7 Sep. 1939), I, 55.

[91]) Memorandum of von Moltke, cited in Rossi, p. 74 and n.l.; cf. Kleist, p. 104.

[92]) Schulenburg to Ribbentrop, 19 Sep. 1939, *NSR*, p. 101; *BDS*, pp. 111-112.

[93]) Ribbentrop to Schulenburg, 22 Sep. 1939, *NSR*, p. 102; *BDS*, p. 112.

side of the line.[94]) A new element was introduced into the picture by Stalin personally on September 25. At an interview to which Schulenburg had been summoned, Stalin suggested that Germany take the province of Lublin and the portion of the province of Warsaw on the west side of the Bug, leaving Lithuania to Russia in return. He asked that this proposal be considered at the forthcoming visit of Ribbentrop.[95]) At the same time there seemed to be evidence of a more friendly attitude by the Russians toward Germany.[96])

Ribbentrop's second trip to Moscow has been described elsewhere in considerable detail.[97]) It will be reviewed here only in outline. The results, however, must be registered. There was a treaty of friendship supplemented by a separate boundary protocol; the first signed by Ribbentrop and Molotov on September 28,[98]) the second by Molotov and Schulenburg on October 4.[99]) There was a confidential protocol providing for the return of Germans to Germany and Ukrainians and Belorussians to the Soviet Union.[100]) A secret protocol stated the agreement of the two powers not to tolerate on their territories any Polish agitation concerning the territory occupied by the other power.[101]) This was, however, considerably affected by yet another secret protocol which provided for the exchange of territory suggested by Stalin, the effect of which was to place the border in Poland very close to the Curzon line and to leave most of the essentially Polish areas to Germany. This protocol also provided that a small portion of Lithuania—the region around Mariampol—would still go to Germany. [102]) This last cession supplemented the Suwalki area which

---

94) Memorandum of Weizsäcker, 26 Sep. 1939, cited in Rossi p. 79.

95) Schulenburg to Ribbentrop, 25 Sep. 1939, NSR, pp. 102-103; BDS, p. 113.

96) Report of German Naval Attaché in Moscow, cited in Skl, A, 1, 163: 25 Sep. 1939, 170 - C, TMWC, XXXIV, 678.

97) Kordt, Wahn und Wirklichkeit, pp. 221-27 and Nicht aus den Akten, pp. 344-54; Rossi, pp. 80-81. Kordt was there himself in the German delegation; Rossi used the as yet unpublished account of the conversations prepared by Hencke.

98) German-Soviet Boundary and Friendship Treaty, NSR, pp. 105-06; BDS, pp. 116-17.

99) "Zusatzprotokoll zwischen Deutschland und Union der S.S.R.," in Seidl, pp 133-138.

100) NSR, p. 106; BDS, pp. 117-118.

101) NSR, p. 107; BDS, p. 119.

102) NSR, p. 107. There is some evidence to indicate that the Germans may have allowed the Russians to have Lithuania at least in part because of the refusal of the latter to participate in the war on Poland. Ernest J. Harrison, Lithuania's Fight for Freedom (New York, 1945), pp. 20-21; cf. Kleist, p. 101; Wiley to Hull, 17 September 1939, United States, Department of State, The Soviet Union, 1933-1939, p. 938.

The Lithuanians later apparently found out that they had been traded to the U.S.S.R. by Germany. Norem to Hull, 13 October 1939, United States, Department of State, The Soviet Union, 1933-1939, p. 968.

Molotov had promised Germany as a consolation for the loss of the oil region. The regulation of these claims had to be clarified by two later exchanges of letters, both on October 8, 1939.[103]) The Mariampol question was to give rise to all sorts of complications later.

Two other things came out of the second Moscow conference. The first of these was a joint German-Soviet public declaration calling for an end to the war.[104]) This document launched the joint German-Soviet peace offensive to be discussed in detail in the next chapter. The other matter was the exchange of two letters between Ribbentrop and Molotov concerning future economic relations between the two states.[105]) In this connection it should be pointed out that one of these letters included among other things a Soviet promise to deliver to Germany additional oil supplies equal to the annual production of the often mentioned Borysław-Drohobycz area.[106]) The other aspects of these letters will be considered in the next chapter in the discussion of economic cooperation.

When Ribbentrop returned to Berlin he spoke enthusiastically of his trip.[107]) It is quite clear that Ribbentrop was greatly impressed. This was his great diplomatic triumph, and he therefore quite naturally became an ardent advocate of the Pact policy, at least for the time being.

German-Soviet cooperation provided the opportunity for the unleashing of the war and the partition of Poland. It was now to enter a new period of continuing practical mutual support in the political, naval, and economic spheres.

Supplementary Note to Chapter IV:

The Russo-Turkish Negotiations; September, October, 1939.

The negotiations for a treaty of mutual assistance between the Soviet Union and Turkey which had been one of the main subjects of Potemkin's trip to Ankara in the spring of 1939 were resumed in

---

[103]) The letters concerning Suwalki are referred to in Rossi, p. 76 and n. 2. The two letters concerning the part of Lithuania are given in Seidl, pp. 144 and 145; only the one from Molotov to Schulenburg appears in *NSR*, pp. 118-19, *BDS*, pp. 131-32; cf. Schulenburg to Ribbentrop, 3 Oct. 1939, *NSR*, p. 112; *BDS*, pp. 124-25; Ribbentrop to Schulenburg, 4 Oct. 1939, *NSR*, pp. 113-14; *BDS*, pp. 126; Schulenburg to Ribbentrop, 4 Oct. 1939, *NSR*, p. 114; *BDS*, p. 127; Ribbentrop to Schulenburg, 4 Oct. 1939, *NSR*, p. 115-16; *BDS*, p. 127-29.

[104]) *NSR*, pp. 108-109; *BDS*, pp. 120-121.

[105]) *NSR*, pp. 108-09; *BDS*, pp. 120-21.

[106]) *NSR*, p. 109; the translation here does not quite bring out the sense of the original German — "entspricht" (*BDS*, p. 121) should be translated as "corresponding to" rather than "commensurate with".

[107]) See, e.g. Schmidt, p. 471; Galeazzo Ciano, *The Ciano Diaries, 1939-1943*, ed. Hugh Gibson (New York, 1946), 2 Oct. 1939, p. 154.

September when Turkish Foreign Minister Saracoglu went to Moscow. These negotiations are related to the subject of German-Soviet relations because of the possibility that Turkey, which was linked to the Western Powers, might provide an indirect link between the Soviets and the West—the very thing Germany wanted least. The details of these negotiations have been recorded elsewhere[108]) and a recital of them would only interrupt the main thread of Russo-German relations. By way of summary, though, it is important to record that in spite of Saracoglu's long visit to Moscow—September 23 to October 18—no agreement was reached, partly because of the urgings of the German government in Moscow. Turkey then signed a mutual assistance treaty with England and France with a proviso that she would not be obligated to fight the Soviet Union.[109])

---

[108]) Kordt, *Wahn und Wirklichkeit*, p. 226; Beloff, II, 297-302; Dallin, pp. 105-11; Gafencu, *Vorspiel zum Krieg im Osten*, pp. 346-54; Rossi, pp. 100-102.

[109]) Schulenburg to Weizsäcker, 5 June 1939, *NSR*, p. 20; *BDS*, p. 22; Memorandum of Hencke, 24 Aug. 1939, *NSR*, pp. 73-74; *BDS*, 81-82; Schulenburg to Ribbentrop, 17 Sep. 1939, *NSR*, p. 97; *BDS*, pp. 106-107; Weizsäcker to Ribbentrop, 18 Sep. 1939, *NSR*, p. 97; *BDS*, p. 102; Ribbentrop to Schulenburg, 2 Oct. 1939, *NSR*, p. 110; *BDS*, p. 122; Ribbentrop to Papen, 2 Oct. 1939, *NSR*, pp. 110-11; *BDS*, p. 123; Schulenburg to Ribbentrop, 3 Oct. 1939, *NSR*, p. 113; *BDS*, p. 125; Ribbentrop to Schulenburg, 7 Oct. 1939, *NSR*, pp. 117-18; *BDS*, p. 120; Schulenburg to Ribbentrop, 8 Oct. 1939, *NSR*, p. 120; *BDS*, pp. 133-34; SK1, A, 2, 193: 24 Oct 1939, 170 - C, *TMWC*, XXXIV, 680.

CHAPTER FIVE

FROM THE PEACE OFFENSIVE TO THE ATTACK IN THE WEST

A. THE PEACE OFFENSIVE

On September 28, 1939, Ribbentrop and Molotov issued a joint public statement on behalf of their governments which stated that their definitive settlement of the Polish question had created the basis for a lasting peace in Eastern Europe and called for an end to the war between Germany and the Western Powers. Mutual consultations were provided in case the war did continue.[1]) This statement touched off the Soviet-German peace offensive.

Before the details of this peace offensive are summarized, the motives of the two countries sponsoring it might be examined briefly. Germany's desire for the conclusion of a peace agreement is easily understood. Germany had obtained what she wanted at that time, and if she could keep it without any further fighting—so much the better. An explanation of Soviet Russia's willingness to push a peace campaign at that time is more difficult to advance. Perhaps the leaders of the Soviet Union believed that Russia would profit whether or not the peace offensive succeeded, while the support given to German policy would produce additional benefits from that side. If the peace offensive failed, German troops would move out of Eastern Europe to the western front and the capitalistic countries would go through a blood-bath like that of 1914-18, thus leaving the Soviet Union in a relatively stronger position. If some sort of peace or truce were arranged, the Soviets still would gain. At the peace table they would be in a strong position—they had carefully provided for a line dividing Poland so that the part held by them was the part once recognized by England as essentially Russian in accordance with the Curzon Line. In the period of uneasy balance following any peace treaty, the Soviet Union would presumably benefit from her position of being sought by both sides as an ally in the new difficulties and

---

[1]) *NSR*, p. 108; *BDS*, pp. 119-20.

crises which would certainly arise. Whatever the reasons, the actual events of the peace offensive are fairly clear.

The border between Germany and Soviet Russia had been drawn and was to be considered final.[2]) The friendship between the two countries had been, as Stalin was to express it,[3]) "cemented with blood."[4]) Now Germany wanted peace and in this she was to have the support of the Soviet Union.

A peace offensive had been anticipated by the British Prime Minister as early as September 10.[5]) Chamberlain answered the German-Russian declaration of September 28 in the House of Commons on October 3. He stated that the British Government would examine any proposals made, but that Britain could accept "no mere assurances from the present German Government."[6]) This position was supported by the leaders of the Labor [7]) and Liberal [8]) parties while the Communist member supported the idea of ending the war forthwith.[9])

Hitler made his peace bid in a speech to the Reichstag on October 6. The proposals were turned down on October 12 by the British government after consultations with the Dominions, France, and Poland.[10]) Chamberlain was very definite.

> The German Chancellor had made his speech.... I must now state the position of His Majesty's Government.... I must ask hon. Members to recall for a few moments the background....
> It is after this wanton act of aggression [against Poland].... that the German Chancellor now puts forward his proposals....
> We must take it, then, that the proposals which the German Chancellor puts forward for the establishment of what he calls "the certainty of European security" are to be based on recognition of his conquests and of his right to do what he pleases with the conquered.

---

[2]) Germany Oberste Befehlshaber der Wehrmacht, OKW, WFA, L I (Hitler), "Weisung Nr. 5," 30 September 1939, PS - 439 (photostat, 4pp.), p. 2.

[3]) Stalin to Ribbentrop, 22 Dec. 1939, R. Umiastowski, *Russia and the Polish Republic, 1918-1941* (London, [1945]), p. 182.

[4]) Presumably a reference to Russian casualties in the attack on Poland; Molotov acknowledged over 2,500 in his *Report to the Supreme Soviet of the USSR, 31 October 1939* (New York, 1939), p. 10.

[5]) Keith Feiling, *The Life of Neville Chamberlain* (London, 1946), p. 417; cf. *ibid.*, p. 424.

[6]) Hansard, *Parliamentary Debates* (fifth series), CCCLI, cc. 1856-57.

[7]) *Ibid.*, c. 1862.

[8]) *Ibid.*, cc. 1865-66.

[9]) *Ibid.*, cc. 1896-1901.

[10]) *Ibid.*, CCCLII, cc. 172, 563-66.

It would be impossible for Great Britain to accept any such basis....[11])

In the meantime, on October 10, the Soviets had attempted to push with the United States the idea of a peace based on the *status quo* through a communication from the Soviet to the American minister in Brussels.[12]) The American government was not impressed.[13])

The general line which the Soviet government had already been following for some time was explained by Molotov in his *Report to the Supreme Soviet of the USSR* on October 31, 1939. He began by clarifying the new outlook of the Soviet government:

> ....in the past few months such concepts as "aggression" and "aggressor" have acquired a new concrete connotation, a new meaning. It is not hard to understand that we can no longer employ these concepts in the sense we did, say, three or four months ago. Today, as far as the European great powers are concerned, Germany is in the position of a state which is striving for the earliest termination of the war and for peace, while Britain and France, which only yesterday were declaiming against aggression, are in favor of continuing the war and are opposed to the conclusion of peace. The roles, as you see, are changing.[14])

Molotov then summarized Russo-German relations as follows:

> As I have said, our relations with Germany have radically improved. Here the development has proceeded along the line of strengthening our friendly relations, extending our practical cooperation and rendering Germany political support in her efforts for peace.[15])

The last of these points, that of political support for Germany, was exemplified in the speech itself by a denunciation of the lifting of the United States arms embargo.[16])

Molotov made further speeches containing contributions to the

---

[11]) *Ibid.*, cc. 363-65; excerpts from those parts of this speech dealing in a rather general way with British war aims were put together in a written message conveyed through Switzerland to the German opposition to Hitler to show the German generals that the Western Powers would not take military advantage of any confusion in Germany resulting from an attempt to overthrow the Hitler government (Erich Kordt, *Nicht aus den Akten*, pp. 367-69 and Anhang; Testimony of Theo Kordt, U.S. v. Weizsäcker, E.T. 12272-82.

[12]) Davies to Hull, 10 October 1939, Joseph Davies, *Mission to Moscow* (New York, 1941), p. 462.

[13]) Hull, I, 710-12; cf. Weizsäcker to Thomsen, 10 October 1939, NG - 1424, trans. OCCWC (mimeo, 1 p.).

[14]) Molotov, p. 4-5.

[15]) *Ibid.*, p. 7-8.

[16]) *Ibid.*, p. 23.

peace campaign on November 6, 1939[17]) and March 29, 1940.[18]) Stalin contributed some statements on the peace offensive which were published in *Izvestia* on November 29, 1939. The communist movement throughout the world demanded an end to the war and condemned the British and French governments for their refusal to begin peace negotiations immediately.[19])

Though the peace offensive may have had considerable influence on such matters as the strength of France, its effect in regard to bringing about peace was nil. This constituted the condition for further Russo-German consultations according to the joint declaration of September 28. These consultations, however, never took place.[20]) Germany and Russia were engaging in more "practical cooperation."

B. ECONOMIC COOPERATION

Soviet-German economic cooperation is one of the least understood, though most important, aspects of German-Soviet relations in the period of the Non-Aggression Pact. Two main factors are responsible for this. One is the limited amount of reliable and comprehensive evidence which is available. The State Department's *Nazi-Soviet Relations, 1939-1941*, for example, purposely omitted "the bulky details of economic relations."[21]) The other factor is the persistent tendency for the economic negotiations and relations to be so intertwined with other developments as to make a separation almost impossible. In the case of naval affairs, the interconnection with economic problems is so complex as to make a separate, integrated treatment of that field necessary; in regard to other forms of economic relations, an effort will be made to record the outlines in so far as the evidence permits. The following account goes only to the summer of 1940 in detailing the negotiations; in regard to actual cooperation, material through the spring of 1941 is included.

At the end of Ribbentrop's second visit to Moscow, two written

---

[17]) *Bulletin of International News,* XVI (1939), 1249.

[18]) *Ibid.,* XVII (1940), 418.

[19]) Since a somewhat similar communist peace offensive is in progress as this is being written, it seems unnecessary to enter into all the details of the peace campaign of 1939 - 1941 here. Accounts and material will be found in Beloff II, 287-92; Rossi, pp. 91-97, 111-21 (also Angelo Rossi, *Physiologie du parti communiste français* [Paris, 1948]; Angelo Rossi, *Les communistes français pendant la drôle de guerre; une page d'histoire* [Paris, 1951]); Dallin, pp. 78-79; Schwarz, pp. 174-175, 178-79; Canada, Royal Commission to investigate disclosures of secret and confidential information to unauthorized persons, *The Report of the Royal Commission* (Ottawa, 1946), pp. 101-02, 113, 219; Georgi Dimitroff, *The War and the Working Class of the Capitalist Countries* (New York, 1939).

[20]) Kordt, *Wahn und Wirklichkeit,* p. 228, n. 1.

[21]) Editor's Foreword, *NSR,* p. iv (see *BDS,* p. IV).

exchanges concerning economic matters took place between him and Molotov. In the first, which was made public, the Soviet Union agreed to new economic negotiations designed to further more extensive trade relations—the Soviet Union was to send raw materials in exchange for manufactured goods delivered "over an extended period."[22]) In the second, which remained secret, the Soviet government, aside from promising more oil, as indicated before, affirmed its intention to facilitate German transit trade across its newly acquired Polish territories from Rumania, and across the Soviet Union herself from the Middle and Far East.[23])

The new economic negotiations began on October 8, 1939, and lasted, with minor interruptions, for over four months, until February 11, 1940. In the first part of the negotiations Schnurre seems to have played the leading role on the German side; later Ritter was the chief German representative.

The German economic mission arrived in Moscow on October 8 and was received by Molotov on the same day.[24]) Dr. Schnurre had prepared an outline he planned to follow in the talks. This outline has been published, though without its annexes.[25]) Schnurre planned to leave the economic agreement of August 19, 1939, intact, but to obtain an additional agreement greatly expanding the volume of trade. The Soviets would be expected to increase their deliveries in return for a grandiose German compensation scheme—involving the construction of plants in the Soviet Union by Germany—which would run over a period of five years. Since the supplies to be asked of the Soviet Union would cut into Soviet supplies and consumption, thus going beyond the sending of exportable surpluses, Schnurre anticipated —correctly as will be seen—that the political intervention of the highest Soviet authorities would be needed to secure agreement. He also intended to examine the question of transit shipments from the Middle and Far East to Germany.

As the negotiations concerning these various points dragged on over a considerable period of time, some of the issues were settled by separate agreements. One subject in which Germany was very much interested was the supplying of grain fodder by the Soviet Union.[26]) This matter was settled by an agreement signed in Moscow on October

---

[22]) Ribbentrop to Molotov, 28 September 1939, *NSR,* pp. 108-09; *BDS,* pp. 120-21.
[23]) *Ibid.,* p. 109; *BDS,* p. 121.
[24]) Schwarz, p. 160; Beloff, II, 293.
[25]) *NSR,* pp. 119-29; *BDS,* pp. 132-33; Beloff calls this document "Schnurre's instructions" (II, 293); not an accurate description in view of its title, contents, and style.
[26]) Germany, Ministerrat für die Reichsverteidigung, "Niederschrift über die Sitzung des Ministerrats für die Reichsverteidigung am 16. Oktober 1939," PS - 2852, *TMWC,* XXXI, 235.

24, which provided among other things for the delivery of one million tons of feed grains by Soviet Russia.[27]) Deliveries under this agreement seem to have started on December 18, 1939.[28]) The other special agreements will be dealt with later in this section.

Negotiations in Moscow were continued, not only by the official German delegation, but by representatives of individual concerns in areas under German control as well.[29]) Furthermore, on October 26 a rather large Soviet trade delegation arrived in Berlin.[30])

The next two months witnessed considerable difficulties. The requests of the Russians seemed excessive to the German military leaders who brought immediate complaints to the German Foreign Ministry.[31]) The Soviets were apparently making very substantial demands for German military equipment.[32]) On December 4 General

---

[27]) Schwarz, p. 160; Beloff, II, 293. The full text of the agreement is not yet available.

[28]) See entry under "Wirtschaftliche Nachrichten," in Sk1, A, 5, 20: 4 January 1940, C - 21 (photostat, 260pp). Beloff fails to give any source for his statement (II, 293) that the deliveries began in November.

[29]) Germany, Reichsgruppe Industrie, Ausfuhrgemeinschaft für Kriegsgerät, "Sitzung des engeren Beirats der A.G.K. in Berlin am 29.9.39," NI - 919 (photostat, 2pp.), p. 2, and "A.G.K. an Auswärtiges Amt, Reichswirtschaftsministerium, Wehrwirtschaftsamt und Vierjahresplan; 'Russland-Verhandlungen, Protektorat Altreich'," 30 September 1939, NI - 919 (photostat, 2pp.), p. 1. For an example of the relations of individual German corporations to the course of the negotiations, see the following documents emanating from I.G. Farben: I.G. Farben Technischer Ausschuss, Büro (Ter Meer), "Ter Meer an Ambros und andere; Betreff: Russland-Verhandlungen," 17 November 1939, NI - 6505 (mimeo, 2pp); I.G. Farben, Technischer Ausschuss, Büro (Ter Meer, Ambros), "I.G. Farben an Professor Dr. C. Krauch, Generalbevollmächtigter des Ministerpräsidenten Generalfeldmarschall Göring für Sonderfragen der chemischen Erzeugung; Betreff: Verhandlungen mit den Delegationen der U.d.S.S.R.," 15 November 1939, NI - 6505 (mimeo, 4pp.); I.G. Farben, Technischer Ausschuss, Büro, "Anlage zum Schreiben der I.G. Farben-industrie Aktiengesellschaft vom 15. November 1939 betreffend Verhandlungen mit den Delegationen der U.d.S.S.R.," 15 November 1939, NI - 6505 (mimeo, 5pp.); I.G. Farben, Kaufmännischer Ausschuss, "Niederschrift über die 28. Sitzung des K.A. am 13. Dezember 1939," 22 December 1939, NI - 9501 (photostat, 3pp.), p. 2.

[30]) Schwarz, p. 160. For information concerning the visit of this Russian commission and its tours of German industrial establishments, see Germany, OKW, Wi Rü Amt, Wi VII (Becker), "W.Wi. VII, 11381/39, Betreff Russland, an OKH, OKM, RdL," 24 October 1939 (2pp. typescript in the Library of Congress, Aeronautics Division), p. 2; Germany, OKL, GL, "Bericht über den Besuch der russischen Luftfahrtkommission bei den Lizenzwerken des Motorenbaues, zu 1409/39 vom 17.11.39," 12 January 1940 (5pp. typescript in the Library of Congress, Aeronautics Division); Germany, OKW, Wi Rü Amt, Wi VII, "Betreff Russen, Besuche der Kommissionen am 8.11.39," 8 November 1939, NIK - 9235 (photostat, 3pp.) (see also the Staff Evidence Analysis, mimeo, 2pp.).

[31]) Memorandum of Weizsäcker, 1 November 1939, NSR, p. 127; BDS, p. 141.

[32]) See for example the seven page long list attached to Germany, OKW, Wi Rü Amt, Wi VII (Becker), "W.Wi. VII, 11381/39, Betreff Russland, an OKH, OKM, RdL," 24 October 1939 (typescript in the Library of Congress, Aeronautics Division).

Thomas, Chief of the War Economy and Armaments Office of the High Command of the Armed Forces, stressed the critical nature of Germany's economic situation under wartime conditions in a conference with General Keitel.[33] On the following day Keitel called Weizsäcker to complain about the "more and more voluminous and unreasonable" requests of the Russians. Weizsäcker replied that the Foreign Ministry intended to curb their demands, though it had not yet decided on the appropriate procedure.[34] On December 11 Ribbentrop spoke to the Soviet Ambassador about the Russian demands and indicated in a rather guarded manner that Germany, being at war, could not supply everything that was wanted.[35]

The negotiations in Moscow were conducted on the German side by Ritter, Schulenburg, Schnurre, and Hilger; and on the Soviet side by Mikoyan, Commissar for Foreign Trade, Babarin, the Soviet trade delegate to Berlin, and Stalin himself.[36] The Germans had been instructed to work for an agreement designed to become the first of a series to be drawn up at yearly intervals.[37] Stalin agreed to this procedure,[38] and the agreement was eventually drawn up in this manner.[39]

In the last week of December a few more issues were settled by separate agreements. On December 23, 1939, a railway agreement was signed between Germany and the Soviet Union to facilitate traffic between the two countries and to secure the smooth flow of supplies from Rumania to Germany across Russian-occupied Poland.[40] The latter of these points had been one of the stipulations

---

[33] Germany, OKW, Wi, Rü Amt (Thomas), "Aktennotiz, Besprechung Thomas-Keitel 4 Dezember 1939," PS - 1456 (photostat, 2pp.), p. 1.

[34] Memorandum of Weizsäcker, 5 December 1939, *NSR*, pp. 128-29; *BDS*, p. 143; cf. "Vortrag Chef Wehrwirtschaftsstab beim Ob. d. M. über die Rohstofflage," Skl, A, 4, 44: 7 December 1939, C - 27 (photostat, 236pp.); "Vortrag Chef M. Wa. beim Ob. d. M. über die sowjetrussischen Rüstungsforderungen, die äusserst hoch sind und zum Teil Terminsetzungen enthalten, die selbst im Frieden unerfüllbar sind," Skl, A, 4, 44-45: 7 December 1939, C - 27 (summarized in C - 170, *TMWC*, XXXIV, 682).

[35] Memorandum of Ribbentrop, 11 December 1939, *NSR*, p. 131; *BDS*, p. 145.

[36] Testimony of Ritter, U.S. v. Weizsäcker, G.T. 11916; "Vortrag Hauptamts-chef M. Wa. beim Ob. d. M. über Ergebnis Wirtschaftsverhandlungen Botschafter Ritter in Moskau," Skl, A, 5, 62: 10 January 1940, C - 21.

[37] Testimony of Ritter, U.S. v. Weizsäcker, G.T. 11915-17.

[38] *Ibid.*, G.T. 11916.

[39] Memorandum of Schnurre, 26 February 1940, *NSR*, pp. 131, 133; *BDS*, pp. 146-149; Germany, Beauftragter für den Vierjahresplan, "7. Sitzung des General-rats vom 28. Februar 1940 unter Vorsitz von Staatssekretär Körner," NI - 7474 (photostat, 7 pp.), p. 1.

[40] Dallin (p. 422) and Beloff (II, 293) give the date as December 24, but see Germany, Auswärtiges Amt, *Vertrags-Verzeichnis,* Item 1985, p. 648.

of the exchange of letters of September 28.[41]) Also on December 23, 1939, an agreement regulating air transport between the two countries was signed in Moscow.[42]) The Soviet-German trade and payments agreements of March 1, 1938, which had been renewed on December 19, 1938, was extended to the end of 1940 by an exchange of notes on December 31, 1939.[43])

There were, however, several obstacles to the signing of the main agreement. Germany wanted delivery of such non-ferrous metals as copper, nickel, and tin, in time to save Germany from dipping into her own stocks for the production of goods to be shipped to Russia.[44]) This desire was not fulfilled; the agreement provided for the delivery of these metals by the Soviet Union within the general framework of the Russian deliveries.[45]) Another point on which Germany made a substantial concession at Hitler's personal order was the granting of Stalin's demand for a number of new, secret military weapons and items of equipment, together with plans and specifications.[46]) These concessions were granted by Hitler when Ritter flew back to Berlin during the course of the negotiations in January, 1940.[47]) On the other hand, some important concessions were made by the Soviet Union. In the first place, the German demands for supplies were very large, and meeting these involved Soviet Russia's willingness to dip into her own reserves. Also of great significance was the question of timing the deliveries. The Germans wanted a longer period to pay for the Soviet deliveries which they required immediately.[48]) In spite of the exchange of letters of September 28, the Russians insisted that the

---

[41]) Ribbentrop to Molotov, 28 September 1939, *NSR*, p. 109; *BDS*, p. 121.

[42]) Germany, Auswärtiges Amt, *Vertrags-Verzeichnis*, Item 1984, pp. 647-48; cf. Beloff, II, 293.

[43]) Germany, Auswärtiges Amt, *Vertrags-Verzeichnis*, Item 1991, p. 649.

[44]) Germany, Beauftragter für den Vierjahresplan, "3. Sitzung des Generalrats vom 10. Januar 1940 unter Vorsitz von Staatssekretär Körner," NI - 7474 (photostat, 6pp.), p. 5; Memorandum of Schnurre, 26 February 1940, *NSR*, p. 133; *BDS*, p. 148.

[45]) Germany, Beauftragter für den Vierjahresplan, "7. Sitzung des Generalrats vom 28. Februar 1940 unter Virsitz von Staatssekretär Körner," NI - 7474, p. 2; Memorandum of Schnurre, 26 February 1940, *NSR*, p. 133; *BDS*, p. 148. This was provided for in an exchange of letters between Mikoyan and Schnurre attached to the treaty; Germany, Auswärtiges Amt, "Wirtschaftsabkommen zwischen dem Deutschen Reich und der Union der Sozialistischen Sowjet-Republiken," 11 February 1940, NIK - 11361 (photostat, 78pp.) (hereafter cited as "Wirtschaftsabkommen"), pp. 64-65.

[46]) Testimony of Ritter, U.S. v. Weizsäcker, G.T. 11917.

[47]) *Ibid.*, cf. Halder (19 January 1940), III, 32.

[48]) Memorandum of Schnurre, 26 February 1940, *NSR*, pp. 131-32; *BDS*, pp. 146-47.

deliveries balance constantly.[49]) The final agreement provided for
Soviet deliveries over a period of eighteen months and compensating
German deliveries over a period of twenty-seven months, with a
balancing along this ratio required every six months.[50]) Even though
some such scheme must have been contemplated in the negotiations
of September 28 ("compensation.... over an extended period"), a
personal letter from Ribbentrop to Stalin on February 3, 1940, was
required to secure this settlement.[51])

The commercial agreement was finally signed on February 11, 1940.
Aside from the details already mentioned, the agreement provided
for large quantities of oil, cotton, phosphates, chrome ore, iron,
platinum, manganese ore, and lumber to be sent to Germany.[52])
Prices were apparently to be based on the August, 1939, level. The
Soviet Union promised to try to buy metals and other goods for
Germany abroad.[53]) She agreed to the transit of one million tons of
soybeans from the Far East with a fifty percent reduction of the
freight charge.[54]) Germany also was assured transit rights for supplies
from the Middle and Far East across the Russian railway system.
Article 9 of the treaty provided for Soviet oil shipments to compensate
for the oil from the Boryslaw-Drohobycz region and specified the
form of German payment.[55]) Schnurre estimated in his memorandum
of February 26, 1940, that, including deliveries under the agreement
of August 19, and deliveries from the Soviet Union to the Protectorate
of Bohemia and Moravia, total Soviet deliveries and services to Germany would amount to about eight hundred million Reichsmark
during the first twelve months of the new treaty.[56])

The treaty of February 11 stipulated large deliveries from Germany to the Soviet Union according to several detailed lists.[57])
The naval items included will be taken up in the next section of this
chapter. The various schemes for the construction of whole plants in
the Soviet Union seem never to have materialized.[58]) As for actual

---

[49]) Reports of Ritter summarized in Sk1, A, 5, 205: 25 January 1940, C - 21; cf.
C - 170, *TMWC*, XXXIV, 683.
[50]) Memorandum of Schnurre, 26 February 1940, *NSR*, pp. 131-32; *BDS*, pp.
146-47; Germany, Auswärtiges Amt, "Wirtschaftsabkommen," pp. 1-5.
[51]) Memorandum of Schnurre, 26 February 1940; Langer and Gleason, p. 387 and
n. 26.
[52]) See List 1 attached to the treaty (Germany, Auswärtiges Amt, "Wirtschaftsabkommen," pp. 8-9).
[53]) Confidential protocol attached to the treaty, *ibid.*, p. 7.
[54]) See especially Article 12 of the treaty, *ibid.*, p. 5.
[55]) *Ibid.*, p. 3.
[56]) *NSR*, p. 133; *BDS*, p. 147.
[57]) Germany, Auswärtiges Amt, "Writschaftsabkommen," pp. 10-63, 68-74.
[58]) I.C. Farben, Vorstand "Niederschrift über die 26. Vorstandssitzung am 10.

deliveries, aside from these two categories, coal appears in fact to have predominated, together with some special deliveries of military equipment.[59])

The problem facing Germany in meeting the required deliveries while herself at war was apparently a rather difficult one. A special inter-ministerial committee was established to coordinate all work on the deliveries.[60]) On March 30, 1940, Hitler issued a special directive according to which industrial orders for the Soviet Union were, if necessary, to take precedence over those of the German armed forces.[61]) Certain problems which arose in 1940 and 1941 concerning German deliveries will be considered at another point. Three important matters still to be examined here are the actual extent of Soviet economic aid to Germany, the transit trade question, and the importance of Soviet-German trade to the German war effort.

Only scattered sources provide statistics on Soviet deliveries to Germany, but some indication of what happened can be derived from them. In March, 1940, the first full month under the new agreement, Germany issued licenses for 37.4 million Reichsmark of imports from Eastern Europe; 27.8 million of it from the Soviet Union and the rest from the Baltic States. This was 9.6 % of Germany's total imports. By June, 1940, the imports from Eastern Europe had risen to 108.7 million Reichsmark, constituting 21.8 % of total imports.[62])

Juli 1941," 10 July 1941, NI - 8077 (photostat, 8pp.), p. 4. An excellent example of the planning for one of these construction projects is in the Manuscripts Division of the Library of Congress: I.G. Farben, *Allgemeine Bemerkungen zu den Angeboten für die U.d.S.S.R. auf Anlagen zur Herstellung von Fliegerbenzin aus Steinkohle bzw. Braunkohle bzw. Kräckrückständen* (November, 1939), 7pp., "Streng vertraulich".

[59]) According to an annex to the minutes of the "Regierungssitzung im neuen Regierungssaal der Burg am 26. Oktober 1943," in the diary of Hans Frank, the railway system in Poland carried 3056 train-loads of coal and 70 train-loads of other goods to the U.S.S.R. in the period 1939-1941 (PS - 2233, *TMWC*, XXIX, 633). See also Germany, Reichsgruppe Industrie, Ausfuhrgemeinschaft für Kriegsgerät, "Geschäftsbericht 1939/40," 14 August 1940, NIK - 11360 (photostat, 13pp.), pp. 3, 6, 13; F. Krupp, Abteilung für Kriegsgerät, "Report for the Fiscal Year 1939/40 of the Department for War Material," NIK - 11625 (mimeo, 68pp.), trans. United States, OCCWC, pp. 21, 55, 66-67.

[60]) Germany, Beauftragter für den Vierjahresplan, "7. Sitzung des Generalrats vom 28. Februar 1940 unter Vorsitz von Staatssekretär Körner," NI - 7474, p. 2.

[61]) Testimony of Ritter, U.S. v. Weizsäcker, G.T. 11933; Germany, OKW, Wi Rü Amt (Thomas), "Grundlagen für eine Geschichte der deutschen Wehr- und Rüstungswirtschaft," PS - 2553, p. 314, in *TMWC*, XXX, 272. The writer has not been able to find a copy of this order of Hitler. A copy of an order on this subject of the same date, but by Göring, is in the Aeronautics Division of the Library of Congress: Germany, Ministerrat für die Reichsverteidigung (Göring), "Generalfeldmarschall Göring an das Oberkommando der Wehrmacht; Betreff: Russland-Vertrag, Export," 30 March 1940 (typescript, 1p.).

[62]) Germany, Statistisches Reichsamt, Abteilung VI, "Germany's Payments to

In the period from April to July, 1940, the U.S.S.R. was Germany's leading supplier of grain (70 million RM), and second in timber (35 million RM), base metals (14 million RM), and oil (32 million RM).[63] Apparently this general rate of deliveries continued to the fall of 1940.[64]

One of the most important features of Soviet-German economic cooperation was the transit traffic of goods across the Soviet Union to Germany. It was to a large extent in this manner that Germany hoped to escape the effects of the British blockade. Germany now had access to the countries of the Middle and Far East and even of the Western Hemisphere.[65] The transit trade was significant in several fields. This was the way in which the Soviet Union expected to purchase non-ferrous metals for delivery to Germany.[66] Of particular interest to Germany was the supply of soybeans from Manchuria. On October 16, 1939, Göring had called for an investigation of the possibilities in this field.[67] As has been mentioned already, the Soviet Union agreed to the transit of one million tons of soybeans at half the regular freight charge. In the winter of 1939-1940 a special mission of German business men, with the approval of the official German agencies, checked the transit situation and the supply possibilities in the Far East on the spot.[68] The mission found that the main trouble would be in obtaining the desired quantities from the Manchurian and Japanese authorities, rather than in transporting the supplies to Germany.[69] They found that one of the reasons for the difficulty was the pressure on Japan from England, which had dis-

Foreign Countries from April, 1940, until June, 1940," 20 September 1940, NG - 927, trans. United States, OCCWC (mimeo, 5 pp), p. 3.

[63] *Ibid.,* pp. 4-5.

[64] Memorandum of Schnurre, 28 September 1940, *NSR,* p. 201; *BDS,* p. 224

[65] Dallin, pp. 525-26; I.G. Farben "Memorandum, 23 April 1941," NI-6123 (photostat, 3pp.), p. 1. The failure to call attention to the possibility of Soviet economic aid to Germany by providing transit facilities is the main defect of the otherwise generally excellent analysis and amazingly accurate forecast of Soviet policy in case of a new European war, in Moscow British Embassy to the Foreign Office, 20 February 1939, *BD,* IV, 611-14.

[66] Germany, Beauftragter für den Vierjahresplan, "7. Sitzung des Generalrats vom 28. Februar 1940 unter Vorsitz von Staatssekretär Körner," NI-7474, p. 2.

[67] Germany, Ministerrat für die Reichsverteidigung, "Niederschrift über die Sitzung des Ministerrats für die Reichsverteidigung am 16. Oktober 1939," PS - 2582, *TMWC,* XXXI, 235.

[68] I.G. Farben, Wirtschaftspolitische Abteilung, "Handelspolitische Beziehungen zur Mandschurei," 17 May 1940, NI - 1096 (photostat, 3pp.), p. 2.

[69] [Sostmann], "Bericht über die von Herrn Dähn und mir im Auftrage der Deutschen Oelmühlen-Rohstoffe G.m.b.H., Berlin, durchgeführte Reise nach dem Fernen Osten zum Studium und der Lösung der Transport- und Einkaufsfragen von Soyabohnen und Soyaöl," 29 April 1940, NI - 1096 (photostat, 8pp.), pp. 4-8.

covered that substantial quantities of goods were reaching Germany from ships loaded in Japanese ports and later transshipped over the Transsiberian Railway.[70]) A substantial volume of soybeans and related products did, however, reach Germany in the transit trade. In the period April-July, 1940, Japan was Germany's second most important supplier in the milk, oils, fats, category (soybeans and oil came under this classification) with shipments valued at 24 million Reichsmark—more than Germany's neighbour Holland.[71]) In the month of March, 1941, Germany received over 10 million Reichsmark worth of milk products, oils, and fats from the Far East.[72]) Considerable support was thus given to the German economy.[73])

Of even greater importance than the soybean trade was the transit trade in rubber. This war-essential commodity was desperately needed by Germany, which had no adequate stockpiles. At the outbreak of war in 1939, Germany's rubber supply, including natural and synthetic rubber, was sufficient for only about *two months*.[74]) With careful economizing this period could be stretched somewhat, but imports were essential. These had to come from the rubber-producing areas of the Far East through Japanese intermediaries and across the Soviet Union. The great importance of this is repeatedly stressed in the German documents.[75]) At one time, in 1941, the Soviets even provided a special train for transporting rubber to Germany.[76]) The subject of rubber transit deliveries will be referred to again repeatedly, particularly in connection with the German decision to attack the Soviet Union.[77])

---

[70]) *Ibid.*, p. 4.

[71]) Germany, Statistisches Reichsamt, Abteilung VI, "Germany's Payments to Foreign Countries from April, 1940, until June, 1940," NG - 927, p. 4.

[72]) Germany, Statistisches Reichsamt, Abteilung VI, "Approved Imports of Goods in March, 1941," 8 May 1941, NG - 927 (mimeo, 4pp.), trans. United States, OCCWC, p. 1.

[73]) Total transit shipments in 1940 are given as ca. 220,000 tons to Germany and 45,000 tons from Germany in Helmut Wohlthat, "Wirtschaftsverhandlungen mit Japan und Mandschukuo," 27 March 1942, International Military Tribunal for the Far East, Document 4038, p. 2.

[74]) Germany, OKW, Wi Rü Amt (Hedler), "Kautschuk und die Versorgungslage im Kriege," 31 March 1941, NI - 6194 (photostat, 36pp.), p. 23.

[75]) See for example, Germany, OKW, Wi Rü Amt, "Vortrag Obstlt. Tietze beim Amtschef," 7 February 1941, PS - 1456 (photostat, 5pp.), p. 2; Germany, OKW, Wi Rü Amt (Thomas), "Aktennotiz, Besprechung beim General Feldmarschall Keitel am 8.2.41," PS - 1456 (photostat, 2pp.), p. 1.

[76]) Memorandum of Schnurre, 5 April 1941, *NSR*, p. 318; *BDS*, p. 357; cf. Memorandum of Schnurre, 15 May 1941, *NSR*, p. 340; *BDS*, p. 381.

[77]) For information on German demands for shipments of graphite from Madagascar and rubber and wolfram from French Indo-China to Vladivostok for transit to Germany, see France, Delegation française auprès de la Commission allemande d'armistice, Recueil de Documents, I (29 June - 29 September, 1940) (Paris, 1947), 379,

Of course, some exports went from Germany across the Soviet Union to foreign countries, but this was limited by the burden placed on the Soviet transportation system by the reciprocal Russo-German deliveries.[78] For example, the total volume of trade between Germany and Iran for the year 1939/40 was almost the same as for the year 1938/39, but a far larger proportion of the volume (393 out of 553 million Rials, instead of 290 out of 558) consisted of Iranian exports to Germany.[79]

The question of the importance of the aid Germany received from the Soviet Union as a result of the economic agreements is very difficult to answer. In the first place, the available evidence does not include a total of all the goods and services provided to Germany; it does not even offer reliable subtotals for any one of the services or categories of supplies. In the opinion of the writer, the evidence which is available does not make it possible to derive any moderately reliable estimate.[80] Of even greater difficulty is the second problem, that of estimating the importance of the specific goods and services to the German war effort. There is no necessary relation between this and their bulk or monetary value. Small quantities of rubber, for example, could make a great deal of difference to the German war economy, since without the natural rubber vast amounts of synthetic rubber and reclaimed rubber would be useless.[81] The alloys used in the production of steel furnish another good example. Other instances of disparity between monetary value and real importance to a war economy could be given, but the point should be clear.[82]

The Germans themselves certainly considered the economic aid received from the Soviet Union as of the greatest importance.[83]

403-05, 410-11; II (30 September - 23 November, 1940) (Paris, 1950), 162, 215-16, 500-02. More material will, no doubt, appear in the volumes of this series yet to be published.

[78] Germany, OKW, Wi Rü Amt (Reute), "Besprechung am 19. Dezember 1939 über Lage und Aussichten der deutschen Ausfuhr," PS - 1456 (photostat, 9pp.), p. 3.

[79] George Lenczowski, *Russia and the West in Iran, 1918-1948* (Ithaca, 1949) pp. 95, 328. Rial = $ .0824.

[80] Dallin's attempt along these lines (pp. 426-27) relates only to the value of direct Soviet exports to Germany and is quite unconvincing even for that.

[81] Germany, OKW, Wi Rü Amt (Hedler), "Kautschuk und die Versorgungslage im Kriege," 31 March 1941, NI - 6195, *passim.*

[82] The complete failure of Dallin to consider this aspect of the problem has led him to state in terms as definite as they are untenable, that "Soviet-German trade.... was more significant politically than economically. In the German struggle against the British blockade, it was far too weak as a weapon and its propaganda value in no way corresponded to the actual volume of the trade turnover (Dallin, p. 427)."

[83] Memorandum of Ciano, 10 March 1940, Ciano, *Ciano's Diplomatic Papers* p. 347; Gafencu, *Vorspiel zum Krieg im Osten,* p. 55; Germany, Beauftragter für

The various materials cited in this section combine to give an impression of a real and tangible support of the German war effort. Much more research on as yet unavailable documents needs to be done; but even the evidence available to this writer leaves open the question of whether without Soviet aid, particularly in the matter of oil supplies and rubber transit, the German attack in the West in 1940 would have been as successful as it was,[84]) and the attack on the Soviet Union would have been possible at all.

C. NAVAL COOPERATION[85])

The naval cooperation between Germany and the Soviet Union is the subject of a separate section because, though a direct part of the economic and political developments of the years 1939 to 1941, it becomes almost unintelligible if not presented in a connected account. In such an account, one can trace the development of German-Soviet cooperation in one field almost as a sample; and at the same time, one can gain some insight into what became one of the main motivating factors in the opposition of the German navy to the attack on the Soviet Union.

Important aspects of naval cooperation were involved in the economic negotiations of the winter 1939-40. The German navy took the position that Soviet Russia's generous offer of economic aid to Germany required a corresponding willingness on the part of Germany to make substantial deliveries.[86]) Thus already on November 1, 1939,

---

den Vierjahresplan, "7. Sitzung des Generalrats vom 28. Februar 1940 unter Vorsitz von Staatssekretär Körner," NI - 7474, p. 2. For an interesting discussion of the great value to Germany of Soviet economic aid, both direct aid and transit facilities, see the excerpts from a speech of Dr. Schlotterer, a high official of the German Ministry of Economics (Reichswirtschaftministerium), to the officers of the Reichsgruppe Industrie, in: I.G. Farben, Einkaufsabteilung (Weiss), "Vertrauliche Niederschrift zum Umlauf," 14 January 1941, NI - 6734 (mimeo, 17 pp.), pp. 2-3.

[84]) On the importance of Soviet oil to the German campaign in the West, see Germany, OKL, Reichsminister der Luftfahrt und Ob.d.L., GL 5 (Heemswerder [?]), "GL 5 an das OKW, Wi Rü Amt (Griebel); Betreff: Einfuhr von Flugbenzin (No. 5819/40)," 18 May 1940 (typescript, 1p.), in the Library of Congress, Manuscripts Division.

[85]) This section is based largely on the diary system of the German navy. Several complete volumes and many portions, excerpts, and summaries have been available to the writer. On the whole, these diaries constitute one of the most valuable and reliable sources on German-Soviet relations. The sections of the diary system used are Part A—General; Part C, VII—Führer Conferences (also published separately by the U.S. Navy); and Part C, VIII—Political Matters. The volumes of Part A are numbered by the month of the war, starting with September, 1939. The volumes of the latter two are indicated by the year covered; thus "C VII/40, 61" would refer to page 61 of the volume on Führer conferences in 1940.

[86]) Sk1, C VIII/39, 162: 26 October 1939, cited in C - 170, TMWC, XXXIV, 680.

there was agreement that the uncompleted German cruiser "Luetzow" would be placed at the disposal of the Russians.[87] The Russians however, wanted the cruiser "Seydlitz" as well. Admiral Raeder, Commander in Chief of the German Navy, would not agree to this.[88] Hitler also insisted that the naval deliveries to the Soviet Union must not weaken Germany's own military strength.[89] As the negotiations in Moscow continued, larger Russian demands were presented. These included the cruiser "Prinz Eugen" as well as the two previously named, and big naval turrets, naval blue-prints, and naval equipment. Many of these demands were met, but the "Prinz Eugen" was also withheld. The navy declared itself ready, however, to provide the Russians with the plans for the battleship "Bismarck" and with plans for destroyers and submarines. Hitler wanted this matter examined further before making a decision.[90] In a conference between Raeder and Ritter, the Admiral declared his willingness to sell the blue-prints of the battleship "Bismarck" provided the price were high enough. He was willing to take the chance of having them fall into the hands of the English and was prepared to let out the fact that the ship when planned was designed in a manner violative of Germany's treaty obligations.[91]

In the continuing negotiations, the Soviets substantially lowered their demands. While grateful for the willingness of Germany to sell the "Luetzow", the Russians continued to ask for heavy caliber naval turrets and other important items of naval equipment.[92] These demands were, to a considerable extent, agreed to by the Germans. It is clear from the various lists of planned German deliveries attached to the Soviet-German economic treaty of February 11, 1940, that naval equipment was to constitute a very large part of the German repayment for Soviet raw materials. Included in the extensive

---

[87] Germany, OKM, *Fuehrer Conferences on Matters Dealing with the German Navy*, trans. U.S. Navy Department, Office of Naval Intelligence (Washington, 1947) (hereafter cited as Fuehrer Conferences), 1939, p. 33.

[88] Sk1, A, 3, 5: 4 November 1939, cited in C - 170, *TMWC*, XXXIV, 681.

[89] Germany, OKM (Raeder), "Vortrag beim Führer am 10. XI. 1939," C - 100, *TMWC*. XXXIV, 319.

[90] Germany, OKM, "Vortrag Chef M. Wa. beim Ob. d. M. über die sowjet-russischen Rüstungsforderungen....," Sk1, A, 4, 44-45: 7 December 1939, C - 27 (summarized in C - 170, *TMWC*, XXXIV, 682); Germany, OKM, "Report of the Commander in Chief, Navy to the Fuehrer 8 December 1939," Führer Conferences 1939, p. 47; cf. C - 170, *TMWC*, XXXIV, 682, and C - 27, p. 58.

[91] Ritter to Ribbentrop, 15 December 1939, NG - 3164 (photostat, 1p.). In this document the "Bismarck" is referred to as a cruiser, but see Germany, Auswärtiges Amt, "Wirtschaftsabkommen," p. 12.

[92] Germany, OKM, "Vortrag Hauptamtschef M. Wa. beim Ob. d. M. über Ergebnis Wirtschaftsverhandlungen Botschafter Ritter in Moskau," Sk1, A, 5, 62-63. 10 January 1940, C - 21 (summarized in C - 170, *TMWC*, XXXIV, 683).

lists of German delivery obligations were the cruiser "Luetzow", the plans for the "Bismarck", plans for a large destroyer, a long schedule of ship-building materials, various kinds of naval guns and gun equipment, hydrographic equipment, several small ships, naval turrets of the heaviest caliber, and other categories of material for the Soviet Navy.[93] In these ways the Germans were to contribute to the building up of the Russian navy.[94]

Exactly how much naval equipment Germany actually turned over to the Soviets under the agreement is not known as no comprehensive summaries are as yet available. It is clear from the evidence which is available that the deliveries were quite substantial. Aside from the "Luetzow", a great part of the promised naval equipment was sent. At least large sections of the turrets were delivered, as well as much heavy-caliber naval ammunition, submarine equipment, and many other items from the various lists attached to the economic treaty.[95] The cruiser "Luetzow", which was sold for one hundred million Reichsmark, was towed to Kronstadt in May or June of 1940, still incomplete. The additional parts and the turrets were sent by German firms by rail.[96] These were fitted under the supervision of personnel

---

[93] The following sections of the economic treaty, all taken from Germany, Auswärtiges Amt, "Wirtschaftsabkommen," contain the most important information on this point: Liste 2, A. Kriegsschiffbau (pp. 11-12); Liste 2, B. Schiffbaumaterialien (pp. 13-20); Liste 2, C. Marineartillerie (pp. 21-22); Liste 2, D. Minen- und Torpedo-Ausrüstung (p. 23); Liste 2, E. Hydroakustische Apparatur (p. 24); Liste 2, F. Hydrographische Geräte (pp. 25-28); Liste 2, I. Nachrichtenmittel (p 41); Liste 3, IX. Schiffe (p. 61); Liste 4, A. Kriegsschiffbau (p. 69); Liste 4, B. Marineartillerie und andere Marine-Ausrüstung (pp. 70-71); Liste 4, C. Hydrographische Geräte (p. 71); Liste 5, VII. Schiffe (p. 74); Geheime Anmerkungen zu den Listen 2 und 4 (Kriegsgerät) (p. 78).

[94] In the years 1937-1940 the Soviet Union had made considerable efforts to purchase warships in the United States. Information on this will be found in United States, Department of State, *The Soviet Union, 1933-1939*, pp. 457-91, 670-708, 869-903 (note especially Kirk to Hull, 17 December 1939, p. 707, for Soviet interest in heavy naval turrets.); Hull, I, 743. For general information on the Soviet navy in the years 1939 and 1940, see H.G. Thursfield (ed.), *Brassey's Naval Annual, 1939* (London, 1940), pp. 42-44, and *Brassey's Naval Annual, 1940* (London, 1941), pp. 39-41.

[95] The following references contain information on actual German deliveries to the Soviet Union: Testimony of Schulte-Möntig, *TMWC*, XIV, 316; *PHKV*, XIV, 351; Testimony of Wagner, *TMWC*, XIII, 476; *PHKV*, XIII, 32; F. Krupp (Reiff), "Niederschrift des Herrn Reiff über die Besprechung in Essen am 21. Juni 1940," NI - 920 (photostat, 3pp.); F. Krupp, Abteilung für Kriegsgerät, "Report for the Fiscal Year 1939/40 of the Department for War Material," NIK - 11625, pp. 21, 55.

[96] It would seem that at the time of the German invasion of the Soviet Union some items had not been delivered; Germany, Reichsgruppe Industrie, Ausfuhrgemeinschaft für Kriegsgerät (Kloenne), "Aktenvermerk zu einer Unterredung mit

from the Krupp company and German naval experts.[97]) The Germans were ready to assist in the training of Russian officers to run the "Luetzow",[98]) and agreed to a Soviet request for German naval instructors to train the specialists needed to operate the ship.[99])

It is interesting to note, on the other hand, that the repeated requests of the German navy for permission to purchase submarines from the Soviet Union and the Baltic States were refused by Hitler, perhaps mainly because he did not want the Soviets to see any weakness in German naval power.[100])

The field of naval supplies was one in which Germany was providing most of the aid, while Russia was sending aid in the form of materials like oil which have been discussed already. Russia did, however, provide Germany with extensive naval assistance of other kinds. Of great direct benefit to German naval warfare was the help given to the Germans at Murmansk. This Russian port was of importance to Germany both from the standpoint of her own merchant shipping and for her naval war against British ships. German shipping which was in the North Atlantic when war broke out went to Murmansk. From there the ships slipped back to Germany along the Murman and Norwegian coasts.[101]) When such German ships left Murmansk the Russians would delay any British or other Allied ships until the German ships were safe.[102]) This, of course, would prevent shadowing of the German ships. The most famous case of this kind was that of the great German liner "Bremen". This ship had slipped through the British blockade to Murmansk. When the Germans had everything ready to protect her passage from Murmansk to the Reich,

---

Herrn Kapitän Schottky am 29.9.1941; Betrifft: Abrechnung der Russland Geschäfte," 30 September 1941, NIK - 9244 (mimeo, 3pp.), p. 2.

[97]) United States, OCCWC, Evidence Division, Interrogation Branch, Krupp Trial Team, "Interrogation of Georg Schild," 3 October 1947, Interrogation Summary No. 3670 (mimeo, 2pp), p. 2; United States, OCCWC, Evidence Division, Interrogation Branch, Military Division, "Interrogation of Otto Schniewind," 21 November 1947, Interrogation Summary No. 4271 (mimeo, 4pp.), p. 2; Memorandum of Schnurre, 15 May 1941, NSR, p. 340; BDS, p. 351.

[98]) Skl, A, 17, 214: 17 Januari 1941, cited in C - 70, TMWC, XXXIV, 697.

[99]) Skl, A, 19, 389: 27 March 1941, NOKW - 2556 (photostat, 2pp.), p. 2; Skl, A, 19, ?: 28 March 1941, cited in C - 170, TMWC, XXXIV, 701.

[100]) Germany, OKM (Raeder), "Unterredung Chef der Skl mit dem Führer am 23.9. [1939] in Zoppot," C - 100, TMWC, XXXIV, 316; Skl, C VII/39, 11: 10 October 1939, in Fuehrer Conferences, 1939, p. 12, and TMWC, XXXIV, 679; "Report of the Commander in Chief, Navy, to the Fuehrer on 22 November 1939," Fuehrer Conferences, 1939, p. 40 (summarized in C - 170, TMWC, XXXIV, 681); cf. Testimony of Schulte-Möntig, TMWC, XIV, 316; PHKV, XIV, 351.

[101]) See, e.g., Skl, A, 2, 34: 3 Oct. 1939, C - 122 (photostat, 8pp.), p. 7.

[102]) Skl, A, 2, 203: 25 Oct. 1939, summarized in C - 170, TMWC, XXXIV, 680; Assmann, p. 199.

the Russians held up all Allied ships in Murmansk for three days, and by this and other forms of aid helped secure the safe passage of the "Bremen" back to Germany.[103]) Another, though somewhat different, case which attracted considerable attention at the time was the case of the American ship "City of Flint" in which Russia aided Germany in violation of the rules of international law.[104]) Less spectacular, but probably more important to Germany, was the use of Murmansk as a stopping place for blockade breakers.[105])

The cooperation of the Russians at Murmansk was also useful to the Germans in the matter of equipping auxiliary cruisers for attacks on British shipping. Raeder first raised this issue with Hitler on September 23, 1939.[106]) By October 10 one such auxiliary cruiser was already being equipped at Murmansk.[107]) For all these services Raeder repeatedly thanked the Soviet navy. The Naval Commissar, when given a letter of thanks from the German admiral, said that "his answer would consist not of empty words, but of deeds, and that only after their completion would he address an answer to the Commander in Chief [of the German Navy]."[108])

The use of Murmansk in German operations seems to have been important mainly in 1939. While the events described above were going on, there were negotiations for a more substantial form of Soviet aid to Germany. This is the question of the "Basis Nord", the German naval base on Soviet territory. Originally Raeder had thought in general terms of using Russian ports.[109]) Then he raised the question of combined German-Soviet pressure on Norway to secure a naval base in that country for Germany. The German navy was very eager to obtain such a base in order to expand the operational possibilities of German naval warfare. Some thinking along these lines had apparently already been done when Raeder discussed the matter with

[103]) Sk1, C VIII/39, 175ff.: 2 Nov. 1939, cited in C - 170, *TMWC*, XXXIV, 681; Sk1, A, 4, 68: 9 Dec. 1939 and 72: 10 Dec. 1939, C - 27; Germany, OKM (Raeder), "Vortrag Ob. d. M. beim Führer 12. XII. 39., Betrifft: Angelegenheit Norwegen," C - 64, *TMWC*, XXXIV, 273; Sk1, A, 4, 85: 12 Dec. 1939, C - 27, summarized in C - 170, *TMWC*, XXXIV, 682; Adolf Ahrens, *Die Siegesfahrt der "Bremen"* (Berlin, 1940), pp. 117-53.

[104]) Hull, I, 704-05; United States, Department of State, *The Soviet Union, 1933-1939*, pp. 984-1013.

[105]) See, e.g., Sk1, A, 4, 192: 24 Dec. 1939, 214: 28 Dec. 1939, 234: 31 Dec. 1939, C - 27.

[106]) Germany OKM, (Raeder), "Unterredung Chef der Sk1 mit dem Führer am 23.9. [1939] in Zoppot," C - 100, *TMWC*, XXXIV, 316, cited in C - 170, *ibid.*, p. 678.

[107]) Sk1, C VII/39, 10 October 1939, cited in C - 170, *TMWC*, XXXIV, 679.

[108]) Sk1, C VIII/39, 175ff: 2 Nov. 1939, cited *ibid.*, p. 681.

[109]) Germany, OKM (Raeder), "Unterredung Chef der Sk1 mit dem Führer am 23.9. [1939] in Zoppot," C - 100, *ibid.*, p. 314.

his section chiefs on October 3, 1939. He stated that he considered it necessary to bring this problem to Hitler's attention and at the same time ordered that the various aspects of the matter be investigated.[110] At his conference with Hitler on October 10, Raeder pointed out the value of gaining a base in Norway, perhaps at Trondheim, with the aid of Soviet pressure; and Hitler agreed to consider the matter.[111] This did not result in anything concrete because the Russians, apparently on their own initiative, offered the Germans a base on Russian territory near Murmansk. The first mention of this on October 10, 1939, was accompanied by the statement that the offer would be investigated.[112] When Raeder saw Hitler again on October 16, he stated that the place was well situated, some investigation with maps having presumably been made in the meantime.[113] The base, referred to under the code name "Basis Nord" in the naval documents, was to be at Zapadnaya Litza Bay or Western Litza Bay.[114] Western Litza Bay is the name of the port of a small fishing village (population 100 - 250) about thirty-five miles northwest of Murmansk. It is situated at the point where the Western Litza River enters into an inlet about ten miles long.[115] The harbor facilities were probably not very extensive, in spite of the good location; but from the beginning, the Germans planned to station a repair ship there.[116] Preparations for the use of the base were under way by October 17,[117] and were carried out with the support of the Soviet Navy.[118]

When the commander of Germany's submarine fleet, Admiral Dönitz, was asked what he thought about such a base, he stressed

[110] This account is based on Sk1, A, 2, 28: 3 Oct. 1939, C - 122 p. 1 (partly in *TMWC*, XXXIV, 423-24; summarized *ibid.*, p. 679), and Testimony of Schniewind, U.S. v. Leeb, G.T. 4719.

[111] Sk1, C VII/39, 11: 10 Oct. 1939, cited in C - 170, *TMWC*, XXXIV, 679; see also Germany, OKM, Befehlshaber der Unterseeboote, "Dönitz an das Oberkommando der Kriegsmarine, 1 Abt. Sk1," 9 Oct. 1939, C - 5, *ibid.*, pp. 159-61.

[112] Fuehrer Conferences 1939, p. 12; cf. *TMWC*, XXXIV, 679, and XXXV, 629.

[113] Germany, OKM (Raeder), "Vortrag Ob.d.M. beim Führer am 16.10.1939," C - 100, *TMWC*, XXXIV, 317.

[114] Alfred Jodl, "Tagebuch 13 October 1939 - 30 Januar 1940," PS - 1811 (photostat, 100pp.), 19 November 1939, p. 43. Originally Molotov had offered the use of the port of Teriberka, East of Murmansk; see Anthony E. Sokol, "The Cruise of 'Schiff 45'," *United States Naval Institute Proceedings*, LXXVII (1951), 477.

[115] Leningrad, Geografo-ekonomicheskii nauchno-issledovatel'skii institut, Murmanskii filial [Economic geography scientific research institute, Murmansk branch] *Ekonomicheskii atlas Musmanskogo okruga, Leningradskoi oblasti* [Economic atlas of the Murmansk okrug of the Leningrad oblast] (Leningrad, 1935).

[116] Germany, OKM (Raeder), "Vortrag Ob.d.M. beim Führer am 16.10.1939," C - 100, *TMWC*, XXXIV, 317.

[117] Sk1, A, 2, 135: 17 October 1939, cited in C - 170, *ibid.*, p. 680.

[118] Sk1, C VIII/39, 175ff.: 2 November 1939, *ibid.* It should be noted, however, that the Germans seem to have continued stopping at Murmansk.

its great importance to the furtherance of the submarine campaign against Great Britain and worked out a memorandum about the requisite equipment of such a naval base.[119]) Soon after, orders for trials of the base were issued.[120]) By the beginning of 1940, a somewhat garbled version of the whole affair had reached the Western Powers.[121])

The full extent to which the Germans used this base and its over-all importance to their effort are not known. Answers to such questions could be derived only from a very careful examination of large parts of the records of the German Navy which are now held in England. The following summary of information now available may serve as a basis for future investigation.

"Basis Nord" was used by the Germans mostly as a stopping place for their submarines.[122]) An indication of the importance attached to it by the German Navy is the fact that the possible interruption of the "important sea communication with Basis Nord" by Britain as the result of a German attack on Norway was given by the Naval War Staff (Seekriegsleitung) as one of the arguments against such an attack.[123]) Another sign of the high value placed upon this base by the Germans was the suggestion of Admiral Raeder that in return for the service thus rendered Germany, the Germans should not occupy Tromsö when attacking Norway, but should leave it as a base for the Russians. Hitler turned down this proposal as he preferred "not to have the Russians sitting so close."[124])

While the invasion of Norway was being planned, the problem of supplying German forces in Northern Norway was considered especially difficult. It must be remembered that the port of Narvik in North Norway—the loading place for iron from Sweden—was a focal point in the whole operation. Raeder suggested the possibility of using "Basis Nord" as a supply base for the northern group of the German attacking force at his conference with Hitler on February

---

[119]) Germany, OKM (Dönitz), "Kriegstagebuch des Befehlshabers der Unterseeboote, 1. - 15. 11. 1939," pp. 2-3, 3 November 1939, Dönitz - 3, *TMWC*, XL, 7-9; cf. *TMWC*, XIII, 219-21; *PHKV*, XIII, 245-47.

[120]) Skl, A, 3, ?: 17 November 1939, Dönitz - 4, *TMWC*, XL, 9.

[121]) Skl, A, 5, 19: 4 January 1940, C - 21.

[122]) Walther Hubatsch, *Die deutsche Besetzung von Dänemark und Norwegen 1940* (Göttingen, 1952), p. 23. Hubatsch obtained this information from the Chief of the Operations Sections of the Seekriegsleitung (p. 23, n. 44).

[123]) Skl, A, 5, 83: 13 January 1940, C - 21, also in *TMWC*, XXXIV, 185; cf. *ibid.*, p. 334.

[124]) See the extract from Skl, C VII/40, 102: 23 February 1940, in D - 881, *TMWC*, XXXV, 633-34; Skl, C VII/40, 103: 9 March 1940, in C - 170, *TMWC*, XXXIV, 684.

23, 1940.[125]) In the final operational plan, three tankers were to supply the German squadron convoying troops to Narvik—two to be sent from Germany, and one, the "Jan Wellem", from "Basis Nord". Only the "Jan Wellem" actually arrived in Narvik; and though it could not avert the eventual destruction of the ten German destroyers there, it is clear that the supplies provided by this ship enabled the Germans to inflict severe losses on the British in the battles fought in the Narvik area.[126])

After the conquest of Norway and the Atlantic coast of France, Germany no longer needed the base at Western Litza Bay. Ambassador Schulenburg was instructed on September 5, 1940, to inform the Soviet government that the German Navy intended to abandon the base, and to express the thanks of the German government for the valuable aid the Soviets had extended.[127]) Raeder also wrote a letter of thanks to the Soviet government which replied by indicating its pleasure at having been able to help.[128]) The Germans were to return to Western Litza Bay in 1941 when their offensive on Murmansk bogged down along the Western Litza River for the duration of the Eastern campaign.[129])

As soon as the arrangements for "Basis Nord" seemed well along the way to fruition, the German Navy had started to look beyond it to the Northeast passage—the seaway around Siberia to the Pacific. Negotiations for the use of this seaway by German ships, necessarily aided by Soviet ice-breakers, were already in progress by December 30, 1939.[130]) The negotiations were conducted by the German naval attaché in Moscow.[131]) The Germans wanted to use the seaway mainly for two purposes. In the first place, they wanted to send auxiliary cruisers to the Pacific to attack Allied shipping. These could

[125]) Germany, OKM (Raeder), "Vortrag des Ob.d.M. beim Führer am 23.2.40," C - 100, *TMWS*, XXXIV, 334.

[126]) See Assmann, pp. 135, 143; Hubatsch, p. 111; OKM, WFSt, "Lagebericht des Wehrmachtführungsstabes, Lagemeldung Kriegsmarine 7.4.40," in Hubatsch, p. 269; cf. Sk1, C VIII/40, 169: 5 April 1940, C - 170, *TMWC*, XXXIV, 684. The decisive role of "Jan Wellem" is emphasized in Walther Hubatsch's excellently documented study of the Scandinavian operation by the statement (p. 174) that this ship "made the resistance [at Narvik] possible in the first place (hat den dortigen Widerstand überhaupt erst ermöglicht)."

[127]) Woermann to Schulenburg, 5 September 1940, *NSR*, p. 185; for the file marks, see *BDS*, p. 208.

[128]) Sk1, A, 13, 119: 10 September 1940, cited in C - 170, *TMWC*, XXXIV, 690.

[129]) Waldemar Erfurth, *Der finnische Krieg, 1941-1944* (Wiesbaden, 1950), pp. 48-49.

[130]) Germany, OKM (Raeder), "Vortrag des Ob. d. M. beim Führer am 30.XII.39," C - 100, *TMWC*, XXXIV, 322.

[131]) Sk1, A, 5, 24: 5 Jan. 1940, C - 21.

thus avoid interception by British blockade ships before reaching their general area of operations—the South Atlantic, Indian, and Pacific Oceans. In addition, the Germans hoped to secure the return of merchant ships in the Pacific area to Germany by this route. It was anticipated that they might carry some of the goods Germany was getting from the Far Eastern part of the Soviet Union and would thus relieve the pressure on the Soviet transportation system. There was also the possibility of delivering German goods to Far Eastern Russia in this manner.[132] The Germans evidently anticipated a favorable Soviet reply, for they soon started to issue orders to German ships tied up in the Dutch East Indies and the Western Hemisphere to try to reach Japan for a passage over the arctic seaway from there.[133]

A positive outcome of the negotiations was indicated by January 19, 1940; no political difficulties were expected, but some problems in actual use of the seaway were considered likely to arise.[134] By January 26 the political questions were apparently settled, and only the practical details remained to be worked out.[135]

There is absolutely no evidence to show whether any German merchant ships used the northern passage. In the absence of any evidence, it seems safe to assume that very few, more likely none, did. One auxiliary cruiser, however, did make the trip. It was one of the raiders, disguised as a merchant ship, on which the German navy, not without good reason, placed considerable hope. The ship was the "Komet", referred to in the naval documents under the code name "Schiff 45".

According to a report from the German naval attaché in Moscow on February 4, 1940, the outlook for the use of the seaway was good; and the navy accordingly planned to send out "Schiff 45" by this route.[136] The ship was prepared for the trip, and Raeder reported to Hitler on June 20, 1940, that it would be ready to leave Germany at the beginning of July.[137] The Russians helped in the later stages of the preparations.[138] On August 12, 1940, the ship, supported in

---

132) This is outlined in great detail in Sk1, A, 5, 82-83: 12 January 1940, C - 21; a one sentence summary is in C - 170, *TMWC*, XXXIV, 683.

133) Sk1, A, 5, 108-09: 14 January 1940, 151: 18 January 1940, C - 21.

134) Sk1, A, 5, 153: 19 January 1940, C - 21.

135) Sk1, A, 5, 220: 26 January 1940, C - 21; cf. Fuehrer Conferences, 1940. I, 1.

136) Sk1, A, 6, 49: 6 Feb. 1940, summarized in C - 170, *TMWC*, XXXIV, 684; Sokol, p. 478.

137) Fuehrer Conferences, 1940, I, 57.

138) Sk1, A, 11, 206: 18 July 1940, summarized in C - 170, *TMWC*, XXXIV, 687.

various ways by the Russians, started along the passage.[139]) Assisted
by a Soviet ice-breaker, the "Schiff 45" made the passage to the Bering
Straits and entered the Pacific on September 5, 1940.[140])

Once this merchant raider had reached the Pacific, the prob-
blems of bases and supplies remained. It seems that at one time there
was some discussion of a German base analogous to "Basis Nord" in
Far Eastern Russia.[141]) This matter is, however, not at all clear.
Arrangements for transporting across the Transsiberian railroad the
crews of ships captured by the German merchant raiders in the Pacific
do seem to have been made.[142]) The Germans also wanted to use
the Siberian railway for sending supplies to "Schiff 45" and another
raider which had joined it after a trip across the South Atlantic. One
shipment was sent successfully; but the Russians refused to transmit
the second, ostensibly because they thought it incompatible with their
neutrality, more likely because by then the disappearance of British
ships in the Pacific was being noticed in the press.[143]) Other means
of supply had to be worked out.[144]) Eventually a system of supply
from Japanese ports through other German ships was established.[145])
In any case, "Shiff 45", in conjunction with the other raider, sank or
captured 64,000 tons of Allied shipping before returning to Germany
around South America.[146])

German-Soviet naval cooperation took a number of other forms
as well. A series of incidents involving attacks by Russians on German
ships at the time of the Soviet-Finnish war were settled after German
protests without too much difficulty.[147]) The Germans restricted their

---

[139]) Skl, A, 12, 143: 12 August 1940, summarized *ibid.*, p. 689; Skl, A, 13, 155: 12
Sep. 1940, summarized *ibid.*, p. 690.

[140]) Fuehrer Conferences 1940, II, 18; Samuel E. Morison, *History of United
States Naval Operations in World War II*, Vol. III, *The Rising Sun in the Pacific,
1931-April, 1942* (Boston, 1950), pp. 50-51; Winston Churchill, *The Second World
War*, Vol. II, *Their Finest Hour* (London, 1949), p. 526; Sokol, pp. 478-84.

[141]) Skl, C VIII/40, 169: 5 April 1940, summarized in C - 170, *TMWC*, XXXIV,
684-85; Sokol, p. 477.

[142]) Skl, A, 16, 138: 11 December 1940, 151-52: 12 December 1940, C - 105 (photostat, 346 pp.).

[143]) Skl, A, 16, 174: 14 December 1940, C - 105.

[144]) Skl, A, 16, 289: 26 December 1940, C - 105.

[145]) Skl, A, 22, 58-59: 6 June 1941, 128: 12 June 1941, 189: 17 June 1941, 253-54:
12 June 1941, C - 37 (photostat, 411pp.).

[146]) Morison, pp. 50-51; for an account of the trip of "Schiff 45" based on statements by her captain, see Washington *Daily News*, 29 Oct. 1947, p. 5; for an account
clearly based on documents of the Naval War Staff, see Sokol, pp. 484-89.

[147]) Skl, A, 4, 86: 12 December 1939, C - 27 (summarized in C - 170, *TMWC*,
XXXIV, 682); Skl, A, 4, 97-98: 13 December 1939, 117: 15 December 1939, 129:
16 December 1939, 154: 19 December, 171: 21 December 1939, C - 27; Skl, C VII/39
68: 30 December 1939, C - 100, *TMWC*, XXXIV, 321-22.

naval operations in the Baltic[148]) and in the Black Sea[149]) to avoid incidents with the Soviet Union. The Germans persistently tried to exclude Soviet ships from the effects of their intensive submarine warfare.[150]) In return, the Russians arranged their trade agreements with England in such a manner as not to interfere with the German war effort. Some of the goods Russia received were reexported to Germany, while the goods Soviet Russia sent to England went along routes open to German attack.[151]) The Russians protested violently against the British blockade and refused to discuss their deliveries to Germany with the English.[152])

A variety of similar instances of cooperation could be listed, but this would not add materially to the picture which the foregoing account presents. In the field of naval, as in that of economic, cooperation it is most difficult to draw a balance or offer any over-all conclusions. The recital of the main forms of naval cooperation does, however, leave the clear impression that in this sphere of activity a great deal was done. The German navy was in many ways the weakest branch of Germany's armed forces. The aid given it by the Soviets materially raised its fighting effectiveness and supported its efforts.

D. THE SOVIET-FINNISH WAR

In the period between the second visit of Ribbentrop to Moscow and the German attack in the West various diplomatic moves were made by the Soviet Union that had some repercussions on German-Soviet relations. Some of these, such as those involving the countries of South-East Europe—particularly Bulgaria and Rumania—and the three small Baltic states will be taken up later in connection with the developments of the summer of 1940. However, the fact that the attempts of Soviet Russia to secure various concessions from Finland led to the outbreak of a war, which in its later stages seemed likely to merge with the war between Germany and the Western

---

[148]) Skl, C VIII/39, 168, 173: 26 October 1939, summarized in C - 170, *TMWC*, XXXIV, 680; Skl, A, 4, 65: 9 December 1939, C - 27; Germany, OKM (Raeder), "Vortrag des Ob.d.M. beim Führer am 23.2.40," C - 100, *TMWC*, XXXIV, 331; Skl, C VIII/40, 159: 1 April 1940, summarized in C - 170, *TMWC*, XXXIV, 684.

[149]) Skl, C VIII/40, 256: 8 May 1940, summarized in C - 107, *TMWC*, XXXIV, 685.

[150]) See *TMWC*, XXXIV, 312-35, *passim*, and 614; cf. Ritter to Schulenburg, 6 December 1939, NG - 3913 (photostat, 2pp.).

[151]) Skl, A, 2, 93: 11 October 1939, summarized in C - 170, *TMWC*, XXXIV, 679; cf. Skl, A, 4, 13: 3 December 1939, C - 27.

[152]) Text of the Russian note on the British blockade in Schwarz, pp. 339-40; for official German comment on the note see *ibid.*, pp. 340-41. See also Dallin, pp. 104-05 and Skl, A, 9, 2: 1 May 1940, summarized in C - 170, *TMWC*, XXXIV, 685.

Powers, makes it desirable to discuss the effects of the Russo-Finnish War on German-Soviet relations at this point. The implications of the Soviet-Finnish War for the relations between the Axis partners will be examined in more detail in the next section of this chapter; the main theme of this section will be the attitude of Germany to the winter war.

Finland had been assigned to the Soviet sphere of interests by the Secret Protocol of August 23, 1939.[153] The changes made by the Secret Protocols of September 28 left the status of Finland unaffected.[154] It seems important to stress at this point that the line drawn in these protocols was a strictly geographical one as regards the Baltic area—Finland was in no way differentiated from Estonia and Latvia in regard to possible treatment by the Soviet Union.

The Finns tried to find out in Berlin what had been decided about Finland at Ribbentrop's second visit on October 2, but were left uninformed.[155] Alarmed by the Russian moves toward the Baltic States which had resulted in new agreements between them and the Soviet Union—agreements obviously concluded under Russian pressure—the Finns again turned to the German government on October 9.[156]. The call of the Finnish Minister had been announced beforehand, presumably on instructions from Finnish Foreign Minister Erkko after the latter had told the Soviet Ambassador in Helsinki on October 8 that the Finnish negotiator Paasikivi would leave for Moscow the following day.[157] Weizsäcker spoke to the Finnish Minister along lines previously worked out and sent to the German Minister in Finland.[158] If Weizsäcker followed the prepared outline closely, and there is no reason to doubt that he did, the Finnish minister could hardly have been left in doubt as to the real situation.

> In Moscow.... the well-known definitive line of demarcation was fixed. West of this line lie the German interests, east of it we have registered no interests. We are therefore not informed as to what demands Russia intends to make on Finland.... But after the developments cited above we would hardly be in a position, in any case, to intervene in the Russian-Finnish conversations.[159]

---

[153] *NSR*, p. 78; *BDS*, p. 86.
[154] *NSR*, p. 07; *BDS*, p. 117.
[155] Memorandum of Weizsäcker, 2 October 1939, *NSR*, p. 111; *BDS*, pp. 123-24.
[156] Memorandum of Weizsäcker, 9 October 1939, *NSR*, p. 121; *BDS*, pp. 134-35.
[157] Memorandum of Erkko, 8 October 1939, Finland, Ministry of Foreign Affairs, *The Development of Finnish-Soviet Relations during the Autumn of 1939*, (Helsinki, 1940), p. 45.
[158] Weizsäcker to Blücher, 9 October 1939, *NSR*, p. 122; *BDS*, pp. 135-36.
[159] *Ibid.* For the proposed German-Finnish pact referred to in this conversation,

The Swedish Minister who saw Weizsäcker on the same day did not receive a similarly honest reply.[160])

On October 10, the German Minister in Finland, Wipert von Blücher, warned the German government that Finland would fight if the Russian demands went beyond some islands in the Gulf of Finland. He urged that, in view of the serious economic consequences of a Russo-Finnish war for Germany, the German government should intervene with the Soviets to advise moderate demands.[161]) Blücher's pro-Finnish attitude almost led to his dismissal by Ribbentrop.[162])

The details of the Soviet-Finnish negotiations during October and November are not relevant to this study.[163]) Because of the importance of the war which followed, however, some discussion of the Russian motivation is essential. It is most important that the date when the Soviets first requested the sending of a Finnish emissary be remembered. That date was October 5.[164]) At that time the German-Soviet peace offensive was just getting under way, and the Soviets were probably not certain what its outcome would be. If peace were to "break out," it probably seemed wise to the Soviet leaders to gather in the fruits of the Moscow agreements just as soon as possible. If, on the other hand, the Western Powers continued the war, a long and unpredictable conflict would surely ensue. Whatever turn such a war might take, or whatever its outcome might be, would it not be wisest to take quickly what could be taken—to batten down the hatches, so to speak—and to prepare for all eventualities? Once the Soviets had committed themselves in Molotov's speech of October 31, to take action about Finland, it probably seemed essential to them to go on. It seems clear that a swift collapse of Finland was expected; perhaps the business would be finished in a few days. As has happened at other times, the Soviets misjudged the country they were dealing with and the likely reactions of other nations to their own initiative; and the determined Finnish resistance with its international implications at first caught them off balance.

This explanation of the Soviet actions in regard to Finland is the

---

see Wipert von Blücher, *Gesandter zwischen Diktatur und Demokratie* (Wiesbaden, 1951), pp. 142-43.

[160]) Memorandum of Weizsäcker, 9 October 1939, *NSR*, p. 123; *BDS*, p. 136; cf. Weizsäcker, p. 281. The discussion of this matter in Hubatsch (p. 12) is somewhat misleading on the information given to the Swedes.

[161]) Blücher to Ribbentrop, 10 October 1939, *NSR*, p. 123; *BDS*, p. 132.

[162]) Testimony of Kessel, U.S. v. Weizsäcker, E.T. 9487; Weizsäcker, p. 281.

[163]) The Soviets apparently informed the Germans about the course of the negotiations. Schulenburg to Ribbentrop, 15 October 1939, cited in Langer and Gleason, p. 325, n. 49.

[164]) Yrjö-Koskinen to Erkko, 5 October 1939, Finland, p. 42.

simplest; and therefore, in the opinion of the writer, the one most likely to be correct. In any case, it requires none of the historical metaphysics advanced by writers like Schuman and Dallin to bolster their very detailed projections of Soviet policy formulation.

When the Soviet-Finnish War broke out on November 30, 1939, Germany announced her neutrality. Instructions were sent to German missions abroad on the position to take toward the conflict. The second of these specifically directs that sympathy be expressed for the Soviet point of view.165) Since Finland had been assigned to Soviet Russia's sphere, it was incumbent upon Germany to favor the latter, or at least to do nothing to hinder her. The Germans quickly realized, however, that this attitude would hurt them in the eyes of her friends—Italy and Spain.166)

The leadership of the German navy strongly recommended that absolutely nothing be done to help Finland, and that any proposed Italian aid to Finland not be allowed to cross Germany.167) At a conference with Hitler on December 12, Raeder spoke to the Führer to this effect. Hitler declared himself in full agreement. Keitel told them that Sweden was being informed that weapons would be supplied to Sweden only on the written guarantee of the Swedish government that they were actually to be used only by the Swedish armed forces.168)

When Tass, the official Soviet news agency, gave currency to reports that Germany was allowing transit to Italian planes and other equipment for Finland across Germany, Ribbentrop summoned the Soviet Ambassador, denied all the stories, and in righteous indignation reproved the Soviet government for spreading the reports.169) It seems most likely that the Tass report was designed to feel out German policy by getting some definite reaction, or possibly to head off the sort of shipments it referred to. In any case, when the Italians a few days later tried to ship planes, that had been ordered before the war broke out, across Germany to Finland, the Germans refused to permit transit.170)

One of the most interesting indications of German policy toward the conflict is supplied by the German reaction to a Soviet request for help in blockading Finland. The Soviet blockade was announced on

---

165) Weizsäcker to Schulenburg, 6 December 1939, *NSR*, p. 130; *BDS*, p. 144; cf. Weizsäcker to German Missions, 2 December 1939, *NSR*, pp. 127-28; *BDS*, pp. 141-42.

166) Sk1, A, 4, 7: 2 Dec. 1939, C - 27.

167) Sk1, A, 4, 59: 9 Dec. 1939, C - 27.

168) Germany, OKM (Raeder), "Vortrag Ob.d.M. beim Führer 12. XII 39.," C - 64, *TMWC*, XXXIV, 272.

169) Memorandum of Ribbentrop, 11 December 1939, *NSR*, pp. 130-31; *BDS*, p. 144; see, however, Langer and Gleason, p. 340 and n. 106.

170) See Léonardo Simoni [pseud.], *Berlin ambassade d'Italie*, trans. C. D. Jonquières (Paris, 1947), 12 Dec. 1939, pp. 49-50, 13 Dec. 1939, p. 50.

December 8.[171]) Two days later the Soviets asked whether German ships would supply food and fuel to their submarines operating in the Gulf of Bothnia, compensating supplies for Germany being promised. The German navy recommended that the project be carried out, and Hitler gave his approval the same day.[172]) On December 12, however, after the Germans had already made considerable preparations to provide the aid requested, the Soviets called it all off without stating any reason.[173]) Because of their interest, the relevant sections of the diary of the German Naval War Staff are translated in full in AP-PENDIX I. The most interesting thing about them is what they do not say. There is absolutely no reference whatever to German-Finnish relations. The recognition of Soviet Russia's exclusive interest in Finland seems axiomatic. Support for Soviet naval action is readily offered; yet it was at this very time that the Germans felt obliged to impose restrictions on their own naval warfare in the Baltic and to suffer from various incidents as discussed in the preceding section.

As the war continued for several weeks, and the Soviets suffered set-backs, various new possibilities arose. The Western Powers talked much—and did little—about helping Finland. The Germans viewed with alarm the possibility that Allied aid to Finland would involve shutting off of the vital steel shipments from Sweden. It was anticipated that the drain of the war would reduce Soviet deliveries to Germany. It was therefore in Germany's interest to have the war ended soon. The role of Germany in the attempts to bring about a peace settlement is still not quite clear. The most definite evidence concerns a German sounding of the Soviets in Janary, 1940. At the request of the Finnish government, the Germans raised the question of possible German mediation with the Soviet government. Schulen-burg saw Molotov twice; the answer was negative. The German minister in Finland was therefore instructed to inform the Finnish government that there seemed to be no immediate prospects of ending the war in this manner.[174]) A further, extremely vague, attempt in February also failed.[175])

As the Soviet-Finnish War continued into February and March, even greater complications appeared on the horizon. The Western Powers were developing plans for a general activation of the war

---

[171]) Sk1, A, 4, 54-55: 8 Dec. 1939, C - 27.

[172]) Sk1, A, 4, 73: 10 Dec. 1939, C - 27; cf. *TMWC*, XXXIV, 272.

[173]) Sk1, A, 4, 88: 12 Dec. 1939, C - 27.

[174]) Blücher, pp. 165-67; see also Sk1, A, 5, 95: 13 January 1940, 127: 17 January 1940, C-21; John H. Wuorinen (ed.). *Finland and World War II, 1939-1944* (New York, 1948), p. 73; Halder (19 January 1940), III, 32; Simoni (20 January 1940), p. 76.

[175]) Blücher, pp. 172-77.

against Germany. The various details of these plans are not directly relevant to this study, but the following partial outline will show why they would exercise considerable influence on Soviet-German relations. One of the main points was, of course, to help Finland; but this became merely a secondary aspect of a scheme aimed primarily, though indirectly, at Germany.[176]) Germany's iron supply was to be cut by an Allied expeditionary force to Scandinavia, and her oil supplies were to be cut by Allied attacks on the Rumanian and Russian oil fields in the South.[177]) These schemes soon came to the attention of the German government.[178]) In general, the Germans were quite pleased to have the Russians pushed more to their side by events,[179]) but the prospect of having their vital war supplies cut off was hardly welcomed. German intelligence reports on the Allied plans were passed on to the Russians.[180])

The Russians, no doubt, had their own sources of information. They had no desire to be involved in a world war, and therefore wanted a favorable but swift settlement of the Finnish venture. They presumably feared that once they became involved in hostilities with the Western Powers, the Allies and the Germans would get together in that ever-feared nightmare of the Soviet leadership—the joint attack of the "capitalistic" powers on the Soviet Union. There is not a shred of evidence to support the theory that anything of the kind was about to happen, but the Soviets acted on it anyway.

The Russians dropped the "People's Government of the Democratic Republic of Finland," which they had established to lead the Finnish masses that were supposed to revolt against the "White Guardist" government, and dealt with the real government of Finland. Having broken through the Mannerheim Line in a big offensive, the Russians could probably have occupied all of Finland in a comparatively short time, but they preferred to negotiate lest they become involved in war with the Western Powers. Peace was signed on March 12.

As propaganda attacks and the military planning of the West continued along the lines previously stated even after March 12, the Soviets tried to clear themselves in the eyes of the West by restricting their aid to Germany. At the end of March, beginning of April, 1940, the Soviets took various steps to limit their support of the German war effort. In all areas they created difficulties, and for a short time

---

[176]) See Chamberlain to Lindley, 1 January 1940, Feiling, pp. 427-28.

[177]) Germany, Auswärtiges Amt, *Die Geheimakten des Französischen Generalstabes* (German White Book, No. 6) (Berlin, 1940); *Voprosy Istorii* [Questions of History], 1949, No. 2, pp. 101-08.

[178]) See e.g. Papen to Ribbentrop, cited in Halder (26 February 1940), III, 99.

[179]) Halder (14 Dec. 1939), II, 6, (27 March 1940), III, 133.

[180]) Halder (6 March 1940), III, 113.

deliveries to Germany were suspended.[181]) The German attack on Norway changed all that and, along with a lifting of all the Soviet restrictions on aid to Germany, introduced a new period in German-Soviet relations.[182])

E. GERMAN-SOVIET COOPERATION AND THE AXIS[183])

The Italian government had declined to enter the war on Germany's side at the end of August, 1939, and during the months that followed, the Axis partnership was at times rather strained. The agreement between Germany and Russia was to contribute substantially to Italian dissatisfaction. This somewhat vague uneasiness in Italy came to the surface with the Russian attack on Finland and Germany's attitude toward the attack.

The Germans had expected that their position in Italy would be hurt by the events in Scandinavia.[184]) The reaction in Italy came quickly. A few days after the Russians attacked Finland, demonstrations for Finland took place in Italy.[185]) The Italian press sided with the Finns.[186]) The effect of Germany's attitude in the Soviet-Finnish War on the Italian position toward Germany was examined at a conference of the German Naval War Staff on December 6 in which the German naval attaché to Rome participated.[187]) It was considered possible that further German-Soviet cooperation might well, in case of a Soviet-Russian advance in the Balkans, lead to a swing by Italy from a position of benevolent to one of hostile neutrality.

Diplomatic repercussions followed rapidly. Presumably because of the anti-Soviet demonstrations, the new Russian Ambassador to Italy, Nikolai Gorelkin, was recalled from Rome on December 9.[188]) Gorelkin had been scheduled to present his letters of credence on December

---

[181]) Sk1, C VIII/40, 169: 5 April 1940, cited in C-170, *TMWC*, XXXIV, 684-85; Memorandum of Schulenburg, 11 April 1940, *NSR*, pp. 138-40; *BDS*, pp. 154-56; Schulenburg to Ribbentrop, 1 April 1940, cited in *BDS*, p. 156, n. 1; Sokol, p. 478; Germany, OKW, Wi Rü Amt, Wi VII (Keitel), "Wi VII 6206/40; Betreff: Russlandvertrag - Export," 3 April 1940 (typescript, Library of Congress, Aeronautics Division, 1 p.).

[182]) Schulenburg to Ribbentrop, 9 April 1940, *NSR*, p. 138; *BDS*, p. 154; Memorandum of Schulenburg, 11 April 1940, *NSR*, pp. 139-40; *BDS*, pp. 154-156.

[183]) A great amount of additional material on this subject has now been published in Mario Toscano, *Una mancata intesa italo-sovietica nel 1940 e 1941* (Firenze, 1953). No significant changes are required by this new material, and those interested in more details are therefore referred to Toscano's very fine monograph.

[184]) Sk1, A, 4, 7: 2 December 1939, C-27.

[185]) Ciano, *The Ciano Diaries* (2-4 December 1939), pp. 174-75.

[186]) Sk1, A, 4, 29: 5 December 1939, C-27.

[187]) Sk1, A, 4, 34-37: 6 December 1939, C-27.

[188]) Ciano, *Diaries* (9 December 1939), p. 177.

12; he informed Ciano that he would leave Rome on December 11,[189]) and actually did so.[190]) This left the Soviet embassy in Rome in the hands of the Chargé d'Affaires, Leon Helfand, whose role will come under review in connection with the German efforts to bring Italy and Russia together again.

During December, 1939, and January, 1940, various plans to help Finland were worked out in Rome,[191]) though, as has been pointed out previously, Italian supplies to Finland were held up by Germany. At the end of December, 1939, the Italian Ambassador to Moscow, Augusto Rosso, was recalled.[192]) The Italians twice asked Berlin in the most agitated manner whether it was true that German technicians were going to help the Russians.[193]) Ciano's foreign policy speech to the Chamber of Fasces and Corporations on December 16 had a distinctly anti-German tone and produced a very hostile reaction in Germany.[194]) A good indication of Italian feeling can be seen in the way Ciano congratulated the British Ambassador on the capture of the German ship Altmark in Norwegian territorial waters.[195]) The Italian step which produced a concrete, though delayed, German reaction was a letter Mussolini sent to Hitler on Januari 4.[196]) Mussolini urged the reconstitution of some sort of Poland. He took the side of Finland in the winter war. He argued at great length against continued cooperation with the Russians.

Berlin's immediate reaction to the letter was a defense of the Soviet action against Finland.[197]) Finally Hitler answered Mussolini in a letter dated March 8 and carried to Italy by Ribbentrop in person.[198]) Hitler's letter contains a long general exposition of the

---

[189]) *Ibid.*

[190]) *New York Times,* December 14, 1939, p. 1.

[191]) Ciano, *Diaries* (8 December 1939), p. 177, (19 December 1939), p. 180, (2 January 1940), p. 191, (15 January 1940), p. 196, (27 January 1940), p. 201.

[192]) *Ibid.,* (28 December 1939), p. 185; cf. *ibid.* (10 January 1940), p. 194.

[193]) Simoni (27 December 1939), p. 59, (30 December 1939), p. 61. Difficulties between Germany and Italy over similar rumors at that time are well illustrated by the texts of the Italian intercepts of telephone conversations between the German Embassy in Rome and the Ministry of Foreign Affairs in Berlin (U.S. National Archives, Italian Documents, Microfilm Reel 419, frames 009752-835, *passim*).

[194]) For the text of Ciano's speech, see Galeazzo Ciano, *An Account of the International Situation in Recent Years. Speech in the Chamber of Fasces and Corporations, December 16, 1939* (Rome, 1939); cf. Ciano, *The Ciano Diaries,* pp. 178-80. For the reaction in Germany, see Simoni (19 December 1939), p. 55, (28 December 1939), p. 59, (29 December 1939), p. 61; Hassell (25 December 1939), p. 112.

[195]) Ciano, *Diaries* (19 February 1940), p. 209.

[196]) Text in Adolf Hitler and Benito Mussolini, *Les Lettres secrètes échangées par Hitler et Mussolini* (Paris, 1946), pp. 47-58.

[197]) Simoni (8 January 1940), pp. 66-67, (10 January 1940), pp. 68-69, (2 February 1940), pp. 81-82; cf. Halder (10 January 1940), III, 21, (11 January 1940) III, 23-24.

[198]) Kordt, *Wahn und Wirklichkeit,* p. 240.

reasons for a limited cooperation with the Soviet Union. Turning specifically to the Finnish affair, Hitler justified the Soviet demands and explained sympathetically the reasons for their military difficulties.[199]

Ribbentrop was in Rome March 10 and 11, conferring with Ciano and the Duce. On March 10 Ribbentrop attempted a long and detailed explanation of the German policy toward the Soviet Union. He stated that there was no more danger from the Soviet Union which was now nationalistic, had thrown the Jews out of office, and was no longer interfering in internal German affairs.[200] He explained that the Soviet-Finnish War was the result of diplomatic mistakes and had been forced on Russia. He defended the Russian action.[201] Finally, he stressed Soviet economic aid to Germany in the form of direct deliveries, purchases abroad, and the transit trade.[202] On the following day Ribbentrop and Mussolini discussed the possibilities for improving Italian-Soviet relations, and both agreed to work toward such an improvement.[203] It was at this time, apparently, that Ribbentrop was told that the Soviet chargé, Leon Helfand, was generally oriented against a policy of cooperation with the Axis.[204] Helfand had been in Italy for many years and belonged to the Litvinov school of Russian diplomats.[205]

Immediately upon his return to Berlin, Ribbentrop began to work for a Soviet-Italian rapprochement. He apparently wanted a renewed exchange of ambassadors and the recall of Helfand. On March 13 Ribbentrop had a long conversation with the Soviet Ambassador in Berlin. He gave the latter an account of his trip to Rome and the subjects discussed there. He stressed the importance and mutual desirability of better relations between Italy and Russia, informed the Russian that Mussolini had specifically stated his desire for such an improvement, expressed his regret at the absence of the two ambassadors from their respective posts, and offered his own services for a restoration of good relations.[206] There was also a good deal of rather reticent sparring about Helfand—nothing definite came out, but the Russian must have been left with the impression that something in regard to this man needed examination.

---

[199] Hitler to Mussolini, 8 March 1940, 1833 - PS, trans. United States, OCCWC (mimeo, 7pp.), pp. 4-5.

[200] Ciano, *Diplomatic Papers*, pp. 342-43.

[201] *Ibid.*, pp. 343-45.

[202] *Ibid.*, p. 347; cf. Gafencu, *Vorspiel zum Krieg im Osten*, pp. 55-56.

[203] Ciano, *Diplomatic Papers*, pp. 350-51, 356.

[204] Ribbentrop to Schulenburg, 21 March 1940, Seidl, p. 165.

[205] Reynolds and Eleanor Packard, *Balcony Empire* (New York, 1942), p. 208; cf. Ciano, *Diaries* (20 Sep. 1939), p. 148.

[206] Memorandum of the German Foreign Office, 13 March 1940, Seidl. pp. 160-63.

On the same day, or on one of the days immediately following, Ribbentrop seems to have instructed Schulenburg to report to Molotov about the Rome conversations and ask about a possible improvement in Italian-Soviet relations.[207]) Schulenburg saw Molotov on or before March 18; his report on the conversation is not available, but Molotov seems to have been noncommittal.[208])

On March 18, 1940, Hitler and Mussolini met at the Brenner pass. They went over much the same ground previously covered at Ribbentrop's visit, including the relations of the Axis partners with the Soviet Union.[209])

Ribbentrop sent Schulenburg a summary of the Brenner conversations for Molotov[210]) and at the same time instructed him to take up the question of Italian-Soviet relations again when delivering this information. In a long instruction on this, Ribbentrop went over all the details.[211]) The observation which Molotov had apparently made, to the effect that there was no sign of an Italian desire for improved relations, was to be answered by the desire for such improvement expressly stated to Ribbentrop by Mussolini. The German Foreign Minister suggested that the best way to start the rapprochement was to return the ambassadors to their posts, and that this might be done without loss of prestige to either side if the Russians would indicate their willingness for a simultaneous return of the Ambassadors through Ribbentrop. At length Ribbentrop informed Schulenburg about the Helfand problem and suggested that a private letter from himself to Schulenburg, a copy of which he enclosed, might be used by the latter to sound out the Soviet leaders about this man.

Schulenburg saw Molotov on march 26.[212]) There is no reference to Helfand in the report on this conversation. Molotov thanked Schulenburg for the information and, at the urgent request of the latter, promised to submit the question of improving Italian-Soviet relations to his government. Schulenburg received the impression that Molotov wanted some concrete signs from Italy and suggested that a few friendly articles about the Soviet Union in the Italian press would provide these signs. Ribbentrop therefore instructed Mackensen, German ambassador in Rome, to see Ciano and, in accordance with Schulenburg's advice, ask that the appropriate instructions be given

---

[207]) *Ibid.*, p. 161; cf. Ribbentrop to Schulenburg, 21 March 1940, Seidl, p. 164.
[208]) Schulenburg to Ribbentrop (Moscow No. 530), 18 March 1940, cited in Ribbentrop to Schulenburg, 21 March 1940, Seidl, p. 164.
[209]) Ciano, *Diplomatic Papers*, pp. 364-65.
[210]) Ribbentrop to Schulenburg, 21 March 1940, Seidl, pp. 166-67.
[211]) Ribbentrop to Schulenburg, 21 March 1940, *ibid.*, pp. 164-66.
[212]) Schulenburg to Ribbentrop, 26 March 1940, *ibid.*, p. 168.

to the Italian press.[213]) Ciano, however, had gleefully noted some anti-Italian comments in Molotov's speech of March 29 and planned to use these to counter the German plans for a rapprochement.[214]) When Mackensen saw Ciano, therefore, on April 1, the latter refused the German request, but upon Mackensen's insistence agreed to put the matter before the Duce.[215]) Mussolini supported Ciano's position.[216])

After this incident, nothing happened for about a month. In spite of an inconclusive conversation between Ciano and Helfand on April 29,[217]) both sides began to express an interest in improved relations again at the beginning of May.[218]) When Mackensen again urged Ciano to work for the rapprochement on May 20, the latter declared that Italy had no objections.[219]) On June 8, 1940, agreement on the return of the ambassadors was reached; Ciano commented in his diary that "Ribbentrop will be happy over this, since it was one of the great objectives of his policy."[220])

Even before the ambassadors returned, Molotov started to push for a Soviet-Italian agreement covering the Balkans.[221]) Ribbentrop, however, did not want such an agreement.[222]) On June 17 and 20, Rosso had his first interviews with Molotov,[223]) and on June 22, Gorelkin was received by Ciano.[224]) At these meetings the Russians reopened the question of a Soviet-Italian agreement about the Balkans, Molotov discussing the matter again with Rosso on June 25. The Russians proposed that if Italy recognized Soviet hegemony in the Black Sea, they would recognize Italian hegemony in the Mediterranean. Rosso recommended acceptance of the proposals, but for some time Rome did not answer.

By now, however, the time had come for Helfand's recall. Whether

---

213) Mackensen to Ribbentrop, 1 April 1940, *ibid.,* pp. 171-72.

214) Ciano, *Diaries* (31 March 1940), p. 229.

215) Mackensen to Ribbentrop, 1 April 1940, Seidl, p. 172.

216) Ciano, *Diaries* (1 April 1940), p. 230.

217) Ciano, *Diaries* (29 April 1940), p. 241.

218) For the Russian side, see Halder (6 May 1940), III, 191; for the Italian side, Ciano, *Diaries* (1 May 1940), p. 242.

219) Ciano, *Diaries* (20 May 1940), p. 253.

220) *Ibid.* (8 June 1940), p. 262; cf. Simoni (10 June 1940), p. 151.

221) Molotov-Schulenburg conferences on June 3 and 7, 1940. Schulenburg to Ribbentrop, 3 June 1940, *NSR,* p. 144 (see *BDS,* p. 161, n. 3, for an indication that a telegram from Berlin was then sent to Mackensen); Schulenburg to Ribbentrop, 6 June 1940, *NSR,* p. 144; *BDS,* p. 162; Schulenburg to Ribbentrop (Moscow No. 1094, 7 June 1940, cited in *NSR,* p. 148; *BDS,* p. 166, and Rossi, p. 156, n. 3.

222) Ribbentrop to Schulenburg, 16 June 1940, *NSR,* p. 148; *BDS,* p. 166; see also the English edition of Rossi's book (London, 1950), p. 145.

223) Schulenburg to Ribbentrop, 26 June 1940, *NSR,* p. 160; *BDS,* p. 180.

224) Ciano, *Diaries* (22 June 1940), pp. 267-68.

as a result of hints from Germany or reports from Gorelkin, or both, on July 14 Helfand informed Ciano that he had been ordered to Moscow.[225] Fearing for his life, Helfand secured help from Ciano, flew to Portugal and thence across the Atlantic.[226]

In August, Mussolini came back to the idea of an agreement with Russia.[227] On consulting Berlin, however, the Italians received a German veto and accordingly dropped their plans.[228] This incident will be reviewed in connection with German-Soviet relations in autumn 1940. The Italo-Soviet rapprochement had gone even further than Germany herself wanted.

---

[225] *Ibid.* (14 July 1940), pp. 375-76; it is interesting to note that the Italians had secured the recall of Ulrich von Hassell and the Germans that of Bernardo Attolico because of their hostile attitude toward the projects of the Axis.

[226] Packard, p. 209.

[227] Ciano, *Diaries* (4 August 1949), p. 280, (6 August 1940), p. 281.

[228] *Ibid.* (17 August 1940), p. 285; Simoni (17 August 1940), pp. 191-92, (18 August 1940), pp. 193-94, (19 August 1940), p. 194.

CHAPTER SIX

FROM THE ATTACK ON NORWAY
TO JULY 19, 1940

On April 9, 1940, Germany attacked Norway and Denmark. The successes quickly gained by the German forces had an immediate effect on German-Soviet relations. At the end of March, beginning of April, 1940, there had been a distinct cooling off in these relations, and severe restrictions had been imposed by the Russians on the practical cooperation they were willing to furnish Germany.[1]) This has been examined in connection with the Soviet-Finnish war. When Schulenburg saw Molotov on April 9 to inform him of Germany's action in Scandinavia, Molotov did an "about-face" and was most friendly again. In the eyes of the Soviet leaders, the German action was welcome for two interrelated reasons. First, the Finnish question was very likely to be closed, especially if Germany won in Norway. Secondly, the Allies would now be occupied with Germany directly— since Germany had gone on the offensive, the Allies would probably lack the need and resources for such adventures as the attack on Baku.[2])

The German attack in the West on May 10 was different from that in Scandinavia, not only in degree but also in character. While the latter had been an attempt to safeguard supplies and secure bases, the former was designed to knock out the Western Powers directly and immediately. The attitude of the Soviet Union toward such a major effort was of the greatest importance. Norway was obviously not a theater for the commitment of vast masses of troops. The Western front, however, would require the commitment of the overwhelming majority of the German divisions, in particular the most

---

[1]) Sk1, C VIII/40, 169: 5 April 1940, cited in C-170, *TMWC*, XXXIV, 684-85; Memorandum of Schulenburg, 11 April 1940, *NSR*, pp. 138-39; *BDS*, p. 156, n. 1.

[2]) Memorandum of Schulenburg, 11 April 1940, *NSR*, pp. 138-40; *BDS*, pp. 154-56. For the telegram Schulenburg to Ribbentrop, 9 April 1940 (No. 648), concerning notification of the Soviets about the invasion of Norway and Denmark, which is not printed in *NSR* (p. 138, n. 63), see Denmark, Rigsdagen, Folketinget, Kommission af 25. October 1950 i henhold til Grundlovens 45, *Beretning til Folketinget*, Vol. XII, *Bilag, Tyske Dokumenter* (Copenhagen, 1951), p. 182.

highly trained and best equipped. What would Russia do while these troops were engaged in action in the West?

This problem was one of those posed by the military leaders in Germany who were opposed to an attack on France. General Leeb, the commanding general of Army Group C, had warned on October 11, 1939, that a German commitment in the West would give Soviet Russia a free hand.[3]) On October 31, 1939, General Rundstedt, commanding general of Army Group A, warned that once Germany's offensive strength had been used up in the West, as he was sure it would be, anything could happen in the East.[4]) Hitler, however, was not only confident of victory in the West, he was also rather certain that the Soviet Union would not move for some time and that he was therefore free to attack.[5]) He was probably strengthened in this assumption by the belief that the Russian army would first have to repair some of the damage incurred in the Soviet-Finnish War.[6]) Accordingly, the Germans had left along the eastern border on May 7, 1940, only four regular and nine territorial (Landesschützen) divisions.[7])

Of course, if Germany were to carry out an attack in the West, leaving such weak forces in the East, it was necessary for her to keep relations with Soviet Russia in a fairly friendly condition, particularly in the Balkans where Germany would be unable to intervene in defense of her interests. This was no doubt one element leading the Germans to work for the Italian-Soviet rapprochement described in the preceding chapter.[8]) When the High Command of the German Army raised the question of a quick occupation of Rumania by transporting troops across Hungary in April, 1940, Hitler turned the project down since he was trying "by all means to keep the Balkans quiet." [9]) Similarly, the Germans took pains to restrict the activities of Ukrainian nationalists.[10])

---

[3]) Leeb to Brauchitsch, "Denkschrift über die Aussichten und Wirkungen eines Angriffs auf Frankreich und England unter Verletzung der Neutralität Hollands, Belgiens und Luxemburgs," 11 October 1939, NOKW - 3433, trans. United States, OCCWC (mimeo, 12pp.), pp. 7, 11; cf. U.S. v. Leeb, G.T. 9944.

[4]) Rundstedt to Brauchitsch, 31 Oct. 1939, NOKW - 511 (photostat, 6pp.) p. 4.

[5]) Adolf Hitler, "Denkschrift und Richtlinien über die Führung des Krieges im Westen," 9 October 1939, L-52 TMWC, XXXVII, 470; Adolf Hitler, "Besprechung beim Führer," 23 Nov. 1939, PS - 789, TMWC, XXVI, 331.

[6]) Skl, A, 4, 199-200: 27 December 1939, C-27, partly quoted in C-170, TMWC, XXXIV, 682-83 (note mis-dating to 17 Dec. 1939); Skl, A, 4 225-26: 30 December 1939, C-27, cited in C-170, TMWC, XXXIV, 683 (mis-dated to 31 December).

[7]) Germany, OKW, WFA, "Übersicht [über die deutsche Heeresverteilung]," 7 May 1940, 1783 - PS (photostat, 1p.).

[8]) See Halder (1 Jan. 1940), III, 16.

[9]) Germany, OKW, Wi Rü Amt, "Besprechungsnotiz, Vortrag Amtschef bei Gen. Oberst Keitel," 26 Apr. 1940, PS - 1456 (photostat, 3 pp.), p. 1.

[10]) Hans Frank, "Tagebuch," 12 Apr. 1940 (Abteilungsleitersitzung), PS - 2233,

Once it had become clear, however, that the Germans were winning great victories in the West, the Russians stepped up their diplomatic activities. The obviously imminent entrance of Italy into the war removed another obstacle to Soviet policy—once involved in the war, Italy, with her poor economy, would no longer be a free agent.

The Soviets moved in three places—the Baltic states, Finland, and the Balkans. Under the provisions of the agreements with Germany, the Soviets had secured agreements with the three Baltic states providing for their partial military occupation in the fall of 1939. In accordance with the spirit of the settlement of September 28, the people of German descent in these areas were moved to Germany.[11]) This was the status of those states at the end of May, 1940. With regard to Estonia and Latvia, Russia had complete freedom under her agreements with Germany, while a section of Lithuania had been reserved to Germany in case of full Russian military occupation.

In June and July of 1940, the Russians in several stages fully incorporated these states into the Soviet Union as the Germans had anticipated.[12]) The complete occupation and annexation of Lithuania, however, produced difficulties with Germany. The Russians asked for German agreement to an occupation of all of Lithuania in return for compensation and insisted that they should henceforth have the use of the free port in Memel previously accorded to Lithuania. Since the negotiations concerning these matters dragged along over a very considerable period of time they will be dealt with in a later chapter. The Finnish question also fits more appropriately into a later section, as its repercussions on German-Soviet relations did not become significant until September, 1940. Russian moves in the Balkans, on the other hand, were to lead to immediate and important negotiations.

The Soviet demand for the cession of Bessarabia did not come unexpectedly. In October, 1939, at the time that she was pushing forward in regard to Finland and the Baltic states, Russia also began to move in the Balkans. The Soviets did not approach Rumania directly. They offered a treaty of mutual assistance to Bulgaria. The Bulgarians declined the Russian offer.[13]) It was apparently at this time, furthermore, that the Soviet government indicated to Bulgaria that they would support Bulgarian demands on the Dobrudja, the south-east corner of Rumania, and defined this area to include the

---

TMWC, XXIX, 373-74; Rintelen to Ziemke, 8 June 1940, *NSR*, p. 145; *BDS*, pp. 162-63.

[11]) The population exchange agreements were signed on January 10, 1941, Germany, Auswärtiges Amt, *Vertrags-Verzeichnis*, Items 2140, 2142, 2143, pp. 692-93.

[12]) SkI, A, 10, 43: 5 June 1940, cited in C-170, *TMWC*, XXXIV, 686; SkI, A, 10, 15 June 1940, *ibid.*

[13]) Memorandum of Weizsäcker, 12 October 1939, *NSR*, p. 124; *BDS*, pp. 137-38.

cities of Constanza and Tulcea. Such a revision of the Bulgarian-Rumanian border would have meant that after the cession of Bessarabia to the Soviet Union, Rumania would have had no port directly on the Black Sea and Russia would have bordered directly on Bulgaria —and through Bulgaria on European Turkey. The Bulgarians declined this offer also and so informed the Rumanian government.[14]

The Russians did not persist in this part of their general diplomatic policy of late 1939, clearly designed to isolate Rumania, tie Bulgaria to the Soviet Union, and threaten Turkey simultaneously, for the reason that they became very deepy involved in the Finnish aspect of their advance. The Russians probably believed, and believed correctly, that if the Finnish question resulted in a war, the Germans would stand by unconcerned; while any hostilities involving Rumania with its all-important oil resources would certainly precipitate a quick German reaction.[15] Once the Soviet-Finnish War had broken out, Russia concentrated on that to the exclusion of the Balkans. Furthermore, at this time Italy was clearly assuming a protective role toward the Rumanian minister.[16] There was, nevertheless, considerable uneasiness about possible complications in the Balkans.[17]

By the time Soviet diplomacy again started moving in the Balkans as a result of the German attack in the West, the Rumanians knew that the Germans had agreed to let Russia take Bessarabia,[18] and that the British guarantee would, in effect, not be upheld by England against Russia.[19] The short period of Soviet reticence before the German attack on Norway, repeatedly referred to already, may account for the assurances given by the Russians to the United States on April 2, 1940, that they intended no action in regard to Bessarabia.[20] Once Germany attacked through the Low Countries, how-

---

[14] Gafencu, *Vorspiel zum Krieg im Osten,* p. 356.

[15] For German concern about Rumanian oil at this time see Keppler to Himmler, 5 December 1939, NG - 2593, trans. United States, OCCWC (mimeo, 1 p.); Keppler to Himmler, 8 Dec. 1939, quoting in full Fabricius to Ribbentrop, 7 December 1939, NG - 2593, trans. United States, OCCWC (mimeo, 2pp.); Himmler to Keppler, 12 Dec. 1939, NG - 2593, trans. United States, OCCWC (mimeo, 1p.); cf. Hagen, p. 284.

[16] Ciano, *Diaries* (23 December 1939), p. 182, (26 December 1939), p. 183, (28 December 1939), p. 185, (6-7 January 1940), pp. 192-93, (25 March 1940), p. 226; Ciano, *Papers,* (26 December 1939), p. 330, (6-7 January 1940), p. 331; Gafencu, pp. 369-71.

[17] Compare the interesting reports of the German naval attachés in Italy and Turkey: "Besprechung Marineattaché in Rom (Kapitän zur See Löwisch) bei der Skl," Skl, A, 4, 37: 6 December 1939, C-27; "Besprechung mit Marineattaché Ankara (Konter-admiral v. d. Marwitz)," Skl, A, 219: 29 December 1939, C-27.

[18] Gafencu, pp. 344-46; evidence concerning an attempt by Germany to mediate the Russo-Rumanian differences in the winter of 1939-40 is not adequate for definite interpretation (Halder [1 January 1940], III, 16).

[19] Gafencu, pp. 366-70.

[20] Hull, I, 743-5; this was also the time when a possible trip of Molotov to Berlin did not materialize, see *NSR,* pp. 134-37; *BDS,* pp. 151-53.

ever, it became clear that the Russians would apply pressure; and this was fully recognized in Germany.[21])

The rapidity of the German advance in the West probably startled the Russians as much as the rest of the world. The Germans, however, felt that the attitude of the Russians continued to be loyal and that the Soviets were maintaining a "positive attitude" toward the German victories.[22]) On the evening of June 17 Molotov congratulated the Germans on their "splendid success." At the same time he informed them of the Russian moves in the Baltic states.[23])

On June 22 the Moscow radio broadcast a Tass communiqué denying rumors of German-Soviet friction.[24]) This communiqué was to serve the function, among other things, of paving the way for Russo-German cooperation in the solution of the Bessarabian problem.[25]) On June 23 Molotov informed Schulenburg that the Bessarabian problem required an immediate solution and that the Soviets also intended to claim Bukovina because of its Ukrainian population.[26]) He said further that the Soviets expected German support for their demands and that an answer from Germany should reach Moscow by June 25.[27]) On June 24 the problem was discussed in Berlin,[28]) and Italy was informed.[29]) In a rather evasively worded memorandum Ribbentrop explained to Hitler the relevant sections of the Secret Protocol of August 23, 1939.[30])

The official German reply was telephoned to Schulenburg at 6:00 P.M. on June 25. The note stated that Germany was not interested in Bessarabia except for the Germans living there, that the

[21]) Halder (22 May 1940), IV, 29; Sk1, A, 9, 285: 28 May 1940, cited in C-170, *TMWC*, XXXIV, 685; cf. Sk1 C VIII/40, 359; 28 June 1940, cited in C-170, *TMWC*, XXXIV, 687.

[22]) There is evidence of three reports of Schulenburg to this effect: one is a digest of a summary in Sk1, A, 9, 210: 21 May 1940, in C-170, *TMWC*, XXXIV, 685; the second is summarized in Sk1, A, 9, 270: 27 May 1940, NOKW - 2545 (photostat, 6pp.), p.2; the third is given in Schulenburg to Ribbentrop, 29 May 1940, *NSR*, p. 143.

[23]) Schulenburg to Ribbentrop, 17 June 1940, *NSR*, p. 154; *BDS*, p. 173.

[24]) Schulenburg to Ribbentrop, 24 June 1940, Moscow No. 1212, *NSR*, p. 156; *BDS*, pp. 175-76.

[25]) Schulenburg to Ribbentrop, 24 June 1940, Moscow No. 1213, *NSR*, p. 157; *BDS*, p. 176.

[26]) Schulenburg to Ribbentrop, 23 June 1940, Moscow No. 1205, *NSR*, p. 155; *BDS*, p. 174.

[27]) Schulenburg to Ribbentrop, 23 June 1940, Moscow No. 1208, cited in Rossi, p. 146, n. 3.

[28]) Simoni (24 June 1940), pp. 162-63.

[29]) Ciano, *Diaries* (24 June 1940), p. 269; Rosso conferred with Molotov on June 25 (Schulenburg to Ribbentrop, 26 June 1940, Moscow No. 1235, *NSR*, pp. 160-61).

[30]) Memorandum of Ribbentrop for Hitler, 24 June 1940, *NSR*, pp. 157-58; *BDS*, p. 177.

claim to Bukavina was something new, and that Germany had great
economic interests in the rest of Rumania and was therefore greatly
concerned lest that country become a theatre of war. Germany agreed
to support the Russian claim to Bessarabia with the Rumanians.
Ribbentrop asked Schulenburg to stress the desire of Germany that
there be a peaceful settlement.[31]) That same evening Schulenburg
delivered this message to Molotov. The latter thanked him for the
support of Germany and stated that the Soviet Union too, was
interested in a peaceful solution. There was some argument about
the question of Bukovina which left Schulenburg with the impression
that on this point some changes might be made. Molotov further
agreed to the return of the *Volksdeutsche* from areas occupied by
Russia to the Reich.[32])

During the morning of June 26 the Soviets examined the situation
and made their decision. Although, as will appear later, they were not
prepared to give up their claim to all of Bukovina, they thought it
wise to moderate their immediate demands in view of the German
objections and ask for only the northern part of Bukovina. On the
afternoon of June 26, Molotov informed Schulenburg of this and said
that now Soviet Russia expected the Germans to advise Rumania to
yield when the demands were filed with the Rumanian ambassador in
Moscow.[33]) The Germans immediately informed the Italians through
Mackensen, and Ciano thereupon saw the Soviet ambassador to tell
him that Italy had "no objections to the liquidation of this problem"
but would prefer to see it settled without war.[34])

The Russians were clearly in a hurry. That evening at 10 o'clock,
a few hours after the Molotov-Schulenburg conference, the Rumanian
minister was given an ultimatum demanding the cession of Bessarabia
and northern Bukovina; an answer was expected on the next day,
June 27.[35]) Molotov immediately informed Schulenburg of this
step.[36]) Schulenburg's message on it arrived in Berlin at 6:30 A.M.,
June 27; at 10:30 A.M. Ribbentrop ordered the German minister in
Bucharest to advise the Rumanian government to yield to the Soviet
demands.[37])

The question was now one for Rumania. When the general problem

---

[31]) Ribbentrop to Schulenburg, 25 June 1940, *NSR*, pp. 158-59; *BDS*, pp. 178-79.
[32]) Schulenburg to Ribbentrop, 25 June 1940, Moscow No. 1233, *NSR*, pp. 159-60; *BDS*, pp. 179-80.
[33]) Schulenburg to Ribbentrop, 26 June 1940, Moscow No. 1236, *NSR*, pp. 161-62; *BDS*, pp. 180-81.
[34]) Ciano, *Diaries* (26 June 1940), p. 270.
[35]) Gafencu, pp. 386-88.
[36]) Schulenburg to Ribbentrop, 26 June 1940, Moscow No. 1241, *NSR*, p. 163; *BDS*, p. 153.
[37]) Ribbentrop to Fabricius, 27 June 1940, *NSR*, p. 163; *BDS*, pp. 183-84.

of defending Rumanian neutrality and independence had been discussed in a crown council on April 19, 1940, it had been decided that Rumania would fight against Germany or Russia, should either attack her.[38]) Once the defeat of France made Western support impossible, however, this policy was reviewed; and on May 29 it was decided that to counter the danger from the Soviet Union, Rumania would have to fit herself into the German scheme of things.[39])

The Russian ultimatum came as a surprise—there had been no warning of its imminence or terms from Germany.[40]) The Rumanians were urged to give in by both Germany and Italy.[41]) The Axis wanted a quick and peaceful settlement and demanded the immediate granting of Russia's demands. The Rumanians had no alternative; on the evening of June 27 they sent their answer. It was worded in a manner that seemed to seek further negotiations, so the Germans quickly assured the Soviet government that it was in fact a complete acceptance of the Soviet demands.[42]) The German attitude at that time is best summarized in an entry in the Halder diary:

> Russia wants Bessarabia. We are not interested in Bessarabia. The issue of the Bukowina raised by Russia is new and goes beyond our agreements with the Russians. In any event, it is imperative for our interests that there should be no war in the Balkans.[43])

Some problems in Soviet-German relations raised by the Soviet move against Rumania were soon settled. On July 17 Molotov formally recognized German economic interests in Rumanian oil production,[44]) and the people of German descent in the areas acquired by Russia were eventually evacuated to Germany.[45])

The most significant immediate effect of the Russian move against Rumania was to set off a series of events which greatly disturbed German-Russian relations. It is important that it was this series of

---

[38]) Gafencu, p. 376.

[39]) *Ibid.*, pp. 377-82; Foreign Minister Gafencu resigned immediately.

[40]) *Ibid.*, p. 387.

[41]) For details, see *ibid.*, pp. 389-90, 454-55; Ciano, *Diaries* (28 June 1940), p. 270; Skl, A, 10, 270ff.: 26 June 1940, cited in C-170, *TMWC*, XXXIV, 687.

[42]) Gafencu, p. 391.

[43]) Halder (25 June 1940), IV, 95.

[44]) Schulenburg to Ribbentrop, 17 July 1940, Moscow No. 1405, cited in Rossi, p. 153 and n. 2.

[45]) Agreements of 29 July and 5 September, 1940, Germany, Auswärtiges Amt, *Vertrags-Verzeichnis*, Item 2090, p. 677. For an interesting, though not very reliable, account of the return of these Germans, see Kleist, pp. 107-14.

In the summer of 1940 there had also been two Russo-German agreements concerning border incidents; Germany, Auswärtiges Amt, *Vertrags-Verzeichnis*, Items 2052, 2088, pp. 664, 676.

subsequent events, rather than the Bessarabia-Bukovina issue itself, which clouded the relations between the two countries. Had there still been a desire in Germany for long-term agreement with the Soviet Union, Hitler could probably have directed these developments into other channels. The details of all this will be examined later.

The long-term effect of the Russian action was undoubtedly to push Rumania firmly into the camp of the Axis,[46] just as Finland had earlier been put into a frame of mind which was to make an alliance with Germany seem to be the only hope of safety. It might therefore be said that the two flanks of the German attack on Soviet Russia were secured for Hitler by the foreign policy of Moscow.

In the meantime, the campaign in the West had moved on very swiftly. The history of that campaign will not be examined here. The point which must be stressed is that starting from May 28, 1940, there is a vast amount of reliable and detailed evidence showing that Germany intended to carry out a substantial reduction of her army immediately after the defeat of France. The war against England, if it had to be continued, would require mainly naval and air efforts; the army was to be reduced by releasing a number of divisions—originally forty, later the figure was cut to seventeen.[47] This aspect of German military history is of great significance because the developments in this sphere in the summer of 1940 will provide some of the most important clues toward an understanding of the changes in German policy and the specific time at which these changes occurred.[48]

With France down, Germany began to think of peace. At the time of the armistice negotiations, Ciano met Ribbentrop and made the following comments in his memorandum on the conversation:

---

[46] Gafencu, pp. 390-92.

[47] The following list of references provides a sampling of the most important evidence: Halder (28 May 1940), IV, 40, (7 June), IV, 58, (12 June), IV, 72, (15 June), IV, 78, (16 June), IV, 80, (18 June), IV, 82-3, (19 June), IV, 85; Germany, OKW, Wi Rü Amt, Thomas, "Aktennotiz über die Entwicklung der Rüstungslage im Sommer 1940," [Sep. 1940?], PS - 1456 (photostat, 3pp.), p. 2; Germany, OKW, Wi Rü Amt, "Aktennotiz, Betreff Abteilungs Chefbesprechung am 12.6.40," 12 June 1940, PS - 1456 (photostat, 7pp.), p. 4; Germany, OKW, Wi Rü Amt, "Notiz über Aussprache im Führerhauptquartier," 14 June 1940, PS - 1456 (photostat, 1p.); Germany, OKW, WFA, "Gliederung des Heeres," 1 July 1940, PS - 1793 (photostat, 2pp.), p. 1; Skl, C VII/40, 221: 4 June 1940, cited in C-170, TMWC, XXXIV, 686; Vinzenz Müller, "Erklärung von Müller," 8 January 1946, USSR-149 (photostat, 12 pp.), p. 2 (quoted at length in TMWC, VII, 267; PHKV, VII, 287-88); Greiner, p. 110.

[48] From this point on there will be a number of instances like the preceding footnote in which a considerable number of rather technical military documents will be cited as evidence for some specific statement. Since this is not a military history, the text merely abstracts from the military details the directly relevant material concerning the over-all development of German-Russian relations.

I [Ciano] must add at this point that von Ribbentrop expressed himself in terms which are absolutely new in his vocabulary. He spoke of humanity's need for peace, of the need for reconstruction, of the need for bringing together the nations, whom the war has separated so much, to live together in harmony.

I put the question to him bluntly: Does Germany at the present moment prefer peace or the prosecution of the war? Without hesitation Ribbentrop replied: "Peace".[49]

In this, Ribbentrop was clearly reflecting the views of Hitler, as he did on all important matters, and was probably quoting the Führer's phraseology. Hitler seems to have wavered for a while, since on June 30 a directly contrary position was taken by Ribbentrop.[50] But in his speech to the Reichstag on July 19, 1940, Hitler made a "peace offer" of the vaguest sort. The British press and radio reaction was immediate and negative—to Hitler's regret according to Ciano who was in Berlin at the time.[51]

---

[49] Ciano, *Diplomatic Papers* (19 June 1940), p. 373; cf. Schmidt, pp. 484-85.

[50] Memorandum of Weizsäcker, 30 June 1940, NG - 1718 (photostat, 1p.); cf. Schmidt, pp. 491-92.

[51] Ciano, *Diaries* (19 and 20 July 1940), p. 277; see Winston Chruchill, *The Second World War*, Vol. II, *Their Finest Hour* (London, 1949), pp. 230-31. See also Langer and Gleason, pp. 653-54.

CHAPTER SEVEN

JULY 20, — AUGUST 27, 1940

After the conclusion of the campaign against France, fundamental decisions had to be made in Germany about the future conduct of the war.[1]) For that reason, the period covered by this chapter is in many ways the most important of the whole study, and a word about the sources used in its preparation wiuld, therefore, seem advisable. The important occurrences of this period are almost all of a largely military nature, and the evidence concerning them comes mainly from military sources. These sources are of two kinds—written, contemporary records, and subsequent statements and testimony. The contemporary records which are now available provide a reliable outline and establish the main events, but they are not adequate for a full understanding of developments. It is, therefore, necessary to use the statements and testimony of participants. These individuals, particularly Keitel, Jodl, Warlimont, and Halder, have been questioned about a few events repeatedly and in detail. Their evidence is often conflicting, sometimes self-contradictory, sometimes clearly erroneous. Several of them were on trial for their lives. Often they were simply unable to reconstruct in detail the occurrences of day to day affairs which took place six to eight years before the interrogations. The testimony of these men presents the historian with a maze of material. An effort will be made to construct out of it, in conjunction with contemporary records and some other sources, an accurate account of these fateful days. At all points the evidence weighed will be cited. If that evidence is incorrectly interpreted, its complexity is the writer's only excuse.[1a])

The chronological framework of the crucial period in the summer of 1940 is most readily revealed by a comparison of two of Hitler's directives on the conduct of the war—one of July 16 and the other of August 1. The first, directive number sixteen, opens with the following phrase:

> Since England, despite her militarily hopeless situation still

---

[1]) The author has also examined this problem in an article, "Der Deutsche Entschluss zum Angriff auf die Sowjetunion," *Vierteljahrshefte für Zeitgeschichte,* I (1953), 301-18.

[1a]) Many problems of the day to day events may be solved if more of the German military diaries become available, particularly those of the *Wehrmachtführungsstab* and the Operations Section of the General Staff of the Army.

shows no sign of willingness to come to terms, I have decided to prepare a landing operation against England, and if necessary to carry it out.... The preparations for the entire operation must be completed by mid-August.[2])

The second, directive number seventeen, starts this way:

In order to prepare the ground for the final crushing of England I intend to intensify air and sea warfare against the British Isles.[3])

The different approach—"prepare a landing" and "prepare the ground for the final crushing"—is indicative of the change in the thinking of the highest German leadership which will now be examined.

At the time order number sixteen was issued and the British were showing no signs of recognizing their supposed final defeat, German military thinking[4]) was devoted to three main subjects—the invasion of England, the strengthening of German forces in the East, and a reduction in the size of the German army. The last of these three has been examined already and will be taken up again later.

The invasion of England, under study at naval headquarters since November, 1939, had been discussed between Hitler and Raeder on May 21, 1940.[5]) The details of this matter will not be outlined here. It is important to keep in mind, however, that there was little real teamwork in the planning, that the project looked more and more difficult, the more closely it was examined, and that there was never any great enthusiasm for it. The German navy had been fatally weakened in the Norwegian campaign.[6]) All therefore depended on the *Luftwaffe,* and Hitler seems to have recognized its failing long before other German leaders.[7])

While this problem was being studied, plans were drawn up to send back to the East in a routine transfer some of the very large number of divisions concentrated in France and Belgium. These divisions are listed as already in the East in the deployment schedule of July 1, 1940,

---

[2]) Germany, Oberste Befehlshaber der Wehrmacht, OKW, WFA, L (Hitler), "General Order No. 16 on the Preparation of a Landing Operation against England," 16 July 1940, PS - 442, trans. United States, Chief of Counsel for the Prosecution of Axis Criminality (hereafter referred to as CCPAC) (mimeo, 3pp.), p. 1; also cited in Churchill, II, 267; cf. Halder (19 July 1940), IV, 121.

[3]) Germany, Oberste Befehlshaber der Wehrmacht, OKW, WFA, L (Hitler), "Order No. 17 on the Conduct of Air and Sea Warfare against England," 1 August 1940, PS - 443, trans. United States, CCPAC (mimeo, 1p.); cf. Churchill, II, 285.

[4]) The term "military" is used to refer to all branches of the German armed forces, not just the army.

[5]) "Report of the Commander in Chief, Navy to the Fuehrer on 21 May 1940," Fuehrer Conferences, 1940, I, 51.

[6]) At the end of June the German navy could bring into action no more than one heavy cruiser, two light cruisers, and four destroyers (Churchill, I, 657).

[7]) Raeder, "Raeder Memorandum for Assmann," 30 January 1944, C - 66, *TMWC,* XXXIV, 277.

though they were then still actually in France.[8]) Discussion of the re-assignment of these divisions seems to have begun on or before June 16.[9]) The unit to be sent east was the Eighteenth Army. Its commander, General von Küchler, and its chief of staff, General Marcks (of whom more later), were oriented on their mission by General Halder on July 4.[10]) The officer in charge of military railway transportation estimated that the armor of the Eighteenth Army could start moving on July 18.[11]) The headquarters of this army were moved around the middle of July.[12]) The actual orders for the movement of the first transports of Eighteenth Army troops seem to have been issued near the end of July because the orders of Küchler on the orientation to be given the troops thus transferred are dated July 22, 1940.[13]) This transfer of the Eigh-teenth Army has been recorded in a rather detailed manner because this must be the "return transports" Keitel testified about at Nuremberg;[14]) they have been confused by some, who did not know the chronological background, with the later transfer for the war on Russia.[15]) On the other hand, this transfer of troops leaves the later transfers of August and September 1940 in a separate category—a factor of the greatest importance.[16])

In the meantime, a new interpretation of England's attitude toward Germany begins to appear in the documents. In the early summer of 1940 the Germans expected the whole world to share their belief in their own invincibility and to draw the necessary conclusions; the evident failure or refusal of the English to do this left them rather surprised. The invasion of England was often thought of more as an occupation after surrender or obvious collapse, than as the way to bring about the defeat

---

[8]) Germany, OKW, WFA, "Gliederung des Feldheeres," 1 July 1940, PS - 1783 (photostat, 2pp.), p. 1.

[9]) Halder (16 June 1940), IV, 80; cf. Halder (25 June 1940), IV, 95.

[10]) Halder (4 July 1940), IV, 103.

[11]) Ibid., p. 104; cf. Halder (11 July 1940), IV, 113.

[12]) Georg von Küchler, "Erklärung von Generalfeldmarschall von Küchler," 10 April 1947, NOKW - 1038 (photostat, 4pp.), p. 3; United States, OCCWC, Evidence Division, Interrogation Branch, "Interrogation of GFM von Kuechler," 29 March 1947, Interrogation Summary No. 1650 (mimeo, 3pp.), p. 2; cf. Simoni (13 July, 1940), p. 179.

[13]) Germany, AOK 18, Ic, Küchler, "2489/40," 22 July 1940, NOKW - 1531 (mimeo, 2pp.), trans. United States, OCCWC. This order also cited an order of Brauchitsch which was passed on the units of the 18th Army on the same day; cf. Halder (20 Aug. 1940), IV, 167; Germany, XVII. AK, "Korpsbefehl Nr. 1," 23 July 1940, NOKW - 2437 (photostat, 3pp.).

[14]) Testimony of Keitel, TMWC, X, 525, PHKV, X, 590.

[15]) See, e.g., Müller, "Erklärung von Müller," 8 January 1946, USSR - 149, p. 2.

[16]) If this is kept clearly in mind, many inaccuracies and obfuscations in the testimony at Nuremberg can be resolved, e.g. Testimony of Halder, U.S. v. Leeb, G.T. 1879-80; Testimony of Halder, U.S. v. Weizsäcker, G.T. 20536, 20549-50; Testimony of Brauchitsch, TMWC, XX, 577; PHKV, XX, 630.

of that country.[17]) As July brought neither a surrender nor a collapse, the German leaders began to wonder about the reasons for this. The British just seemed unwilling to do the "reasonable thing."[18]) Weizsäcker had offered the idea that one more demonstration of German military power would do the trick.[19]) The possibility of an Anglo-Russian rapprochement was already being considered.[20]) More serious was the related thought that Britain was hoping that Russia would not stand aside unconcerned forever. This theme first comes out in the conference between the army leaders and Hitler on July 13 at which the order to start invasion preparations was issued. Commenting on Hitler's attitude, Halder wrote in his diary,

> The Fuehrer is greatly puzzled by Britain's persisting unwillingness to make peace. He sees the answer (as we [Brauchitsch and Halder] do) in Britain's hope on Russia, and therefore counts on having to compel her by main force to agree to peace. . . .[21])

This matter no doubt acquired greater significance in Hitler's mind as a result of Britain's refusal of his "peace offer" of July 19. In any case, Hitler must have examined the whole problem of the future conduct of the war and the relations of Germany with Russia in the days around July 19 because he had arrived at some fairly definite conclusions by July 21. Because of the very specific nature of some of his statements on July 21 it is likely that Hitler had consulted some of his military advisors in the High Command of the Armed Forces (OKW) during these days.[22])

On July 21, 1940, there was a meeting between Hitler and the highest military leaders. There are two reports on it; one by Raeder and one from Brauchitsch as recorded by Halder.[23]) The two reports are basically in agreement, though Halder gives far more details. Because of its significance, the most important sections of Halder's record are quoted here:

22 July 1940, 10 00 *Conference with Ob.d.H.* [Brauchitsch]

2) Ob.d.H. summarizes his Berlin *Conference with the Fuehrer* on 21 July.

. . . .

---

[17]) See Germany, OKW, Chef WFA (Jodl), "Die Weiterführung des Krieges gegen England," 30 June 1940, PS - 1776, *TMWC*, XXVIII, 301-03.

[18]) Halder (22 June 1940), IV, 91.

[19]) *Ibid.*, (30 June 1940), p. 98.

[20]) *Ibid.*, (11 July 1940), p. 114.

[21]) *Ibid.* (13 July 1940), p. 117; cf. Assmann, pp. 204ff; Greiner, pp. 116-17, 292.

[22]) Testimony of Halder, U.S. v. Weizsäcker, E.T. 20748.

[23]) Raeder's report will be found in Fuehrer Conferences, 1940, I, 81, and in C - 170, *TMWC*, XXXIV, 688; Halder's record is in Vol. IV of his diary under the date of July 22, pp. 126-28; parts of it are also translated in U.S. v. Weizsäcker, E.T. 20748.

c) Reasons for continuance of war by Britain:
1) Hope for a change in America....
2) Puts hope in Russia.

. . . .

e) Crossing the Channel appears very hazardous to the Fuehrer. On that account, invasion is to be undertaken only if no other means is left to come to terms with Britain.

f) Britain perhaps sees the following possibilities:
1) Create trouble on the Balkans through Russia, to cut us off from our fuel source, and so paralyze our Air Force.
2) To gain the same ends by inciting Russia against us.
3) To bomb our synthetic oil plants.

. . . .

h) If Britain persists in waging war, efforts will be made to confront her with a solid political front, embracing Spain, Italy, Russia.[24])

6) Fuehrer will decide by middle of the week, after Raeder's report, whether invasion will be carried through *this fall*. If not now, not before May next. We shall probably know conclusively by the end of the week....

7) Stalin is flirting with Britain to keep her in the war and tie us down, with a view to gain time and take what he wants, knowing he could not get it once peace breaks out. He has an interest in not letting Germany become too strong, but there are no indications of any Russian aggressiveness against us.

8) Our attention must be turned to tackling the Russian problem and prepare planning. The Fuehrer has been given the following information:

a) German assembly will take at least 4 – 6 weeks.

b) Object: To crush Russian Army or slice as much Russian territory as is necessary to bar enemy air raids on Berlin and Silesian industries. It is desirable to penetrate far enough to enable our Air Force to smash Russia's strategic areas. (Check with Foreign Armies East.)[25])

c) Political aims: Ukrainian State
Federation of Baltic States
White Russia—Finland[26])
Baltic States as a permanent thorn in the flesh.

d) Strength required: 80-100 divisions. Russia has 50-75 good Divs. If we attack Russia this fall, pressure of the air war on England

---

[24]) This point may be the germ of the proposals made to Molotov in November 1940.

[25]) This is probably a note of Halder's to himself; the assignment involved is discussed later in this chapter. "Foreign Armies East" refers to the Eastern Intelligence Department of the General Staff of the Army.

[26]) This seems to refer to the participation of Finland in a war on Russia; the rest of point 8, c, presumably foreshadows the later division of the occupied eastern territories into its main territorial subdivisions.

will be relieved. United States could supply both Britain and Russia.

e) Operations: What operational objective could be attained? What strength have we available? Timing and area of assembly? Gateways of attack: Baltic States, Finland, Ukraine.— Protection of Rumanian oil fields. (Check with Op. Sec.)[27])

Three important points about Hitler's discourse should be noted— first, the whole discussion of Russia comes as a result of England's continuance of the war; second, a decision about an invasion of England in the fall of 1940 is to come in a few days; and third, the projected attack on Russia seems to be assigned as yet, though not explicity, to the fall of 1940. These points will be the focus of attention during the following ten days.[29])

As a result of this conference Brauchitsch, when giving the quoted report to Halder, instructed the latter to have the various relevant problems investigated.[30]) Halder looked into the matter to some extent himself.[31]) He instructed the chief of the Eastern Section of the Intelligence Department to prepare a report on the situation in regard to Soviet military strength and dispositions.[32]) He also told two high officers, Gener-

---

[27]) Refers to the Operations Section of the General Staff of the Army (OKH, Gen.St.d.H., Op.Abt.). This matter will be discussed later in this chapter.

For discussion of these diary entries see Testimony of Halder, U.S. v. Weizsäcker, G.T. 20524-26, E.T. 20748; Testimony of Halder, U.S. v. Leeb, G.T. 1882. Halder's testimony about the huge Russian forces facing the German border and Rumania can be largely discounted; he was comparing Russian strength as indicated on a German intelligence map for 23 April and 1 June *1941* with German strength in July *1940;* Testimony of Halder, U.S. v. Weizsäcker, E.T. 20705, 20761-62; G.T. 20527, 20633, should be compared with Testimony of Halder, U.S. v. Weizsäcker, E.T. 20715; G.T. 20537-39, 20619-20, 20631; and Koerner Document 405, Exhibit 98.

[29]) From here on matters become even more complicated because of the organizational structure of the German military commands. Hitler was Supreme Commander of the Armed Forces and as such had his own military staff—the High Command of the Armed Forces, or OKW, in which the most important generals were Keitel, Jodl, and Warlimont. Each of the three branches of the armed forces at this time had its own separate commander in chief with a staff. The High Command of the Army, or OKH, was headed by Brauchitsch with Halder as Chief of Staff. Hitler dealt sometimes with the OKW, sometimes with the OKH. This system, of course, makes it very difficult to follow the course of events since it is not always clear which office did what and whether in a given instance one office knew what the other was doing. It should be added that this was one purpose of the whole arrangement.

[30]) Testimony of Halder, U.S. v. Weizsäcker, G.T. 20525.

[31]) *Ibid.,* Halder (24 July 1940), IV, 130. For possible earlier work on this by Halder at Brauchitsch's suggestion see footnote *** to Halder (2 July 1940), IV, 100 on page 5 of the notes.

[32]) For details of the work of Kinzel of *Fremde Heere Ost* see Halder (22 July 1940), IV, 129, (26 July 1940) 132; Hans Pieckenbrock, "Statement of Pieckenbrock," USSR - 228, quoted in *TMWC*, VII, 263; *PHKV*, VII, 283.

al Greiffenberg of the Operations Section of the General Staff of the Army and General Marcks, Chief of Staff of the Eighteenth Army, to work out independently some operational plans for the attack.[33]

During the period between July 21 and 29 Hitler apparently discussed the proposed attack on the Soviet Union with Keitel or Jodl or both. These discussions, which may have included the preparation of a memorandum by Keitel, persuaded Hitler that an attack on Russia in the fall of 1940 was impractical—the troop concentration would take too long and the transportation and supply facilities were inadequate—and that an attack would have to take place, if at all, in the spring of 1941. On July 29 Hitler told Jodl that he had reached this conclusion. On the same day Jodl passed this information on to the highest officer on his staff: General Warlimont, and the three senior officers of Warlimont's department. He told them that Hitler was planning to attack the Soviet Union in the spring of 1941 and asked them to prepare some studies for himself so that he might be able to examine the attendant problems in detail without reference to the High Command of the Army. At this conference also, Jodl directed his staff to prepare an order for the improvement of the transport and supply facilities in the East. In this manner the obstacles which made an attack impossible in 1940 were to be surmounted. This order was drafted and issued on August 9, 1940, under the title of "Aufbau Ost" or Reconstruction East.[34]

———— — —

[33] The details of this are interesting and essential to an understanding of the German campaign in the East but will not be examined here. For Greiffenberg's work, see Halder (22 July 1940), IV, 129, (27 July 1940) 134, (1 August 1940) 146, (18 August 1940) 165, (19 August 1940) 165, (26 August 1940) 174; Testimony of Halder, U.S. v. Weizsäcker, G.T. 20526, E.T. 20750. For the work of Marcks, see Halder (29 July 1940, IV, 136, (1 August 1940) 146, (5 August 1940) 150, (6 August 1940) 151; Testimony of Halder, U.S. v. Weizsäcker, G.T. 20525-26, 20530.

[34] There is perhaps no contemporary evidence on the conference of July 29. The writer has tried to construct an account out of the following evidence: Testimony of Halder, U.S. v. Weizsäcker, G.T. 20526-27; Walter Warlimont, "Deposition of Warlimont" 13 November 1945, USSR - 263 in *TMWC*, VII, 249-50, and XV, 516-17, *PHKV*, VII, 279-80 and XV, 564: "Interrogation of Warlimont," 12 October 1945, United States, CCPAC, *Nazi Conspiracy and Aggression, Supplement B* (Washington, 1948), pp. 1635-36; Testimony of Warlimont, U.S. v. Leeb, G.T. 6287, 6366-68, 6370, 6372-73; Warlimont, "Erklärung von Warlimont," 1 November 1946, NOKW - 152 (photostat, 5pp.), p. 3; United States, OCCWC, Evidence Division, Interrogation Branch, "Interrogation of Walter Warlimont," 21 October 1946, Interrogation Summary No. 324 (mimeo, 3pp.), p. 2; Warlimont, "Eidesstattliche Erklärung des Walter Warlimont," 21 November 1945, PS - 3031 (mimeo, 1p.); Warlimont "Erklärung von Warlimont," 21 November 1945, PS - 3032 (mimeo, 1p.); Testimony of Keitel, *TMWC*, X, 524-25, 604-05; *PHKV*, X, 589-90, 676-77; Testimony of Jodl, *TMWC*, XV, 390-91, 515-18; *PHKV*, XV, 428, 562-65; Jodl, "Erklärung von Jodl," 26 September 1946, NOKW - 65, p. 9; United States, OCCWC, Evidence Division, Interrogation, "Interrogation of Alfred Jodl," 6 September 1940, Interrogation Summary No. 87 (mimeo, 8pp.), p. 5; Wolf Junge, "Affidavit of Junge," 1 October 1947, NG - 2665 (mimeo, 3pp.)

In the meantime, the plans for the invasion of England were not progressing well. On the evening of July 28, the High Command of the Army received a memorandum from the navy which provided for a much smaller landing area in England than the army had requested, and which in other ways brought the grandiose schemes of the army within the physical capacities of the German navy.[35]) When Brauchitsch and Halder discussed this on the evening of July 30, they came to the conclusion that the navy would probably not provide them with the means for a successful invasion that fall.[36]) The two leaders of the German army then examined the various lines of action open to them, assuming that invasion in the fall should be impossible, and in this connection considered the proposal of attacking the Soviet Union which Hitler had raised on July 21. Their views contrast in a very interesting manner with Hitler's opinion as expressed on the following day, and they are therefore quoted in full.

> The question whether, if a decision cannot be forced against Britain, we should in the face of a threatening British-Russian alliance and the resulting two-front war turn first against Russia, must be answered to the effect that we should keep on friendly terms with Russia. A visit to Stalin would be desirable. Russia's aspirations to the Straits and in the direction of the Persian Gulf need not bother us. On the Balkans, which falls within our economic sphere of interest, we could keep out of each other's way. Italy and Russia will not hurt each other in the Mediterranean. This being so, we could deliver the British a decisive blow in the Mediterranean, shoulder them away from Asia, help the Italians in building their Mediterranean Empire and, with the aid of Russia, consolidate the Reich which we have created in Western and Northern Europe. That much accomplished, we could confidently face war with Britain for years.[37])

At this point it would be well to summarize the situation just before the important conference of July 31. The possibility of invading Eng-

---

trans. United States, OCCWC, p. 1; Junge, "Affidavit of Junge," 15 April 1948, Warlimont - 103, p. 8; Ernst Köstring, "Affidavit of Köstring," 20 November 1945, PS - 3014, United States, CCPAC, *Nazi Conspiracy and Aggression*, V, 734; Bernhard von Lossberg, *Im Wehrmachtführungsstab* (Hamburg, 1950), pp. 105-06. The account of these events recently published by Helmuth Greiner (pp. 293-94) is especially valuable as Greiner kept the war diary of the Wehrmachtführungsstab and seems to have based this section of his book, which includes the best summary of the "Aufbau Ost" order, on contemporary notes.

[35]) Halder (28 July 1940), IV, 135.

[36]) *Ibid.* (30 July 1940), p. 140.

[37]) *Ibid.*, p. 141.

land in the fall of 1940 already seemed dim. Britain was thought to be
relying on American aid and the possibility of Russian intervention of
some sort. The advisability of attacking the Soviet Union before a pincer
attack could be mounted was therefore being weighed. The Commander
in Chief and the Chief of Staff of the Army did not consider such an
attack necessary. Staff studies of an attack on Russia were, however,
being prepared by several people in the High Command of the Army
(OKH) as well as in the High Command of the Armed Forces (OKW)[38])
Hitler seems to have come rather close to a decision. Having examined
the project for about two weeks, he had already discussed the problems
of timing with his staff and had evidently been persuaded by them that
an attack in 1940 was not feasible. An order to remedy the deficiencies
that forced a postponement of any offensive to the spring of 1941 was
already in preparation, though its issuance may not have been finally
decided.

On July 31, 1940, a conference of perhaps decisive importance in the
history of the Second World War took place at the Berghof. Present
were Hitler, Keitel, Jodl, Raeder, Brauchitsch, Halder, and Puttkamer,
naval adjutant in Hitler's headquarters. The first part of the conference
was devoted to a discussion of the invasion of England—both Raeder's
and Halder's records of this part are available.[39]) The only point of interest in this discussion is Raeder's repeated recommendation that the
invasion be postponed to the following spring.[40]) Hitler decided that
preparations for the invasion should continue and its launching in the
latter part of September, 1940, made dependent upon the success of the
air force. If this did not work out right, then the invasion was to be postponed until May, 1941.[41]) It is obvious, however, that Hitler was not at
all enthusiastic about the idea of an invasion.[42])

The discussion then shifted to other possible actions. For this part we
have only the detailed account of Halder.[43]) Again it is probably best to
quote from Halder's notes at length.

----

[38]) The dispute between the drive on Moscow and the drive into the Ukraine which
was to be of such great importance in the fall of 1941 is already heralded in discussions
in the OKH on July 27, 1940. Halder (27 July 1940), IV. 134.

[39]) Raeder's account and an annex are printed in Fuehrer Conferences, 1940, II,
9-13; Halder's record, presumably made while Hitler was speaking, is in his diary, Vol.
IV, pp. 141-44.

[40]) Fuehrer Conferences, 1940, II, 9, 11; Halder, IV, 141.

[41]) Fuehrer Conferences, 1940, II, 11-12.

[42]) See also "Report of the Commander in Chief, Navy to the Fuehrer on 23 August
1940 at 1720," ibid., p. 14.

[43] Halder, IV, 144-45. (Raeder had left the room after the discussion of the invasion of England).

31 July 1940   Berghof   1130

. . . .

Fuehrer: . . . .

d) In the event that invasion does not take place, our action must be directed to eliminate all factors that let England hope for a change in the situation. To all intents and purposes the war is won. France has stepped out of the set-up protecting British convoys. Italy is pinning down British forces.

Submarine and air warfare may bring about a final decision, but this may be one or two years off.

Britain's hope lies in Russia and the United States. If Russia drops out of the picture America, too, is lost for Britain, because elimination of Russia would tremendously increase *Japan's power* in the Far East.

Russia is the Far Eastern sword of Britain and the United States pointed at Japan. Here an evil wind is blowing for Britain. Japan, like Russia, has her program which she wants to carry through before the end of the war.

Russia is the factor on which Britain is relying the most. Something must have happened in London! The British were completely down; now they have perked up again. Intercepted telephone conversations. Russia is painfully shaken by the swift development of the Western European situation.

All that Russia has to do is to hint that she does not care to have a strong Germany, and the British will take hope, like one about to go under, that the situation will undergo a radical change within six or eight months.

With Russia smashed, Britain's last hope will be shattered. Germany then will be master of Europe and the Balkans.

Decision: Russia's destruction must therefore be made a part of this struggle. Spring 1941.

The sooner Russia is crushed, the better. Attack achieves its purpose only if Russian state can be shattered to its roots with one blow. Holding part of the country alone will not do. Standing still for the following winter would be perilous. So it is better to wait a little longer, but with the resolute determination to eliminate Russia. This is necessary also because of contiguity on the Baltic. It would be awkward to have another major power there. If we start in May 41, we would have five months to finish the job in. Tackling it this year still, would have been best, but unified action would be impossible at this time.

Object is destruction of Russian manpower. Operation will be divided into three actions:

First thrust: . . . .

Second thrust: . . . .

Finally: . . . .

Successively: . . . .

Ultimately: Ukraine, White Russia, Baltic States to us. Finland extended to the White Sea.

7 Divs. will stay in Norway....

50 „ in France.

3 „ in Holland and Belgium.

_____

60 Divs.

120 Divs. for the East

_____

180 Divs.

=====

. . . .

Projected Balkan settlement. Proposed arrangement between Hungary and Romania, to be followed by guarantee for Romania.[44])

This report on Hitler's talk should make it quite clear that the decision to attack the Soviet Union was made on July 31 or just before that date. It cannot be argued that these were just random speculations of the Fuehrer; the military and diplomatic implications of this decision were *immediately* realized and implemented by the highest agencies of the Reich. Before we trace these, a further discussion of the facts recited so far seems appropriate.

The motivation for the attack on Russia which appears in the conferences of July, 1940, is directly connected with the war on England and the failure to bring that war to a speedy conclusion. The thoughts of Brauchitsch and Halder, as well as Hitler, to the effect that it might take considerable time to bring about an end of hostilities have been quoted. The question for the leaders of Germany in July, 1940, was, what next? The army advocated a war on England centered in the Mediterranean theatre.[45]) In the annex to this chapter two other answers to the question will be presented—that of the German navy and that of Rudolf Hess. Hitler decided to attack Russia. Why?

At that time there was little evidence of any Anglo-Soviet rapprochement. The proposal of the British to send Sir Stafford Cripps as special trade negotiator had been turned down by Moscow.[46]) He was then made ambassador but still did not succeed in accomplishing anything.[47]) The Soviets informed Germany of his proposals and their own reactions.[48]) Russia's unwillingness to work with England was understood

[44]) For discussion of this conference, see Testimony of Halder, U.S. v. Weizsäcker, G.T. 20525-26, E.T. 20749-50; cf. Greiner, pp. 294-95.

[45]) From Raeder's report on the July 31 conference one can infer that Brauchitsch suggested to Hitler the strategy he had worked out with Halder the day before (Fuehrer Conferences, 1940, II, 12).

[46]) Skl, A, 9, 295: 29 May 1940, cited in C - 170, *TMWC*, XXXIV, 685; Schulenburg to Ribbentrop, 29 May 1940, *NSR*, p. 143; *BDS*, pp. 159-60; Beloff, II, 326.

[47]) Churchill, II, 119-20; Hull, I, 811; Langer and Gleason, pp. 644-45, 728.

[48]) Schulenburg to Ribbentrop, 13 July 1940, *NSR*, pp. 166-68; *BDS*, pp. 187-88.

and appreciated in Germany.[49]) But Hitler seems to have paid no attention to all this. He simply could not believe that the "decadent" British meant to fight it out to the end regardless of what the Soviet Union might or might not do. Embittered by the refusal of England to acknowledge defeat, he hoped to encompass her collapse by first crushing Russia and thus making himself stronger. After the great victories in the West, Hitler had lost all sense of proportion and was willing to take on the Soviet Union right away. Pure greed came into this picture more and more as time passed, and finally the policy of systematic enslavement and extermination was presented to the world as "anti-communism" by the German propaganda machine.

The discussions of July, 1940, which have been quoted show clearly that communism had nothing to do with Hitler's decision. This was to be confirmed by later events in the East.[50]) In 1940 no ideological factors appear in the discussions. For example, Russia's claim to Bukovina may have been something new and it may have upset the Germans, but it certainly had little or nothing to do with communism.

Before leaving these speculations to return to the events of July and August 1940, it is interesting to note that the British Prime Minister accurately foresaw the decision Hitler would make. Confident about the outcome of any attempted invasion before the Germans became disheartened, Churchill wrote to the Prime Minister of the Union of South Africa on June 27, 1940:

> Obviously, we have first to repulse any attack on Great Britain by invasion, and show ourselves able to maintain our development of airpower. This can only be settled by trial. If Hitler fails to beat us here he will probably recoil eastwards. Indeed, he may do this even without trying invasion, to find employment for his Army, and take the edge off the winter strain upon him.[51])

Two weeks later he had thought out an answer to the problem posed by this possibility. On July 8 he wrote to the Minister of Aircraft Production, Lord Beaverbrook:

In the book by Hans-Günther Seraphim, *Die deutsch-russischen Beziehungen, 1939-1941* (Göttinger Beiträge für Gegenwartsfragen, Heft 1) (Hamburg, 1949), pp. 25-27, the transmission of this information by the Soviets to Germany is regarded as a veiled threat; a somewhat dubious interpretation. On the whole, this publication is a rather poor apologia for German foreign policy—the German equivalent of the Soviet Information Bureau's *Falsificators of History* (Washington, 1948) on which it is largely based and with which it stands on about the same level of historical writing.

[49]) Halder (22 July 1940), IV, 129; Skl, A, 11, 261: 23 July 1940, cited in C- 170, *TMWC*, XXXIV, 688.

[50]) The subject is well beyond the scope of this study but see for example Memorandum of Bräutigam, 25 October 1942, PS - 294, *TMWC*, XXV, 331-42; Political Report by Dr Paul W. Thomson, 19 October 1942, PS - 303, *TMWC*, XXV, 342-46; the list could be extended indefinitely.

[51]) Churchill to Smuts, 27 June 1940, Churchill, II, 200.

In the fierce light of the present emergency the fighter is the
need, ... But when I look around to see how we can win the war I
see that there is only one sure path. We have no continental army
which can defeat the German military power. The blockade is
broken and Hitler has Asia and probably Africa to draw from.
Should he be repulsed here or not try invasion, he will recoil east-
ward, and we have nothing to stop him. But there is one thing that
will bring him back and bring him down, and that is an absolutely
devastating, exterminating attack by very heavy bombers from this
country upon the Nazi homeland. We must be able to overwhelm
them by this means, without which I do not see a way through. We
cannot accept any lower aim than air mastery. When can it be obtained?[52])

The events of July, 1940, were to have effects apparent to the outside
world only after a considerable period of time had elapsed,[53]) but they
quickly had repercussions on German military and diplomatic policy
which will now be examined. These repercussions also reflect on the nature of the decisions of July, 1940, for they show them to have been not
simply vague allusions to possible developments, but rather the spur to
immediate action.

The first sphere to feel the impact of the momentous decision to attack the Soviet Union was that of the military establishment. Up to this
time a reduction in the size of the German army had been planned as
discussed in the preceding chapter. On July 31, however, Hitler had
talked about 120 divisions for the East alone, 60 more being assigned to
Norway and the West.[54]) This of course precluded the planned reduction
to a 120 division army; and at the end of July Keitel told General
Thomas, Chief of the War Economy and Armaments Section of the High
Command of the Armed Forces, that the reduction scheme would presumably not be carried out.[55]) At a meeting on August 2 Keitel told
Thomas that "the Fuehrer now viewed the whole situation differently
and that one had to prepare oneself for any possible political situation
for 1941."[56]) While the preparations for the invasion of England were to
continue, it was now Hitler's opinion that the 120 division army would
be insufficient and that the armament program would have to be based
on the expectation of an army of about 180 divisions. General Thomas
deduced these changes, with great accuracy, from

---

[52]) Churchill to Beaverbrook, 8 July 1940, Churchill, II, 567.

[53]) Members of the opposition seem to have found out rather quickly - Hassell (10
August 1940), p. 159; Weizsäcker, p. 299; cf. Hull, II, 967.

[54]) Halder (31 July 1940), IV, 145.

[55]) Germany, OKW, Wi Rü Amt, Thomas, "Aktennotiz über die Entwicklung der
Rüstungslage im Sommer 1940," [September? 1940], PS - 1456, p. 2. This meeting must
have been after July 21, whether it was before or on July 31 is not known; most likely it
was just before and corresponds to Jodl's meeting with his staff on July 29.

[56]) Ibid.

the recognition [by the highest leadership] that

1) one may under some conditions no longer count on the collapse of England in 1940,
2) in the year 1941 the intervention of the United States may occur (in Frage kommen kann),
3) the relations with Russia may undergo a change in 1941.[57])

Instead of disbanding some divisions, the army furloughed some units for work in war industry.[58]) The commencement of work on the armaments program for the 180 division army was ordered by Keitel on August 17.[59]) By August 21 the planning was already on the basis of a possible number of 200 divisions.[60])

In the meantime the order "Aufbau Ost" had been prepared and ordered released. It was issued on August 9.[61]) We have already seen that this order was designed to provide the transportation and supply facilities needed for an attack on Russia. Planning was also begun at this time for the establishment of a general headquarters for the army in East Prussia.[62]) Plans were made for the occupation of Rumania.[63]) This project was held up temporarily at the request of the Foreign Ministry,[64]) but will come up again in connection with the Vienna award and guarantee.

The most important move in the military sphere was of course the transfer of more troops to the East. The details of this are slightly confused, and not too important anyway; the main fact is that as a result of orders of August 27 and September 6 at least fifteen more divisions were ordered to the East.[65]) The different character of these movements from the transfers ordered in July has already been indicated.

---

57) *Ibid.*, p. 3.

58) Germany, OKW, WFA, "Stellenbesetzung der H.Gr.Kdos., AOKs, Gen.Kdos. und Höheren Kommandos z.b.V., Stand 10.8.40," 10 August 1940, PS - 1783 (photostat, 8pp.), pp. 5-7; Müller, "Erklärung von Müller," 8 January 1946, USSR - 149, p. 2.

59) Germany, OKW, Wi Rü Amt, Thomas, "Aktennotiz über die Entwicklung der Rüstungslage im Sommer 1940," [September?, 1940], PS - 1456, p. 3. See also Germany, OKW, WFSt, L, "1650/40; Heeresaufbau auf 180 Divisionen," 10 September 1940, cited in Gordon A. Harrison, *United States Army in World War II, The European Theater of Operations—Cross-Channel Attack* (Washington, 1951), p. 130, n. 12.

60) Germany, OKW, Wi Rü Amt, "Aktennotiz Betreff Vortrag des Amtschefs beim Gen. F. M. Keitel am 21.8.40," PS - 1456 (photostat, 1p.).

61) Testimony of Warlimont, U.S. v. Leeb, G.T. 6373.

62) Halder (7 August 1940), IV, 152, (14 August 1940) 160.

63) *Ibid.* (15 August 1940), p. 161.

64) *Ibid.* (23 August 1940), p. 170.

65) Testimony of Brauchitsch, *TMWC*, XX, 577; Testimony of Bentivegni, *TMWC*, VII, 263; Testimony of Jodl, *TMWC*, XV, 391; 428 Testimony of Halder, U.S. v. Weizsäcker, G.T. 20549-50; Müller, "Erklärung von Müller," 8 Jan. 1946, USSR - 149, p. 2; Raeder, "Die Vorbereitungen zum Kriege mit der Sowjet-Union," July and August 1945, PS - 1451 (photostat, 9pp.), p. 2, also USSR - 460, *IMWC*, XXXIX, 521, Germany, OKW, "Weisung vom 27. 8. 40," in C - 170, *TMWC*, XXXIV, 690; Germany,

The navy was also affected directly. Raeder had asked on July 11 that he be warned of any expected complications in the East.[66]) On August 13 Hitler told him to have the northern Norwegian fjords more heavily fortified "so that Russian attacks there would have no chance of success."[67]) This task was carried out cooperatively by the army and the navy,[68]) and Raeder reported on the work to Hitler on September 6.[69])

The economic implications of these military measures were discussed by Thomas with Göring on August 14. Göring commented that now the armaments program would really begin. It was agreed at Göring's request that efforts would be made to supply the deliveries to the Soviet Union on schedule until the spring of 1941. After that the Germans would no longer be interested in satisfying Soviet Russia.[70])

Other military details will be reviewed in connection with the diplomatic repercussions of the July decisions. The technical military matters have been discussed in some detail because they reflect rather strongly on the nature of the decisions which had been made. At later points the purely military affairs will be examined further though not always at such length.

The decision to attack Russia brought with it several very important decisions in the diplomatic field. It has already been shown that at the conference of July 31 Hitler had stated that Germany would settle the differences between Rumania and Hungary and then grant the former a guarantee. This move will be covered in the next chapter though an account of the connecting events will then be necessary. Germany's relations to Finland were also affected; here too the tie to the decision to attack Russia is quite clear.[71]) The change in German-Finnish relations will be examined more closely in the section dealing with German-Soviet relations in September, 1940.

The third area of diplomatic activity affected was that of Germany's

OKH, Gen.St.d.H. Op.Abt. (Brauchitsch), "496/40," 6 September 1940, NOKW - 1744 (mimeo, 8pp.), trans. United States, OCCWC, p. 1 and U.S. v. Leeb, G.T. 1311-12; Testimony of Salmuth, U.S. v. Leeb, G.T. 3878; Halder (26 Aug. 1940), IV, 174; Kordt, p. 298.

[66]) Skl, C VII/40, 226: 11 July 1940, in C - 170, *TMWC*, XXXIV, 687.

[67]) Fuehrer Conferences, 1940, II, 14; also in C - 170, *TMWC*, XXXIV, 689; cf. Greiner, p. 296.

[68]) Halder (18 and 19 Aug. 1940), IV, 165; Greiner, p. 297.

[69]) Fuehrer Conferences, 1940, II, 17.

[70]) Germany, OKW, Wi Rü Amt (Thomas), "Aktennotiz; Betreff: Besprechung bei Reichsmarschall Göring am 14. 8. 1940," PS - 1456 (photostat, 2pp.); cf. Germany, OKW, Wi Rü Amt (Meendsen-Bohlken), "Vortragsnotiz über Besprechung bei Reichsminister Dr. Todt," 22 August 1940, PS - 1456 (photostat, 5pp.), p. 1.

[71]) E.g. Halder (22 July 1940), IV, 128, (31 July 1940) 145, (12 August 1940) 157, (22 August 1940) 168, (26 August 1940) 174, (31 August 1940) 179; Germany, OKW, Wi Rü Amt (Thomas), "Aktennotiz; Betreff: Besprechung bei Reichsmarshall Göring am 14. 8. 1940," PS - 1456, p. 2.

attitude toward the rapprochement between Italy and the Soviet Union
—a rapprochement for which Ribbentrop had worked with great energy
and quite unusual diplomatic finesse. When Hasso von Etzdorf, liaison
man of the Foreign Ministry to the High Command of the German
Army, discussed the diplomatic situation with Halder on August 23, he
summarized Germany's attitude to the effect that Hitler wanted "German-Italian talks under exclusion of [*sic*, while excluding] Russia."[72])
It was in accordance with this policy that Germany had vetoed the
Italian-Russian negotiations for a delineation of spheres of influence on
August 17.[73]) Germany had its own plans for the Balkans.

Still another area of diplomatic activity was the problem of Lithuania.
The Russians had occupied all of that country and now asked to be relieved of the obligation of ceding the section around Mariampol to the
Germans.[74]) Neither this problem in itself, nor the connected one of
Soviet Russia's claim to the use of the free port in Memel previously
accorded to Lithuania, is of very great significance; but the almost interminable delay by the Germans in settling this matter was indicative of
the changed attitude toward the Soviet Union. The tedious details of
this affair will not be related, but the dates of the evidence illustrate the
length of time needed for a settlement of these minor matters.[75])

By the end of August the important decisions had been made. The repercussions on German-Soviet relations were quick to make themselves
felt. They were to appear in a very significant manner first at the two
ends of the area lying between Germany and the Soviet Union—
Rumania and Finland.

---

[72]) Halder (23 August 1940), IV, 170; this entry is dated after the events of August
16-18, but from the context it is a summary of the Italian-Russian discussions, with the
quoted statement being an explanation for Germany's attitude towards these talks.

[73]) Ciano, (17 August 1940), p. 285; Simoni, (17 August 1940), pp. 191-92, 18 August
1940), pp. 193-94, (19 August 1940), p. 194; Memorandum of Schmidt, 20 September
1940, PS - 1842, *TMWC*, XXVIII, 575-76; Gafencu, pp. 75-76; Kordt, p. 273, n. 1;
Rossi, p. 159 and n. 1. For additional details, see Mario Toscano, *Una mancata intesa
italo-sovietica nel 1940 e 1941* (Firenze, 1953), pp. 54-58.

[74]) Schulenburg to Ribbentrop, 13 July 1940, *NSR*, p. 166; *BDS*, pp. 186-87.

[75] Ribbentrop to Schulenburg, 2 August 1940, *NSR*, p. 174; *BDS*, p. 196; Martius to
Schulenburg, 9 August 1940, *BDS*, p. 198 (*NSR*, p. 176, gives Schnurre as the signer of
this note; the German edition is probably correct.); Schulenburg to Ribbentrop, 12
August 1940, *NSR*, p. 176; *BDS*, pp. 198-99; Ribbentrop to Schulenburg, 24 August
1940 (Berlin No. 1513), cited in Rossi, p. 250 and n. 1; Schulenburg to Ribbentrop,
30 August 1940, *NSR*, pp. 177-78; *BDS*, p. 200; Memorandum of Meyer-Heydenhagen,
2 September 1940, Seidl, pp. 203-04; Schulenburg to Ribbentrop, 4 September 1940,
NSR, p. 184; *BDS*, p. 207; Ribbentrop to Schulenburg, 5 September 1940, *NSR*, pp.
186-87; *BDS*, p. 210; Schulenburg to Ribbentrop, 11 September 1940, *NSR*, p. 188;
BDS, p. 211; Molotov to Schulenburg, 21 September 1940, *NSR*, p. 193; *BDS*, p. 217;
Memorandum of Schmidt, 15 November 1940, *NSR*, p. 237; *BDS*, p. 269; Memorandum of Sommer, 22 December 1940, Seidl, pp. 302-04; Secret Protocol of January 10,
1941, *NSR*, pp. 267-68; *BDS*, p. 300; cf. Kordt, pp. 274-75.

ANNEX

Alternatives to the Attack on Russia

It has been shown that when confronted with the problem of what to do if England could not be conquered in 1940 Hitler decided to attack Russia. This decision was not the first choice of many other German leaders and may appear in somewhat clearer perspective if the alternatives advocated are examined.

The proposal of Brauchitsch and Halder has been quoted. Its main point was a continuation of the war against England exclusively, by fighting mainly in the Mediterranean area with particular emphasis on the capture of the Suez Canal. The German navy advocated a very similar line. Raeder constantly stressed the importance of the Mediterranean theatre and the possibility of striking a decisive blow there. He added to this recommendation a more energetic prosecution of the submarine war against England to be aided by the development of a real naval-air arm. It was the Navy's opinion that England could be defeated only by these means and that all else should wait until after this had been accomplished.[76] Furthermore, the leadership of the German navy was very strongly opposed to a war with Soviet Russia which would divert strength from the navy and air force to the army, thus permanently hindering the fight against Britain.[77]

A radically different approach occurred to Rudolf Hess. Hess had in the past taken Hitler's professions of friendship for England quite seriously, and had even realized that Ribbentrop was often working in an opposite direction.[78] One of his most important political advisors was Albrecht Haushofer, the son of the famous geopolitician. Haushofer, in working for the overthrow of the Nazi regime, was using his contacts with Hess for anti-Nazi activities, and was later executed by the Gestapo.[79] Apparently to some extent under Haushofer's influence, Hess in

---

[76] Fuehrer Conferences, 1940, II, 19; *ibid.*, pp. 24-28, cited in *TMWC*, XXXIV, 691; Fuehrer Conferences, 1940, II, 41, cited in *TMWC*, XXXIV, 693; Skl, A, 16, 234-40: 20 December 1940, C - 105 (photostat, 346pp.), cited in *TMWC*, XXXIV, 694; Fuehrer Conferences, 1940, II, 68-80, cited in *TMWC*, XXXIV, 694-96; Raeder, "Die Vorbereitungen zum Kriege mit der Sowjet-Union," July and August 1945, PS - 1451, p. 3 (the dates in this memorandum are all two months later than they should be); Raeder, "Memorandum for Assmann," 30 January 1944, C - 66, *TMWC*, XXXIV, 277.

[77] For a more detailed account of the differences of the German navy with the official policy laid down by Hitler in regard to relations with Russia, see Gerhard L. Weinberg, "Research Problems in German-Russian Relations 1939-1941" (Unpublished M.A. thesis, Dept. of History, University of Chicago, 1949), Part I, A, 2, "The Navy and the official policy," pp. 13-17.

[78] Herbert von Dirksen, *Moskau, Tokio, London* (Stuttgart, 1950) pp. 229-30; Weizsäcker, pp. 170-71.

[79] A good, but uncritical, biography is Rainer Hildebrandt, *Wir sind die Letzten* (Berlin, 1949); cf. Hassell (16 May 1941), p. 185, (18 May 1941), p. 204, (2 August 1941),

the summer of 1940 decided, probably before hearing of the plan to attack Russia, that he would try to work for a peace with England. There is evidence of a letter of Hess to Haushofer about this on September 10, 1940—obviously the letter must have been based on previous conversations between them. Haushofer answered at length in a letter to Hess of September 19.[80]) As a result of this exchange Haushofer wrote a letter for Hess to the Duke of Hamilton on September 23, 1940, which the Duke actually received.[81]) At the same time that Haushofer was urging Hess onward and doing other things on the side, Hess was also playing a double game. In the winter of 1940-41 he himself prepared a long letter to the Duke of Hamilton.[82]) Eventually, while Haushofer was working on various schemes through Switzerland, Hess himself flew to England.

The evidence which is available now[83]) makes it clear that Hess, without authorization from Hitler, thought that he could somehow establish rapport between the leaders of Germany and England after the Churchill government had been either removed or circumvented and could thus bring about a peace in which Germany would gain a free hand in Europe (which he said did not include Russia), while the British Empire would remain untouched except for the return of Germany's colonies. The knowledge of the forthcoming war with Russia, which he probably

---

p. 215; Testimony of Hildebrandt, U.S. v. Weizsäcker, G.T. 20270; see also the reference to Haushofer crossed out in Memorandum of Schmidt, 14 May 1941, PS - 1866, *TMWC*, XXIX, 31, n. 10.

[80]) Haushofer to Hess, 19 September 1940, PS - 1670 (photostat, 4pp.); see also Haushofer to Hitler, 12 May 1941, PS - 1671 (photostat, 1p.); Albrecht Haushofer, "Englische Beziehungen und die Möglichkeit ihres Einsatzes," 12 May 1941, PS - 1671 (photostat, 12pp.).

[81]) Duke of Hamilton, "Report on Interview with Herr Hess," 11 May 1941, M - 116, *TMWC*, XXXVIII, 175-76.

[82]) Testimony of Bohle, U.S. v. Weizsäcker, E.T. 13497-98; Testimony of Leitgen, U.S. v. Weizsäcker, E.T. 13965.

[83]) The material already cited and the following: Testimony of Leitgen, U.S. v. Weizsäcker, E.T. 13938-39, 13951-52; United States, OCCWC, Evidence Division, Interrogation Branch, "Interrogation of Alfred Hess," (13 August 1947, Interrogation Summary No. 3128 (mimeo, 3pp.) p. 3; Churchill, *The Second World War*, Vol. III, *The Grand Alliance* (Boston, 1950), pp. 48-55; Ivone Kirkpatrick, "Record of an Interview with Herr Rudolf Hess," 13 May 1941, M - 117, *TMWC*, XXXVIII, 177-80; Kirkpatrick, "Record of an Interview with Herr Hess on May 14th [1941]," M - 118, *TMWC*, XXXVIII, 181-82; Kirkpatrick, "Record of a Conversation with Herr Hess on May 15th, 1941," M - 119, *TMWC*, XXXVIII, 182-84; Hildegard Fath, "Affidavit of Fath," Hess - 13, *TMWC*, XL, 278-79; Lord Simon, "Minutes of a Conversation between Lord Simon and Hess," 10 June 1941, Hess - 15, *TMWC*, XL, 279-92 and X, 4-7; Memorandum of Schmidt, 14 May 1941, 1866 - PS, *TMWC*, XXIX, 29-32; Halder (15 May 1941), VI, 117-18; Ciano, *The Ciano Diaries* (13 and 14 May 1941), pp. 350-52; J. R. Rees (ed.), *The Case of Rudolf Hess* (New York, 1948), pp. 17-19, 22-23, 39-43, 52, 54-55, 57, 96-129, 168, 174-75, 206-07, 210; Kordt, *Wahn und Wirklichkeit*, p. 322 and nn. 1-4.

did not possess when he began to work along this line, may have urged him along in his efforts; but there is no basis whatever to the stories that he tried to get British agreement for a joint front against the Soviets; on the contrary, he carefully evaded answering questions of British interrogators who tried to find out whether or not a Soviet-German war was impending.

CHAPTER EIGHT

FINLAND, RUMANIA, AND THE DANUBE

The first really important effects on Soviet-German relations of the decision to attack Russia were the outcome of policies Germany adopted because of that decision toward Finland and Rumania. Before these policies and the reactions of the Russians to them are examined, it might be well to summarize the military preparations for the attack on the Soviet Union which were made in the last part of August and in September along that part of the frontier, directly under German control, between the two countries at the ends.

The various improvements in the railways, roads, and airports which had been ordered by the "Aufbau Ost" directive were now under way as were the troop movements already referred to.[1] In addition, more anti-aircraft guns were moved east, both to protect German industry against British planes and to show the Russians that Germany could defend herself against air attack from any quarter.[2]

It was thought in Germany that all this activity might alarm the Russians into thinking that a German attack on Russia was impending. An order for the camouflaging of the preparations was therefore issued on September 6 to the Abwehr, the military intelligence and counter-intelligence office.[3] A translation of the text of this order is given in Appendix II. It can be seen, if the document is studied carefully, that the Germans hoped to deter the Russians from any action in the Balkans and from any attack on Germany while the latter was preparing her own offensive; the first, by giving the "impression" that the heaviest concentrations were toward the South, and the second by exaggerating the armored strength and stressing the anti-aircraft defenses in the East. The improvements in the transportation system made under "Aufbau Ost" were to be explained away as routine and of a commercial nature. When the text of this order is examined in connection with the military preparations then already under way, it becomes clear that this is not just a cover-up for defensive measures.[4]

---

[1] See also Halder (30 August 1940), IV, 178, (1 September 1940) 180.

[2] Germany, OKW, Wi Rü Amt, "Aktennotiz: Betreff: Vortrag Amtschef beim Gen.F.M. Keitel am 21. 8. 40," PS - 1456, p. 1.

[3] Germany, OKW, WFSt, L (Jodl), "WFSt an Ausl. Abw.; Betreff: Unterlagen für den Nachrichtendienst," 6 September 1940, PS - 1229, *TMWC,* XXVII, 72-73.

[4] See Testimony of Jodl, *TMWC,* XV, 390, *PHKV,* XV, 428, and compare Köstring,

In the meantime the long-range planning in the High Command of the Army entered a new phase. On September 3 General Paulus was appointed *Oberquartiermeister* I in the general staff of the army and immediately began work on the plans for the attack on Russia.[5]) He worked out a detailed plan for the distribution of divisions between East and West and among the three army groups to be used in the East. His plans were discussed in the High Command of the Army on September 17[6]) and September 19.[7]) On the following day, Army Group B (Fieldmarshal von Bock) took over command of the Eastern Front from Küchler's Eighteenth Army.[8]) It will be seen later that it was on the basis of the detailed plans of Paulus that the actual operational orders were drafted.[9])

From the very beginning, German plans for the attack on Russia involved the participation of Finland. This is suggested in the conference of July 21[10]) and clearly stated in that of July 31.[11]) Under these circumstances the Germans were naturally worried when it seemed as if a new crisis in Soviet-Finnish relations were about to develop in the late summer of 1940. In 1939 the Germans had, in accordance with the Secret Protocol of August 23, 1939, carefully refrained from aiding Finland; in fact, they were, as has been shown, prepared to aid in the blockade of that country. In July and August of 1940 Finland was as much in the sphere assigned to Russia by the Protocol as before; but now Germany wanted Finnish help in the attack on Russia, believed that because of the winter war of 1939-40 Finland would be prepared to cooperate, and was therefore unwilling to allow the Soviets to retain a free hand in that area.[12]) When it seemed as if Russia were about to do in Finland what she had previously done in the Baltic states, Germany viewed with alarm what she had observed with detached interest in 1939.[13])

"Affidavit of Köstring," 20 November 1945, PS - 3014, United States, CCPAC, *Nazi Conspiracy and Aggression*, V, 734-35.

[5]) Testimony of Paulus, *TMWC*, VII, 254; *PHKV*, VII, 284; Testimony of Halder, U.S. v. Weizsäcker, G.T. 20528. Halder says that Paulus worked out his own plans independently, while Paulus claims that he worked on a study which must have been in preparation for several weeks before he saw it (*TMWC*, VII, 301, *PKHV*, VII, 335).

[6]) Halder (17 September 1940), IV, 198-99.

[7]) *Ibid.* (20 September 1940), p. 201; cf. *ibid.* (29 October 1940), p. 252.

[8]) *Ibid.* (20 September 1940), p. 202.

[9]) See also Müller, "Erklärung von Müller," 8 January 1946, USSR - 149, p. 3.

[10]) Halder (22 July 1940), IV, 128.

[11]) *Ibid.* (31 July 1940), p. 145.

[12]) See the handwritten paragraph at the end of Göring's letter to Eric Rosen (his Swedish brother-in-law), 21 November 1940, PS - 1985 (photostat, 4pp.), p. 4.

[13]) Skl. A, 11, 249: 22 July 1940, cited in C - 170, *TMWC*, XXXIV, 688; Skl, A, 11, 330: 28 July 1940, cited *ibid*; Sk1, A, 12, 1: 1 August 1940, cited *ibid.*, p. 689; Sk1, A, 12, 41: 4 August 1940, cited *ibid*; Sk1, C VII/40, 270: 13 August 1940, cited *ibid*; Sk1, A, 12, 372: 31 August 1940, cited *ibid*; Halder (9 August 1940), IV, 154, (12 August 1940) 157, (14 August 1940) 159.

Some quick action would have to be taken if Finland were still to be in existence at the time of the scheduled attack on Russia. By August 14 certain decisions had been made in Germany. Hitler wanted "a quick and strong supplying of Finland as he did not wish to deliver Finland into the hands of the Russians." The first thing the Finns were to be sent, was large quantities of anti-tank mines. An aide of Göring, Colonel Veltjens, was to discuss the matter with the Finnish Marshal Mannerheim and report back the Finnish wishes.[14]). On August 18 Veltjens saw Mannerheim, signed an arms-purchase agreement, and at the same time obtained Finnish approval of the sending of some *Luftwaffe* personnel across Finland to the Kirkenes area of Norway. The technical negotiations for this culminated in an agreement signed on September 12.[15])

In the meantime, on August 22, the German military attaché in Helsinki, General Rössing, had conferred with General Halder. They discussed the new attitude of Hitler toward Finland, including the approval of supply shipments and the negotiations for the transit of two mountain divisions across Finland to Kirkenes.[16]) These problems seem to have been reviewed at a conference between Hitler and Brauchitsch on August 26 when German intervention to occupy Petsamo in case of a Russian attack on Finland was agreed upon.[17]) On August 29 speedy supplies to Finland were discussed by Thomas and Göring,[18]) and on the next day Thomas informed the leading officers of his department of the new policy.[19]) While the Russians were to be allowed to find out about all this, so that they might be deterred from action against Finland,[20]) the whole thing was to be explained as directed against the British.[21]) At this time Ribbentrop also alluded rather cautiously to German interest in Soviet-Finnish relations in some talks with the Russian Ambassador in Berlin.[22])

---

[14]) Germany, OKW, Wi Rü Amt (Thomas), "Aktennotiz; Betreff: Besprechung bei Reichsmarschall Göring am 14. 8. 1940," PS - 1456, p. 2.

[15]) Wuorinen, p. 92; Blücher, p. 198; Greiner, pp. 297-98; Carl Gustav Mannerheim, *Erinnerungen,* trans. H. von Born-Pilsach (Zurich, 1952), pp. 425-26. According to the testimony of Risto Ryti (President of Finland at that time) at the Finnish War Crimes Trial, the Finnish government was not informed about the agreement of September 12, 1940, by the military authorities. See Hjalmar J. Procopé, *Sowjetjustiz über Finnland* (Zürich, 1947, pp. 136-37.

[16]) Halder (22 August 1940), IV, 168.

[17]) *Ibid.* (26 August 1940), p. 174.

[18]) Germany, OKW, Wi Rü Amt (Thomas), "Aktennotiz, Besprechung bei Reichsmarschall Göring," 29 August 1940, PS - 1456 (photostat, 2pp.), p. 2.

[19]) Germany, OKW, Wi Rü Amt, "Aktennotiz, Besprechung beim Amtschef am 30. 8. 40," PS - 1456 (photostat, 2 pp.), p. 1.

[20]) *Ibid.*

[21]) Halder (31 August 1940), IV, 179; for naval supplies to Finland, see Skl, A, 13 ?: 23 September 1940, NOKW - 2557 (mimeo, 4pp.), trans. United States, OCCWC, p. 4).

[22]) Memorandum of Meyer-Heydenhagen, 2 September 1940, Seidl, p. 203.

A German-Finnish diplomatic agreement covering the transit of German troops and equipment was signed on September 22.[23]) All of this activity was probably in contravention of the Secret Protocol of August 23, 1939. Ribbentrop in an instruction of September 16 had planned to have Schulenburg inform the Soviets of the agreement the day before it was concluded.[24]) This was, however, apparently cancelled by a later instruction, for on September 26 Molotov asked the German chargé about the German troops in Finland.[25]) It is obvious from the agitated diplomatic correspondence which followed that the Russians were very seriously disturbed by the German action, all the more so since they had not been informed beforehand.[26]) Probably to some extent because of the German actions, the tensions between Russia and Finland eased somewhat in October.[27])

A real rift had been made in the relations between Germany and the Soviet Union. This question was to be raised insistently by Molotov on his visit to Berlin in November and seems to have been one of the points about which he was most concerned. This will be reviewed in the context of the Molotov visit; but it might be interesting to mention here that of the thirty-six pages comprising the memoranda on Molotov's conversations with Hitler and Ribbentrop in the State Department publication, seven are taken up by rather acrimonious debate about the respective interests of Russia and Germany in Finland. Before the decision to attack Russia, Germany had been willing to see the Soviets conquer that country; now they meant to protect it as an ally for the coming war.

Another serious rift in German-Soviet relations was opened by the German actions in regard to Rumania. While it is true that the Germans had been surprised by the swiftness of Russia's action in June and by the unexpected claim to Bukovina, the specific steps now taken by Germany seem to stem from the decision to attack the Soviet Union and expand

---

[23]) For text see *NSR*, p. 202, *BDS*, p. 227; Wuorinen, p. 93; see also Blücher, pp. 200-01; Greiner, p. 298.

[24]) Ribbentrop to Schulenburg, 16 September 1940, *NSR*, pp. 188-89, *BDS*, p. 212; cf. Ribbentrop to Blücher, 16 September 1940, *NSR*, p. 189; *BDS*, p. 212.

[25]) Tippelskirch to Ribbentrop, 26 September 1940, *NSR*, pp. 198-99, *BDS*, pp. 222-23. Schulenburg was then in Berlin.

[26]) Ribbentrop to Tippelskirch, 2 October 1940, *NSR*, pp. 201-02, *BDS*, pp. 226-27; Tippelskirch to Ribbentrop, 4 October 1940, *NSR*, pp. 203-04, *BDS*, pp. 227-28; Memorandum of the German Foreign Office, 8 October 1940, *NSR*, p. 205, *BDS*, p. 230; Tippelskirch to Ribbentrop, 9 October 1940, *NSR*, p. 207, *BDS*, p. 239; Ritter to Schulenburg, 14 October 1940, NG - 3187, summarized in U.S. v. Weizsäcker, E.T. 808 cited in Testimony of Ritter, U.S. v. Weizsäcker, G.T. 11936; Schulenburg to Ribbentrop, 1 November 1940, *NSR*, p. 217, *BDS*, p. 244.

[27]) SkI, C VIII/40, 561: 6 October 1940, cited in C - 170, *TMWC*, XXXIV, 692; Wuorinen, p. 94.

German influence in the Balkans; they would probably have taken place even if Russia had never claimed Bukovina.[28])

The general policy to be followed had been laid down by Hitler at the conference of July 31. He had stated that Germany would settle the differences between Hungary and Rumania and then give a guarantee to the latter.[29]) Plans for the dispatch of German troops to Rumania were in preparation by August 15,[30]) but were held in abeyance until needed.[31]) Preparations were also made to secure the industrial facilities of Rumania in case of German occupation.[32])

In the last days of August events moved quickly. On August 24 the Germans tried to frighten the Rumanians into obedience to them by spreading rumors of Russian troop concentrations on the Rumanian border. The Italians, Rumanians, and Hungarians were quickly summoned to Vienna, and on August 30 Hungary was awarded parts of Transylvania while Germany extended a guarantee to the rest of Rumania. The details of the Vienna settlement are relevant here only in regard to the following two aspects: first, the German action was taken without previous consultation with the Soviet Union, and second, the guarantee had some very important implications for German-Soviet relations in the Balkans. The other aspects of the settlement must be passed over.[33])

While the Vienna negotiations were in progress, the Russians had tried to warn the Rumanians not to overlook the interest of the Soviet

---

[28]) The presentation of the German-Soviet clashes in the Balkans as an outcome, rather than the cause, of the German decision to attack the Soviet Union is contrary to the well-known interpretation of Gafencu who deduced the German decision from these clashes. Although this writer has the greatest admiration for Gafencu's work on the background of the German-Soviet war, the interpretation it presents simply does not fit the facts. Gafencu calls the German guarantee of Rumania the first rift in German-Soviet relations. Perhaps it was, but that does not alter the fact that the guarantee was an outcome of Hitler's decision to attack the Soviet Union.

The thesis of Gafencu that Hitler—an unpredictable and emotional individual—had not finally made up his mind until the spring of 1941 is not supported by presently available evidence. Although the characterization of Hitler as one who often vacillated and changed "decisions" already made in sound as a general thesis, the decision to attack the Soviet Union is, interestingly, one of the few exceptions. Probably in no other major question of policy did Hitler adhere as closely to a plan of action determined so far in advance.

[29]) Halder (31 July 1940), IV, 145.

[30]) *Ibid.* (15 August 1940), p. 161.

[31]) *Ibid.* (23 August 1940), p. 170.

[32]) Germany, OKW, Wi Rü Amt, "Aktennotiz, Besprechung beim Amtschef am 30. 8. 40," PS - 1456, p. 1.

[33]) Gafencu, p. 81. For the Vienna award and related details see *ibid.*, pp. 80-84; Halder (26 August 1940), IV, 174, (28 August 1940) 176, (29 August 1940) 177; Simoni (31 August 1940) p. 196; Ciano, *Diaries* (26 August 1940) p. 287, (27 August 1940) p. 287, (29 August 1940) pp. 388-89, (30 August 1940) p. 389; Schmidt, pp. 495-96

Union in her neighbor by some rather confusing diplomatic maneuvers in the night of August 29.[34]) Immediately after the negotiations ended, the storm really broke. Ribbentrop sent Schulenburg instructions to inform Molotov in a long telegram of August 30.[35]) When Schulenburg saw Molotov on August 31, the latter was very reserved and asserted that Germany had violated the consultative provision (Article III) of the Non-Aggression Pact.[36]) Ribbentrop protested against this assertion in a detailed memorandum explaining Germany's actions as in accord with the Pact.[37]) Schulenburg saw Molotov again on September 9 to deliver the memorandum. Molotov announced that the Soviet government considered the matter of such importance that it would answer in writing; he could state right away, however, that the USSR still believed that Germany had failed to consult them as it was obligated to do.[38]) Before leaving Moscow to report to Berlin, Schulenburg had a meeting with Molotov on September 21. At that time Molotov handed him a long Soviet memorandum which answered the earlier German one.[39])

The Soviet memorandum dealt with several disputed points. The Soviet government insisted that it should have been and could have been informed about the Vienna negotiations beforehand. At the same time the Soviets indicated their willingness to negotiate the question of amending or deleting the consultative clause in the Non-Aggression Pact. The Soviets further protested vehemently against the guarantee given to Rumania. On this the Soviet position could be attacked as somewhat inconsistent, but the Germans were diplomatic enough to overlook the point. The Russians insisted on the one hand that the guarantee was an unnecessary step which was being interpreted as directed against them, when in fact Germany could have assured itself, simply by asking the Soviets, "that the U.S.S.R. does not intend to threaten the territorial integrity of Rumania."[40]) At the same time they were asserting that the Germans had promised to support the Russian claim to Southern Bukovina when that question was reopened.[41]) Schulenburg disputed the correctness of this assertion and Molotov

---

[34]) Gafencu, pp. 82-84.

[35]) Ribbentrop to Schulenburg, 30 August 1940, *NSR*, pp. 178-80, *BDS*, pp. 201-03

[36]) Schulenburg to Ribbentrop, 31 August 1940, *NSR*, pp. 180-81, *BDS*, p. 203; cf. Memorandum of Meyer-Heydenhagen, 2 September 1940, Seidl, pp. 204-04.

[37]) Ribbentrop to Schulenburg, 3 September 1940, *NSR*, pp. 181-83; *BDS*, pp 204-06; Schulenburg to Ribbentrop, 4 September 1940, *NSR*, pp. 183-84, *BDS*, p. 206-07; Ribbentrop to Schulenburg, 5 September 1940, *NSR*, pp. 185-87, *BDS*, pp 208-10.

[38]) Schulenburg to Ribbentrop, 9 September 1940, *NSR*, p. 187, *BDS*, p. 210-11.

[39]) Memorandum of Schulenburg, 21 September 1940, *NSR*, pp. 189-90, *BDS*, pp. 213-14; Molotov to Schulenburg, 21 September 1940, *NSR*, pp. 190-94, *BDS*, pp. 214-18

[40]) *NSR*, p. 191, *BDS*, p. 215; cf. Gafencu, p. 74.

[41]) *NSR*, p. 193; *BDS*, p. 217.

somewhat modified his language, but the intentions of the Soviets in this matter were certainly made clear. In the concluding sections of the memorandum, the Soviets again called attention to the importance of strict observance of the consultative clause. Schulenburg was asked to make sure that the German government appreciated the position of the Soviets. This subject also was to be discussed in November when Molotov was in Berlin.

By the time of this last interview, German measures for the dispatch of troops to Rumania were already well under way. Details were discussed on August 28, 29, and 30.[42] All sorts of conferences and secret trips in the first three weeks of September prepared the ground for the German military mission to Rumania.[43] By about September 20 all was ready; it had been decided to send not just the training troops asked for by Rumania but a full division with more to follow. By the end of September, rumors about these troops were appearing in the press; and the Germans felt obliged to inform the Soviet Union as well as other countries about the "training troops" being sent to "instruct" the Rumanian army.[44] The purpose of these troop transports was made clear in an order outlining the function of the military mission to Rumania. This documents states that the mission is ostensibly to help train the Rumanian army, but that its "real task" is to prepare for the commitment of German and Rumanian troops against Russia from Rumanian territory.[45]

This affair greatly antagonized the Russians who suddenly saw

---

[42] Halder, IV, 176-77.

[43] Halder (9-10 September 1940), IV, 189, (12 and 13 September 1940) 192, (14 September 1940) 195, (18 September 1940) 201, (20 September 1940) 202; Weizsäcker to Canaris, 14 September 1940, with "Entwurf einer Dienstanweisung für die deutsche Militärmission in Rumanien," NG - 3824 (photostat, 4pp.); Canaris to Weizsäcker, 20 September 1940, NG - 4649, United States, OCCWC, Staff Evidence Analysis (Mimeo, 1p.).

[44] Memorandum of Weizsäcker, 3 October 1940, NG - 3823 (photostat, 2pp.); Gerstenberg and Fabricius to Ribbentrop, 7 October 1940, NG - 3761 (mimeo, 1p.); Ritter to Ribbentrop, 8 October 1940, NG - 3761 (mimeo, 3pp.); Halder (23 September 1940), IV, 204-05, 207, (26 September 1940) 209, (2 October 1940) 216, (7 October 1940) 223; Testimony of Ritter, U.S. v. Weizsäcker, G.T. 11857-58; Falkenstein to ?, 29 October 1940, PS - 376 (photostat, 4pp.), p. 2; Germany, OKW, WFSt, L(1), "00845/40," 10 October 1940, cited in OKH, Gen.St.d.H., Op.Abt. (Brauchitsch), "810/41, Betreff: Verlegung A.O.K. 11 nach Rumänien," 6 May 1941, NOKW - 99 (photostat, 2pp.), p. 1; United States, OCCWC, Evidence Division, Interrogation Branch, "Interrogation of Generalleutnant Hermann Hoelter," 19 June 1947, Interrogation Summary No. 2543 (mimeo, 4pp.), p. 1; Sk1, A, 13, ?: 23 September 1940, NOKW - 2557, trans. United States OCCWC, p. 3; Hagen, p. 285; Ribbentrop to Tippelskirch, 9 October 1940, NSR, p. 206, BDS, p. 231; Tippelskirch to Ribbentrop, 10 October 1940, NSR, pp. 206-07, BDS, pp. 232-33. For a good account of these events, see Greiner, p. 299-307.

[45] Germany, OKW, WFSt, L, Keitel, "33248/40," 20 September 1940, C - 53 (photostat, 3pp.), p. 1.

themselves excluded from further participation in Balkan affairs by what looked like a diplomatic and military barrier at their southern border. The annoyance of the Russians was recognized in Berlin and Rome.[46]) The Italians, as the Germans soon found out, were not pleased either. The German actions in regard to Rumania produced two echoes in the Balkans. The Italians, who were displeased by Germany's sole occupation of Rumania, decided to demonstrate their independence of Germany by launching their ill-fated attack on Greece.[47]) Even before, the Russians had reacted by demanding a share in the settlement of the Danubian question.

The Danube was legally under the control of two international organizations. The lower (maritime) Danube from Braïla to the Black Sea was under the European Commission which in 1940 consisted of England, France, Germany, Italy, and Rumania. Established by the Treaty of Paris of 1856 and strengthened at the Congress of Berlin in 1878, the European Commission had wide powers of control over the delta of the Danube. On the other hand, the Danube from Ulm to Braïla (the fluvial Danube) was under the International Commission established by the Treaty of Versailles. It consisted at this time of the riparian states together with Italy, England, and France, but had only technical functions and powers. Russia had been dropped from the European Commission in 1917 and was never a member of the International Commission. She had already shown an interest in the affairs of the European Commission in the spring of 1940.[48])

At the beginning of September, 1940, the Germans summoned a conference at Vienna of the riparian states belonging to the International Commission (thus excluding England and France). This conference adjourned on September 13, having decided to dissolve the International Commission and to provide a provisional regime pending the adoption of some definitive new agreement.[49]) The Soviets seized this occasion as an opportunity to announce their claims and to assert the position in the Danube basin to which they considered themselves entitled and at the same time gave notice that they would not permit themselves to be excluded from the discussion of problems affecting the Balkan area.[50])

[46]) Sk1, A, 13, 102: 8 September 1940, cited in C - 170, *TMWC*, XXXIV, 690; Ciano, *Diaries* (19 September 1940), p. 293.
   [47]) Ciano, *Diaries* (8 October 1940), p. 299, (12 October 1940), p. 300, (14 October 1940), p. 301, (22 October 1940), p. 303; Halder (18 November 1940), V, 29.
   [48]) Beloff, II, 324; Dallin, pp. 210-11. A useful summary of the various treaties governing the control of the Danube river is given in *Foreign Relations of the United States: The Paris Peace Conference, 1919*, XIII (Washington, 1947), 664-67.
   [49]) Rossi, p. 154.
   [50]) For some reason, the editors of *Nazi-Soviet Relations* have omitted *all* the documents covering the negotiations concerning the Danube from that publication. The account given here is based mainly on the following sources: Gafencu, Chapter III, "Der

On September 11, Deputy Commissar for Foreign Affairs Andrei Vyshinsky expressed to Schulenburg the surprise of the Soviet Union at its not having been invited to the conference. When Schulenburg pointed out that only the upper Danube was involved, Vyshinsky replied with the statement that the Soviet Union was interested in all questions affecting the Danube.[51]) On being informed of this, Ribbentrop told the Soviet Ambassador in Berlin that the problem of the International Commission would be settled by Germany, but that Germany was prepared to help Russia secure a seat on the European Commission again. Molotov thereupon summoned Schulenburg on September 14 and handed him a memorandum outlining the Soviet position and proposals. The Soviet government suggested the abolition of both Commissions. A single new one was to be established to govern the Danube from Bratislava, where it leaves German territory, to the Black Sea. The members of the commission were to be the riparian states only—this would exclude Italy as well as England and France. Molotov insisted that the Danubian clauses of the treaty settlements of 1856, 1878, and 1920 should be abolished and proposed that this be done in the manner outlined.

The Russians must have felt that the guarantee to Rumania had been, in effect, an attempt to exclude them from the forthcoming rearrangements in the Balkans; they hoped to come back into the picture in this manner. At the same time they hoped to gain an entrance into Central Europe and more power over the Danube than Russia had ever possessed under the Tsars.

The Germans were not particularly pleased by this turn of events. They decided, presumably at the time that Schulenburg was in Berlin, to make the following proposal to the Soviets: Germany would agree to the substitution of one new commission for the two old ones. A conference of delegates from Germany, Italy, Russia, and Rumania would meet at Bucharest and establish a provisional regime. This provisional regime would control the Danube until the new commission had been established as a result of further negotiations. By this offer the Germans hoped to please the Russians, drive the French and English out of the European Commission, exacerbate the relations between the latter and the Soviet Union, and at the same time leave the question of the ulti-

Kampf um die Donaumündung," pp. 92-117, the best account available; a survey in Kordt, *Wahn und Wirklichkeit*, pp. 273-74; an entry in the Halder diary (16 September 1940), IV, 197; some side references in *NSR*, pp. 211, 244, 252; and the 19 complete or excerpted documents on the Bucharest conference released in 1944 by the German Foreign Office, which are printed, with a brief introduction, in Peter (pseud.), "Dokumentarischer Bericht - Die Sowjetregierung und die Donaumündung Ende 1940," *Hamburger Monatshefte für Auswärtige Politik*, XI, Nos. 1/2 (January-February 1944) pp. 22-39. Some of the Italian documents have been published in Toscano, *Una mancata intesa italo-sovietica nel 1940 e 1941*.

[51]) Cf. Skl, A, 13, 349: 26 September 1940, cited in C - 170, *TMWC*, XXXIV, 691.

mate settlement open. This German answer was delivered about October 18; in the meantime the Russians had reacted to the German military occupation of Rumania by seizing some islands in the Danube delta from Rumania and thus obtaining control of the Chilia channel.[52]) By October 26 agreement on the German proposal had been reached, and the convening of the Bucharest Conference was publicly announced for October 28.

The course of the conference will not be recounted. The opposite purposes of the Russians and Germans ruled out agreement from the start since neither side seemed eager to compromise. The Germans wanted to keep the Russians out of any real position on the Danube; the U.S.S.R. wanted to secure full control of the maritime Danube and great influence on the fluvial Danube. Interrupted by long recesses, the conference moved along slowly for almost two months. At the beginning, the British protested the Soviet action in participating with the Axis in breaking international agreements as unneutral conduct. The Soviets published a sharp and hostile reply.[53]) After discussion of various more or less intricate proposals had failed to produce any substancial agreement, the conference adjourned on December 21. Neither side was willing to make concessions on the basic issues, and the Germans were content to let the matter rest unsolved until they could impose a settlement by force of arms.

---

[52]) This technical violation of Rumanian territorial integrity was ignored by Germany in spite of the guarantee previously given to Rumania. After their own actions in this area, the Germans perhaps believed that they should not antagonize Russia further by raising this question Gafencu, pp. 103-05; see also Greiner, p. 310; U.S. National Archives, Italian Documents, Microfilm Reel 1290, frame 107681.

[53]) See Beloff, II, 257; cf. Sk1, C VIII/40, 610: 5 November 1940, cited in C - 170, TDWC, XXXIV, 693.

CHAPTER NINE

FROM THE TRIPARTITE PACT TO THE END
OF 1940

On September 27, 1940, Germany, Italy and Japan signed the Tripartite Pact in Berlin. Unlike the situation in 1938-1939, agreement among the three powers had been reached this time in less than six weeks of negotiations. The main terms of the Pact provided for a recognition of the respective primacy of Germany and Italy in Europe and of Japan in Eastern Asia (Articles I and II); an agreement to aid each other if attacked by a power not yet involved in the European or the Sino-Japanese conflict (Article III); and a declaration that this Pact in no way affected the relations of the individual partners with the Soviet Union (Article V).[1] The Pact seems to have been largely the idea of Ribbentrop who secured first the approval of Japan and then that of Italy.[2] The two main purposes of the treaty were to draw the three participating powers more closely together and to frighten the United States away from intervention in the European or Pacific war.[3]

In the last few days before the actual signing of the treaty, Schulenburg had arrived in Berlin where he did his best to urge a more considerate attitude toward the Soviet Union.[4] It was anticipated that the reaction of the Soviets to the news of the Tripartite Pact would be unfavorable, but that they would take no direct action.[5] The Soviet government was to be informed on the day before the signing of the treaty.[6] Tippelskirch, the German chargé in Moscow, was also instruc-

---

[1] For full text see PS - 2643, *TMWC*, XXXI, 56-57. The original draft of the text was in English; its main clauses will be found in Feis, pp. 119-20.

[2] See the excellent account in Feis, pp. 112-21.

[3] Weizsäcker, p. 299.

[4] No documents on Schulenburg's stay in Berlin are available; see, however, the discussion in Gafencu, pp. 133-36.

[5] Memorandum of Schmidt, 20 September 1940, *TMWC*, XXVIII, 574-76, 579-80.

[6] Ribbentrop to Tippelskirch, 26 September 1940, *BDS*, pp. 219-20. The copy printed in *NSR* is neither the telegram sent to Moscow nor the message actually delivered to Molotov. Changes, indicated only in the German edition, were made in Moscow before delivery. These written-in changes involved the removal of all references to the specifically anti-American character of the Pact, with general references to the democratic countries and those wanting to expand the war being substituted. These changes seem to have been ordered by another instruction to Tippelskirch as a similar procedure was used in

ted to inform Molotov that Ribbentrop had received the Soviet memorandum of September 21 and that he intended to reply in a letter to
Stalin which would include an invitation for Molotov to come to Berlin.

On the evening of September 26, Tippelskirch took these messages to
Molotov.[7]) It was at this meeting that Molotov asked about the German
troop transports through Finland. In regard to the Tripartite Pact, he
demanded to see the text before it was signed, as he considered the
Soviet Union entitled to consultation under the consultative clause of
the Non-Aggression Pact. When Weizsäcker informed the Russian Ambassador in Berlin of the course of events on September 28, he stressed
the desire of the German government for better relations between the
powers of the Tripartite Pact, particularly Japan, and the Soviet
Union.[8]) Ribbentrop's answer to the request of Molotov for consultation before the signing of the pact was sent *after* the signing on October
2. It argued that because of the provisions of Article V of the Tripartite
Pact the Soviets were not entitled to previous consultation and added
that there were "no secret protocols or any other secret agreements."
The letter to Stalin was announced as coming in a few days.[9]) Molotov
replied to Ribbentrop's statements by reserving his answer to the German interpretation of the consultation clause.[10])

The reaction of the Soviet Union to the Tripartite Pact was correct[11])
but not friendly. The Russians probably felt left out and a bit uneasy
about this apparent revival of the Anti-Comintern Pact in a stronger
form.[12]) The possible adherence of the Soviet Union to the Tripartite

---

informing the Russian Ambassador in Berlin (Memorandum of Weizsäcker, 28 September 1940, NG - 3074 [mimeo, 2pp.], p. 1). Feis (p. 117) has been misled by the defi-
ciences of the American edition.

It should also be noted that the text in the American edition is taken from a draft of
September 25 in the files of the Foreign Minister and is an English version of the
document in Seidl, pp. 218-20. The text in *BDS* is taken from the telegram as sent to
Moscow on September 26 and found in the files of the Moscow Embassy. The most important difference between the two German texts (other than the written alterations) is
the omission in the Moscow copy of the phrase "gegenüber Amerika" which appear as
"against America" in the first sentence of point 3) in the American edition (p. 195).
There were then three texts—draft, telegram, and delivered message. The American
edition gives the draft; the German edition gives the actual telegram, indicates the
changes made before delivery, and cites the draft.

[7]) Tippelskirch to Ribbentrop, 26 September 1940, *NSR*, pp. 197-99, *BDS*, pp.
222-23; cf. Gafencu, p. 126.

[8]) Memorandum of Weizsäcker, 28 September 1940, NG - 3074, pp. 1-2.

[9]) Ribbentrop to Tippelskirch, 2 October 1940, *NSR*, pp. 201-03, *BDS*, pp. 227-28.
The quoted statement is false, see Feis, pp. 120-21 and n. 25.

[10]) Tippelskirch to Ribbentrop, 4 October 1940, *NSR*, p. 204, *BDS*, pp. 228-29.

[11]) Sk1, C VIII/40, 544: 29 September 1940, cited in C - 170, *TMWC*, XXXIV, 691
(the reference to A, 13, 1 in this entry would refer to October 1).

[12]) Gafencu, Chapter IV, pp. 118-32.

Pact was to be one of the topics of conversation at Molotov's visit to Berlin and will be reviewed in that connection.

Before the Molotov visit can be discussed, it is necessary to picture the framework of military preparations within which the visit took place. Failure to consider the military developments which preceded the Molotov visit and excessive emphasis on one military order issued after the visit, have led many writers to very questionable conclusions concerning the course of German-Soviet relations.

The operational studies of General Paulus were nearing an end. The operational plan was finished at the beginning of November, 1940.[13] Military exercises on some of the problems raised in these plans took place in November and the early part of December.[14] Paulus reported on the progress of his work on November 8 and again on November 13.[15] Before these dates, however, an important conference had taken place at the High Command of the Armed Forces on November 4. At this conference, on which we have only indirect evidence, a number of operations were discussed—an attack through Spain, an attack on Greece, the attack on Soviet Russia. It was made clear that the preparations for the attack on Russia were to go on in spite of the forthcoming Molotov visit.[16] The decisions of Hitler on the various problems discussed at that conference were brought together in Directive 18 on the conduct of the war. A draft of this order was sent out on November 7.[17] The final copy was issued on November 12, though clearly prepared before that date.[18] The dates are extremely significant because November 12 was the date on which Molotov arrived in Berlin and the order refers to his visit. The passage about Russia in this order reads as follows:

Russia

Political discussions for the purpose of clarifying the attitude of Russia in the immediate future are being started. Regardless of what outcome these conversations will have, all preparations for the East already orally ordered, are to be continued.

[Written Führer] directives concerning this will be issued as soon

---

[13] Testimony of Paulus, *TMWC*, VII, 254, *PHKV*, VII, 280-81.

[14] *Ibid.*; Testimony of Halder, U.S. v. Weizsäcker, G.T. 20528-29, E.T. 20750-51.

[15] Halder (8 November 1940), V, 14, (13 November 1940) 20.

[16] Testimony of Jodl, *TMWC*, XV, 391-92, *PHKV*, XV, 428-29; "Conference of the Chief, Operations Division, Naval Staff with the Chief, Operations Staff, Armed Forces High Command, General Jodl on 4 November 1940," Fuehrer Conferences, 1940, II, 33, 35 (cited in *TMWC*, XXXIV, 691).

[17] Halder (7 November 1940), V, 13; see the reference to the draft of November 7 in the covering note to the copy of November 12 in Heinz Holldack, *Was wirklich geschah* (Munich, 1949), p. 425.

[18] Germany, Oberste Befehlshaber der Wehrmacht, OKW, WFSt, L (Hitler), "Weisung Nr. 18," 12 November 1940, PS - 444, *TMWC*, XXVI, 40-46; note that the number of the day is written in on the typed document (this is very clear on the photostat).

as the basic outlines of the operational plan of the army have been submitted to me and approved by me.[19])

On the basis of this order, prepared and issued before the conversations with Molotov, Halder gathered the plans which had been prepared. The railway development was progressing according to plan, and the schedules for the supply and troop build-up had been worked out and were already in operation.[20]) The High Command of the Army (OKH) warned the High Command of the Armed Forces (OKW) of the time restrictions imposed on other planned operations by the requirements of the attack on Russia.[21]) At the end of November the military exercises conducted under the direction of General Paulus were almost finished. On the basis of these and the other studies which had been prepared, Halder reported the plans of the army, called for in the directive of November 12, at a conference with Hitler on December 5, 1940. After detailed discussion Hitler agreed to the army's proposals and directed that these proposals along with plans for other branches of the armed forces be codified by his own staff. This was done, and the codification was issued as Directive 21 on December 18, 1940.[22])

Directive 21, which is entitled "Case Barbarossa" after the code name for the attack on the Soviet Union, is, if viewed in the context of pre-

---

[19]) The German text is as follows:

"Russland

Politische Besprechungen mit dem Ziel, die Haltung Russlands für die nächste Zeit zu klären, sind eingeleitet. Gleichgültig, welches Ergebnis diese Besprechungen haben werden, sind alle schon mündlich befohlenen Vorbereitungen für den Osten fortzuführen.

"Weisungen darüber werden folgen sobald die Grundsätze des Operationsplanes des Heeres mir vorgetragen und von mir gebilligt sind."

Oral orders refer to the orders Hitler gave to the generals personally and which the latter then carried out directly or put into written form. "Weisungen" refers to the numbered written directions on the conduct of the war periodically issued by Hitler.

[20]) Halder (11 October 1940), IV, 228, (7 November 1940) V, 12-13, (8 November 1940) 15, (12 November 1940) 18, (3 December 1940) 50; Greiner, pp. 310-12; Harrison, p. 130.

[21]) Halder (18 November 1940), V, 27; cf. *ibid.* (27 November 1940), p. 43.

[22]) This summary of the events of November and early December, 1940, is based on the following sources: Halder (19 November 1940), V, 31, (4 December 1940) 53 (5 December 1940) 55-56, (13 December 1940) 68; Testimony of Halder, U.S. v. Weizsäcker, G.T. 20529-30, E.T. 20752; Testimony of Paulus, *TMWC*, VII, 255, *PHKV*, VII, 281; Germany, OKW, WFSt, KTB 6a, Anlage, 1, "Vortrag beim Führer am 5. 12. 40," PS - 1799, *TMWC*, XXXVIII, 393-95; Testimony of Warlimont, U.S. v. Leeb, G.T. 6287, 6373, 6375-77; Jodl, "Erklärung von Jodl," 26 September 1946, NOKW - 65, pp. 9-10; Warlimont, "Erklärung von Warlimont," 1 November 1946, NOKW - 152, pp. 3-4; the following interrogations by United States, OCCWC, Evidence Division, Interrogation Branch - "Interrogation of Jodl," 6 September 1946, Interrogation Summary No. 87, p. 5; "Interrogation of Keitel," 13 September 1946, Interrogation Summary No. 117; "Interrogation of Dr. Wilhelm Scheidt," 4 October 1946, Interrogation Summary No. 215 (mimeo, 4pp.), p. 3; and "Interrogation of Warlimont," 21 October 1946, Interrogation Summary No. 324, pp. 2-3; Greiner, pp. 325-31.

ceding preparations, merely a summing up of plans already worked out.[23]) The military details are those in the planning stage since July, and the tasks assigned to Finland and Rumania are also those visualized in the July conferences. The section dealing with the army operations is specifically labeled as in accordance with the plans suggested by Halder on December 5. These, in turn, were the outcome of the studies of Paulus, started at the beginning of September and finished after the order of November 12. It can be seen from this that the timing of the order of December 18 and the Molotov visit have nothing to do with each other. The impression to the contrary is perhaps largely due to the confusion of ordinary orders with the "Weisung" or Hitler directive, and to the seriously misleading editing of the State Department's publication. By inserting among the 261 diplomatic documents one military document—Directive 21—right after the documents on the Molotov visit and Molotov's subsequent proposals, the impression was created that the Germans decided to attack because of the course taken by those talks. In this manner, former Secretary of State James Byrnes seems to have been misled by his own staff;[24]) Winston Churchill has not been similarly deluded.[25])

During December, before and after the issuance of Directive 21, the military preparations continued. The problem of Bulgaria, a very involved military and diplomatic affair to be taken up in more detail later, now entered the sphere of military preparations, as the Bulgarians requested military aid from Germany for fear of Russian attacks if Bulgaria were to help the Axis. In December a military mission paved the way for German occupation of that country as had earlier been the case in Rumania.[26])

Believing that the Soviet Union could be beaten in a few months, Hitler wanted to settle all the military problems on the continent in 1941.[27]) As will be seen in the next chapter, the orders to the individual army groups for the attack on Russia were prepared in January, 1941.

---

[23]) Text in *TMWC*, XXV, 47-52; *BDS*, pp. 291-95. The text printed in *NSR* is incomplete.

[24]) James Byrnes, *Speaking Frankly* (New York, 1947), pp. 288-89.

[25]) Churchill, II, 518-19.

[26]) Germany, OKW, WFSt, L (Warlimont), "Nr. 001082/40; Betreff: Bulgarien," 4 December 1940, NOKW - 3347 (photostat, 1p.); Germany, OKH, Gen.St.d.H., Op.Abt. (Halder), "720/40 an Attaché Abteilung," 10 December 1940, NOKW - 3347 (photostat, 1p.); Germany, OKH, Gen.St.d.H., Att.Abt. "67/40 an OKW Ausland; Betreff: Erkundungen in Bulgarien," 13 December 1940, NOKW - 3347 (photostat, 1p.); Interrogation of Warlimont, 16 October 1945, United States, CCPAC, *Nazi Conspiracy and Aggression, Supplement B*, p. 1639; Skl, A, 16, 44: 4 December 1940, C - 105; Skl, A, 16, 261-62: 23 December 1940, C - 105; Halder (26 November 1940), V, 38, (12 December 1940) 66.

[27]) Germany, OKW, WFSt, L (von Lossberg), "Besprechung Führer-Chef W F St am 17. 12. 40," 21 December 1940, PS - 1799 (photostat, 2pp.), p. 2.

This is the framework of military preparations within which the Molotov visit must be studied.

In the latter part of September, 1940, the Germans had again taken up the question of having Molotov visit Berlin. The negotiations for the Tripartite Pact were almost completed, and it was thought best to invite the Soviets to participate lest they be excessively offended. It was believed in Germany, no doubt partly because of Schulenburg's emphasis on this point, that it would be wise to attempt to smooth over some of the difficulties which had arisen and were certain to continue to arise as a result of the moves Germany considered necessary in preparation for the attack on Soviet Russia. There was the thought that a show of unity by the totalitarian powers might frighten England into making peace. It seemed wise to find out what the attitude of Russia would be in the coming months. This became even more important when, after the Russian acceptance and shortly before the visit itself, Germany began plans for an attack on Greece. Finally, Hitler probably wanted to see whether there was any chance of a new fundamental agreement with the Soviet Union; should this prove impossible as expected, the visit would still serve German interests by providing Germany with real or fabricated statements of Russian demands which might be used to secure or keep in line reluctant allies in the coming struggle.[28]

Ribbentrop had indicated on September 25, 1940, in the draft of the instruction concerning the Tripartite Pact, that he would write to Stalin, inviting Molotov to Berlin.[29] The letter was given to Schulenburg to take back with him when he returned to Moscow on October 15.[30] The letter itself is dated October 13.[31] It begins with a detailed review of the events since Ribbentrop's second visit to Moscow. For Stalin's benefit, the captured French documents about allied plans, especially in regard to the Caucasus oil fields, are discussed in detail. The war is declared won; the Axis has only to wait for the British to acknowledge their collapse. While waiting, Germany and Italy have found it necessary to consolidate their positions and secure their sources of supply. This is the explanation for the troop movements across Finland and for the Vienna award. The movement of troops into Rumania (which could not be explained by the alleged presence of British troops in Greece until Greece had been attacked by Italy two weeks later) was explained as needed to safeguard German interests and as a preventive measure against pos-

---

[28] Weizsäcker, p. 304; Gafencu, *Vorspiel zum Krieg im Osten, pp. 136-38, 140-42;* Memorandum of Schmidt, 20 September 1940, PS - 1842, *TMWC,* XXVIII, 576, also PS - 1865, United States, CCPAC, Staff Evidence Analysis.

[29] Draft of Ribbentrop, 25 September 1940, *NSR,* p. 196, Seidl, pp. 218-20.

[30] Simoni (15 October 1940), p. 206; Schulenburg to Ribbentrop, 19 October 1940, *NSR,* p. 215, *BDS,* pp. 241-42.

[31] Ribbentrop to Stalin, 13 October 1940, *NSR,* pp. 207-13, *BDS,* pp. 233-40.

sible English action against the oil wells. In this connection, Ribbentrop announced that a favourable reply to the Russian proposals concerning the Danube would be forthcoming. A discussion of the Tripartite Pact follows, stressing its purpose of keeping other democracies out of the war, and the complete compatibility of this treaty with the friendly relations of Germany and her partners with the Soviet Union.

In conclusion, Ribbentrop invites the Soviet Union to share in the division of the world with Germany, Italy, and Japan and requests that Molotov come to Berlin to discuss these matters. For further discussions Ribbentrop suggested another visit by himself to Moscow later for talks with Stalin, possibly with representatives of Italy and Japan coming to Moscow also.[32]

Schulenburg delivered the letter to Molotov on October 17, presumably in the evening.[33] Molotov admitted that he owed a visit to Berlin but reserved an answer until after he had studied the letter. On the evening of October 19 Molotov informed Schulenburg that Stalin's reply, which would be ready on October 21, would be favorable; that Molotov would come to Berlin in November after the celebrations of November 7 and 8.[34] Stalin's answer was handed to Schulenburg on October 21.[35] In it Stalin agreed with the desirability and possibility of further agreements and stated that Molotov could arrive in Berlin between November 10 and 12. He welcomed the idea of a later visit to Moscow by Ribbentrop but stated that the suggestion of joint consultations with Italy and Japan would require previous examination. Schulenburg added in his report to Ribbentrop that the Russians had requested secrecy and that Hilger would come to Berlin, carrying Stalin's original letter, to discuss the details of the trip.

Hilger went to Berlin and returned to Moscow by October 30. He brought instructions concerning the communiqué to be issued to announce the visit of Molotov. Apparently he had also been given an instruction to Schulenburg according to which the latter was to inform Molotov of the intended adhesion of Hungary, Rumania, Slovakia, and Bulgaria to the Tripartite Pact. Schulenburg recommended that Ribbentrop do this himself during Molotov's visit.[36] This was done, but in a very different form, as will appear later. The details of the communiqué and other matters relating to the trip were settled in the next

---

[32] It took the Moscow embassy two days to prepare a translation of this long missive. Ribbentrop to Schulenburg, 18 October 1940, *NSR*, p. 214, *BDS*, p. 241; Schulenburg to Ribbentrop, 19 October 1940, *NSR*, p. 213, *BDS*, pp. 241-42; Ribbentrop to Schulenburg (Berlin No. 1890), 21 October 1940, Seidl, p. 240.

[33] Schulenburg to Ribbentrop, 17 October 1940, *NSR*, p. 214, *BDS*, p. 240.

[34] Schulenburg to Ribbentrop, 19 October 1940, Seidl, p. 239; cf. Rossi, p. 172, n. 2.

[35] Schulenburg to Ribbentrop, 21 October 1940, *NSR*, p. 216, *BDS*, pp. 242-43.

[36] Schulenburg to Ribbentrop, 30 October 1940, Seidl, p. 241.

few days.[37]) Ribbentrop asked Molotov to bring along a portrait of Stalin, and Molotov speedily agreed.[38])

In the discussions between the Axis partners which preceded the Molotov visit, two general themes were dominant—that an effort should be made to divert the Soviets from the Balkans to the Persian Gulf area, and that if Russia would adhere to the Tripartite Pact, a protocol for that adhesion and the definition of the respective spheres of interests would later be signed by the four powers in Moscow.[39])

Molotov arrived in Berlin on the morning of November 12 and spent many hours in conversations with Ribbentrop and Hitler on that and the following day.[40]) These talks have become well known, and it is therefore not necessary to summarize each one; however, a number of the important aspects of the conversations will be considered.

The German leaders spent much time reviewing the course of the war and declaring that they had won it. When first speaking to Molotov, Hitler also made an effort to justify such steps as the troop movements through Finland in terms of German's military needs during the war. These actions would cease with the end of the war. The Tripartite Pact was explained in most vague terms, and Ribbentrop indicated in somewhat veiled language that some other countries might join—he did not specify which ones.[41]) The Germans asked the Soviet Union to join the Tripartite Pact and suggested that Russia, like the three other powers, turn southward for her expansion, securing an outlet to the Ocean on the Persian Gulf rather than the Mediterranean. These were the main themes of the German approach.

Molotov consistently attempted to reduce the vague formulations of the Germans into specific details; for example, he repeatedly asked for clarification of the Tripartite Pact and the meaning and size of the "Greater East Asia Sphere" assigned to Japan. It is of great significance

---

[37]) Schulenburg to Dörnberg, 30 October 1940, *ibid.*, p. 243; Ribbentrop to Schulenburg, 31 October 1940, *ibid.*, pp. 243-44; Schulenburg to Ribbentrop, 1 November 1940 *ibid.*, pp. 244-45.

[38]) The telegrams are cited in Rossi, p. 173 and n. 3.

[39]) Memorandum of Schmidt, 20 September 1940, PS - 1842, *TMWC*, XXVIII, 575; Ciano, *Diplomatic Papers* (28 October 1940), pp. 402-04; (4 November 1940), 406; see also reference to what was probably a report of Schulenburg shortly after his return to Moscow on October 15, 1940, in Sk1, A, 214: 19 October 1940, C - 170, *TMWC*, XXXIV, 692. There are some details on the German preparations for the conversations with Molotov in Frans von Papen, *Der Wahrheit eine Gasse* (Munich, 1952) pp. 526-27; but because of the unreliability of the source these details must be viewed with great caution.

[40]) The records of the conversations kept by the Germans are in *NSR*, pp. 217-54, *BDS*, pp. 247-87; see also the very interesting account in Schmidt, pp. 516-25. For a brief account of Molotov's meetings with Hess and Göring on November 13, see Hilger and Meyer, p. 323, n. 8.

[41]) See *NSR*, p. 220, *BDS*, p. 250; the translation of this veiled language is accurate.

that already at the first, preliminary, discussion with Ribbentrop, Molotov alluded to the Finnish question as the only one remaining open from the 1939 settlement and announced that he intended to discuss it in detail later.[42])

Once Molotov really had an opportunity to speak, he immediately launched into the Finnish question and Russian interests in regard to Bulgaria, Rumania, and Turkey, referring in this to specific instructions given him by Stalin. The discussion of Finland between Hitler and Molotov was very long and very acrimonious. Molotov insisted on the strict observance of the Secret Protocol of August 23, 1939. Hitler talked about German economic interests in Finland and some rather far-fetched notions about American intervention in case of another war in the Baltic. Molotov had stated that Russia intended to settle the Finnish question in the same manner as the question of Bessarabia and the Baltic states (Randstaaten)—i.e. by annexation.[43]) The Germans kept harping on the danger of another war in the Baltic which they wanted to avoid. Molotov indicated his amazement at the change in the position of Germany which had not worried about such a war in 1939, but which now, when she considered herself victorious, seemed so alarmed by this unlikely contingency.

In principle, Molotov was willing to agree to the idea of joining the Tripartite Pact, but he insisted that first the existing issues must be clarified. He had already raised the question of Southern Bukovina. Now he attacked the guarantee of Rumania and asked that it be revoked. This Hitler declined to do. The big issue Molotov raised next was a Russian guarantee of Bulgaria. This question was evaded by the Germans with the counter-question of whether the Bulgarians had requested such a guarantee and by references to the need to consult Mussolini on such an issue. There was also much rather general talk about such subjects as the Straits, Soviet-Japanese relations, the Sino-Japanese conflict, and the danger from England at Salonika.[44])

---

[42]) *NSR*, p. 225, *BDS*, p. 255.

[43]) *NSR*, p. 240, *BDS*, p. 272.

[44]) The question of the Straits was brought up originally by Ribbentrop at his first meeting with Molotov (*NSR*, pp. 222-23; *BDS*, pp. 252-53). Molotov gave no reply to the detailed plans for "certain special privileges to Russia" proposed by Ribbentrop at this meeting. When Hitler first asked for the Soviet plans in regard to the Straits and offered German help in "an improvement for Russia in the régime of the Straits," Molotov avoided answering (*NSR*, pp. 232-33; *BDS*, pp. 263-64). At the second Hitler-Molotov meeting, the latter raised the question of a Soviet guarantee of Bulgaria as a means of securing Soviet interests in the Straits. Molotov expressed confidence in the possibility of settling the Straits issue itself satisfactorily by direct negotiations with Turkey (*NSR*, pp. 244-45; *BDS*, pp. 276-77). At the final meeting between Molotov and Ribbentrop there was some more rather general discussion of a change in the status of the Straits (*NSR*, pp. 247-48, 250, 252-53; *BDS*, pp. 280, 282-85).

What light is shed on German-Soviet relations by these talks? By the time the conference was held the German decision to attack the Soviet Union was already definite and not to be shaken except by some totally unforeseeable event. This can be deduced from the discussion of Finland. The German-Soviet agreement explicitly assigned Finland to the Soviet sphere, and the Germans did not try to deny that. Hitler may well have felt for reasons not connected with the attack on Soviet Russia that he could make no major concessions in the *Balkans*. The oil of Rumania and the Greek adventure of Italy were of real importance. There was then, however, no really important German interest in *Finland* other than that country's predetermined role in the war on Russia.[45] The German troop movement through Finland, which were the main cause of the Russian complaints, resulted, as we have seen, from the decision to attack Russia. The obstinate insistence of Molotov on this issue must have shown the Germans the importance attached to it by the Soviets. Hitler, however, was unwilling to modify, not to mention abandon, his plans for the attack. The horror stories about a war in the Baltic sound no more convincing than the question of whether Bulgaria had asked for a Russian guarantee. The complete unwillingness of the Germans to abide by the terms of the Secret Protocol in spite of Russian insistence is a clear indication that no new political agreement was really desired, at least not by Hitler.[46]

Soviet policy at this time seems have been oriented toward a long war. The lack of eagerness to participate in the division of the British Empire is probably to be accounted for by the belief that this division was not as imminent as the Germans pretended. It is clear also that the Russians were most interested in further gains in the Balkans. These, as will be seen presently, they were to attempt to secure by negotiations with Germany, Bulgaria, and Italy—only to be blocked directly or indirectly by Germany in each case. Adherence to the German-Soviet agreement of 1939 in regard to Finland was made the touchstone of future collaboration with the Reich. In any case, the Germans received the impression that they could count on the Russians not to break with them in the immediate future.[47]

After Molotov's visit there were some further negotiations between Germany and Soviet Russia about the issues raised in Berlin. The initiative remained with Moscow; Berlin simply did not answer.[48] There is

---

[45] There were, of course, the nickel deposits of Petsamo; but in case of a new German-Soviet settlement, an agreement on nickel supplies analogous to the one about the Boryslaw-Drohobycz oil could undoubtedly have been worked out.

[46] It is by no means certain that Ribbentrop knew at this time of the scheduled attack on Russia.

[47] Halder (14 November 1940), V, 22, (16 November 1940) 26.

[48] Testimony of Ribbentrop, *TMWC*, X, 291, 314-15, *PHKV*, X, 329, 356-57. The

no evidence showing that the Germans, as they claimed, were in consultation with Italy about the Soviet suggestions.

The problem in which the Russians seemed most interested was that of Bulgaria,[49]) particularly as the various Balkan countries seemed about to join the Tripartite Pact. On November 18 Molotov queried the Bulgarian Minister in Moscow on this subject. He promised the support of Russia for Bulgaria's territorial demands on her neighbours and warned that any Axis guarantee of Bulgaria must include the participation of the Soviet Union.[50]) On November 25, the same day on which the Russian proposals for joining the Tripartite Pact were given to Schulenburg,[51]) the Soviet representative at the Bucharest Danube Conference saw the King and Prime Minister of Bulgaria and asked them to accept a treaty of mutual assistance with the Soviet Union,[52]) while Molotov placed these Russian demands before the Bulgarian Minister in Moscow.[53]) On November 30 the Bulgarians declined to sign with Russia, adding that the Soviet Union could hardly be worried about Bulgaria's considering adhesion to the Tripartite Pact when she was thinking of taking that step herself.[54]) There were apparently some further negotications but with no different results.[55]) The position of Bulgaria in Germany's military plans was already fixed by this time. The further details of the negotiations of Russia and Germany with and about that country will be examined in the next chapter.

The Russians may have thought that the renewal of Italian feelers for a rapprochement leading to a delimitation of spheres of influence might provide an opportunity for the realization of Soviet aims in the Balkans. The Italians, who were now in the war and therefore in a very different position from a year before, were trying to get a resumption of trade

---

German draft proposals for agreements with Russia are in *NSR*, pp. 255-58, *BDS*, pp. 244-47; they are dated November 9, 1940, in the German edition (p. 244) and may thus have been prepared in Germany before the Molotov talks. Judging from the file in which they were found, the draft was later sent to Schulenburg. The Russian proposals are in Schulenburg to Ribbentrop, 25 November 1940, *NSR*, pp. 258-59, *BDS*, pp. 288-90 (see also *BDS*, p. 290, n. 4). Molotov's question why Germany had not answered is in Schulenburg to Ribbentrop, 17 January 1941, *NSR*, p. 270, *BDS*, pp. 302-03.

[49]) For a later diplomatic skirmish about Finland, see Memorandum of Meyer-Heydenhagen, 12 December 1940, Rossi, p. 197; cf. Sk1, A, 16, 157: 13 December 1940, C - 105.

[50]) Report of Woerman, 22 November 1940, in Rossi, p. 187-88.

[51]) Schulenburg to Ribbentrop, 25 November 1940, *NSR*, pp. 258-59, *BDS*, pp. 288-90.

[52]) Richthofen to Ribbentrop, 30 November 1940, in Rossi, pp. 188-89; cf. Michael Sokolnicki, *The Turkish Straits* (Beirut, 1950), p. 21, n. 17.

[53]) Halder (26 November 1940), V, 39-40; cf. *ibid.* (28 November 1940), 45.

[54]) Richthofen to Ribbentrop, 30 November 1940, in Rossi, p. 189.

[55]) Halder (10 December 1940), V, 63; Sk1, A, 16, 110: 9 December 1940, C - 105 (cited in *TMWC*, XXXIV, 694).

with Soviet Russia and had begun political discussions to accomplish this. In January, 1941, the Germans interposed a veto in this scheme just as they had done in August of 1940.[56])

Complications in Soviet-German relations had, in the meantime, also arisen in the economic sphere. German deliveries were falling below schedule even before the new armaments program was adopted in August, and the repercussions of the latter were expected to unbalance the accounts even more. In September, at the same time that the Russians were reacting to German steps in other fields, the attitude of the Soviet economic negotiators stiffened. The Soviets cancelled the various long-term projects provided for by the treaty of February 11, 1940, and stated that they would make use of their right to suspend shipments until the treaty-stipulated ratio of deliveries had been attained unless a satisfactory settlement could be reached. The German negotiator, Schnurre, returned to Berlin in the middle of September, 1940, and submitted to Ribbentrop and Göring a report on the delivery situation and the position assumed by the Soviet Government. Along with this, he presented the arguments for assigning deliveries to the Soviet Union the priority ratings needed for the maintenance of Soviet deliveries.[57]) Göring agreed to Schnurre's proposal on September 30.[58]) At the beginning of October, new directives assuring high priority to the deliveries for the Soviet Union were issued; and considerable efforts were made by the government to secure the cooperation of German industrial concerns in the delivery program.[59])

[56]) Ciano, *Diaries* (25 October 1940), p. 304, (1 January 1941, p. 331, (3 January 1941), p. 332; Ciano to Alfieri, 16 December 1940, Ciano, *Diplomatic* Papers, p. 411; *ibid.*, (19 January 1941), p. 419; Halder (16 September 1940), IV, 197; Simoni (5 January 1941), pp. 231-35, (6 January 1941), pp. 235-36, (10 January 1941), p. 238, (16 January 1940), p. 238; Rosso to Alfieri, 16 January 1941, in Simoni (12 January 1941), pp. 239-43; Tonano, 96-109.

[57]) Memorandum of Schnurre, 26 September 1940, *NSR*, pp. 196-97, *BDS*, p. 221; Memorandum of Schnurre, 28 September 1940, *NSR*, pp. 199-201, *BDS*, pp. 294-96; cf. Halder (16 September 1940), IV, 197, (25 September 1940) 208; Gafencu, pp. 86-87, 141.

[58]) Memorandum of Schnurre, 28 September 1940, *NSR*, p. 201, n. 97.

[59]) Greiner, p. 313; Hilger and Meyer, p. 321; Germany, OKW, Wi Rü Amt Thomas, "Grundlagen für eine Geschichte der deutschen Wehr- und Rüstungswirt schaft," PS - 2353, p. 315, in *TMWC*, XXX, 272; Selections from the speech of Dr Schlotterer to the Beirat der Reichsgruppe Industrie on October 3, 1940, in I.G. Farben, Einkaufsabteilung (Weiss), "Vertrauliche Niederschrift zum Umlauf," 14 January 1941, NI - 6734, p. 3; F. Krupp (Eberhardt), "F. Krupp A.G. an das Reichswirtschafts-ministerium; Betrifft: Russland-Vertragsabschluss fuer Lieferung von 6 Stueck 38 cm Schiffgeschuetzturmen und Munition. Freistellung durch das Reich aus Folgen eventueller Eingriffe des Reiches," 8 October 1940, NIK - 11629 (mimeo, 4pp.), p. 2; F. Krupp (Vaillant), "Transcript by Herr Vaillant concerning a Discussion at the High Command of the Navy, on 13 November 1940," 13 November 1940, NIK - 12079 (mimeo, 4pp.), trans. United States, OCCWC; F. Krupp (Vaillant), "Der Reichswirt-

New economic negotiations had been scheduled for December, 1940, at the time of the negotiations one year before.[60]) These negotiations were again marked by considerable difficulties. They were delayed by various minor complications as well as the insistence of the Soviets that the Germans agree to a settlement of the Lithuanian boundary problem. On December 31, 1940, the Soviet-German Trade and Payments Agreement was again renewed, this time until August 1, 1942.[61]) On January 10, 1941, the new economic agreement and the protocol concerning Lithuania were signed.[62]) The economic agreement was considered satisfactory by the German negotiators, but Hitler refused to permit the publicizing of its favorable terms by the German Press.[63])

At the end of 1940, a new crisis in Russo-German relations, similar to that of September, seemed about to start in the lower Balkans. German plans for further military moves in the Balkans through Bulgaria were under way. Because the Soviet government had already indicated its interest in that country, considerable difficulties in Soviet-German relations were to arise. These matters were tied up with the Italian fiasco in Greece, to which defeats in North Africa were added in December. These events enabled England to undertake diplomatic manouvers in the Balkans for an anti-German front, manouvers which were in part seconded by the United States. The Balkan developments which followed will be the subject of the next chapter, but only in so far as they have a direct bearing on German-Soviet relations.

---

schaftsminister an die Friedrich Krupp Aktiengesellschaft; Betrifft: Russland 38 cm Doppeltuerme (Entwurf)," 13 November 1940, NIK - 12080 (mimeo, 3pp.).

[60]) Testimony of Ritter, U.S. v. Weizsäcker, G.T. 11916.

[61]) Germany, Auswärtiges Amt, *Vertrags-Verzeichnis,* Item 2137, pp. 691-92. A set of railway agreements had been signed in Berlin on October 1, 1940 (*ibid.,* Item 2105, p. 682).

[62]) Gafencu, pp. 159-61; Halder (3 December 1940), V, 52; Memorandum of Sommer, 22 December 1940, Seidl, p. 304; Secret Protocol of January 10, 1941, *NSR,* pp. 267-68, *BDS,* p. 300; cf. Memorandum of Schnurre, 5 April 1941, *NSR,* pp. 318-19; *BDS,* pp. 356-57; Memorandum of Schnurre, 15 May 1941, *NSR,* pp. 339-41, *BDS,* pp. 381-52. See also Germany, Auswärtiges Amt, *Vertrags-Verzeichnis,* Items 2139-43, pp. 692-93.

[63]) The text of the economic agreement is not available. For the discussions in Germany about the agreement, see Testimony of Schnurre, U.S. v. Weizsäcker, G.T. 19161-62; Memorandum of Etzdorf, 10 February 1941, NG - 2988 (photostat, 5pp.), p. 1.

CHAPTER TEN

FROM THE BULGARIAN CRISIS TO THE
YUGOSLAV COUP

In the first months of 1941 a series of spectacular events occurred in the Balkans. Their repercussions on German-Soviet relations must be recorded; however, they could hardly affect these relations in any really basic way as the German course was already decided. These matters will, therefore, be reviewed to a large extent because they shed light on the foreign policy of the Soviets by recording their reactions to German military and diplomatic steps.

As in previous chapters, the background of military preparations is a necessary framework for a record of other activities. In the first three months of 1941 the planning already goes down to the level of the individual armies; at the end of this period it received a rude shock from events in Yugoslavia.

The timing of the attack on Russia had been set at "Spring 1941" on July 31, 1940.[1]) The middle of May was considered best by the conference of December 5.[2]) In the latter part of December, 1940, and the first part of January, 1941, the more detailed plans for the three army groups scheduled to make the attack were prepared. A complete draft of the order of the High Command of the Army was ready on January 22 and was formally issued on Januari 31. On Januari 30 the navy issued its first comprehensive order. The headquarters of the army groups worked out the plans, schedules, and requests called for by the High Command and, after receiving approval, issued their own basic orders for the units under them. These orders went out in the middle of February. On the basis of these, the separate armies and panzer groups worked out their plans, and the divisions, theirs.[3]) Naturally, under these circumstances

---

[1]) Halder (31 July 1940), IV, 144.

[2]) Testimony of Halder, U.S. v. Weizsäcker, G.T. 20530.

[3]) It seems unnecessary to present this in great detail. The following documents seem to the writer of the greatest interest—there are many others. It should be remembered that there were generally parallel orders from each Army Group, Army, Division, etc. Germany, OKM, Skl, "94/41 an OKW, WFSt, L; Betrifft: Barbarossa," 30 January 1940, NOKW - 2270 (photostat, 8pp.); Germany, OKH, Gen.St.d.H., Op.Abt. "50/41, Entwurf, Aufmarschanweisung Barbarossa," 22 January 1941, NOKW - 2705 (photostat, 18pp.); Germany, HGrK C, Ia, "8/41, Aufmarschanweisung Barbarossa Teil I," 5 February 1941, NOKW - 2587 (also 2452) (photostat, 7pp.); Germany, HGrK A, Ia,

the half a million men who had been furloughed to work in war industries had to be recalled and an additional half million were to be added to the army—all this by May 1.[4]) The various military conferences of January and February will not be reviewed except for that of February 3. At this conference Hitler reviewed the operational plans in detail; the general lines for concealing the tremendous massing of troops were established, and the principles for contacting the other countries scheduled to participate in the attack were laid down.[5]) The basic order on misleading the enemy concerning German intentions was issued on February 15 and was elaborated by a large number of subsequent directives.[6]) In Appendix III one of the later operational orders on this subject has been translated as it shows one aspect of the attempted concealment in a rather interesting manner. Most of the other orders on this subject provided for an attempt to camouflage the massing of troops in the East as a deceptive measure for the invasion of England or as movements connected with the impending Balkan operations.

Important orders concerning the participation of other states, particularly Finland and Rumania were issued on March 13 and May 1.[7]) The

---

"150/41, Aufmarschanweisung Barbarossa," 15 February 1941, NOKW - 2670 (photostat, 16pp.); Germany, HGrK A (Sodenstern), "151/41 an OKH, Gen.St.d.H. Op.Abt.; Betreff: Barbarossa (Mitwirkung anderer Staaten)," 12 February 1941, NOKW - 2670 (photostat, 3pp.); Germany, OKH, Gen.St.d.H., Op.Abt., "15139/41 an Armeeoberkommando 16," 21 January 1941, NOKW - 2703 (photostat, 1p.); Germany, HGrK C, Ia, "30/41, Operationsstudie im Rahmen einer Heeresgruppe," 23 January 1941, NOKW - 2703 (photostat, 16pp.); Germany, Pz.Gr. 3, Ia, "25/41, Aufmarschanweisung Barbarossa," 12 March 1941, NOKW - 2756 (photostat, 13pp.); Germany, HGrK A, "Kriegstagebuch der Heeresgruppe Süd, 1. Teil, Abt. Ia," 2 February 1941, NOKW - 3432 (photostat, 1p.); a number of additional documents have been included in the bibliography.

[4]) Germany, OKW, Wi Rü Amt (Reute), "Besprechung am 9. Januar 1941, Arbeitseinsatz und Einziehungen in der nicht zum engeren Rüstungsbereich gehörender Wirtschaft," PS - 1456 (photostat, 49pp.), p. 48; cf. I.G. Farben, Vorstand, "Niederschrift ueber die 24. Vorstandssitzung am 5. Februar 1941," NI - 8078 (mimeo, 9pp.), p. 2.

[5]) Germany, OKW, WFSt, "Besprechung über 'Fall Barbarossa' und Sonnenblume," 3 February 1941, PS - 872, *TMWC*, XXVI, 392-99; Testimony of Brauchitsch, *TMWC*, XX, 578, *PHKV*, XX, 630; Testimony of Halder, U.S. v. Weizsäcker, G.T. 20531, 20533-34; Halder (3 February 1941), V, 103; cf. Greiner, pp. 340-45.

[6]) Testimony of Warlimont, U.S. v. Leeb, G.T. 6379-80; OKW, WFSt, L, "Richtlinien für die Feindtäuschung," 15 February 1941 PS - 875 (photostat, 5pp.); Germany OKW, WFSt (Keitel), "400/41 an Reichsminister Todt," draft 9 March, sent 12 March 1941, PS - 874 (also PS - 1747, NOKW - 243) (photostat, 2pp.); Germany, OKW, WFSt, L (Keitel), "44699/41; Betrifft Feindtäuschung," 12 May 1941, PS - 876 (photostat, 2pp.); Sk1, A, 18, 231-32: 18 February 1941, C - 33, *TMWC*, XXXIV, 217-18; Germany, OKW, WFSt, L, "Zeitplan Barbarossa," 1 June 1941, C - 39, *TMWC*, XXXIV, 231; Germany, AOK 17, Ic, "266/41 an die Heeresgruppe Süd; Betreff: Schutzmassnahmen gegenüber der Bevölkerung," 29 May 1941, NOKW - 136 (photostat, 1p.); Halder (8 April 1941), VI, 59, (18 April 1941) 76, (3 May 1941) 96, (5 May 1941) 98, (16 May 1941) 131.

[7]) OKW, WFSt, L (Keitel), "Richtlinien auf Sondergebieten zur Weisung 21," 13

implications for German-Soviet relations of the German decision to have these countries participate in the attack on Russia have already been examined (Chapter VIII). The various implementing negotiations and conferences with these countries will, therefore, not be reviewed, though they form an interesting chapter in German diplomacy.[8])

There were also extensive preparations in the economic field.[9]) Most of this work consisted of preparations for the economic exploitation of the Soviet territories to be occupied. There was, however, another economic problem which attracted considerable attention—the results of losing

---

March 1941, PS - 477, *TMWC*, XXVI, 57; OKW, WFSt, L (Keitel), "44638/41, Beteiligung fremder Staaten an den Vorbereitungen für 'Barbarossa'," 1 May 1941, NOKW - 240 (photostat, 2pp.); cf. Halder (4 May 1941), VI, 97.

[8]) Most of the important evidence concerns Finland; the question of just how much the Finns knew of Germany's intentions at that time will not be answered here. It seems clear, however, that the Finnish military at least knew a good deal more than the two books by Wuorinen and Erfurth (cited at the end of this footnote) indicate. Germany, OKW, WFSt, L, "Besprechung bei Chef L am 30. 4. 1941," 1 May 1941, PS - 873, *TMWC*, XXVI, 400; Kitchmann, "Deposition of Colonel Kitchmann," USSR - 229, *TMWC*, VII, 328, *PHKV*, VII, 362-63; Testimony of Schnurre, U.S. v. Weizsäcker, G.T. 11167-68; Germany, HGrK C, "Operationsstudie im Rahmen einer Heeresgruppe," 23 January 1941, NOKW - 2703, p. 2; Germany, HGrK A, Ia, "151/41 an OKH, Gen.St. d.H., Op.Abt.; Betreff: Barbarossa (Mitwirkung anderer Staaten)," 12 February 1941; Ribbentrop to Blücher, 9 March 1941, NG - 1579 (mimeo, 1p.), trans. United States, OCCWC (cited in U.S. v. Weizsäcker, E.T. 819); Germany, OKW, Wi Rü Amt (Thomas), "Vortrag bei Reichsmarschall Göring am 19. 3. 41," 20 March 1941, PS - 1156 (photostat, 3pp.), pp. 2-3; Germany, OKW, WFSt, L (Warlimont), "Vortragsnotiz: Vorschlag für die Vorbereitung der Besprechungen über Beteiligung Finnlands am Unternehmen Barbarossa," 28 April 1941, NOKW - 241 (photostat, 2pp.); Germany, OKW, WFSt, L (Lossberg), "44638/41; Betreff: Finnenbesprechung," 22 May, 1941, PS - 883 (photostat, 3pp.); Rössing to Mellenthin, 22 May 1941, NG - 4310 (photostat, 1p.); Germany, OKH, Gen.St.d.H., Att.Abt. (Mellenthin), "93/41 an Chef Gen.St.d.H.," 24 May 1941, NG - 4310 (photostat, 2pp.); Germany, OKW, WFSt, L, "975/41 an Heimatsstab Nord, Oberst Buschenhagen," [24 May 1941], NG - 4310 (photostat, 1p.); Germany, OKH, Gen.St.d.H., Op.Abt. (Grolman), "Auszug aus Protokoll der Besprechung mit den Vertretern der finnischen Wehrmacht am 25. 5. 41 in Salzburg," NG - 4310 (photostat, 6pp.); Germany, OKW, WFSt, L, Heimatsstab Nord (Buschenhagen), "Buschenhagen to Jodl," 4 June 1941, NG - 4310 (photostat, 2pp.); Germany, OKH, Fr.H.Ost. (Kinzel), "Protokoll über die Besprechungen in Finnland vom 3.-6. Juni 1941," 10 June 1941, NOKW - 1181 (photostat, 4pp.); Testimony of Warlimont, U.S. v. Leeb, G.T. 6385; Skl, C VII/41, 12: 4 February 1941, cited in C - 170, *TMWC*, XXXIV, 698; Skl, A, 18, 231: 18 February 1941, C - 33, *TMWC*, XXXIV, 217 and 699; Skl, A, 18, 340-41: 25 February 1941, C - 33 (photostat, 394pp.); Fuehrer Conferences, 1941, I, 53-54, 65; Skl, A, 22, 48: 5 June 1941, C - 37 (photostat, 411pp.); Halder (16 December 1940), V, 71; (17 December 1940) 72, (30 January 1941) 101, (14 February 1941) 115-16, (30 April 1941) VI, 90-92, (14 May 1941) 115, (26 May 1941) 133; Wuorinen, pp. 93-99; Erfurth, pp. 25-37. Most of the important evidence involving Rumania has been cited already; that concerning Hungary dates to the last days before the attack.

[9]) For a list of references from *TMWC*, see Weinberg, Appendix III, B, pp. 59-60; there are vast amounts of additional material, mostly unpublished, some of which is included in the bibliography.

the transit route across Siberia. This was particularly important in regard to obtaining rubber from the Far East. The loss of this route was one of the reasons why General Thomas opposed the war on Russia. Hitler's answer to such objections, as repeated by Göring and Keitel, is illuminating; they reported that Hitler would not be influenced in his planning by such economic difficulties.[10]) The rubber problem was taken up with Matsuoka when he came to Berlin and will be referred to again when his visit is discussed; it also played an important role in the economic relations between Germany and Russia in the last months before the attack.

During the months of January and February, 1941, the Germans were laying the groundwork for the attack on Greece and the preceding occupation of Bulgaria. In Bulgaria there were still divergent currents of opinion which the government had to consider. There was the fear that the Soviet Union might attempt an attack on Bulgaria's Black Sea Coast. There was concern lest Turkey would step in to fight against further German advances in the Balkans. These problems made the Bulgarian government cautious in its collaboration with the Germans. At all times it insisted that overt steps, such as the entry of German troops or adhesion to the Tripartite Pact, be taken only when adequate German military protection for Bulgaria was assured. This insistence, which revealed the fear of Russian intervention in particular, led to long and complicated negotiations with the German military and diplomatic authorities. The Bulgarian wishes were observed to a considerable extent as they did not interfere substantially with the German plans.[11])

[10]) Germany, OKW, Wi Rü Amt (Thomas), "Aktennotiz, Besprechung beim General Feldmarschall Keitel am 8. 2. 41," PS - 1456 (photostat, 2pp.), p. 2; Germany, OKW, Wi Rü Amt, "Aktennotiz über Rücksprache Amtschef mit Staatssekretär Landfried; Betreff: Kautschuklage," 12 February 1941, PS - 1456 (photostat, 2pp.), p. 1; on this subject see also Germany, OKW, Wi Rü Amt, "Besprechung Reichsbeauftragter für Kautschuk, Herr Jehle, beim Amtschef mit Obstlt. Tietze," 7 February 1941, PS - 1456 (photostat, 5pp.), p. 2; Germany, OKW, Wi Rü Amt, Thomas, "Aktennotiz über Vortrag beim Reichsmarschall am 26. 2. 41," 27 February 1941, PS - 1456 (photostat, 3pp.), p. 1; Testimony of Huenermann, U.S. v. Weizsäcker, G.T. 23366-67; *TMWC*, XXX, 276.

[11]) The following is a selection of the more important documents: Germany, OKH, Gen.St.d.H., Op.Abt. (Halder), "722/40 an Att.Abt.," 14 December 1940, NOKW - 3347 (photostat, 1p.); Memorandum of Ritter, 2 January 1941, NG - 3144 (photostat, 2pp.); Germany, OKW, Ag.Ausl., "10/41 an Herrn Ritter," 11 January 1941, NG - 3144 (photostat, 1p.); Weizsäcker to Richthofen, 5 January 1941, NG - 3144 (photostat, 2pp.); Ritter to Richthofen, 15 January 1941, NG - 3144 (photostat, 7pp.) (see also NOKW - 2625); Antonescu to Ribbentrop, 15 January 1941, NG - 3764 (mimeo, 12pp.); trans. United States, OCCWC; Weizsäcker to Ribbentrop, 15 January 1941, NG - 5286 (photostat, 2pp.); Memorandum of Ritter, 15 January 1941, NG - 5541 (mimeo, 3pp.), trans. United States, OCCWC; Ritter to Killinger, 16 January 1941, NG - 3765 (mimeo, 1p.), trans. United States, OCCWC; Ritter to Ribbentrop, 23 January 1941, NG - 5530 (mimeo, 1p.), trans. United States, OCCWC; Weizsäcker to Ritter, 24 January 1941,

This time, the Russians reacted swiftly though without success. Early in January the Germans became aware of increased Russian diplomatic activity in Bulgaria.[12]) The attitude of Russia in the event of a German occupation of Bulgaria was not clear to Hitler.[13]) He was to find out quickly. The Russians had not, in spite of suggestions of Schulenburg to this effect, been informed accurately by the Germans of the size and purpose of their troop movements into Rumania which seem to have become particularly heavy in the first part of January.[14]) Left in the dark, the Russians proceeded to scout the situation on their own. All the Russian diplomatic representatives in Southeast Europe were summoned to Moscow.[15]) On January 12 a Tass communiqué reported that there were rumors that German troops were in Bulgaria with the knowledge and consent of the Soviet Union. The communiqué denied in sharp and unqualified terms that Russia had been consulted by Germany or Bulgaria.[16]) The Bulgarians were disturbed by this communiqué[17]) and promptly denied the presence of German troops.[18]) The Russians had probably expected an answer from Germany through diplomatic channels; when none came, they again took the initiative. On January 17 Dekanozov in Berlin and Molotov in Moscow simultaneously presented the Germans with a memorandum concerning the apparently imminent occupation of Bulgaria by German troops.[19]) Referring to reports that the German army was to occupy Bulgaria, Greece, and the Straits, the memorandum stated that Russia "will consider the appearance of any

---

NG - 3144 (photostat, 1p.); Memorandum of Ritter, 27 January 1941, NG - 5239 (mimeo, 3pp.), trans. United States, OCCWC; Germany, OKW, WFSt, L (Warlimont), "44150/41 (to Pol I M 351)," 11 February 1941, NG - 5236 (mimeo, 3pp.), trans. United States, OCCWC; Germany, OKW, WFSt, L, "44150/41," 14 February 1941, NG - 5255 (mimeo, 1p.), trans. United States, OCCWC; Richthofen to Ribbentrop, 15 February 1941, NG - 3874 (mimeo, 2pp.); Richthofen and Bruckman, to OKH, Att. Abt., 17 February 1941, NG - 5539 (mimeo, 1p.); cf. Conference of German and Bulgarian Generals, 8 February 1941, PS - 1746, *TMWC*, XXVIII, 16-21.

[12]) Sk1, A, 17, 68: 6 January 1940, cited in C - 170, *TMWC*, XXXIV, 696.

[13]) Sk1, C VII/41, 6: 8 January 1941, cited *ibid.*; Fuehrer Conferences, 1941, I, 4.

[14]) Ribbentrop to Schulenburg, 7 January 1941, *NSR*, pp. 264-65, *BDS*, pp. 296-97; Schulenburg to Ribbentrop, 8 January 1941, *NSR*, p. 266, *BDS*, pp. 298-99; Ritter to Weizsäcker, 7 January 1941, NG - 5531 (mimeo, 1p.), Staff Evidence Analysis, United States, OCCWC; Marginal note by Weizsäcker, 10 January 1941, to Schulenburg to Ribbentrop, 8 January 1941, *BDS*, p. 299, n. 2; Ribbentrop to Schulenburg, 10 January 1941, *NSR*, p. 267, *BDS*, p. 288.

[15]) Simoni (7 January 1941), p. 237; cf. Memorandum of Weizsäcker, 10 January 1941, NG - 3999 (photostat, 1p.).

[16]) Text in Gafencu, pp. 174-75.

[17]) Skl, A, 17, 149: 12 Jan. 1941, cited in C - 170, *TMWC*, XXXIV, 697.

[18]) Gafencu, p. 178.

[19]) Weizsäcker to Ribbentrop, 17 January 1941, *NSR*, pp. 268-69, *BDS*, p. 301; Schulenburg to Ribbentrop, 17 January 1941, *NSR*, pp. 270-71, *BDS*, pp. 302-03.

foreign armed forces in the territory of Bulgaria and of the Straits as a violation of the security interests of the U.S.S.R."

The German answer to this memorandum was given to Dekanozov on January 22 and Molotov on January 23.[20]) The reply definitely stated that German troops would march through Bulgaria if and when this seemed to Germany to be necessary to prevent the English from gaining a foothold in Greece. What the Russian reaction to this was—aside from general displeasure—is not absolutely clear; but apparently attempts were made to influence the Bulgarians against a final commitment to Germany.[21]) The Bulgarians had, however, already decided, and had, as we have seen, received adequate assurances of protection from Germany.

On February 27, 1941, Schulenburg was instructed to tell Molotov on February 28 of Bulgaria's adhesion to the Tripartite Pact, and on March 1 of the advance of German troops into that country.[22]) The Germans had been, and for some time continued to be, worried about the Russian reaction to their move through Bulgaria on Greece. They were, as has been seen, making arrangements to defend Bulgaria in case of landing attempts. The defenses of Rumania, particularly of the port of Constanza, were strengthened. A Soviet blow at Finland in retaliation for the German occupation of Bulgaria was thought possible. Clearly, the Russian reaction was awaited with interest and some anxiety.[23])

There was a Russian reaction, but of a purely non-violent kind. Molotov protested in very determined language.[24]) On March 4 the Russian Press published the note handed to the Bulgarian Minister on the

[20]) Ribbentrop to Weizsäcker, 21 January 1941, *NSR*, pp. 271-72, *BDS*, pp. 304-06; Memorandum of Weizsäcker, 22 January 1941, *NSR*, p. 273, *BDS*, pp. 306-07; Ribbentrop to Schulenburg, 22 January 1941, cited in *NSR*, p. 272, n. 11, *BDS*, p. 306, n. 4; Schulenburg to Ribbentrop, 23 January 1941, *NSR*, p. 274, *BDS*, p. 307.

[21]) See Skl, A, 18, 132: 11 Feb. 1941, C - 33, cited in C - 170, *TMWC*, XXXIV, 699.

[22]) Ribbentrop to Schulenburg, 27 February 941, *NSR*, pp. 276-77, *BDS*, pp. 310-11; cf. Memorandum of Weizsäcker, 1 March 1941, NG - 3874 (mimeo, 1p.). For an interesting sidelight on Germany's discussion of British troops in Greese in these documents compare Weizsäcker to Schulenburg, 22 February 1941, *NSR*, pp. 275-76, *BDS*, p. 309, with Richthofen and Benzler to Ritter, 12 March 1941, NG - 3874 (mimeo, 11p.) and Greiner, p. 261.

[23]) Important evidence will be found in the following: Ritter to Schulenburg, 21 February 1941, *NSR*, pp. 274-75, *BDS*, p. 308; Germany, OKW, WFSt, L, "44150/41," 14 February 1941, NG - 5255, p. 1; Richthofen to Ribbentrop, 15 February 1941, NG - 3874, p. 2; Skl, A, 17, 232: 18 January 1941, cited in C - 170, *TMWC*, XXXIV, 697; Skl, A, 17, 324: 24 January 1941, cited *ibid.*, p. 698; Skl, A, 18, 3-4: 1 February 1941, 37: 4 February 1941, 134-6: 11 February 1941, 383-84: 28 February 1941, C - 33; Skl, A, 19, 39: 3 March 1941, cited in C - 170, *TMWC*, XXXIV, 700; Halder (7 January 1941), V, 87, (18 January 1941) 88, (25 January 1941) 94, (1 February 1941) 102, (22 March 1941) VI, 33.

[24]) Schulenburg to Ribbentrop, 28 February 1941, *NSR*, pp. 277-78, *BDS*, pp. 311-12, and 1 March 1941, *NSR*, pp. 278-79, *BDS*, pp. 312-13

previous day. This note severely criticized the Bulgarian government for its actions and stated that Bulgaria could expect no further support from the Soviet Union.[25]) Russian policy continued to be marked by great caution, however. No overt steps were taken for several weeks. On March 25 the newly stiffened Soviet attitude came into the open though in a rather indirect manner. The Soviets published an understanding with Turkey to the effect that each would remain neutral should the other be attacked by a third power. This could strengthen Turkey vis-à-vis Germany—it had been the demand of the Russians that Germany be excluded from the application of such an agreement that had contributed largely to the failure of Saracoglu's mission to Moscow in September-October, 1939.[26])

At the time that the Russians were engaging in these somewhat obscure moves to discourage German expansion, while still leaving all possibilities open, Britain was making a determined effort to capitalize on her own successes in North Africa and the Greek successes in Albania by building up an anti-German front in the Balkans.[27]) To a limited extent the United States supported these moves.[28]) It was this combination of circumstances that formed the diplomatic background of the Yugoslav coup of March 27, 1941, in which the Cvetkovic government was overthrown by a military group, supported by mass demonstrations, because of its adhesion to the Tripartite Pact.[29])

The coup of March 27 was probably welcomed in Moscow, but there is no evidence of either Yugoslav Communist influence internally or Soviet Russian influence externally on the coup itself. The scantiness of the material on the Russian steps and plans in the crucial days from March 27 to April 6 resembles the similarly fragmentary evidence concerning Russo-Polish relations around September 1, 1939, in that it allows of a variety of interpretations but adequately supports none.[30]) Until some evidence clarifying the issues becomes available, no more can be said with confidence than that the Russians continued their pol-

---

[25]) Text in Gafencu, pp. 185; see German comment in Skl, A, 19, 53ff.: 4 March 1941, cited in C - 170, *TMWC*, XXXIV, 700.

[26]) Text in Gafencu, pp. 189-90; cf Skl, C VIII/41, 128: 25 March 1941, cited in C - 170, *TMWC*, XXXIV, 701; Papen to Ribbentrop, 1 April 1941, NG - 5738 (mimeo, 1p.).

[27]) See Churchill, *The Second World War*, Vol. III, *The Grand Alliance* (Boston: 1950), pp. 10, 17-19, 29-30, 33-35, 64-77, 94-98, 110, 161, 167-69.

[28]) *Ibid.*, p. 58; Hull, II, 928-34.

[29]) The purely domestic issues involved cannot be examined here.

[30]) What evidence there is, has been made difficult to evaluate properly because of the distortions produced by two other factors: the divergent views of various Yugoslav groups and the Tito-Stalin split. For evidence and discussion of it, see Gafencu, pp. 194-203; Churchill, III, 160-75; Hull, II, 929-34; Hamilton Fish Armstrong, *Tito and Goliath* (New York: 1951), pp. 8-17; Frans Borkenau, *European Communism* (New York, 1953), Chapter XIII; Dallin, pp. 303-05; Beloff, II, 366-67; Hagen, pp. 215-28, 246.

icy of cautious diplomatic activity to hinder the German advance in the Balkans. The Russo-Yugoslav friendship treaty of April 5 was a clearer gesture than the communiqués about Bulgaria and Turkey, but it was still only a gesture.[31]

The Yugoslav coup had some very significant effects on German plans. On March 21 an important conference of the leading generals had been summoned for March 27 to discuss details of the attack on Russia.[32] This conference thus provided a good opportunity for consideration of the changes needed as a result of the events of that day. On hearing of the coup, Hitler decided to attack Yugoslavia as soon as possible, and this decision necessitated various changes in the preparation of the attack on Russia. Of these the one ultimately most important was that of postponing the invasion of Russia for five weeks to June 22.[33] This postponement had very significant effects on the German campaign in the Soviet Union but meant no relaxation of the determination to begin that campaign.

In the early days of the attack on Yugoslavia, there was some concern, as there had been at the time of the occupation of Bulgaria, that the Soviets would intervene, but nothing of the kind happened.[34] At

---

[31]) Schulenburg to Ribbentrop, 4 April 1941, *NSR*, pp. 316-18, *BDS*, pp. 354-56; Ribbentrop to Schulenburg, 6 April 1941, *NSR*, p. 320, *BDS*, pp. 357-58; Schulenburg to Ribbentrop, 6 April 1941, *NSR*, p. 320, *BDS*, p. 357; cf. Hitler-Schulenburg Conversation 28 April 1941, *NSR*, pp. 330-31, *BDS*, pp. 370-72.

[32]) Germany, OKH, Gen.St.d.H., Op.Abt. (Halder), "479/41; Betreff: Besprechung beim OKH," 21 March 1941, NOKW - 2670 (photostat, 2pp.), p. 1.

[33]) Germany, HGrK A, "Kriegstagebuch der Heeresgruppe Süd, Abt. Ia," 27 March 1941, p. 31, 2 April 1941, pp. 39-40, NOKW - 2670 (photostat, 4 pp.); Germany, AOK 12, "227/41; Armeebefehl Nr. 4," 2 April 1941, NOKW - 3432, pp. 1, 9; Testimony of Jodl, *TMWC*, XV, 394, *PHKV*, XV, 432; Germany, OKW, WFSt, L, "Besprechung über Lage Jugoslawien," 27 March 1941, PS - 1746, *TMWC*, XXVIII, 21-25; Testimony of Halder, U.S. v. Weizsäcker, G.T. 20532; Testimony of Halder, U.S. v. Leeb, G.I. 1895; Testimony of Paulus, *TMWC*, VII, 255, *PHKV*, VII, 284; Skl, A, 20, 27ff.: 3 April 1941, in C 170, *TMWC*, XXXIV, 701-02; Skl, A, 19, 389: 27 March 1941, NOKW - 2556 (photostat, 2pp.), p. 2; Halder (27 March 1941), VI, 37-38. For a discussion of the thesis that Hitler decided to attack Russia because of the coup and the Yugoslav-Russian treaty, see below, p. 155.

[34]) Germany, OKH, Gen.St.d.H., Op.Abt., "Aufmarschanweisung für 'Unternehmen 25' sowie ergänzende Weisung für 'Marita'," 30 March 1941, R - 95, *TMWC*, XXXVIII, 253-54; Germany, Oberste Befehlshaber der Wehrmacht, OKW, WFSt, L (Hitler), "Weisung Nr. 26; Zusammenarbeit mit den Verbündeten auf dem Balkan," 3 April 1941, C - 24 (photostat, 5pp.), pp. 1-2; Halder (6 April 1941), VI, 55, (7 April 1941) 57-58, (10 Apr. 1941) 63; see also NOKW - 2691, Staff Evidence Analysis, United States, OCCWC. The fear of Russia may have had more to do with the reluctance of Hungarian intervention (bought with various territorial promises) than Prime Minister Teleki's suicide over the recently signed, German-approved treaty of friendship between Hungary and Yugoslavia. Weizsäcker to Ribbentrop, 4 April 1941, NG - 2693 (mimeo, 3pp.); Erdmannsdorff to Ribbentrop, 6 April 1941, NG - 2693 (mimeo, 2 pp.), p. 1; Erdmannsdorff to Ribbentrop, 9 April 1941, NG - 2732 (mimeo, 2 pp.), trans. United States, OCCWC; Germany, OKW, Ag. Ausl., Ausl. III (Bürkner), "124/41 an Ritter," 10 April 1941, NG - 2730 (mimeo, 1p.); cf. Ribbentrop to Erdmannsdorff, 9 December 1940,

this time, the British government, citing intelligence reports of German troop movements, warned the Soviet Union of the impending German attack.[35]) The United States had received detailed reports on the German plans. At the direction of President Roosevelt, Undersecretary of State Sumner Welles had relayed the substance of this information to the Soviet Ambassador in Washington in February and March, 1941.[36]) The Soviet reaction to this information and to the events following April 6 will be one of the main subjects of the next chapter. It might be said that up to this point the Russian policy had been one of very cautious opposition to German moves for about four months. The Russians had been careful, however, not to commit themselves strongly to anyone. They were obviously not pleased by the German advance in the Balkans, but they were unwilling or unprepared to provide actual support to the forces resisting German expansion or to capitalize on the involvement of German troops by attacking on their own initiative.

It was on the day of the Yugoslav coup that Japanese Foreign Minister Yosuke Matsuoka arrived in Berlin for the first of a series of conversations.[37] A large part of the talks concerned the efforts of the Germans to induce Japan to attack Great Britain. In regard to Russia, the Germans made clear to Matsuoka that their relations with that country had deteriorated, but they did not tell him in so many words that they planned to attack. The question of what Matsuoka's impression on this point was, is complicated by the fact that he must have been impressed by the repeated references to rubber shipments to Germany by sea instead of the Transsiberian Railway, and by the attempts of the opposition in Germany to warn him and his entourage of coming events.[38])

NG - 2712 (mimeo, 1p.), trans. United States, OCCWC; Weizsäcker to Fabricius, 11 December 1940, NG - 2658 (mimeo, 2pp.).

[35]) Churchill, III, 356-61; cf. T. Bor-Komorowski, *The Secret Army* (New York, 1951), pp. 57-58, 62-63.

[36]) Hull, II, 967-69; Sumner Welles, *The Time for Decision* (New York, 1944), pp. 169-71. Later in 1941, the Soviets received warnings of Germany's intentions through their intelligence networks in Switzerland (Alexander Foote, *Handbook for Spies* [New York, 1949], pp. 95, 113-15) and Japan (the evidence on this is somewhat confusing, see U.S. Congress, Senate, *Institute of Pacific Relations,* Hearings before the Subcommittee to Investigate the Administration of the Internal Security Act and other Internal Security Legislation of the Committee on the Judiciary, U.S. Senate, 82d Cong., 1st Sess. [Washington, 1951], pp. 380, 508; U.S. Congress, House of Representatives, *Hearings on American Aspects of the Richard Sorge Spy Case,* Hearings before the Committee on Un-American Activities, House of Representatives, 82d Cong., 1st Sess. [Washington, 1951], pp. 1138, 1197; Charles A. Willoughby, *Shanghai Conspiracy* [New York, 1952], p. 105).

[37]) The German records of the talks are in *NSR*, pp. 281-316, *BDS,* pp. 316-354; cf. Schmidt, pp. 526-37, and see also the excellent account in Feis, pp. 180-87.

[38]) For the rubber problem, see Germany, OKW, Wi Rü Amt, "Besprechung Reichsbeauftragter für Kautschuk, Herr Jehle, beim Amtschef mit Obstlt. Tietze" 7 February 1941, PS - 1456, p. 2; Germany, Wi Rü Amt (Thomas), "Aktennotiz über Vortrag beim Reichsmarschall am 26. 2. 41," 27 February 1941, PS - 1456, p. 1; Göring-Matsuoka

The hints which Ribbentrop and Hitler gave him do not sound as clear in the memoranda of the conversations as in the memoirs of the interpreter, Paul Otto Schmidt. The following summary by one of the department chiefs of the High Command of the Armed Forces, Admiral Bürkner, probably presents the issue in the clearest manner possible:

> Matsuoka was obviously especially interested in finding out how the attitude of the Soviet Union was judged by Germany. On this judgement (Beurteilung) he was given two alternatives:
> a) If the Soviet Union behaved properly, then there was really no problem at all;[39]) but if, on the other hand
> b) it behaved badly, one would have to incapacitate her.
> Matsuoka is not supposed to have revealed by his manner whether he fully comprehends the hint contained in b). Those who know him personally, especially the German Ambassador to Tokyo, Ott, consider Matsuoka too clever to doubt [that he did].[40])

While Matsuoka was in Moscow on his return trip to Japan, the Germans struck at Yugoslavia and Greece. The air attack on Belgrade which opened the attack on Yugoslavia took place a few hours after the signing of the Soviet-Yugoslav treaty. In instructing the German minister to get out of town and to warn the legations of countries friendly to Germany to do the same on April 3, Ribbentrop had omitted Soviet Russia from the list.[41]) The German advance was very rapid and it was soon clear that another German victory was imminent. These facts form the background of the new Russian policy to be discussed in the next chapter.

Conference, 29 March 1941, PS - 1879 (photostat, 9p.), pp. 5-7 (cited in Feis, p. 189, n. 5; Ribbentrop to A.A., 27 February 1941, NG - 4449 (mimeo, 8pp.), trans. United States, OCCWC, pp. 7-8 (note: this is the full account of the Ribbentrop-Oshima conference of 23 February 1941; the passage cited is omitted from the excerpts sent out to the German missions abroad on March 2, 1941 [Ribbentrop to German Missions, 2 March 1941, PS - 1834, *TMWC*, XXVIII, 552-64]; for discussion of the rubber problem with Matsuoka, see *NSR*, pp. 286, 307, *BDS*, pp. 321, 344.

Weizsäcker and Raeder had urged that Matsuoka be informed of the coming attack. Memorandum of Weizsäcker, 24 March 1941, NG - 3825 (mimeo, 2pp.); Skl, C VII/41, 53: 18 March 1941, C - 170, *TMWC*, XXXIV, 700. For the German order not to inform the Japanese see Germany, OKW, WFSt, L (Keitel), "Weisung Nr. 24 über Zusammenarbeit mit Japan," 5 March 1941, C - 75, *TMWC*, XXXIV, 305. For attempts of the opposition to "tip off" Matsuoka see Testimony of Kordt, U.S. v. Weizsäcker, E.T. 7425, 7898-99, 10176; Weizsäcker, pp. 310-11. The efforts of Erich Kordt with one of the officials accompanying Matsuoka (Kordt, *Nicht aus den Akten*, p. 411) seem to have had some effect (Feis, p. 187).

[39]) "Wenn die Sowjetunion sich gut verhielte, dann sei ja eigentlich alles in Ordnung;"

[40]) Germany, OKW, Ag. Ausl., Ausl. III (Bürkner), "Kurze Zusammenfassung von Ausgaben über den Besuch des japanischen Aussenministers Matsuoka nach Mitteilungen des Auswärtigen Amtes und anderen Stellen," 10 April 1941, PS - 1537 (photostat, 2pp.).

[41]) Ribbentrop to Heeren, 2 April 1941, NG - 4266 (photostat, 2pp.), p. 2.

SUPPLEMENTARY NOTE

The Yugoslav Coup, the Soviet-Yugoslav Treaty,
and the German Attack on the Soviet Union

A few hours before the German air attack on Belgrade opened the German war against Yugoslavia, the Soviet Union signed a Treaty of Friendship with the Simovic government—a government which had come to power through a coup d'état against Yugoslav adhesion to the Tripartite Pact.[42]) This treaty has been referred to by some as the crucial factor in the German decision to attack the Soviet Union. It was cited prominently in the German note which served as the declaration of war on the Soviet Union.[43]) It was mentioned in the same manner at Nuremberg by Göring, Ribbentrop, and Jodl.[44])

This line of argument is not particularly convincing. Göring contradicted himself by pointing out that Germany took swift action against Yugoslavia for the very reason that the coup might produce results "which would be detrimental . . . in the conflict with Russia;"[45]) that is, the attack on Yugoslavia was necessary to safeguard the previously established plan to attack the Soviet Union. In his conference on Yugoslavia of March 27, 1941—a week before the Soviet-Yugoslav treaty—Hitler stated that the coup had come at a time fortunate for Germany since "the consequences would certainly have been considerably more serious for us if the overthrow of the [Cvetkovic] government had taken place during the Barbarossa operation."[46])

It should be clear from the foregoing that there is no substance to the myth that the events concerning Yugoslavia led Hitler to decide on an attack on the Soviet Union. The decision to attack the Soviet Union had been made many months before. The Yugoslav coup led to a postponement of the attack from May 15 to June 22. Therefore, if there had been any desire or inclination for a rapprochement with the Soviet Union, the coup, it should be noted, provided an additional five weeks for diplomatic action. As the next chapter will show, and as Gafencu has so clearly pointed out in his book, diplomatic action was just the thing Hitler did not want.

---

[42]) The Soviet government informed Germany of the forthcoming signing on the evening of April 4 (Schulenburg to Ribbentrop, 4 April 1941, *NSR*, pp. 316-18; *BDS*, pp. 354-56). The treaty was signed in the night of April 5-6; the Germans attacked Yugoslavia on the morning of April 6.

[43]) Ribbentrop to Schulenburg, 21 June 1941, Parts II, V, *NSR*, pp. 347-48; *BDS*, pp. 390-91.

[44]) Testimony of Göring, *TMWC*, IX, 334, 605, *PHKV*, IX, 374, 668; Testimony of Ribbentrop, *TMWC*, X, 293-94, *PHKV*, X, 332-33; Testimony of Jodl, *TMWC*, XV, 294, *PHKV*, XV, ...

[45]) Testimony of Göring, *TMWC*, IX, 335, *PHKV*, IX, 375.

[46]) OKW, WFSt, "Besprechung über Lage Jugoslawien," 27 March 1941, PS - 1746, *TMWC*, XXVIII, 22.

CHAPTER ELEVEN

FROM THE RUSSO—JAPANESE PACT TO THE GERMAN ATTACK ON RUSSIA

Matsuoka arrived in Moscow on April 7, 1941 — the day after the German attack on Greece and Yugoslavia. He had discussed the possibility of a non-aggression or neutrality pact on his way through Moscow to Berlin. The hints of German-Russian difficulties may have inclined him more to concessions. In any case, Japanese expansion at that time was primarily southwards, and an agreement with Russia would free her rear and might induce Chiang Kai-chek to negotiate. At the same time the Soviets were being warned of an impending German attack and, with their relations with Germany obviously somewhat strained, may also have welcomed the removal of a Japanese threat to their rear. Furthermore, the Soviets were probably influenced by two other considerations. In the first place, while the Tripartite Pact was supposed not to affect the relations of its signatories with the Soviet Union, there was no knowing what secret clauses had been agreed to; perhaps this treaty could be countered by a pact directly with Japan. In the second place, the Russians may have felt that Japan, her rear secured by agreement with Russia, would more readily turn southwards and, by destroying the existing order in Southeast Asia, would unleash forces on which the Soviets could later capitalize. After several days of negotiations, agreement was finally reached on a number of side issues, and a neutrality pact was signed between Russia and Japan on April 13, 1941.[1]

On the same day that the Soviet-Japanese Pact was signed and Matsuoka left Moscow for Tokyo, Schulenburg went to Berlin for consultations. Before this trip of Schulenburg and the policy of Germany at that time are reviewed, it is important to record and analyze a shift in Soviet

---

[1] For Matsuoka's second visit to Moscow see Feis, pp. 184-87; Joseph C. Grew, *Ten Years in Japan* (New York, 1944), pp. 381-83; Churchill, III, 191-92; Gafencu, pp. 206-14; Ott to Ribbentrop, 6 May 1941, NG - 4422 (c) (mimeo, 2pp.), trans. United States, OCCWC; Schulenburg to Ribbentrop, 9 April 1941, *NSR*, p. 321, *BDS*, pp. 359-60; Schulenburg to Ribbentrop, 9 April 1941, *NSR*, pp. 321-22, *BDS*, pp. 360-61; Schulenburg to Ribbentrop, 13 April 1941, *NSR*, pp. 322-23 and 323-24, *BDS*, pp. 361-62 and 363; Welles to Grew, 29 March 1941, United States, Department of State, *Foreign Relations of the United States; Japan, 1931-1941* (Washington, 1943), II, 183-84; Steinhardt to Hull, 11 April 1941, *ibid.*, pp. 184-85.

policy which seems to date from the period of Matsuoka's second visit to Moscow.

Up to the Soviet-Yugoslav Treaty of Friendship of April 5, the Russian attitude toward Germany had been stiffening, as has been shown. Each step of the Germans in the Balkans had provoked a more sullen Russian response. The Russians had never taken any overt action, but they had certainly made their disapproval clear. Around April 10 there was a distinct shift in Soviet policy which became progressively more pronounced during the following two months and was maintained right up to the outbreak of the war. This shift in policy can be understood best in terms of two developments. First, the danger of war with Germany, and second, the German successes in the Balkans which indicated to some extent what such a war might be like.

The warnings reaching the Soviet Union from abroad have been mentioned in Chapter X. The Soviets may also have recognized the fact and the meaning of the German eagerness to get and keep all Russian commissions out of the eastern part of the European territories occupied by Germany.[2] There were constant rumors of an impending German attack in connection with the German troop movements to the East.[3] On March 21 and again on April 9 the Russian Air Attaché in Berlin tried to sound out one of the German officials concerned with economic relations with Russia about a coming German attack.[4]

Added to these facts were the German successes in the Balkans. The German advance was very rapid; on April 13, the day of the signing of the Soviet-Japanese Pact, the Germans entered Belgrade. The element of fear on the part of the Russians was no doubt of considerable im-

---

[2] Memorandum of Ritter, 13 March 1941, *NSR*, p. 279, *BDS*, pp. 313-14 and note of Woermann to it, 15 March 1941, *BDS*, p. 314, n. 1; Twardowski to German Missions in Riga and Kaunas, 8 March 1941, NG - 5143 (mimeo, 1p.); cf. reference to notes of March 6 and 7, in Tippelskirch to Ribbentrop, 15 April 1941, *NSR*, p. 326, *BDS*, p. 365.

[3] Schmieden to Ribbentrop, 3 April 1941, NG - 3831 (mimeo, 1p.), trans. United States, OCCWC; Woermann to Schulenburg, 16 April 1941 (this is the Pol V, 1495g of April 16 cited but not printed in *NSR*, p. 334, n. 16), NG - 3831 (mimeo, 1p.), trans. United States, OCCWC; Testimony of Woermann, U.S. v. Weizsäcker, G.T. 11302-05; Baumbach to OKM, 24 April 1941, *NSR*, p. 330, *BDS*, pp. 369-70; Schulenburg to Ribbentrop, 2 May 1941, *NSR*, p. 334, *BDS*, p. 374; Kramarz to Schulenburg, 4 May 1941, *NSR*, pp. 334-35, *BDS*, p. 375; Note by Kramarz, 7 May 1941, NG - 4289 (mimeo, 1p.), Staff Evidence Analysis, United States, OCCWC; Kramarz to German Missions, 7 May 1941, NG - 3544 (mimeo, 2 pp.), p. 1; Testimony of Ritter, U.S. v. Weizsäcker, G.T. 11938.

[4] Germany, [NSDAP, APA?], "Aktennotiz, 10 Apr. 1941 [Besprechung Immisch-Skorniakoff, 21 März 1941]," PS - 1023 (photostat, 3pp.); Germany [NSDAP, APA?], "Aktennotiz, 10 Apr. 1941 [Besprechung Immisch-Skorniakoff, 9 April 1941]," PS - 1023 (photostat, 2pp.); both documents are from Rosenberg's files.

port.[5]) The speed of the German military advance and the subsequent freedom of the German troops must have weighed heavily with the Soviet rulers. These factors tended to become stronger as time passed; the Germans could regroup their forces, and the good campaign weather in the East was approaching. The speed of developments in the Balkans during the days while Matsuoka was in Moscow may well have contributed to the Russian decision to sign with Japan in the last few hours before the Japanese Foreign Minister left. As the Soviets became more worried about the danger of embroilment in a war which was obviously going to last a long time, they made an effort to avoid a German attack by withdrawing from the policy of unfriendly criticism of German policy and entering on the road of appeasement.[6])

The policy of appeasement—with appeasement defined as one-sided concession by one country designed to induce the other to desist from hostile action—began at the time of the Matsuoka visit. It first became clear in the economic field. In January and February, 1941, Russian deliveries had been very low; they had risen substantially in March.[7]) At the beginning of April important economic negotiations were conducted in Berlin by Schnurre and Krutikov, First Deputy Commissar for Foreign Trade. In these negotiations Krutikov was very conciliatory, and a large number of complicated issues left over from the economic negotiations leading up to the treaty of January 10, 1941, were settled to the satisfaction of the Germans. An oil delivery contract was signed on April 12, and the Russians promised to provide extra trains for deliveries of rubber from the Far East.[8]) All these agreements were adhered to scrupulously by the Russians who delivered large quantities of extremely valuable supplies to Germany right up into the last hours before the German attack. All the vital rubber supplies, the importance of which has been repeatedly stressed, reached Germany, to a large extent by special trains. The German negotiators were convinced that the Russians were prepared to yield to even greater economic demands if these were raised.[9])

---

[5]) See Skl, A, 20, 99: 8 Apr. 1941, cited in C - 170, *TMWC*, XXXIV, 702.

[6]) The Russian policy of April, May, and June, 1941, provides some very interesting material for a discussion of the appeasement policy of England and France and its denunciation by the Soviets.

[7]) Memorandum of Schnurre, 5 April 1941, *NSR*, p. 318, *BDS*, pp. 356-57; cf. Germany, Statistisches Reichsamt, "Approved Imports of Goods in March 1941," 8 May 1941, NG - 927, p. 4. It is worthy of note that in March the goods reaching Germany by transit across Russia were valued at about 25 mil. RM as compared with direct Soviet deliveries of about 23 mil. RM.

[8]) Memorandum of Schnurre, 5 April 1941, *NSR*, p. 318, *BDS*, pp. 356-57; Protocol of April 18, 1941, *NSR*, p. 327, *BDS*, pp. 366-67; Memorandum of Schnurre, 15 May 1941, *NSR*, pp. 339-40, *BDS*, pp. 351-52; Skl, A, 20, 151: 2 April 1940, cited in C - 170, *TMWC*, XXXIV, 702.

[9]) Greiner, p. 385; Memorandum of Schnurre, 15 May 1941, *NSR*, pp. 340-41, *BDS*,

In the political field, the famous gesture of Stalin on April 13 in greeting the German Ambassador and Acting Military Attaché at the station at Matsuoka's departure,[10]) was followed by more substantial concessions. On April 15 the Soviets gave way completely on the issue of the boundary between Germany and Russia along the northern stretch of the line.[11]) There was a detente in Soviet-Finnish relations.[12]) The Soviets also talked more kindly with the Rumanians.[13])

On May 6, after Dekanozov had reported in Moscow and Schulenburg had returned without any message for the Soviet government, Stalin took over the post of Chairman of the Council of People's Commissars from Molotov. This was regarded everywhere as a sign of a policy of further cooperation with Germany, designed to prevent war, and carried out by Stalin directly in person.[14]) Subsequent events confirmed this interpretation. On May 8 Tass issued a *dementi* of troop concentrations on the Western border. On May 9 Russia withdrew its recognition of the governments-in-exile of Belgium and Norway; in likewise revoking recognition of Yugoslavia the Russians expelled the ambassador with whom they had signed the treaty of friendship one month before. On May 12 the Soviet government announced that since May 3 it had been negotiating with and had recognized the anti-British government set up by Rashid Ali in Iraq. On June 3 the recognition of the Greek government-in-exile was revoked. The Germans had not asked for any of these steps. They were clearly one-sided concessions designed to

pp. 381-82; Skl, A, 22, 29: 4 June 1941, C - 37 (cited in *TMWC*, XXXIV, 705); Germany, Beauftragter für den Vierjahresplan (Bergbohm), "11. Sitzung des Generalrats vom 24. 6. 41 unter Vorsitz von Staatssekretär Körner," NI - 7474 (photostat, 12pp.), p. 4; Germany, OKW, Wi Rü Amt, Thomas, "Grundlagen für eine Geschichte der deutschen Wehr- und Rüstungswirtschaft," 1944, p. 315 in PS - 2353, *TMWC*, XXX, 272.

The Germans in the last two months arranged to withhold their deliveries in various ways. Thomas, "Affidavit of Thomas," 13 November 1945, PS - 2353, in U.S. v. Weizsäcker, G.T. 11934; "Report of the Commander in Chief, Navy to the Fuehrer on 22 May 1941," Fuehrer Conferences, 1941, I, 66-67; Ernst von Raussendorff, "Affidavit of Ernst von Raussendorff;" 28 December 1947, NIK - 13342 (photostat, 1p.).

10) See Schulenburg to Ribbentrop, 13 April 1941, *NSR*, p. 324, *BDS*, pp. 361-62.

11) Tippelskirch to Ribbentrop, 15 April 1941, *NSR*, pp. 325-26, *BDS*, pp. 364-65; the German delay in answering this was connected with their desire not to have a mixed boundary commission in that sector. See Woermann to Schulenburg, 24 May 1941, *NSR*, pp. 343-44, *BDS*, pp. 385-86; Woermann to Ribbentrop, 24 May 1941, *NSR*, p. 344, *BDS*, pp. 385-86.

12) Skl, A, 80, 295: 21 April 1941, cited in C - 170, *TMWC*, XXXIV, 703; Halder (3 June 1941), VI, 141; Blücher, p. 220; Mannerheim, p. 433.

13) Gafencu, pp. 262-63, 227.

14) Skl, A, 21, 66: 6 May 1941, 81: 7 May 1941, cited in C - 170, *TMWC*, XXXIV, 704; Baumbach to OKM cited in Skl, A, 21, 156: May 1941, cited in *ibid.*; Papen to Ribbentrop cited in Skl, A, 21, 235: 17 May 1941, *ibid.*, p. 705; Gafencu, pp. 254-56; Schulenburg to Ribbentrop, 7 May 1941, *NSR*, pp. 335-36, *BDS*, p. 376; Schulenburg to Ribbentrop, 12 May 1941, *NSR*, pp. 336-39, *BDS*, pp. 377-79.

clear the air and show Germany the good-will of the Soviet Union.[15]) This policy of the Soviets was heavily stressed by the reports of the German Ambassador in Moscow.[16]) The British Ambassador, Sir Stafford Cripps, left Moscow in disgust.

What was the reaction to this new policy in Germany? The German press was instructed not to print the news of the Soviet concessions, just as in January and February Hitler had forbidden that the benefits of the new trade agreement be publicized.[17]) No attention was paid to the reports from the Moscow Embassy.[18]) For a real understanding of German policy we must look more deeply into this.

In his memoirs, Weizsäcker characterizes the German leadership at that time as moving "along a mental one-way street against Russia."[19]) This seems to be a very accurate description. The preparations for the attack were continuing in both the military and economic spheres. It was assumed that as a result of the planned economic exploitation of the country millions would die.[20]) After the Balkan campaign, the troops used there were transferred as quickly as possible to the Eastern front,[21]) too quickly, in fact, to do a thorough job of "mopping up" in Yugoslavia—with important consequences for the situation there later.[22]) The next campaign was that of Crete. That island was to be occupied by an airborne invasion which turned into a Pyrrhic victory. The fixed nature of the decision to attack the Soviet Union had great influence on the planning of this stroke. The manner in which the German military operations at that time were circumscribed by the plans for the attack on Russia indicates that Hitler was not to be diverted from his decision. Excerpts from the relevant documents showing this fact are given in Appendix IV.[23])

---

[15]) Schulenburg to Ribbentrop, 12 May 1941, NSR, p. 338, BDS, p. 379; Beloff, II, 378-79; Gafencu, pp. 256-58, 264; Testimony of Weizsäcker, U.S. v. Weizsäcker, E.T. 7901-02; Churchill, III, 364.

[16]) See the Schulenburg telegrams of May 7 and 12 just cited; Schulenburg to Ribbentrop, 24 May 1941, NSR, pp. 344-45, BDS, p. 386; Schulenburg to Ribbentrop cited in Skl, A, 22, 53: 6 June 1941, C - 37 (in TMWC, XXXIV, 706); Testimony of Woermann, U.S. v. Weizsäcker, E.T. 11239.

[17]) Simoni (4 June 1941) p. 275, (6 June 1941) p. 275, (12 June 1941) p. 278.

[18]) Testimony of Ribbentrop, TMWC, X, 377-78, PHKV, X, 426-27.

[19]) Weizsäcker, p. 313.

[20]) Memorandum on Barbarossa, 2 May 1941, PS - 2718, TMWC, XXXI, 84; Werner Bross, Gespräche mit Hermann Göring (Flensburg, 1950), p. 122.

[21]) United States, OCCWC, Evidence Division, Interrogation Branch, "Interrogation of Feldmarschall Maximilian von Weichs," 31 January and 3 February 1947, Interrogation Summary No. 1147 (mimeo, 6pp.), p. 3; Germany, Oberste Befehlshaber der Wehrmacht, OKW, WFSt, L (Hitler), "Weisung Nr. 29," 17 May 1941, PS - 452 (photostat, 5pp.), p. 2.

[22]) Hagen, p. 242.

[23]) See also Testimony of Warlimont, U.S. v. Leeb, G.T. 6381-83; Halder (28 April

In the discussions in Germany at that time the military and diplomatic officials maintained that Soviet Russia was not planning to attack Germany.[24]) In fact, the German operational planning was based on this assumption.[25]) In April, when Schulenburg was in Germany, an effort was made by him with the support of Weizsäcker to persuade Hitler not to make war on Russia. Schulenburg had a conversation on the subject of German-Soviet relations with Hitler in which he tried to explain Russian policy as non-aggressive. He also prepared a memorandum on the subject. Weizsäcker tried to influence Hitler through a memorandum to Ribbentrop written in a Nazi-German style to influence the latter. All of this had no effect.[26]) The effort to use Italy as a brake on German policy also failed.[27]) Hitler himself agreed that Soviet Russia was not about to attack Germany on her own initiative.[28]) It was under these circumstances that Admiral Raeder became convinced that Hitler planned to attack Soviet Russia regardless of that country's attitude.[29])

1941), VI, 87, (29 April 1941) 88, (12 May 1941) 111, (22 May 1941), 131, (27 May 1941) 134, (30 May 1941) 139.

[24]) Testimony of Paulus, *TMWC*, VII, 282, *PHKV*, VII, 313; Rundstedt quoted in B. H. Liddell-Hart, *The German Generals Talk* (New York, 1948), pp. 171-72; Germany, HGrK B, "HGrK B an AOK 4. 17. 18." 3 Apr. 1941, NOKW - 2691 (mimeo, 2pp.), Staff Evidence Analysis, United States, OCCWC. The testimony at Nuremberg on this point is generally self-contradictory—everybody claimed to have been against the war on Russia among other reasons because Russia was not going to attack, and everybody claimed that the war was necessary because the Russians were about to attack. Witnesses carefully evaded answering when the prosecutors pointed out this contradiction.

[25]) Testimony of Paulus, *TMWC*, VII, 259, *PHKV*, VII, 289; Germany, XXX. AK Ia, "75/41, Order for the Preparation of the Deployment for 'Barbarossa'," 4 June 1941, NOKW - 2449 (mimeo, 2pp.), trans. United States, OCCWC, p. 1; Germany, AOK 17, "AOK 17 an die AK's," 8 Apr. 1941, NOKW - 2691, p. 2; Germany, AOK 16 (Unterabschnitt Ostpreussen I) Ia, "155/41, Befehl für die Sicherung der Landesgrenze," 10 May 1941, NOKW - 2701 (photostat, 8pp.), p. 1.

[26]) Testimony of Kordt, U.S. v. Weizsäcker, E.T. 7415-16; Testimony of Weizsäcker, *ibid.*, 7900-01; Testimony of Woermann, *ibid.*, 11239; Kordt, *Wahn und Wirklichkeit*, pp. 297-98; Gaus, "Affidavit of Gaus," 26 December 1947, NG - 4183 (mimeo, 2pp.); Weizsäcker, pp. 314-15; Byrnes, p. 291; Hitler-Schulenburg Conversation, 28 April 1941, *NSR*, pp. 330-32, *BDS*, 370-72; Memorandum of Weizsäcker, 28 April 1941, *NSR*, pp. 333-34, *BDS*, pp. 373-74. Churchill's statement that Schulenburg tried to warn Dekanozov (III, 362) has now been confirmed by Hilger and Meyer, pp. 331-32.

[27]) Testimony of Weizsäcker, U.S. v. Weizsäcker, E.T. 7897; Memorandum of Schmidt, 13 May 1941, PS - 1866, *TMWC*, XXIX, 37; Weizsäcker, pp. 307-08; cf. Ciano (6 June 1941), p. 363. Toscano, however, insists (p. 74, n. 120) that Weizsäcker never informed the Italians about Germany's intentions of attacking the Soviet Union.

[28]) Memorandum of Schmidt, 1 April 1941, *NSR*, p. 291, *BDS*, p. 327; Hitler-Schulenburg Conversation, 28 April 1941, *NSR*, p. 332, *BDS*, p. 372; other examples could be cited.

[29]) Raeder, "Memorandum for Assmann," 30 January 1944, C - 66, *TMWC*, XXXIV, 278.

The decision of Hitler to attack Soviet Russia has been shown to have been made originally in July 1940. The reasons then used were of a kind likely to reinforce themselves over a period of time. If it was necessary to defeat Soviet Russia in order to obtain a free hand to smash England, then the necessary measures for an attack on Soviet Russia would in themselves tend to dictate continued adherence to such a course. The attack on Soviet Russia would be a land operation; and, as has been shown, this required that the plans for a reduction of the army, with emphasis on the navy and air force instead, had had to be scrapped. This of course meant that in each succeeding month materials and man-power had gone into the production of equipment other than that need-ed for the fight against England. Viewed objectively, the Balkan cam-paign did offer an excellent opening for the Mediterranean strategy the German navy had repeatedly urged on Hitler, but the Führer's gaze was fixed on the East; he preferred to use his big army first and to deal with the Mediterranean later.[30])

The economic aid from the Soviet Union may well have had just the opposite effect of what the Russians intended. The Russians fully rea-lized the importance of the oil supplies and the transit of rubber to the German war effort and made concessions in this regard whenever they wanted to please Germany. But if Germany came to depend more and more on supplies from the East to feed Europe and maintain her armies in what looked like a long war, might she not get into a very embarras-sing position should the German army ever again be preoccupied in the West while Soviet Russia took the occasion to press for concessions? Was it not perhaps safer, as Hitler put it, to conquer what one need-ed?[31])

The decision to attack was, thus, definite. Inevitably there were bor-der incidents in the last few weeks, particularly those involving the air reconnaissance of both sides. Planes were shot down and protests ex-changed.[32]) On the German side plans were made in some areas for

---

[30]) See Germany, Oberste Befehlshaber der Wehrmacht, OKW, WFSt, L (Hitler), "Weisung 32, Vorbereitungen für die Zeit nach Barbarossa," 11 June 1941, PS - 1799 (photostat, 5pp.).

[31]) Germany, OKW, Wi Rü Amt, "Aufzeichnung, [Besprechung Amtschef mit Reichs-minister Todt]," 20 June 1940, PS - 1456, *TMWC*, XXVII, 220-21; Testimony of Huenermann, U.S. v. Weizsäcker, E.T. 23664-65. Todt was telling Thomas about a con-versation with Hitler. Equally illuminating was Hitler's statement that a campaign in the East would cost no more in casualties than the number of workers tied up in the synthetic industries—so it would be all right to go ahead!

[32]) Germany, Pz.Div., 6 Ia, "280/41, Befehl für die Bereitstellung zum Angriff," 13 June 1941, NOKW - 2652 (photostat, 4pp.), p. 2; Germany, Inf.Div. 36 (mot.), Ic, "Tätigkeitsbericht Nr. 1, p. 3," 12 June 1941, NOKW - 3408 (photostat, 6pp.), p. 2; Memorandum of Kramarz, 20 June 1941, NG - 4218 (mimeo, 1p.), trans. United States, OCCWC; Tippelskirch to Ribbentrop, 22 April 1941, *NSR*, p. 328, *BDS*, pp. 367-68; Jodl to Ritter, 23 April 1941, *NSR, BDS*, pp. 368-69; Ritter to Schulenburg, 14 May

military action even before the official hour set for the attack.[33])

The diplomatic actions of Germany in the last days before the attack, and in the case of Hungary also in the first days afterward, were connected with notifying and bringing into the war the various allies.[34]) A "White Book" on Soviet Russia, like the ones issued at times of previous aggressions, seems to have been planned but was not issued.[35]) The children of the German diplomats in Russia were sent back, and the Russians also decreased their staffs in Germany.[36])

The Soviet Union in its actions in the last days of peace seems to have been trying to find a way for reopening conversations. The Russians no doubt thought that the Germans would present demands, and that if war did break out, it would be at the end of negotiations of some kind. When Schulenburg did not come forward with any demands or proposals, the Russians tried to get a reaction by issuing a long and involved communiqué on June 13. In it they denied that Germany had made demands on the Soviet Union and that hostile troop concentrations were facing each other along the border.[37]) The expected German reaction did

1941, *NSR*, pp. 341-42; *BDS*, p. 383; Schulenburg to Ribbentrop, 17 May 1941, *NSR*, p. 343, *BDS*, pp. 389-90; Memorandum of Weizsäcker, and Dekanozov to Ribbentrop, 21 June 1941, *NSR*, pp. 353-55, *BDS*, pp. 397-99; Schulenburg to Ribbentrop, 21 June 1941, *NSR*, p. 355, *BDS*, pp. 399-400.

[33]) For details see C - 38, *TMWC*, XXXIV, 225-28; NOKW - 2729, 14 June 1941, (photostat, 1p.); Germany, XXXXI AK (Festungsstab Allenstein), Ia, "165/41 an 6. Pz.Div.," 7 June 1941, NOKW - 2567, trans. United States, OCCWC, p. 1; cf. Germany, OKM, Skl, "Skl an OKW, WFSt," 22 April 1941, NOKW - 2726, Staff Evidence Analysis, United States, OCCWC, p. 1; Germany, OKM, Skl, "580/41 an Gruppe Nord; Betreff: Barbarossa," 3 May 1941, NOKW - 2727 (photostat, 1p.).

[34]) Testimony of Horthy, U.S. v. Weizsäcker, E.T. 2742; Testimony of Woermann, *ibid.*, 11248-49; Hitler to Antonescu, 18 June 1941, C - 150, Staff Evidence Analysis, United States, OCCWC, p. 1; Memorandum of Woermann, 26 June 1941, NG - 2975 (photostat, 1p.); Memorandum of Weizsäcker, 16 June 1941, NG - 4236 (photostat, 1p.); Ribbentrop to Erdmannsdorff, 15 June 1941, NG - 4273 (photostat, 1p.); Erdmannsdorff to Ribbentrop, 24 June 1941, NG - 4306 (mimeo, 4pp.), trans. United States, OCCWC; Halder, "Affidavit of Halder," 15 May 1948, Dokumentenbuch II für Otto von Erdmannsdorff, p. 60; Ludin to Ribbentrop, 21 June 1941, NG - 4530 (photostat, 1p.); Skl, A, 22, 174-75: 16 June 1941, C - 37; Ciano, *The Ciano Diaries* (15 June 1941), p. 367; Hitler to Mussolini, 21 June 1941, *NSR*, pp. 349-53, *BDS*, pp. 392-97. It should be noted that the Germans finally overcame Hungary's reluctance by bombing some Hungarian towns and blaming this on the Russians.

[35]) Grosskopf to Ribbentrop, 30 May 1941, NG - 4431, Staff Evidence Analysis, United States, OCCWC, p. 2; Likus to Gaus, 21 June 1941, NG - 3228 (photostat, 1p.).

[36]) Schulenburg to Ribbentrop, 19 June 1941, NG - 4193 in U.S. v. Weizsäcker, G.T. 901; Dekanozov to Ribbentrop, 21 June 1941, NG - 4234 (photostat, 1p.); Skl, A, 22, 203: 18 June 1941, C - 37. Schulenburg was, however, not definitely told the date of the attack. See Joseph Göbbels, *The Goebbels Diaries, 1942-1943*, trans. and ed. by Louis P. Lochner (Garden City, New York, 1948) p. 87.

[37]) Text in Schulenburg to Ribbentrop, 13 June 1941, *NSR*, pp. 345-46, *BDS*, p. 387; cf. Skl, 22, 149-50: 14 June 1941, C - 37 (cited in *TMWC*, XXXIV, 708); Gafencu, pp.

not occur; at the press conference on June 14 the Head of the Press Section of the German Foreign Ministry carefully dodged all questions about the *dementi*.[38]) After waiting for some days for an echo in the German press or an answer by the diplomatic route, the Russians tried again. On June 18 Dekanozov asked to see Weizsäcker, but as Weizsäcker had no instructions for opening conversations, nothing important was discussed.[39]) On June 21, in the evening, Dekanozov in Berlin and Molotov in Moscow again tried to start conversations.[40]) Hitler and Ribbentrop, however, wanted no talks, and Ribbentrop was declared to be out of town when Dekanozov took to calling for an interview every two hours.[41]) On the morning of June 22, after the attack, the diplomatic announcements of war were given out.

The German attack came as a complete tactical surprise along the whole front. Many important bridges were captured intact. Hundreds of Soviet planes were destroyed on the ground. A German attack was apparently not expected; after all the warnings they had received, the Russians were still caught unprepared.[42])

The question of whether the arrangements discovered behind the Russian lines were of a defensive or offensive character will not be examined here as the evidence is inadequate and inconclusive. No documents indicating offensive Russian intentions seem to have been captured. The only sector of the front on which the information is fairly clear is that facing the northern German army group, for which both contemporary evidence and the later testimony of Field Marshal Leeb, the German commander, indicate defensive intentions on the part of the Russians.[43])

277-80. Until more of Schulenburg's reports are available, it will be impossible to examine whether the handing over of the text of the communiqué by Molotov in this instance differed in any way from the other cases.

[38]) Memorandum of Schindel, 14 June 1941, NG - 5154 (mimeo, 4pp.), pp. 1-2.

[39]) Memorandum of Weizsäcker, 18 June 1941, NG - 4235 (photostat, 1p.); cf. Weizsäcker, p. 317. It is not known what was the basis for the entry of June 20 in the Halder Diary, "Molotov wanted to see the Fuehrer 18 June," (VI, 156).

[40]) Memorandum of Weizsäcker, 21 June 1941, *NSR*, pp. 353-54, *BDS*, pp. 397-98; Schulenburg to Ribbentrop, 21 June 1941, *NSR*, pp. 355-56, *BDS*, pp. 399-400; cf. Weizsäcker, p. 317.

[41]) See two Memoranda of the Büro RAM for Weizsäcker, 21 June 1941, NG - 4242 (photostat, 2pp.); Weizsäcker, p. 317; Schmidt, pp. 539-40.

[42]) Testimony of Halder, U.S. v. Weizsäcker, E.T. 20753-54; Germany, AOK 17, "Kriegstagebuch Nr. 1, 23 April-22 Juni 1941," 22 June 1941, NOKW - 1889 (photostat, 13 pp.), pp. 10, 12; Germany, Inf. Div. 123, Ic, "Tätigkeitsbericht der Abteilung Ic," 22 June 1941, NOKW - 2061 (photostat, 9pp.), 2p. ; Skl, A, 22, 270, 273, 277: 22 June 1941, C - 37; Halder (22 June 1941), VI, 161-62; Germany, AOK 16, Ic, "Vernehmung des Oberbefehlshabers der 6. russ. Armee am 9. 8. 1941," 19 August 1941, parts in NOKW - 2721 (photostat, 4pp.), parts cited in Giovanni Messe, *Der Krieg im Osten* (Zürich, 1948), pp. 14, 17 n. 1, 20 n. 1.

[43]) Halder (23 June 1941), VI, 164-66, (24 June 1941) 166; Testimony of Leeb, U.S.

Thus the Soviet Union was drawn into the war in spite of all her efforts to keep out, and at a time when a second front in Europe had existed twice—each time to fall without the slightest support from the Soviets. As a result of the mistakes of her own diplomacy, Russia now found herself face to face with practically the whole German army—an army with the resources of a continent to draw upon and vastly strengthened by Soviet economic aid. The supplies of oil and the rubber faithfully hauled across Siberia easily carried the Germans across the territories Russia had acquired under the Non-Aggression Pact.

Storming along madly on the road of conquest, the Germans had half opened the door for Russia into Central Europe in 1939. They now took out the door altogether by its hinges and by unbelievable cruelty together with political plans of a strictly colonial character made certain that an aroused Russian army would pour through. The results will long be with them and the rest of the world.

---

v. Leeb, G.T. 2304-05, 2309-10. The Halder diary contains the suggestion that the Russians may have expected the Germans to demand Lithuania and were getting ready to abandon it.

CONCLUSIONS

This study concerns the relations between the two greatest powers on the European continent in the period immediately preceding the outbreak of the Second World War and during its early, and perhaps decisive, years. For almost two years, the leaders of two systems who had previously denounced each other's works in the strongest terms steered their countries along a line of more or less friendly cooperation. Having started by joining to destroy the country which provided each with a barrier against the other, they were eventually to come to grips in a military campaign unprecedented in its ferocity and extent and exacting a terrific cost in life and treasure from both. The account of these events which has been set forth here fills in the picture presented by previous writers by providing additional details at many points. Beyond that, however, certain matters hitherto only dimly recognized have been substantially elucidated while in some cases essentially new findings require real modifications of established interpretations.

While Angelo Rossi has recognized the importance of the policy discussions in Germany in the last week of May 1939 for the later course of events, his perception of the really crucial nature of those days has been vitiated by his overlooking of the immediate reaction in Germany to the Molotov-Schulenburg conversation of May 20.[1]) Molotov had stated that the construction of political bases would be essential before economic negotiations could be resumed. The German answer, sent to the German Ambassador in Moscow the next day, was that nothing more was to be done. It was in the days following this that the highest officials in Germany examined the line of policy to be followed toward Russia and finally came to the conclusion that an attempt to come to some sort of agreement with Russia should be made. This decision produced the Weizsäcker-Astakhov conversation of May 30, a conversation which marks a most important step in the diplomacy of 1939.

While the Russians immediately took note of the German step— Molotov alluded to it in his foreign policy speech the following day— it is hardly sound to argue, as Rossi does, that the Russians had decided to sign with Germany by the time of Stalin's speech of March 10. There is, at any rate, no evidence to support such a thesis. Since the Russians had placed such great stress on political foundations for economic negotiations and had then engaged in long preliminary economic negotia-

---

[1]) See above p. 26, n. 66.

tions before making the official announcement of the resumption of economic negotiations on July 21, it seems safe to argue that it was in the period between July 10 and July 21 that the Soviet decision was made. The fragmentary nature of the evidence on this period, which is stressed at the beginning of Chapter III, makes a more precise dating impossible. The Soviet decision thus falls between the hints of Astakhov, which Rossi had taken to be the sign of a previously determined policy of agreement with Germany; and the middle of August which Namier, perhaps because of the more spectacular character of developments at that time, has fixed upon as the turning point.

Contrary to a widespread assumption, the German-Soviet "marriage" was by no means followed immediately by the "honeymoon." As is clearly demonstrated by the troubles over the date of Russian intervention against Poland and the great Russian suspicion that Germany might not abide by her agreements, the real period of German-Russian friendship is not inaugurated until the second trip of Ribbentrop to Moscow on September 28, 1939. This period of mutual distrust casts much light both backward over the earlier negotiations and forward over the succeeding period. This point is essential if we are to avoid the common mistake of overemphasizing the ease with which agreement between the two countries was reached and underemphasizing the aid which they then proceeded to furnish each other. As the account presented in Chapter V ought to demonstrate, this aid was, after the settlement of September 28, considerably greater than has often been thought. Many of the details of Soviet economic aid to Germany remain to be investigated, but the considerable addition to present knowledge offered in this study certainly shows its vast importance to the German war effort. Even if the material for the derivation of a *monetary* total for the goods and services furnished by Soviet Russia to Germany were available, this would still not give us any real indication on this question. It is in this respect that Dallin's very interesting study of Russo-German economic relations is totally out of focus. The rubber used in the landing gear of a plane may well represent an inconsequential fraction of the cost of the plane; it is still essential if the plane is to take part in the war. The fact which makes monetary computations even less realistic is the point that in the example cited the rubber does not even come from Russia at all—it is shipped across the Transsiberian Railway from the Far East and enters into the German-Russian trade accounts only as a freight charge.

The other side of this Soviet-German collaboration has perhaps been equally underestimated. This comes out most clearly in the entries in the German naval diary, revealed here for the first time, which show Germany totally unconcerned about Finland in the winter of 1939-1940—just as her agreements with Russia required—and even willing to give direct aid to the latter's blockade of Finland.

From the German side a decisive change occurs in July 1940. While in some accounts of the history of this period, particularly that of Winston Churchill, the turn of German policy at that time is indicated, the full details and, of even greater importance, the immediate repercussions, of the German decision to attack the Soviet Union are brought together here for the first time. The decision of July is here shown to be not a generalized discussion of future possibilities, but the conscious adoption of a policy requiring immediate implementation in many fields. The decision itself is a purely military one and so is the early planning. In spite of previous speeches by Hitler and later propaganda by Göbbels, the decision to attack the Soviet Union is here demonstrated to have had nothing to do with the system installed in that country.

The decision to attack the Soviet Union was Hitler's answer to the challenge of England—as it had been Napoleon's—and was elaborated into a blue-print for ruthless aggrandizement. There was never any intention of allowing the Russian people a voice in their own future or even of installing a native Nazi regime in the area occupied. The military plans were designed to smash the Soviet Army; beyond this, the German policy was simply to be one of exploiting, expropriating, and exterminating as much as possible—brown commissars were to replace the red ones.[2] The ultimate fate of these schemes is well known. The old saying that he who sows the wind shall reap the whirl-wind applies more truly to few events in modern history than to the German policy toward the Soviet Union after July 1940. The question of whether a state run the way Germany was could have jumped over its own shadow and adopted a different policy from the one actually pursued is beyond the scope of this study but surely deserves the most serious thought.

It is in connection with the German decision to attack the Soviet Union that the material gathered in this study requires a rather thorough recasting of the generally accepted account of German-Soviet relations during the period of the Non-Aggression Pact. It has been maintained that the friction which occurred in the relations between the two partners of the Pact during the fall of 1940, concerning Finland and the Balkans, led the Germans to decide upon the attack. It would appear that the cause and effect relationship here has been reversed. The Ger-

---

[2] This refers, of course, to the official German policy as ordered and largely carried out; some elements in the German government advocated less brutal policies. The best published work dealing with the German occupation of parts of the U.S.S.R., is George Fischer, *Soviet Opposition to Stalin* (Cambridge, 1952). For a detailed study of German policy in the occupied U.S.S.R., see Alexander Dallin, "German Policy and the Occupation of the U.S.S.R., 1941-1945" (Unpublished Ph. D. dissertation, Dept. of History, Columbia University, 1953), a revised version of which will be published by Columbia University Press.

man plan of attack from the very beginning foresaw the participation of Finland and Rumania on Germany's side. If Finland were to fight on Germany's side, she could not be allowed to fall into Russian hands. This meant a total reversal of the German policy toward Finland—a reversal certain to violate the secret agreements with Russia. As detailed in Chapter VIII, Germany began the delivery of war materials to Finland in August 1940, and in September began troop movements across Finland to Norway; troop movements which were directed ostensibly against England but actually against the Soviet Union. The case of Rumania was somewhat similar, except that matters were complicated by the Rumanian nationalities problem. In connection with the decision to attack Soviet Russia, Hitler, therefore, had decided to settle the differences between Hungary and Rumania and then to give a German guarantee to the latter. Thereupon German troops, again supposedly to protect the country against England but actually to prepare the attack on Russia, were sent to Rumania also. These events—the results, not the causes of the German decision to attack the Soviet Union—produced some sharp Russian reactions which only confirmed Hitler in his views. All this was registered, not originated, at the time of the Molotov visit.

This last point, the cumulative repercussions of the German decision to attack, once it had been taken, goes far to explain the singular inflexibility of German policy after July 1940. The German military occupation of Rumania induced the Italians to start their ill-fated attack on Greece. When the Germans went deeper into the Balkans to secure their own interests in that region and to rescue the Italians from their folly, they gave further offense to the Russians who reacted by a series of increasingly direct and bitter communiqués culminating in the Soviet-Yugoslav Treaty of Friendship of April 5, 1941. Again, these reactions confirmed Hitler in his decision to invade Russia.

The materials brought together in this study also bring out a form of inflexibility affecting Soviet policy in the last months of the Pact—an inflexibility which did not serve Russian interests even if judged exclusively by the standards of Russia's own diplomacy. Soviet policy was clearly aimed at avoiding involvement in the war. As the signs of German danger mounted early in 1941, there was a reversal of the means employed by Soviet diplomacy in its dealing with Germany. Whereas from September 1940 to the signing of the Soviet-Yugoslav Treaty there had been a gradual stiffening, especially in regard to German policy in the Balkans, the Russians now turned to a policy of concessions in the hope of avoiding the German attack of which Soviet Russia had been repeatedly warned. This policy, to judge by the outward manifestations recorded in Chapter XI, emphasized excessively the idea of avoiding war altogether with little regard to the problem of the conditions in which Russia would find herself were she involved in hostilities in spite of her efforts. A diplomacy aimed at keeping out of war while at the same time considering the problem of fighting under the best possible conditions if necessary might not have had to go beyond the Russo-Japanese Neutrality Pact to an actual attack on Germany while the panzer divisions of the latter were tied up in the Balkans; but it would surely have refrained from making economic concessions which would greatly strengthen the German war economy at its most critical points— oil and rubber. If the policy of the Russians represented a policy of the calculated risk, one can only conclude that they miscalculated most seriously.

The over-all picture which emerges from these considerations may well fail to fit some of the patterns with which the events of those years are sometimes stamped. We see no Germany plotting anxiously from the very beginning to bring fire and destruction to the Soviet Union; nor do we see a Germany thoughtfully determined to do away with a communist menace to Europe. We do not see a Russia wickedly scheming to deliver Europe into the hands of the Nazis; nor do we see a Russia carefully searching for the most opportune moment to strike down the Nazi armies and state. Perhaps we do not see these things because they were not there. The impression we get is rather one of two great powers plodding fitfully along the path of expediency; one motivated by vast schemes of conquest, the other by the hope of protecting what it has and adding what can safely be picked up.

Future publications and study will no doubt fill in, alter, and revise both the details and findings of this work. The episode of the Soviet-German Non-Aggression Pact provides much material for a careful consideration of the formulation and execution of foreign policy in the totalitarian state. The writer hopes that the account given here and the manner of presentation will contribute to the founding of such consideration on firm and realistic bases.

APPENDIX I

Germany and the Soviet Blockade of Finland[1])

December 10, 1939

The Soviet Navy Commissariat has informed [us] through [the German] naval attaché Moscow that a submarine blockade of Finland in the Gulf of Bothnia is intended and asks whether German ships going to Northern Sweden could take along fuel and food for Russian submarines to be quietly (unauffällig) transferred at sea. Restitution of the amounts delivered [is promised] wherever we wish, such as, for example, at any Soviet port at which our naval units (Seestreitkräfte) have corresponding needs. The naval attaché recommends that the Russian wishes be *granted* because opportunities for the support of our *own* naval warfare would arise from the Russian compensation.

The naval war staff (Seekriegsleitung) is in basic agreement with the proposal for the same reasons cited by the naval attaché and recommends an immediate and speedy reply to convince the Russians of the goodwill of the German navy.

The ships trading at Lulea are, however, presumably unsuited on account of their lack of oil loading and transferral facilities. The commitment of a special motorboat is therefore intended. Preparations [will] take a few days. [The matter of] getting additional motorboats ready is being examined.

The Führer is informed of the matter in the afternoon of December 10 and declares [himself in] agreement.

The attaché in Moscow is informed accordingly. The Russians should transmit more specific wishes as to fuels, food, etc.[2])

December 12, 1939
1740 hours

Telephone call of the naval attaché in Moscow that all measures concerning the provisioning of Russian submarines by German merchant ships in the Gulf of Bothnia are to be cancelled since the Russians have withdrawn the request.

In the meantime the immediate preparation of the tanker "Medea" (now at Bremerhaven) had been arranged for in this matter. The tank-

---

[1]) The blockade was proclaimed by the Soviet Union on December 8, 1939 (Skl, A, 4, 54-5: 8 December 1939, C - 27).

[2]) Skl, A, 4, 73, C - 27.

er was to be quickly transferred to Pillau. It was planned that the provisions of the Russians would be taken simultaneously from Leningrad to Pillau on the steamer "Utlandshörn" for transferral to the "Medea". The naval group, the Commander of Naval Forces in the Baltic Sea, and the Base Commandant Pillau had been informed. In view of the declination of the Russians, the measures ordered will now be revoked.

The reason for the Russians' declining is unknown. It can be assumed that the prevalence of ice (Eislage) in the Gulf of Bothnia at this time of the year entirely precludes submarine operations.

Possibly the Russians directed this request to Germany merely with the thought of securing a clear view of Germany's willingness to support their interests. Finally, on the other hand, the possibility that the Russians had some second thoughts about accepting from Germany aid obligating them to corresponding services in return cannot be excluded.

In this connection the navy war staff regrets that this support did *not* materialize, since the possibility of immediate counter-requests could have arisen from it.[3]

---

[3] Skl, A, 4, 88, C - 27.

APPENDIX II
The Abwehr Order of September 6, 1940

High Command of the Armed Forces (OKW)
WFSt/Abt. L Nr. 33 264/40   The Führer's Headquarters
TOP SECRET   September 6, 1940
Concerns: Basis for Intelligence
With reference to: Abw. III Nr. 398/40 g.K. of 26 August, and
                    OKH Gen.St.d.H. Op.Abt. Ia Nr. 150231/40 g.K.
                    of 2 September 1940.
To: Military Intelligence and Counter-Intelligence

The eastern territory will be manned more strongly in the coming week. By the end of October, the status which can be seen on the enclosed map is to be attained.

As a result of these troop transfers the impression that we are preparing an offensive in the East must not arise in Russia. On the other hand, Russia will realize that strong and crack (hochwertige) German troops are stationed in the Eastern Provinces as well as in the Protectorate [Bohemia and Moravia] and should draw from that the conclusion that we can protect our interests—especially in the Balkans— with strong forces against Russian incursions at any time.

The following *instructions* apply to the work of our own intelligence service as well as for the answering of questions of the Russian intelligence service:

1. The periodic *total strength* of the German troops in the East is to be veiled as much as possible by issuing news about a frequent change of army units there. This change is to be explained as movements into training camps, regroupings, etc.

2. The impression is to be created that the main point of the concentration of troops is in the *southern* part of the Gouvernement-[General, Central Poland], in the Protectorate, and in the Ostmark [Austria], and that the concentration in the North is comparatively light.

3. On giving out information on the *equipment* of the units, especially of the armored divisions, one is to exaggerate where possible.

4. By the passing out of appropriate information, the impression is to be created that the *anti-aircraft protection* in the East was increased considerably after the conclusion of the campaign in the West, and that it is constantly being strengthened at all important targets with equipment captured in France.

5. Concerning the improvements in *railways, roads, airfields, etc.* it is to be stated that these works are held within normal bounds, are necessitated by the improvement of the newly won Eastern territories, and serve the commercial traffic primarily.

To what extent correct details—e.g. the number of regiments, manning of garrisons, etc.—are to be made available to the Abwehr for counter-espionage is to be determined by the OKH [High Command of the Army].

Distribution: For the Supreme Commander of
[omitted]   the Armed Forces [Hitler]
                                          signed: Jodl[1])

---

[1]) The full German text is in PS - 1229, *TMWC,* XXVII, 72-73.

APPENDIX III

Concealment of German Intentions

High Command of the Army (OKH)   HQ, 19 Mar. 1941
General Staff of the Army, Operations Section
No. 465/41 Top Secret

To Army Group B
for information to: Army Group A and Army Group C

The constantly increasing movements of troops to the East in the coming weeks are to be presented to the Russians as a defensive measure [taken] on account of the strong concentrations of Russian forces at the German-Russian border.

In order to lend to this explanation the necessary emphasis, field fortifications are to be constructed, starting in April, both near the border and in the rear areas, to the extent permitted by the training needs of the troops and their preparation for the forthcoming tasks.

The construction of the field fortifications is assigned to Army Group B for the entire [border] area. The requests of Army Groups A and C are to be fulfilled as much as possible.

It will be important to select for the field fortifications *near the border* those areas where a Russian attack appears likely. Aside from this it appears appropriate for purposes of misleading [the Russians] to pick just those areas where later the main centers of our own attack will be. These field fortifications are to be made by the troops.   [p. 1.]

Our defensive intentions are to be made especially clear to the enemy by the construction of field fortifications in the *rearward* areas. These positions are expected to be built generally along the line of the Galician border, the San-Vistula line, as well as the Ortelsburg forests, the Lötzen position, the Masurian Canal and the Heilsberg-Deime line. For the construction of these positions appropriate numbers of the male civilian population of the Generalgouvernement [Poland] will be employed, so that by this means the enemy will also know of our measures by way of rumors. The Generalgouverneur [Frank] has been instructed by the High Command of the Armed Forces (OKW) accordingly.

Additional construction material is not available. The measures must be carried out with the stocks of building materials available on the spot.

Special attention is needed for the necessity of giving the enemy's air reconnaissance the opportunity to recognize the positions being built and to photograph [them].

Army Group B is requested to have appropriate steps taken in agreement with Army Groups A and C and to inform the High Command of the Army (OKH) concerning its intentions by March 25.

By order
s. Halder.[1])

---

[1]) NOKW-2670 (photostat, 2pp.). The various marginal notes made on this copy—that of Army Group A—have been omitted, as have the distribution and the certificate of correctness.

The Attack on Soviet Russia and the Invasion of Crete

The Führer and Supreme Commander
            of the Armed Forces   Führer HQ, 25 April 1941
No. 44581/41 Top Secret
  WFSt/Abt. L (I Op)

Directive No. 28
(Operation Merkur)

1) As a base for the air war against England in the Eastern Mediterranean the *occupation of the island Crete* is to be prepared (Operation Merkur).

. . . .

3) All means are to be used to assemble the airborne corps, including the 22d Division which is again under the control of the Commander in Chief of the Air Force, in the collection area to be designated by the latter. The necessary truck space is to be made available by the High Command of the Army and Air Force to the Armed Forces Transportation Chief. [p. 1] The *transportation movements* must not lead to any delay in the deployment "Barbarossa".

. . . .

s. Adolf Hitler 1)

National Defense Section   Führer HQ, 28 April 1941
No.: 44 618/41 Top Secret L (I Op)

Memorandum for Report!
Concerning: Drawing together of forces
for operation "Merkur"

On April 28 a conference was held at the National Defense Section, under the chairmanship of the Section Chief, with representatives of the three branches of the armed forces concerning the drawing together of forces for the operation "Merkur".
Participants: . . . .

---

1) PS - 450 (photostat, 3pp.), pp. 1-2.

A) *Transport of the 7th Airborne Division, including corps troops of the IX. Airborne Corps.*

7th Airborne Division will be moved by train.... and will be ready for commitment on May 17. This is also the latest time in view of the commitment of the transport groups to "Barbarossa".

. . . .

B) *Movement of the 22d Division.*

The division is now .... in the Bucharest area. It is to be moved into the area Athens-Larissa.

Possibilities:

1) *Air transport:*

According to a report from the air force this is impossible because . . . .

2) *Rail transport:*

Use of the Bulgarian route is impossible....

Use of the route Belgrade-Nish-Greek border .... is out because the rolling stock found there will be fully occupied by the transport of the caterpillar sections of the Panzer division which are needed for "Barbarossa".

3) *Truck transport:*

. . . .

Accordingly, the 22d Division will be available May 27 at the earliest. But the truck transport regiment used which is absolutely needed for the supply needs of the Panzer troops for "Barbarossa", will be usable again after return and repairs only on July 3 according to the High Command of the Army.

4) *Marching*

By marching the division will arrive .... about the middle of June.

5) *Ship transport:*

.... out because of lack of suitable shipping space.

6) *The following expedients were discussed:*

a) Use of the transport space of the 13th and 16th Panzer Divisions must be refused as then .... the divisions cannot be employed in the first line in "Barbarossa".

. . . .

Thus all possibilities for moving the 22d Division to the jumping-off point without affecting the schedules "Merkur" and "Barbarossa" have been exhausted.

C) *Substitution for the 22d Division* by an army division located in the southeast area.

For this the 6th Mountain Division is.... suited.[2] Concerning its movement.... no difficulties exist....

----

[2] Marginal note: "Could one not add the 125th Infantry Regiment? K[eitel]."

The Commander in Chief of the Air Force who is basically in agreement with the proposal of the High Command of the Army still wants parts of the 22d Division moved up later as a third wave for "Merkur".

The High Command of the Army, on the other hand, requests that because of these movements in the southeast area the 22d Division be committed in "Barbarossa" within the framework of the army (11th Army)....

D) *Position of the National Defense Section:*

1) The *timely* movement of the 22d Division is impossible by any means.

. . . .

It is therefore suggested that the 22d Division be made available to the army.[3])

2) The use of the 6th Mountain Division instead of the 22d Division is possible....

. . . .

3) The enclosed draft of an order is therefore suggested.

[s] Warlimont[4])

OKW/WFSt/Abt.L (I Op)   Führer HQ,   29 April 1941
No. 00 785/41 Secret
                    To:
                    1) High Command of the Army....
                    2) Commander in Chief of the Air Force....
                    3) Chief of Armed Forces Transportation
                    for Information Commander in Chief of the Navy....

Contrary orders of Directive 28 are revoked.

The timely transport of the 22d Division for "Merkur" has proved to be impossible under the established conditions.....................

. . . .

(s) W[arlimont] 29/4[5])

---

[3]) Marginal note in Jodl's handwriting: "No." Underneath "High Command of the Armed Forces (OKW) Reserve! K[eitel]."

[4]) Germany, OKW, L, PS - 451 (photostat, 5pp.). Underneath Warlimont's signature is the following written notation by Jodl: "Führer agreed on 29 April. 125th Infantry Regiment is to be added to the 6th Mountain Division. 22d Division is to become OKW reserve and not to be used as ground troops in Barbarossa. J[odl]." The draft promised in D, 3 was enclosed. It is in the form of an amending order to Directive No. 28 and was replaced by the following document.

[5]) PS - 450 (photostat, 1p.). The document is also initialled by Keitel and Jodl. The Distribution has been omitted.

BIBLIOGRAPHY

Listed in the bibliography are the materials found useful in the preparation of this study. All unpublished documents consulted have been listed, whether or not they were cited in the text, so that the research of others may be facilitated.

Except for some documents of the "NI" series—consulted in the Library of Congress —the Nuremberg materials used, both documents and transcripts, are from the Law Library of the University of Chicago. The documents can be located only by the use of the document number and series; e.g. NG - 2852 is document number 2852 in the "NG" series and cannot be found under any author or subject classification. At Nuremberg, the documents were prepared in four forms—photostat, mimeographed copy, translation (if the original was not in English), and Staff Evidence Analysis (cited as SEA). The value of these forms for research is in the order indicated, and the best form available has been used. The SEA is very frequently inadequate, but, on the other hand, often contains useful information on such matters as the source of a document or the identification of initials and signatures.

Diplomatic documents and affidavits are listed under the name of the author. Personal documents by military leaders and Hitler's numbered directives on the conduct of the war are listed under the author's name; other military documents appear under the name of the military office or unit. Abbreviations and technical terms are explained in the section following the index.

Primary Sources: Documents, Affidavits, Trial Transcripts, Interrogations

Antonescu, Ion. "Memorandum on German-Rumanian Cooperation," 15 January 1941. NG - 3764. Translated by United States, OCCWC. Pp. 12 (mimeographed).

Bilmanis, Alfred (ed.). *Latvian-Russian Relations, Documents.* Washington, D.C.: The Latvian Legation, 1944.

Bürkner, Leopold. "Affidavit of Bürkner," 29 September 1947. NG - 2681. Pp. 3 (photostat).

Canada, Royal Commission to Investigate Disclosure of Secret and Confidential Information to Unauthorized Persons. *The Report of the Royal Commission.* Ottawa: Edmund Cloutier, 1946.

Ciano, Galeazzo. *An Account of the International Situation in Recent Years, Speech in the Chamber of Fasces and Corporations, Rome, December 16, 1939.* Rome: Italian Ministry of Foreign Affairs, 1939.

——. *Ciano's Diplomatic Papers.* Translated by Stuart Hood; edited by Malcolm Muggeridge. London: Odhams Press, Limited, 1948.

Dekanozov, Vladimir G. "Note Verbale to the German Foreign Ministry," 21 June 1941. NG - 4234. P. 1 (photostat).

Denmark, Rigsdagen, Folketinget, Kommission af 25. Oktober 1950 i henhold til Grundlovens No. 45. *Beretning til Folketinget.* Vol. XII. *Bilag, Tyske Dokumenter.* Copenhagen: J. H. Schultz, 1951.

Dimitrov, Georgi. *The War and the Working Class of the Capitalist Countries.* New York: Workers Library Publishers, 1939.

Dirksen, Herbert von. "Affidavit of Dirksen," 27 August 1947. NG - 3604. Pp. 6 (photostat).

Erdmannsdorff, Otto von. "Erdmannsdorff to Ribbentrop (No. 352)," 6 April 1941. NG - 2693. Pp. 2 (mimeographed).

——. "Erdmannsdorf to Ribbentrop (No. 368)," 9 April 1941. NG - 2732. Translated by United States, OCCWC. Pp. 3 (mimeographed).

Erdmannsdorff, Otto von. "Erdmannsdorff to Ribbentrop," 24 June 1941. NG - 4306 and 2740C. Translated by United States, OCCWC. Pp. 4 (mimeographed).

Etzdorf, Hasso von. "Memorandum of Etzdorf," 10 February 1941. NG - 2988. Pp. 5 (photostat).

Falkenstein, Freiherr von. "Falkenstein to General ?," 20 October 1940. PS - 376. Pp. 4 (photostat).

Finland, Ministry of Foreign Affairs. *Documents concerning Finnish-Soviet Relations during the Autumn of 1939*. Helsinki: Oy. Suomen Kirya, 1940.

——. *Finland Reveals her Secret Documents on Soviet Policy, March, 1940-June, 1941*. New York: Wilfred Funk, Inc., 1941.

France, Délégation française auprès de la Commission allemande d'armistice. *La Délégation française auprès de la Commission allemande d'armistice, Recueil de Documents*. 2 vols. Paris: Imprimerie Nationale, 1947-1950.

——. Ministère des Affaires Étrangères. *The French Yellow Book*. New York: Reynal and Hitchcock, 1940.

Friedrich Krupp, A.G. Abteilung für Russland. "An das Direktorium der FKAG; Betrifft: neues deutsch-russisches Kreditabkommen," 22 August 1939. NI - 921. Pp. 2 (photostat).

——. "An das Direktorium der FKAG; Betrifft: neues Kreditabkommen mit der U.d.S.S.R.," 21 August 1939, NI - 921. Pp. 2 (photostat).

——. "Warenliste für das 'Laufende Geschäft' gemäss dem deutsch-russischen Abkommen vom 19. August 1939," 22 August 1939. P. 1 (photostat).

——. "Warenliste für das 200 Mill-RM Kreditabkommen vom 19. August 1939," 22 August 1939. NI - 921. P. 1 (photostat).

Friedrich Krupp, A.G. (Eberhardt). "F. Krupp A.G. an das Reichswirtschaftsministerium; Betrifft: Russland-Vertragsabschluss für Lieferung von 6 Stück 38cm Schiffsgeschütztürmen und Munition. Freistellung durch das Reich aus Folgen eventueller Eingriffe des Reiches," 8 October 1940. NIK - 11629. Pp. 4 (mimeographed).

Friedrich Krupp, A.G. (Köttgen). "Niederschrift des Herrn Köttgen über die Besprechung am 7. November 1939," 7 November 1939. NIK - 12686. Pp. 2 (photostat).

Friedrich Krupp, A.G. (Reiff). "Niederschrift des Herrn Reiff über die Besprechung in Essen am 21. Juni 1940," 21 June 1940. NI - 920. Pp. 3 (photostat).

Friedrich Krupp, A.G. (Vaillant). "Aktennotiz; Betrifft: Russland-Abwicklung der Verträge," 30 September 1941. NIK - 9244. Pp. (mimeographed).

——. "Entwurf eines Briefes: Der Reichswirtschaftsminister an die Fried. Krupp Aktiengesellschaft; Betrifft: Russland - 38cm Doppeltürme," 13 November 1940. NIK - 12080. Pp. 3 (mimeographed).

——. "Transcript by Herr Vaillant Concerning a Discussion at the High Command of the Navy, on 13 November 1940; re: Russia - 38cm Double-turrets," 13 November 1940. NIK - 12079. Translated by United States, OCCWC. Pp. 4 (mimeographed).

Gantenbein, James, W. (ed.). *Documentary Background of World War II, 1931 to 1941*. New York: Columbia University Press, 1948.

Gaus, Friedrich. "Affidavit of Gaus," 26 September 1947. NG - 4183. Pp. 2 (mimeographed).

——. "Affidavit of Gaus," 25 January 1948. NG - 4556. Pp. 3 (photostat).

Germany,[1]) Auswärtiges Amt. *Dokumente zum Konflikt mit Jugoslawien und Griechenland (Weissbuch 7)*. Berlin: Zentral-Verlag der N.S.D.A.P., 1941.

---

[1]) The following items are from German government and military agencies, arranged in alphabetical order. Army units are at the end of this list. N.S.D.A.P. documents are given under the German name of the party.

——. *Dokumente zur Vorgeschichte des Krieges (Weissbuch 2)*. Basel: Verlag Bink-häuser, 1939.

——. *Die Geheimakten des Französischen Generalstabes 'Weissbuch 6)*. Berlin: Deut-scher Verlag, 1941.

·——. "Memorandum on the Mussolini-Ribbentrop Conversation, 22 September 1940," 22 September 1940. PS - 1865, SEA, United States, OCCPAC. P. 1 (mimeo graphed).

——. "German Memorandum to the Danish Government," 9 April 1940. NG - 113. Pp. 6 (photostat).

——. *Polnische Dokumente zur Vorgeschichte des Krieges (Weissbuch 3)*. Basel: Ver-lag Birkhäuser, 1940.

——. "Protokoll über die Morgenkonferenz mit den ausländischen Pressevertretern am 14. Juni 1941," 14 June 1941. Record by Schindel. NG - 5154. Pp. 4 (mimeo-graphed).

——. *Vertrags-Verzeichnis seit 1920, Stand Oktober 1941*. [Berlin, 1941].

——. "Wirtschaftsabkommen zwischen dem Deutschen Reich und der Union der Sozia-listischen Sowjet-Republiken," 11 February 1940. NIK - 11361. Pp. 78 (photostat).

Germany, Auswärtiges Amt, Büro RAM. "Neue Sprachregelung," 21 June 1941. NG - 4192 and 4242. P. 1 (photostat).

Germany, Beauftragter für den Vierjahresplan, Deutsche Forschungsgemeinschaft (Mentzel). "Deutsche Forschungsgemeinschaft an OKM, Amt HW (Conrad)," 20 March 1940. PB - 13178. P. 1 (typescript). Original in the Library of Congress, Newspaper Division.

Germany, Beauftragter für den Vierjahresplan, Generalrat. "3. Sitzung des General-rats vom 10. Januar 1940 unter Vorsitz von Staatssekretär Körner," 10 January 1940. Record by Gramsch. NI - 7474. Pp. 6 (photostat).

——. "7. Sitzung des Generalrats vom 28. Februar 1940 unter Vorsitz von Staatssekre-tär Körner," 28 February 1940. Record by Gramsch. NI - 7474. Pp. 7 (photostat).

——. "11. Sitzung des Generalrats vom 24. 6. 41 unter Vorsitz von Staatssekretär Kör-ner," 24 June 1941. Record by Bergbohm. NI - 7474. Pp. 12 (photostat).

Germany, Beauftragter für den Vierjahresplan, Geschäftsgruppe Ernährung. "Riecke an Backe; Betreff: Leistungen des Reichskommissariats Ukraine," 17 November 1943. PS - 1294. Pp. 2 (photostat).

Germany, Deutsche Botschaft China. "Abkommen, Frachtenverkehr, Transitverkehr, Frako (WE - 2 - 2a)," 1940—1944. Folder in the Library of Congress, Manuscripts Division.

——. "Postpaketverkehr über Sibirien (WP 5)," 1926-1941. Folder in the Library of Congress, Manuscripts Division.

——. "Reiseverkehr über Sibirien (WV - 6)," 1939 - 1941. Folder in the Library of Congress, Manuscripts Division.

Germany, Dienststelle Rosenberg.[2]) "Aktennotiz über die Unterredung [Rosenbergs] mit Staatssekretär Körner," 8 May 1941. Prepared by Rosenberg. PS - 1018. Pp. 10 (photostat).

——. "Aufzeichnung [über die Stellung der Hauptkommissare in den besetzten Ostge-bieten]," 10 June 1941. Prepared by Bräutigam. PS - 1032. Pp. 3 (photostat).

---

[2]) As this office was officially established on April 20, 1941, all documents from Rosenberg's files concerning the Soviet Union and dated before April 20, 1941, are listed under the Aussenpolitische Amt of the Nazi Party. The Dienststelle Rosenberg later became the Ministry for the Occupied Eastern Territories (Reichsministerium für die besetzten Ostgebiete).

186 BIBLIOGRAPHY

Germany, Dienststelle Rosenberg. "Denkschrift Nr. 3; Betrifft: U.d.S.S.R.," 25 April 1941. PS - 1020. Pp. 15 (photostat).

——. "Grosskopf's Report on the Session at the Rosenberg Ministry on May 29, 1941," 30 May 1941. NG - 4431. SEA, United States, OCCWC. Pp. 2 (mimeographed).

——. "Grosskopf's Report to Weizsäcker and Woermann on Rosenberg's Requests of May 9, 1941," 9 May 1941. NG - 4856. SEA, United States, OCCWC. P. 1 (mimeographed).

——. "Memoranda on a Conference at the Rosenberg Ministry, May 9, 1941." 9 and 19 May 1941. Prepared by Grosskopf. NG - 4434. SEA, United States, OCCWC. Pp. 2 (mimeographed).

——. "Vermerk über eine Unterredung mit Reichsminister Funk am 24. April 1941," 25 April 1941. Prepared by Rosenberg. NG - 3709. Pp. 2 (photostat).

——. "Reichskommissariate Kaukasus, Russland, Baltenland, Ukraine," 18 June 1941. 1035 - PS. Pp. 9 (photostat).

——. "Stellenbesetzung für den Fall einer erweiterten Aktion im Osten," 22 May 1941. Prepared by Grosskopf. NG - 4755. Pp. 3 (mimeographed).

——. "Stellenbesetzung für den Fall einer erweiterten Aktion im Osten [Zusatz]," 4 June 1941. Prepared by Grosskopf. NG - 4633 and 4772. Pp. 6 (photostat).

——. "Unterredung mit Reichsleiter Rosenberg am 19. 6. 1941," 19 June 1941. Prepared by Grosskopf. NG - 4990. Pp. 5 (photostat).

——. "Vermerk über eine Besprechung bei Reichsleiter Rosenberg am Sonnabend, den 21. Juni 1941, von 11-12 Uhr," 21 June 1941. PS - 1034. Pp. 2 (photostat).

Germany, Ministerrat für die Reichsverteidigung, Vorsitzender (Göring). "Ministerrat für die Reichsverteidigung an das Oberkommando der Wehrmacht; Betreff: Russland-Vertrag, Export," 30 March 1940. P. 1 (typescript). Original in the Library of Congress, Aeronautics Division.

Germany, Oberkommando des Heeres, Generalstab des Heeres, Attaché Abteilung. "Att. Abt. an OKW, Abt. Ausl/Abw.; Betreff: Erkundungen in Bulgarien (No. 67/40)," 13 December 1941. NOKW - 3347. P. 1 (photostat).

——. "Att. Abt. (Mellenthin) an Op. Abt. (Grolman); Betreff: Besprechungen mit Finnen (No. 93/41)," 24 May 1941. NG - 4310. P. 1 (photostat).

——. "Att. Abt. (Mellenthin) an Uthmann," 24 February 1941. NG - 4310. P. 1 (photostat).

Germany, Oberkommando des Heeres, Generalstab des Heeres, Abteilung Fremde Heere Ost. "Protokoll über die Besprechung mit Finnland vom 3.-6. Juni 1941; Thema: Beteiligung der Finnen an Barbarossa (No. 71/41)," 10 June 1941. Prepared by Kinzel. NOKW - 1181. Pp. 4 (photostat).

Germany, Oberkommando des Heeres, Generalstab des Heeres, Generalquartiermeister, Abteilung Kriegsverwaltung. "Wirtschaftsorganisation (No. 285/41)," 14 May 1941. Prepared by Wagner. NOKW - 3335. Pp. 4 (photostat).

Germany, Oberkommando des Heeres. Generalstab des Heeres, Operationsabteilung. "Angaben über die Rote Armee, Stand 15. 1 1941," 22 January 1941. PS - 1799. Pp. 4 (photostat).

——. "Arbeitsstäbe für Barbarossa (No. 144/41)," 14 February 1941. NOKW - 2670. Pp. 2 (photostat).

——. "Entwurf; Aufmarschanweisung Barbarossa (No. 050/41)," 22 January 1941. NOKW - 2705. Pp. 18 (photostat).

——. "Auszug aus Protokoll der Besprechung mit den Vertretern der finnischen Wehrmacht am 25. 5. 1941 in Salzburg," 25 May 1941. Prepared by Grolman. NG - 4310. Pp. 6 (photostat).

——. "Besprechung beim OKH am 27. 3. 1941 (No. 479/41)," 21 March 1941 NOKW - 2670. Pp. 2 (photostat).

——. "Brauchitsch an Heeresgruppe A; Betreff: Aufmarschanweisung Gelb (No. 45/40)," 16 January 1940. NOKW - 511. P. 1 (photostat).

——. "Op. Abt. (Halder) an Att. Abt. (No. 720/40)," 10 December 1940. NOKW - 3347. P. 1 (photostat).

——. "Op. Abt. (Halder) an Att. Abt. (No. 722/40)," 14 December 1940. NOKW - 3347. P. 1 (photostat).

——. "Op. Abt. (Halder) an Heeresgruppe A; Betreff: Barbarossa (No. 261/41)," 24 February 1941. NOKW - 2670. Pp. 3 (photostat).

——. "Op. Abt. (Halder) an Heeresgruppe A; Betreff: Barbarossa (Arbeitsstäbe)," 24 February 1941. NOKW - 2670. P. 1 (photostat).

——. "Op. Abt. (Halder) an Heeresgruppe B; nachrichtlich an Heeresgruppen A und C (No. 465/41)," 19 March 1941. NOKW - 2670. Pp. 2 (photostat).

——. "Op. Abt. an AOK 16 (No. 15134/41)," 21 January 1941. NOKW - 2703. P. 1 (photostat).

——. "Order on Moving Troops to the East (No. 496/40)," 6 September 1940. NOKW - 1744. Translated by United States, OCCWC. (Collection consulted has only page 1. SEA is available).

——. "Verlegung AOK 11 nach Rumänien (No. 810/41)," 6 May 1941. NOKW - 099. Pp. 2 (photostat).

——. "Verlegung der Kommandobehörden nach dem Osten, bezw. Westen (No. 440/41)," 19 March 1941. NOKW - 2670. Pp. 5 (photostat).

Germany, Oberkommando der Luftwaffe, Generalluftzeugmeister. "Bericht über den Besuch der russischen Luftfahrtkommission bei den Lizenzwerken des Motorenbaues (zu Nr. 1409/39 vom 17. 11. 39)," 12 January 1940. Prepared by Heyking. Pp. 5 (typescript). Original in the Library of Congress, Aeronautics Division.

Germany, Oberkommando der Luftwaffe, Reichsminister der Luftfahrt und Oberbefehlshaber der Luftwaffe. "GL 5 (Heemswerder[?]) an das OKW, Wi Rü Amt (Griebel); Betreff: Einfuhr von Flugbenzin (No. 5819/40)," 18 May 1940. P. 1 (typescript). Original in the Library of Congress, Aeronautics Division.

Germany, Oberkommando der Marine. *Fuehrer Conferences on Matters Dealing with the German Navy, 1939, 1940, 1941.* Translated by United States, Navy Department, Office of Naval Intelligence. Washington: Navy Department, 1947.

Germany, Oberkommando der Marine, Abteilung H.W. [Hydrographie und Wetter(?)]. "Abt. H.W. (Conrad) an die Deutsche Forschungsgemeinschaft; Betrifft: Schenkung des 'Meteor'-Werkes an sowjet-russische Institute," 13 March 1940. PB - 13178. Pp. 2 (typescript). Original in the Library of Congress, Newspaper Division.

Germany, Oberkommando der Marine, 1. Seekriegsleitung (Assmann). "Kriegstagebuch der Seekriegsleitung, Teil A, Heft 4," 1-31 December 1939. C - 27. Pp. 236 (photostat).

"Teil A, Heft 5," 1-31 January 1940. C - 21. Pp. 260 (photostat).

"Teil A, Heft 9," 1-31 May 1940 (27 May 1940). NOKW - 2545. Pp. 6 (photostat).

"Teil A, Heft 13," 1-30 September 1940 (23 September 1940). NOKW - 2557. Translated by United States, OCCWC. Pp. 4 (photostat).

"Teil A, Heft 16," 1-31 December 1940. C - 105. Pp. 346 (photostat).

"Teil A, Heft 17," 1-31 January 1941. C - 35. Contains pp. 234, 327-28, 401-04, 418 (photostat).

"Teil A, Heft 18," 1-28 February 1941. C - 33. Contains pp. 1-10, 12-13, 15-45, 48, 50-51, 54-57, 82-83, 97, 126-27, 132-37, 146-47, 150-76, 199, 231-33, 248-50, 340-41, 354-56, 358, 376-84, 387-94 (photostat).

"Teil A, Heft 19," 1-30 March 1941 (24 March 1941); NOKW - 2554, pp. 3 (photostat). 26 March 1941); NOKW - 2555, translated by United States, OCCWC, p. 1 (mimeographed). (27 March 1941); NOKW - 2556, pp. 2 (photostat).

"Teil A, Heft 21," 1-31 May 1941 (2 May 1941). NOKW - 2550. Pp. 2 (photostat).

"Teil A, Heft 22," 1-30 June 94. C - 37. Pp. 411 (photostat).

Germany, Oberkommando der Marine, Seekriegsleitung. "Review of an Eastern Campaign against Russia (Fall 'Barbarossa'); Final Version,"30 January 1941. NOKW - 2658. Translated by United States, OCCWC. Pp. 4 (mimeographed). (Excerpts from a 34-page original).

—. "Skl an Gruppe Nord; Betreff: Barbarossa (No. 580/41)," 3 May 1941. NOKW - 2727. Translated by United States, OCCWC. P. 1 (mimeographed).

——. "Skl (Fricke) an Gruppe Nord; Betreff: Barbarossa (No. 352/41)," 20 March 1941. NOKW - 2760. P. 1 (photostat).

——. "Skl an Gruppe Nord, BdK (No. 1008/41)," 14 June 1941. NOKW - 2729. P. 1 (photostat).

——. "Skl (Schniewind) an OKH, Gen.St.d.H., Op. Abt.; Betreff: Kaukasisches Ölgebiet (No. 599/41)," 9 May 1941. NOKW - 2730. Pp. 6 (photostat).

——. "Skl (Schniewind) an OKW, WFSt," 22 April 1941. NOKW - 2726. SEA, United States, OCCWC. P. 1 (mimeographed).

——. "Skl (Schniewind) an OKW, WFSt; OKH, Gen.St.d.H.; Ob.d.L., Führungsstab; Betreff: Barbarossa (No. 94/41)," 30 January 1941. NOKW - 2270. Pp. 8 (photostat).

Germany, Oberkommando der Wehrmacht. "OKW to the Military Mission in Rumania," 16 January 1941 (?). NG - 3765. Translated by United States, OCCWC. P. 1 (mimeographed).

Germany, Oberkommando der Wehrmacht, Amtsgruppe Ausland. "Ag. Ausland (Bürkner) an Auswärtiges Amt, z.Hd. Herrn Botschafter Ritter; Chef Amt Ausland Abwehr; Chef Abwehr III (No. 10/41)," 11 January 1941. NG - 3144. P. 1 (photostat).

——. "Ag. Ausland (Bürkner) an Gen.St.d.H., Att. Abt., z.Hd. Oberstleutnant Mellenthin (No. 49/41)," 22 February 1941. NG - 4310. P. 1 (photostat).

——. "Ausland III (Bürkner) an Ritter (No. 124/41)," 11 April 1941. NG - 2730. P. 1 (mimeographed).

Germany, Oberkommando der Wehrmacht, Ausland Abwehr. "Ausl/Abw. (Canaris) an Auswärtiges Amt (Weizsäcker)," 20 September 1940. NG - 4649. SEA, United States, OCCWC. P. 1 (mimeographed).

——. "Kurze Zusammenfassung von Ausgaben über den Besuch des Japanischen Aussenministers Matsuoka nach Mitteilungen des Auswärtigen Amtes und anderer Stellen (No. 127/41)," 10 April 1941. Prepared by Bürkner. PS - 1537. Pp. 2 (photostat).

Germany, Oberkommando der Wehrmacht, Wehrmachtführungsamt (later called Wehrmachtführungsstab). "Gliederung des Feldheeres," 1 July 1940. PS - 1783. Pp. 2 (photostat).

——. "Stellenbesetzung der H.Gr.Kdos., AOKs., Gen.Kdos. und Höheren Kommandos z.b.v., Stand 10. 8. 1940," 1 August 1940. PS - 1783. Pp. 8 (photostat).

——. "Übersicht [über die deutsche Heeresverteilung]," 7 May 1940. PS - 1783. P. 1 (photostat).

Germany, Oberkommando der Wehrmacht, Wehrmachtführungsstab, Abteilung Landesverteidigung. "Besprechung Führer-Chef WFSt am 17. 12. 40 (No. 33438/40)," 21 December 1940. Prepared by Lossberg. PS - 1799. Pp. 2 (photostat).

——. "Besprechung beim Reichsleiter Rosenberg," 1 May 1941. PS - 866. Pp. 3 (photostat).

——. "Die Beteiligung fremder Staaten an den Vorbereitungen für 'Barbarossa' (No. 44638/41)," 1 May 1941. Issued by Keitel. NOKW - 240. Pp. 2 (photostat).

——. "Bulgarien, 4. 12. 40 (No. 001082/40)," 4 December 1940. Prepared by Warlimont. NOKW - 3347. P. 1 (photostat).

——. "Entwurf zur Weisung 32 und Weisung an Deutschen General beim Hauptquartier der italienischen Wehrmacht," 30 June 1941. Prepared by Warlimont. PS - 456. Pp. 3 (photostat).

——. "Feindtäuschung (No. 44699/41)," 12 May 1941. Issued by Keitel. PS - 876. Pp. 2 (photostat).

——. "Fernschreiben; Betreff: Weisung 28 (Entwurf)," 28 April 1941. Prepared by Warlimont. 451 - PS. P. 1 (photostat).

——. "Fernschreiben; Betreff: Weisung 28, an OKH, Op. Abt.; Ob.d.L., Lw. Fü. St., Ia; Wehrmachttransportchef; nachrichtlich an Ob. d. M., 1. Skl. (No. 00785/41)," 29 April 1941. Prepared by Warlimont. PS - 450. P. 1 (photostat).

——. "Finnenbesprechung, Zusammenstellung der Besprechungspunkte (No. 44638)," 22 May 1941. PS - 883. Pp. 4 (photostat).

——. "Führer Decisions on Marita (No. 44150/41)," 14 February 1941. NG - 5255. Translated by United States, OCCWC. Pp. 2 (mimeographed).

——. "Führerentscheidungen über Rumänien (No. 44780/41)," 23 May 1941. Issued by Keitel. C - 54. Pp. 3 (photostat).

——. "Kommunistische Aufstandsbewegungen in den besetzten Gebieten. (No. 02060/41)," 16 September 1941. Issued by Keitel. PS - 807 and 829. Pp. 4 (photostat).

——. "Richtlinien für die Feindtäuschung (No. 44142/41)," 15 February 1941. Issued by Keitel. PS - 875. Pp. 4 (photostat).

——. "Vortragsnotiz; Betreff: Bereitstellung der Kräfte für Unternehmen 'Merkur' (No. 4461/41)," 28 April 1941. Prepared by Warlimont. PS - 451. Pp. 5 (photostat).

——. "Vortragsnotiz; Vorschlag für die Vorbereitung der Besprechungen über die Beteiligung Finnlands am Unternehmen Barbarossa (No. 44594/41)," 28 April 1941. Prepared by Warlimont. NOKW - 241. Pp. 2 (photostat).

——. "L (Keitel) an das Auswärtige Amt, z. Hd. von Herrn Legationsrat von der Heyden-Rynsch; Betrifft: Anwendung der Begriffe Krieg, Kriegs-Gebiet usw. auf die besetzten polnischen Gebiete (Generalgouvernement)," 15 April 1940. PS - 646. Pp. 2 (photostat).

——. "L an Heimatsstab Nord (Buschenhagen) (No. 00975/41)," 24 May 1941 (?). NG - 4310. P. 1 (photostat).

——. "Heimatsstab Nord (Buschenhagen) an L (Jodl)," 4 June 1941. NG - 4310. Pp. 2 (photostat).

——. "L (Warlimont) an L (Jodl); Betreff: Marita (No. 44150/41)," 11 February 1941. NG - 5236. Translated by United States, OCCWC. Pp. 3 (mimeographed).

——. "L (Keitel, Jodl, Warlimont) an Reichsminister Todt (No. 00400/41)," 9 March 1941. PS - 874 and 1747. Pp. 2 (photostat).

Germany, Oberkommando der Wehrmacht, Wehrwirtschafts- und Rüstungsamt. "Aktennotiz; Besprechung Thomas-Keitel," 4 December 1939. Prepared by Thomas. PS - 1456. Pp. 2 (photostat).[3])

——. "Besprechung am 19. Dezember 1939 über Lage und Aussichten der deutschen Ausfuhr," 19 December 1939. Prepared by Reute. PS - 1456. Pp. 9 (photostat).

——. "Besprechungsnotiz; Vortrag Amtschef bei Generaloberst Keitel," 26 April 1940. PS - 1456. Pp. 3 (photostat).

——. "Aktennotiz; Betreff: Abteilungs Chefbesprechung am 12. 6. 40," 12 June 1940. PS - 1456. Pp. 7 (photostat).

——. "Notiz über Aussprache im Führerhauptquartier," 14 June 1940. PS - 1456. P. 1 (photostat).

---

[3]) This and the following documents listed under the same author are all from a single file of the Wehrwirtschafts- und Rüstungsamt. This file apparently contained a chronologically organized series of reports on important conferences in which the head of the office (General Thomas) had participated. The individual documents from the file which have been used here are, therefore, listed in chronological, rather than alphabetical, order.

Germany, Oberkommando der Wehrmacht, Wehrwirtschafts- und Rüstungsamt. "Aktennotiz; Betreff: Besprechung bei Reichsmarschall Göring am 14. 8. 1940," 14 August 1940. Prepared by Thomas. PS - 1456. Pp. 2 (photostat).

———. "Amtschefbesprechung," 14 or 15 August 1940. Prepared by Jansen. PS - 1456. Pp. 10 (photostat).

———. "Aktennotiz; Betreff: Vortrag des Amtschefs beim Generalfeldmarschall Keitel am 21. 8. 40," 21 August 1940. PS - 1456. P. 1 (photostat).

———. "Vortragsnotiz über Besprechung bei Reichsminister Dr. Todt," 22 August 1940. Prepared by Meendsen-Bohlken. PS - 1456. Pp. 5 (photostat).

———. "Aktennotiz; Besprechung bei Reichsmarschall Göring," 29 August 1940. Prepared by Thomas. PS - 1456. Pp. 2 (photostat).

———. "Aktennotiz; Besprechung beim Amtschef am 30. 8. 40," 30 August 1940. PS - 1456. Pp. 2 (photostat).

———. "Besprechung bei Generalfeldmarschall Keitel am 20. September 1940," 21 September 1940. PS - 1456. Pp. 2 (photostat).

———. "Aktennotiz über die Entwicklung der Rüstungslage im Sommer 1940," September 1940 (?). Prepared by Thomas. PS - 1456. Pp. 3 (photostat).

———. "Besprechung am 9. Januar 1941; Arbeitseinsatz und Einziehung in der nicht zum engeren Rüstungsbereich gehörenden Wirtschaft," 9 January 1941. Prepared by Reute. PS - 1456. Pp. 49 (photostat).

———. "Vortrag Oberstleutnant Tietze beim Amtschef (Besprechung Reichsbeauftragter für Kautschuk, Herr Jehle, beim Amtschef mit Oberstleutnant Tietze)," 7 February 1941. PS - 1456. Pp. 5 (photostat).

———. "Aktennotiz; Besprechung bei Generalfeldmarschall Keitel am 8. 2. 1941," 8 February 1941. Prepared by Thomas. PS - 1456. Pp. 2 (photostat).

———. "Aktennotiz über Rücksprache Amtschef mit Staatssekretär Landfried; Betreff: Kautschuklage," 12 February 1941. PS - 1456. Pp. 2 (photostat).

———. "Aktennotiz über Vortrag beim Reichsmarschall am 26. 2. 1941," 27 February 1941. Prepared by Thomas. PS - 1456. Pp. 3 (photostat).

———. "Vortrag bei Reichsmarschall Göring am 19. 3. 41," 20 March 1941. Prepared by Thomas. PS - 1156 and 1456. Pp. 3 (photostat).

Germany, Oberkommando der Wehrmacht, Wehrwirtschafts- und Rüstungsamt, Oberstleutnant Dr. Hedler. "Kautschuk und die Versorgungslage im Kriege," 31 March 1941. NI - 6194. Pp. 39 (photostat).

Germany, Oberkommando der Wehrmacht, Wehrwirtschafts- und Rüstungsamt, Arbeitsstab Oldenburg. "Aktennotiz; Besprechung beim Herrn Amtschef, General der Infanterie Thomas, am 28. 2. 41; Betreff: Oldenburg," 1 March 1941. PS - 1317. Pp. 2 (photostat).[4]

———. "Note for the Files regarding the Discussion held on 21. 3. 41 at 11 o'clock with the Head of the Department on Barbarossa," 21 March 1941. PS - 1316. Translated by United States, CCPAC. Pp. 2 (mimeographed).

Germany, Oberkommando der Wehrmacht, Wehrwirtschafts- und Rüstungsamt, Landwirtschaftsamt Gotha. "Questions which will still Have to be Ordered by the Reichsmarschall or will Have to be Settled by the Fuehrer," 5 May 1941. PS - 1314. Translated by United States, CCPAC. Pp. 2 (mimeographed).

———. "Table of Organisation and Discussion thereto for the Führungsstab Ost," 30 April 1941. PS - 1313. SEA, United States, CCPAC. P. 1 (mimeographed).

----

[4] This and the following three documents are listed at this point since the incidents and offices concerned were under General Thomas whose main position was that of heading the Wehrwirtschafts- und Rüstungsamt. Arbeitsstab Oldenburg could also be listed under Beauftragter für den Vierjahresplan and Landwirtschaftsamt Gotha could be listed directly under Oberkommando der Wehrmacht.

Germany, Oberkommando der Wehrmacht, Wehrwirtschafts- und Rüstungsamt, Abteilung W. W. VI. "Wochenbericht für die Zeit vom 2.-8. 9. 39." 8 September 1939. NI - 7493. P. 1 (mimeographed).

Germany, Oberkommando der Wehrmacht, Wehrwirtschafts- und Rüstungsamt, Abteilung W. Wi. VII. "W Wi. VII (Becker) an OKH, OKM, RdL; Betreff: Russland (No. 11381/39)," 24 October 1939. Pp. 9 (typescript). Original in the Library of Congress, Aeronautics Division.

——. "Betreff: Russlandvertrag, Export (No. 6206/40)," 3 April 1940. Issued by Keitel. P. 1 (typescript). Original in the Library of Congress, Aeronautics Division.

——. "Betreff: Russen, Besuche der Kommissionen am 8. 11. 39," 8 November 1939. NIK - 9235. Pp. 3 (photostat). SEA, United States, OCCWC, pp. 2 (mimeographed).

Germany, Oberkommando der Wehrmacht, Wehrwirtschafts- und Rüstungsamt, Wehrwirtschafts-Inspektion XVII. "Der Inspekteur (Gautier) an I.G. Farben (Gross)," 29 September 1939. NI - 7786. P. 1 (mimeographed).

Germany, Reichsgruppe Industrie, Ausfuhrgemeinschaft für Kriegsgerät. "Aktenvermerk zu einer Unterredung mit Herrn Kapitaen Schottky am 29. 9. 1941; Betrifft: Abrechnung der Russland-Geschäfte," 30 September 1941. Prepared by Kloenne. NIK - 9244. Pp. 3 (mimeographed).

——. "Geschäftsbericht 1939/40," 14 August 1940. NI - 11360. Pp. 13 (photostat).

——. "Russland-Verhandlungen, Protektorat Altreich 30. 9. 39," 30 September 1939. Prepared by Eltze. NI - 919. Pp. 2 (photostat).

——. "Sitzung des engeren Beirats der AGK in Berlin am 29. 9. 39; Betrifft: Russland," 29 September 1939. Prepared by Pfirsch. NI - 919. Pp. 3 (photostat).

Germany, Reichsgruppe Industrie, Geschäftsführung. "Reichsgruppe Industrie an die Mitgliedfirmen der AGK und an die Meldestellen der AGK; Betreff: Kriegsgeräteausfuhr nach Polen," 17 May 1939. NIK - 11619. Pp. 2 (mimeographed).

Germany, Reichsgruppe Industrie, Wirtschaftsgruppe Eisen Schaffende Industrie. "Bericht über die Beiratsitzung der Wirtschaftsgruppe Eisen Schaffende Industrie am 19. Dezember 1940 in Berlin," 19 December 1940. NIK - 11709. Pp. 24 (mimeographed).

Germany, Statistisches Reichsamt, Abteilung VI. "Approved Imports of Goods in March, 1941," 8 May 1941 (?). NG - 927. Translated by United States, OCCWC. Pp. 4 (mimeographed).

——. "Germany's Payments to Foreign Countries from April, 1940 until June, 1940," 20 September 1940. NG - 927. Translated by United States, OCCWC. Pp. 5 (mimeographed).

Germany, Wehrmacht. (Documents of units of the German army follow; the alphabetically labeled units are given first, then those having numbers.)

Germany, Heeresgruppe A (Süd). "Aktennotiz zum Schreiben des Herrn Ob. d. H. vom 16. 1. 40," 24 January 1940 (?). Prepared by Manstein. NOKW - 511. P. 1 (photostat).

——. "Aufmarschanweisung Barbarossa (No. 150/41)," 15 February 1941. Issued by Rundstedt. NOKW - 2670. Pp. 17 (photostat).

——. "H. Gr. K. A (Sodenstern) an H. Gr. K. B; Betreff: Barbarossa (No. 157/41)," 15 February 1941. NOKW - 2670. Pp. 2 (photostat).

——. "H. Gr. K. A. (Sodenstern) an OKH, Gen. St. d. H., Op. Abt.; Betreff: Barbarossa (Arbeitsstäbe) (No 121/41)," 8 February 1941. NOKW - 2670. Pp. 2 (photostat).

——. "H. Gr. K. A (Sodenstern) an OKH, Gen. St. d. H., Op. Abt.; Betreff: Barbarossa (Mitwirkung anderer Staaten) (No. 151/41)" 12 February 1941. NOKW - 2670. Pp. 3 (photostat).

——. "H. Gr. K. A an OKH, Gen. St. d. H., Op. Abt.; Betreff: Barbarossa (No. 149/41)," 15 February 1941. NOKW - 2670. P. 1 (photostat).

Germany, Heeresgruppe A (Süd). "Kriegstagebuch der Heeresgruppe Süd, Abt. Ia, 1. Teil," 2 February 1941, 27 March 1941, 2 April 1941. NOKW - 3432. Pp. 4 (photostat).

——. "Verlegung des Hauptquartiers und Nachrichtenverkehr (No. 492/41)," 5 April 1941. Prepared by Sodenstern. NOKW - 2670. Pp. 3 (photostat).

——. "Verlegung des Heeresgruppenkommandos (No. 321/41)," 1 March 1941. Prepared by Sodenstern. NOKW - 2670. Pp. 4 (photostat).

——. "Westoffensive (No. 20/40)," 12 January 1940. Prepared by Rundstedt. NOKW - 511. Pp. 10 (photostat).

Germany, Heeresgruppe Süd, Abwehr II. "Voraussetzungen für die Sicherheit des Nachschubes und die Gewinnung höchster Ernährungsüberschüsse in der Ukraine," 28 October 1941. Prepared by Oberländer. PS - 52. Pp. 9 (photostat).

Germany, Heeresgruppe B (Mitte). "H. Gr. K. B and AOK's 4, 17, 18," 3 April 1941. NOKW - 2691. SEA, United States, OCCWC. Pp. 2 (mimeographed).

Germany, Heeresgruppe C (Nord). "Aufmarschanweisung 'Barbarossa' Teil I (Vorbemerkung) an AOK 18 (No. 8/41)," 5 February 1941. Issued by Leeb. NOKW - 2452 and 2587. Pp. 7 (photostat).

——. "H. Gr. K. C an AOK 16," 30 January 1941. NOKW - 2703. P. 1 (photostat).

——. "H. Gr. K. C (Abschnittsstab Ostpreussen) an AOK 16 (Unterabschnitt Ostpreussen I) (No. 415/41)," 17 May 1941. NOKW - 2706. P. 1 (photostat).

——. "H. Gr. K. C (Sodenstern) an Chef Gen. St. d. H. (Halder) (No. 112/39)," 11 October 1939. NOKW - 3315. P. 1 (photostat).

——. "H. Gr. K. C. (Sodenstern) an H. Gr. K. B. (Salmuth) (No. 112/1939)," 11 October 1939. NOKW - 3433. Translated by United States, OCCWC. P. 1 (mimeographed).

——. "Operationsstudie im Rahmen einer Heeresgruppe (No. 30/41)," 23 January 1941. NOKW - 2703. Pp. 6 (photostat).

——. "Operationsstudie Besprechung am 17. 2. 41 (No. 358/41)," 29 January 1941. NOKW - 2703. Pp. 2 (photostat).

Germany, Panzergruppe 3 (Pz. AOK 3). "Aufmarschanweisung 'Barbarossa' (No. 25/41)," 12 March 1941 and 24 May 1941. NOKW - 2756. Pp. 13 (photostat).

——. "Befehl für die Bereitstellung zum Angriff am B-Tag (No. 201/41)," 9 June 1941. NOKW - 2704. Pp. 6 (photostat).

——. "Kräftezuführung und Regelung der Bewegungen zum Antreten, Neufassung vom 27. 5. 41," 27 May 1941. NOKW - 2756. Pp. 3 (photostat).

——. "Pz. Gr. 3 an H. Gr. K. B (No. 15/41)," 4 March 1941. NOKW - 2450. Translated by United States, OCCWC. P. 1 (mimeographed).

——. "Tätigkeitsbericht Nr. 2 (Ic), Januar-Juli 1941." NOKW - 2672. Translated by United States, OCCWC. Pp. 4 (mimeographed).

Germany, 6. Panzer-Division. "Befehl für die Bereitstellung zum Angriff (No. 280/41)," 13 June 1941. NOKW - 2652. Pp. 4 (photostat).

——. "Divisionsbefehl für den Angriff, Divisionsbefehl Nr. 1 (No. 294/41)," 16 June 1941. NOKW - 2652. Pp. 10 (photostat).

——. "Divisionsbefehl für den Angriff, Entwurf (No. 234/41)," 5 June 1941. NOKW - 2652. Pp. 10 (photostat).

——. "Planspiel am 11. 6. 41 in Allenstein (No. 236/41)," 5 June 1941. NOKW - 2652. P. 1 (photostat).

——. "Tätigkeitsbericht der 6. Panzer-Division, Abteilung Ic, 22 April 1941-10 May 1941." NOKW - 2640. Pp. 3 (photostat).

Germany, 6. Schützen-Brigade. "Kriegstagebuch Nr. 3: 21. 6. 41—22. 11. 41." NOKW - 2639. Pp. 3 (photostat).

Germany, Armeeoberkommando 11. "AOK 11 (Woehler) to H. Gr. K. A; Subject: Reconnaissance of the Pruth Border (No. 2227/41)," 21 May 1941. NOKW - 3031. Excerpts translated by United States, OCCWC. Pp. 2 (mimeographed).

——. "Order for the Defense of the River Moldau until the Assembly of the German Forces Has Been Completed (No. 2308/41)," 26 May 1941. Prepared by Woehler. NOKW - 3054. Excerpts translated by United States, OCCWC. P. 1 (mimeographed).

Germany, Armeeoberkommando 12. "Armeebefehl Nr. 4 (No. 0227/41)," 2 April 1941. NOKW - 3432. Pp. 2 (photostat).

Germany, Armeeoberkommando 16 (Unterabschnitt Ostpreussen I). "Befehl für die Sicherung der Landesgrenze (No. 155/41)," 10 May 1941. NOKW - 2701. Pp. 8 (photostat).

——. "Vernehmung des Oberbefehlshabers der 6. russischen Armee am 9. 8. 1941," 18 August 1941. NOKW - 2721. Pp. 4 (photostat).

Germany, XVII. Armeekorps. "Korpsbefehl Nr. 1 (No. 278/40)," 23 July 1940. NOKW - 3437. Pp. 3 (photostat).

Germany, Armeeoberkommando 17. "AOK 17 an die AK's," 8 April 1941. NOKW - 2691. SEA, United States, OCCWC. Pp. 2 (mimeographed).

——. "AOK 17 an H. Gr. K. A (Süd); Betreff: Schutzmassnahmen gegenüber der Bevölkerung (No. 266/41)," 29 May 1941. NOKW - 136. Pp. 2 (photostat).

——. "Kriegstagebuch Nr. 1, 23 April—22 Juni 1941." NOKW - 1889 (for identification, see SEA, United States, OCCWC; Pp. 3 [mimeographed]). Pp. 13 (photostat).

Germany, 26. Infanterie-Division. "Aufmarsch und Kampfanweisung 'Barbarossa'," 16 June 1941. NOKW - 2451. Translated by United States, OCCWC. Pp. 3 (mimeographed).

Germany, XXX. Armeekorps. "Order for the Preparation of the Deployment 'Barbarossa' (No. 075/41)," 4 June 1941. NOKW - 2449. Translated by United States, OCCWC. Pp. 2 (mimeographed).

Germany, 32. Infanterie-Division. "Vorbemerkungen zur 'Studie Barbarossa' (No. 020/41)," 5 June 1941. NOKW - 2702. P. 1 (photostat).

Germany, 35. Infanterie-Division. "Tätigkeitsbericht (Ic) vom 1. 4. 1941—1. 3. 1942." NOKW - 2356. P. 1 (photostat).

Germany, 36. Infanterie-Division (mot.). "Tätigkeitsbericht (Ic) Nr. 1, 25. 5. 41—31. 5. 42." NOKW - 3408. Pp. 6 (photostat).

Germany, XXXXI. Armeekorps (Festungsstab Allenstein). "XXXXI. AK to 6. Pz. Div.; Committing of the Regiment for Special Duties (No. 165/41)," 7 June 1941. NOKW - 2567. Translated by United States, OCCWC. P. 1 (mimeographed).

——. "Kampfanweisung für Operationsbefehl (No. 83/41)," 11 May 1941. NOKW - 2510. Pp. 9 (photostat).

——. "Korpsbefehl für den Angriff, Barbarossa Studie (No. 96/41)," 19 May 1941. NOKW - 2567. Translated by United States, OCCWC. P. 1 (mimeographed).

——. "Vorbereitung der Operation 'Studie Barbarossa', 21. 4. bis 21. 6. 1941," 21 April-2 May 1941. NOKW - 1168. Pp. 2 (photostat).

Germany, LVII. Armeekorps (mot.). "Korpsbefehl für das Einrücken in die Bereitstellung und die Bereitstellung (No. 107/41)," 9 June 1941. NOKW - 2719. Pp. 13 (photostat).

——. "Kriegstagebuch, 15. 2. 41—31. 10. 41." NOKW - 2673. Pp. 10 (photostat).

Germany, 114. Schützen-Regiment. "Kriegstagebuch Nr. 1, 22. 4. 41—19. 5. 42." NOKW - 2652. Pp. 2 (photostat).

Germany, 123. Infanterie-Division. "Tätigkeitsbericht der Abteilung Ic," 22 June 1941. NOKW - 2061. Pp. 9 (photostat).

Germany, 454. Sicherungs-Division. "Anlage 41 - Kommandeur-Besprechung vom 20. 6. 41 - in Anlageband Nr. 1 zum Kriegstagebuch (Führungsabteilung) Nr. 1, 15. 5.—31. 12. 1941," 20 June 1941. Pp. 2 (photostat).

Gerstenberg, Alfred, and Fabricius, Wilhelm. "Gerstenberg and Fabricius to A.A., Pol I M (No. 1729)," 7 October 1940. NG - 3761. P. 1 (mimeographed).

Gilbert, Felix (ed). *Hitler Directs His War, The Secret Record of His Daily Military Conferences.* Selected, edited, and translated by F. Gilbert. New York: Oxford University Press, 1950.

Göring, Hermann. "Göring to Erich Rosen," 21 November 1940. PS - 1985. Pp. 4 (photostat).

Great Britain, Foreign Office. *The British War Blue Book.* New York: Farrar and Rinehart, 1939.

——. *Documents on British Foreign Policy, 1919-1939.* Edited by E. L. Woodward and Others. Third Series, Vol. III, *1938-39.* Vol. IV, *1939.* Vol. V, *1939.* Vol. VI, *1939.* London. H. M. Stationery Office, 1950-53.

Haushofer, Albrecht. "Englische Beziehungen und die Möglichkeit ihres Einsatzes," 12 May 1941. PS - 1671. Pp. 12 (photostat).

——. "Haushofer to Hess," 19 September 1940. PS - 670. Pp. 4 (photostat).

——. "Haushofer to Hitler," 12 May 1941. PS - 1671. P. 1 (photostat).

Heeren, Viktor von. "Heeren to Ribbentrop (No. 6)," 5 January 1941. NG - 3245. Pp. 2 (photostat).

Heydrich, Reinhard. "Heydrich to Lammers," 21 January 1940. NG - 3507. Translated by United States, OCCWC. Pp. 5 (mimeographed).

Himmler, Heinrich. "Himmler to Keppler," 12 December 1939. NG - 2593. Translated by United States, OCCWC. P. 1 (mimeographed).

Hitler, Adolf. "Erlass des Führers über die Wirtschaft in den neubesetzten Ostgebieten," 29 June 1941. PS - 12. P. 1 (photostat).

——. "Hitler to Antonescu," 18 June 1941. C - 150. SEA, United States, CCPAC. P. 1 (mimeographed).

——. "Hitler to Mussolini," 8 March 1940. PS - 1833. Translated by United States CCPAC. Pp. 7 (mimeographed).

——. "Hitler to Mussolini," 3 April 1941. PS - 1836. Pp. 9 (photostat).

——. "Richtlinien für die Verfolgung von Straftaten gegen das Reich oder die Besatzungsmacht in den besetzten Gebieten," 7 December 1941. PS - 666. Pp. 2 (photostat).

Hitler, Adolf (Germany, Oberster Befehlshaber der Wehrmacht). "Weisung Nr. 5 (OKW, WFA, L, No. 171/39)," 30 September 1939. PS - 439. Pp. 4 (photostat).[4]

——. "General Order No. 16 on the Preparation of a Landing Operation against England (OKW, WFA, L, No. 33160/40)," 16 July 1940. PS - 442. Translated by United States, CCPAC. Pp. 3 (mimeographed).

——. "Order No. 17 on the Conduct of Air and Sea Warfare against England (OKW, WFA, L, No. 33210/40)," 1 August 1940. PS - 443. Translated by United States, CCPAC. P. 1 (mimeographed).

——. "Weisung Nr. 24 über Zusammenarbeit mit Japan (OKW, WFSt, L, No. 44282/41)," 5 March 1941. C - 75 and NOKW - 2670. Pp. 4 (photostat).

——. "Weisung Nr. 26, Zusammenarbeit mit den Verbündeten auf dem Balkan (OKW, WFSt, L, No. 44395/41)," 3 April 1941. C - 24. Pp. 5 (photostat).

——. "Weisung Nr. 28, Unternehmen Merkur (OKW, WFSt, L, No. 44581/41)," 25 April 1941. PS - 450. Pp. 3 (photostat).

——. "Weisung Nr. 29 (OKW, WFSt, L. No. 44717/41)," 17 May 1941. PS - 452. Pp. 5 (photostat).

——. "Top Secret Fuehrer Order No. 30 re Iraq," 23 May 1941. PS - 453. SEA, United States, CCPAC. Pp. 2 (mimeographed).

——. "Weisung Nr. 32, Vorbereitungen für die Zeit nach Barbarossa," 11 June 1941. PS - 1799. Pp. 5 (photostat).

---

[4]) Hitler's directives on the conduct of the war are given here in numerical (chronological) order.

Hitler, Adolf, and Mussolini, Benito. *Les Lettres secrètes échangées par Hitler et Mussolini.* Paris: Éditions du Pavois, 1946.

Holldack, Heinz. *Was wirklich geschah.* Munich: Nymphenburger Verlagsbuchhandlung, 1949.

Huelle, N. "A Note Concerning the Preparation of the Barbarossa Court Martial Jurisdiction Order," 28 April 1941. NOKW-3464. Translated by United States, OCCWC. P. 1 (mimeographed).

I. G. Farben (Interessengemeinschaft Farbenindustrie Aktiengesellschaft). *Allgemeine Bemerkungen zu den Angeboten für die U.d.S.S.R. auf Anlagen zur Herstellung von Fliegerbenzin aus Steinkohle bzw. Braunkohle bzw. Kräckrückständen.* Special print by I. G. Farben, November, 1939. Pp. 7. Original in the Library of Congress, Manuscripts Division.

——. "Memorandum," 23 April 1941. NI - 6123. Pp. 3 (photostat).

I. G. Farben, Einkaufsabteilung (Weiss). "Vertrauliche Niederschrift zum Umlauf," 14 January 1941. NI - 6734. Pp. 17 (mimeographed).

I. G. Farben, Filmfabrik Wolfen (Riess). "Aktennotiz ueber die Besprechung in Abwehrangelegenheiten in Frankfurt/M. am 2. Mai 1941," 4 May 1941. NI - 14312. Pp. 2 (mimeographed).

I. G. Farben (von der Heyde). "Sitzungsbericht in Frankfurt/M. am 2. 5. 1941; Betreff: Zusammenarbeit zwischen Abwehr I Wi und I. G.," 20 May 1941 NI - 14271. Pp. 4 (mimeographed).

I. G. Farben, Kaufmännischer Ausschuss. "Niederschrift über die 19. Sitzung des Kaufmännischen Ausschusses am 17. Feb. 1939," 17 February 1939. NI - 6081. Pp. 4 (photostat).

——. "(Vorläufige) Niederschrift über die 24. Sitzung des Kaufmännischen Ausschusses am 11. August 1939 in Frankfurt/M.," 11 August 1939. NI - 5945 (quoted in NI - 9454). Pp. 5 (photostat).

——. "Niederschrift über die 25. Sitzung des Kaufmännischen Ausschusses am 13. September 1939 in Berlin," 13 September 1939. NI - 5946 (quoted in NI - 9454). Pp. 3 (photostat).

——. "Niederschrift über die 28. Sitzung des Kaufmännischen Ausschusses am 13. Dezember 1939," 13 December 1939. NI - 9501. Pp. 3 (photostat).

I. G. Farben, Technischer Ausschuss, Büro. "Anlage zum Schreiben der I. G. Farbenindustrie Aktiengesellschaft vom 15. November 1939 betreff Verhandlungen mit den Delegationen der U.d.S.S.R.," 15 November 1939. NI - 6505 (mimeographed).

——. "I. G. Farben an Professor Dr. C. Krauch, Generalbevollmächtiger des Min. Präs. Generalfeldmarschall Göring für Sonderfragen der chemischen Erzeugung; Betreff: Verhandlungen mit den Delegationen der U.d.S.S.R.," 15 November 1939. NI - 6505. Pp. 4 (mimeographed).

I. G. Farben, Technischer Ausschuss, Büro (Ter Meer). "Ter Meer an Ambros und Andere; Betreff: Russland-Verhandlungen," 17 November 1939. NI - 6505. Pp. 2 (mimeographed).

I. G. Farben, Vorstand. "Niederschrift über die 24. Vorstandssitzung am 5. Februar 1941," 5 February 1941. NI - 8079. Pp. 9 (mimeographed).

——. "Niederschrift über die 26. Vorstandssitzung am 10. Juli 1941," 10 July 1941, NI - 8077. Pp. 8 (photostat).

I. G. Farben, Wirtschaftspolitische Abteilung. "Handelspolitische Beziehungen zur Mandschurei," 17 May 1940. NI - 1096. Pp. 3 (photostat).

International Military Tribunal. *Trial of the Major War Criminals.* 42 vols. English edition. Nuremberg, 1946-48.

International Military Tribunal for the Far East. *Judgement of the Military International Tribunal for the Far East.* 3 parts and 6 annexes in 8 vols. November, 1948.

Italy, Ministry of Foreign Affairs. *I Documenti Diplomatici Italiani.* Eighth Series: 1935-1939. Ed. by Mario Toscano. *Vol. XII (23 maggio-11 agosto 1939).* Rome: La Libreria dello Stato, 1952.

———. *Vol. XIII (12 agosto - 3 settembre 1939).* Rome: La Libreria dello Stato, 1953.

———. Microfilms of Italian Documents. U.S. National Archives, Record Group 242.

Jasper. "Jasper to Weizsäcker," 21 June 1941. NG - 4242. P. 1 (photostat).

Jodl, Alfred. "Erklärung von Jodl," 26 September 1946. NOKW - 65. Pp. 10 (photostat).

Junge, Wolfgang. "Affidavit of Junge," 1 October 1947. NG - 2665. Translated by United States, OCCWC. Pp. 3 (mimeographed).

Keppler, Wilhelm. "Keppler to Himmler," 5 December 1939. NG - 2593. Translated by United States, OCCWC. P. 1 (mimeographed).

———. "Keppler to Himmler," 8 December 1939. NG - 2593. Translated by United States, OCCWC. P. 1 (mimeographed).

———. "Keppler to Himmler," 12 August 1940. NG - 2587. Translated by United States, OCCWC. P. 1 (mimeographed).

Kordt, Erich. "Affidavit of Kordt," 25 September 1947. NG - 3605. Pp. 6 (photostat).

Kramarz, Hans. "Kramarz to Attachés in Ankara, Bern, Helsinki, Lisbon, Pressburg, Stockholm, Teheran, Tokyo," 7 May 1941. NG - 3544. Pp. 2 (mimeographed).

———. "Kramarz to Weizsäcker," 21 January 1941. NG - 3765. Translated by United States, OCCWC. P. 1 (mimeographed).

———. "Memorandum by Kramarz," 18 April 1941. NG - 3432. Pp. 2 (photostat).

———. "Note on German Aerial Reconnaissance over Russian Territory," 20 June 1941. NG - 4218. Translated by United States, OCCWC. P. 1 (mimeographed).

———. "Note on an Order to German Military Attachés on Rumors of a German Attack on Russia," 7 May 1941 NG - 4289. SEA, United States, OCCWC. P. 1 (mimeographed).

Küchler, Georg von. "Erklärung von Küchler," 10 April 1947. NOKW - 1038. Pp. 4 (photostat).

Lammers, Hans. "Lammers to Rosenberg," 30 June 1941. PS - 12. P. 1 (photostat).

Leeb, Wilhelm von. "Leeb to Brauchitsch," 11 October 1939. NOKW - 3433. Translated by United States, OCCWC. P. 1 (mimeographed).

———. "Denkschrift über die Aussichten und Wirkungen eines Angriffs auf Frankreich und England unter Verletzung der Neutralität Hollands, Belgiens und Luxemburgs," 11 October 1939. NOKW - 3433. Translated by United States, OCCWC. Pp. 7 (mimeographed).

Leverkuehn, Paul (ed.). "Dokumentbuch V fuer Warlimont (U.S. v. Leeb)." Pp. 147 (mimeographed).

Likus, Rudolf. "Likus to Gaus," 21 June 1941. NG - 3228. P. 1 (photostat).

Ludin, Hans. "Ludin to Ribbentrop," 21 June 1941. NG - 4530. P. 1 (photostat).

Mackensen, Hans von. "Mackensen to Ribbentrop," 23 August 1939. International Military Tribunal for the Far East, Defense Document 1634, Exhibit 2726. Transcript of Proceedings, pp. 24190-92.

Magee, Warren E., and Becker, Hellmut (eds.). "Widerstand, Dokumentbuch V für Ernst von Weizsäcker (U.S. v. Weizsäcker)." Pp. 113 (mimeographed).

Moraht. "Moraht to the German Consulate Shanghai," 19 January 1940. P. 1 (typescript). Original in the Library of Congress, Manuscripts Division: German Embassy in China, "Abkommen, Frachtenverkehr, Transitverkehr, Frako (WE - 2 - 2a)."

Molotov, Vyacheslav M. *The International Situation and Soviet Foreign Policy, 31 May 1939.* Moscow: Foreign Languages Publishing House, 1939.

———. *The Meaning of the Soviet-German Non-Aggression Pact, 31 August 1939.* New York: Workers Library Publishers, Inc., 1939.

——. *Report to the Supreme Soviet, 31 October 1939*. New York: Workers Library Publishers, Inc., 1939.

Müller, Vinzenz. "Erklärung von Müller," 8 January 1946. USSR - 149. Pp. 12 (photostat).

Nationalsozialistische Deutsche Arbeiterspartei, Aussenpolitisches Amt. "Afghanistan; Bewaffnung der afghanischen Armee," 11 January 1937. Prepared by Malletke. PS - 1360. Pp. 4 (photostat).

——. "Afghanistan; Unterhaltung zwischen Rosenberg und dem afghanischen Gesandten am 16. Januar 1936," 17 January 1936. PS - 1359. P. 1 (photostat).

——. "Afghanistan: Unterhaltung zwischen Strunk und dem afghanischen Ministerpräsidenten, November, 1935," 17 January 1936. PS - 1359. P. 1 (photostat).

——. "Afghanistan; Zielsetzung des Aussenpolitischen Amtes der N.S.D.A.P.," 18 December 1939. PS - 916. Pp. 16 (photostat).

——. "Aktennotiz; Besprechung Immisch-Skorniakoff am 21. März 1941," 10 April 1941. PS - 1023. Pp. 3 (photostat).

——. „Aktennotiz; Besprechung Immisch-Skorniakoff am 9. April 1941," 10 April 1941. PS - 1023. Pp. 2 (photostat).

——. "Aktennotiz; Besuch des afghanischen Wirtschaftsministers am 1. März 1941," 21 March 1941. Prepared by Rosenberg. PS - 915. Pp. 3 (photostat).

——. "Aktennotiz über die Tätigkeit des Gesandten v. Hentig im Auswärtigen Amt," 8 July 1941. PS - 281. Pp. 17 (photostat).

——. "APA an die Adjutantur des Führers, z. Hd. Wiedemann," 2 January 1937. PS - 1360. P. 1 (photostat).

—— "Denkschrift Nr. 2; Betrifft: U.d.S.SR," 7 April 1941 Prepared by Rosenberg. PS - 1018. Pp. 46 (photostat).

——. "Fortschreitende Zusammenarbeit mit der jetzigen afghanischen Regierung," 18 December 1939. PS - 916. Pp. 3 (photostat).

——. "Memorandum on the German Plans for Afghanistan," 12 December 1939. PS - 1287. SEA, United States, CCPAC. Pp. 2 (mimeographed).

——. "Rosenberg to Lammers," 21 March 1941. PS - 915. P. 1 (photostat).

——. "Rosenberg to Lammers," 12 July 1941. PS - 281. P. 1 (photostat).

"Niederschrift der Quartalbesprechung vom 3. 7. 1940 in Frankfurt a.M. über den anorganischen Fabrikationsplan und den Voranschlag für Laboratoriums- und Versuchskosten für das 3. Vierteljahr 1940," 3 July 1940. NI - 5684. Pp. 5 (photostat). (From I.G. Farben files?)

Ott, Eugen. "Ott to Ribbentrop," 6 May 1941. NG - 4422(c). Translated by United States, OCCWC. Pp. 3 (mimeographed).

Papen, Franz von. "Papen to Ribbentrop," 1 April 1941. NG - 5738. P. 1 (mimeographed).

Peter (pseudonym?). "Dokumentarischer Bericht - Die Sowjetregierung und die Donaumündung Ende 1940," *Hamburger Monatshefte für Auswärtige Politik*, XI, No. 1/2 (January-February, 1944), 22-39.

Poland, Foreign Office. *Weissbuch der Polnischen Regierung*. Basel: Verlag Birkhäuser, 1940.

Raeder, Erich. "Die Vorbereitungen zum Kriege mit der Sowjet-Union," 10 July 1945. PS - 1451 (Part II of USSR - 460). Pp. 9 (photostat).

Raussendorff, Ernst von. "Affidavit of Ernst von Raussendorff," 28 December 1947. NIK - 13342. P. 1 (photostat).

Ribbentrop, Joachim von. "Ribbentrop to Blücher," 9 March 1941. NG - 1579. Translated by United States, OCCWC. Pp. 2 (mimeographed).

——. "Ribbentrop to Erdmannsdorff," 9 December 1940. NG - 2712. Translated by United States, OCCWC. P. 1 (mimeographed).

——. "Ribbentrop to Erdmannsdorff," 15 June 1941. NG - 4273. P. 1 (photostat).

Ribbentrop, Joachim von. "Ribbentrop to the Foreign Ministry on a conversation with Oshima on February 23, 1941," 27 February 1941. NG - 4449. Translated by United States, OCCWC. Pp. 8 (mimeographed).

——. "Ribbentrop to Heeren," 2 April 1941. NG - 4266. Pp. 2 (photostat).

——. "Ribbentrop to Lammers," 13 June 1941. NG - 1691. Pp. 4 (mimeographed).

——. "Ribbentrop to Missions on a Conversation with Oshima on February 23, 1941," 3 March 1941. NG - 3826. Translated by United States, OCCWC. Pp. 5 (mimeographed).

——. "Ribbentrop to Ott," 17 June 1941. PS - 1827. Pp. 6 (photostat).

——. "Ribbentrop to Schulenburg," 8 January 1941. NG - 3822. Pp. 3 (mimeographed).

Richthofen, Herbert von. "Richthofen to Ribbentrop," 15 February 1941. NG - 3874. Pp. 2 (mimeographed).

——. "Richthofen and Benzler to Ritter," 12 March 1941. NG - 3874. P. 1 (mimeographed).

——. "Richthofen and Bruckmann to OKH, Gen. St. d. H., Att. Abt.," 17 February 1941. NG - 5539. P 1 (mimeographed).

Rintelen, Emil von. "Affidavit of Rintelen," 4 June 1947. NG - 3622. Translated by United States, OCCWC. Pp. 2 (mimeographed).

Ritter, Karl. "Memorandum of Ritter (für den bevorstehenden Besuch des bulgarischen Ministerpräsidenten)," 2 January 1941. NG - 3144. Pp. 2 (photostat).

——. "Memorandum of Ritter," 15 January 1941. NG - 5541. Translated by United States, OCCWC. Pp. 3 (mimeographed).

——. "Memorandum of Ritter (on Marita)," 27 January 1941. NG - 5239. Translated by United States, OCCWC. Pp. 3 (mimeographed).

——. "Ritter to Fabricius," 16 January 1941. NG - 3765. Translated by United States, OCCWC. P. 1 (mimeographed).

——. "Ritter to Jodl," September 1942. NG - 2791. Translated by United States, OCCWC. Pp. 6 (mimeographed).

——. "Ritter to Killinger," 23 May 1941. NG - 3172. Pp. 3 (mimeographed).

——. "Ritter to Ludin," 23 April 1941. NG - 3468. Pp 2 (mimeographed).

——. "Ritter to Missions," 6 January 1937. Pp. 3 (typescript). Original in the Library of Congress, Manuscripts Division: German Embassy in China, "Deutsch-Russische Verträge (DW 2, Band I)."

——. "Ritter to Ribbentrop," 15 December 1939. NG - 3164. P. 1 (photostat).

——. "Ritter to Ribbentrop," 23 January 1941. NG - 5530. Translated by United States, OCCWC. P. 1 (mimeographed).

——. "Ritter to Richthofen," 15 January 1941. NG - 3144. Pp. 7 (photostat).

——. "Ritter to Schulenburg," 6 December 1939. NG - 3913. Pp. 2 (photostat).

——. "Ritter to SS Obersturmbannführer Schulze for Ribbentrop," 8 October 1940. NG - 3761. Pp. 3 (mimeographed).

——. "Ritter to Weizsäcker," 7 January 1941. NG - 5531. SEA, United States, OCCWC. P. 1 (mimeographed).

Rössing. "Rössing to OKH, Gen. St. d. H., Att. Abt. (Mellenthin) (No. 51/41)," 22 May 1941. NG - 4310. P. 1 (photostat).

Roosevelt, Franklin D. *F.D.R., His Personal Letters,* Vol IV, *1928-1945.* Edited by Elliot Roosevelt and Joseph P. Lash. New York: Duell, Sloan, and Pearce, 1950.

Rundstedt, Gerd von. "Rundstedt to Brauchitsch," 31 October 1939. NOKW - 511. Pp. 5 (photostat).

——. "Rundstedt to List," 15 February 1941. NOKW - 2670. Pp. 2 (photostat).

Russia, Embassy in the United States. *Soviet War Documents.* Washington, D.C.: Embassy of the U.S.S.R., 1943.

Russia, Ministry of Foreign Affairs. *Documents and Materials Relating to the Eve of the Second World War.* Vol. I. *November 1937-1938,* Vol. II. *Dirksen Papers (1938-1939).* Moscow: Foreign Languages Publishing House, 1948.

Russia, Soviet Information Bureau. *Falsificators of History (An Historical Note).* Washington, D.C.: The Information Bulletin of the Embassy of the Union of Soviet Socialist Republics, 1948.

Schilf, Alfred (ed.). "Dokumentbuch Woermann I (U.S. v. Weizsäcker)." Pp. 98 (mimeographed).

Schmidt, Paul Karl. "Affidavit of Schmidt," 12 December 1947. NG - 4332. Pp. 4 (mimeographed).

——. "Schmidt to Schulenburg," 20 February 1940. NG - 4979. SEA, United States, OCCWC. P. 1 (mimeographed).

Schmidt, Paul Otto. "Aufzeichnung über die Unterredung Göring-Matsuoka am 29. März 1941," 31 March 1941. PS - 1879. Pp. 9 (photostat).

Schmieden, Werner von. "Schmieden to Ribbentrop," 3 April 1941. NG - 3831. Translated by United States, OCCWC. P. 1 (mimeographed).

Schnurre, Karl. "Schnurre to Missions," 9 March 1938. Pp. 3 (typescript). Original in the Library of Congress, Manuscripts Division: German Embassy in China, "Deutsch-Russische Verträge (DW 2, Band I)."

Schröder, Kurt von. "Schröder to Pfirsch, Rademacher, Hobrecker, Lewis," 10 April 1941. NIK - 3994. P. 1 (photostat).

Schulenburg, Friedrich Werner von der. "Schulenburg to Ribbentrop," 20 September 1939. NG - 5776. Translated by United States, OCCWC. Pp. 2 (mimeographed).

——. "Schulenburg to Weizsäcker," 21 May 1941. NG - 4305. P. 1 (photostat).

——. "Schulenburg to Woermann," 31 March 1941. NG - 3868. SEA, United States, OCCWC. P. 1 (mimeographed).

Seidl, Alfred (ed.). *Die Beziehungen zwischen Deutschland und der Sowjetunion, 1939-1941.* Tübingen: H. Laupp'sche Buchhandlung, 1949.

Skodawerke, Aktiengesellschaft vormals. "Protokoll No. 8 über die am 7. Juli 1939 bei der Aktiengesellschaft vormals Skodawerke stattgefundene Besprechung," 17 July 1939. NID - 9395. Pp. 5 (photostat).

Sostmann. "Bericht über die von Herrn Dähn und mir im Auftrage der Deutschen Oelmühlen-Rohstoffe G.m.b.H., Berlin, durchgeführte Reise nach dem Fernen Osten zum Studium und der Lösung der Transport- und Einkaufsfrage von Soyabohnen und Soyaöl," 29 April 1940. NI - 1096. Pp. 8 (photostat).

Steengracht von Moyland, Gustav Adolf. "Steengracht to Weizsäcker," 15 January 1941. NG - 3764. Translated by United States, OCCWC. P. 1 (mimeographed).

Stephan, Werner, F. "Affidavit of Stephan," 20 November 1947. NG - 3706. Translated by United States, OCCWC. Pp. 8 (mimeographed).

Tippelskirch, Werner von. "Erklärung von Tippelskirch," 8 January 1947. NOKW - 643. Pp. 4 (photostat).

Toynbee, Arnold J. (ed.). *Documents on International Affairs, 1939-1946.* Vol. I. *March-September 1939.* Royal Institute of International Affairs. London: Oxford University Press, 1951.

Twardowski, Fritz von. "Twardowski to the German Missions in Riga and Kaunas," 18 March 1941. NG - 5143. P. (mimeographed).

United States, Congress. House Committee on Un-American Activities. *Hearings on American Aspects of the Richard Sorge Spy Case.* Washington: Government Printing Office, 1951.

United States, Congress, Senate. Committee on the Judiciary, Subcommittee to Investigate the Administration of the Internal Security Act and other Internal Security Laws. *Hearings on the Institute of Pacific Relations.* Parts I and II. 82d Congress, 1st Session. Washington: Government Printing Office, 1951.

United States, Department of State. *Documents on German Foreign Policy, 1918-1945.* Series D. Vol. I (German edition). *Von Neurath zu Ribbentrop (September 1937-September 1938).* Vol. II (German edition). *Deutschland und die Tschechoslowakei, 1937-1938.* Baden-Baden: Imprimerie Nationale, 1950. Vol. III (English edition). *Germany and the Spanish Civil War, 1936-1939.* Washington: Government Printing Office, 1950. Vol. IV (English edition). *The Aftermath of Munich, October, 1938-March, 1939.* Washington: Government Printing Office, 1951. Vol. V (German edition). *Polen, Südeuropa, Lateinamerika, Klein- und Mitelstaaten (Juni 1937-März 1939).* Baden-Baden: Imprimerie Nationale, 1953.

———. *Das Nationalsozialistische Deutschland und die Sowjetunion, 1939-1941.* Edited by E. M. Carroll and F. T. Epstein. Berlin: Druckhaus Tempelhof, 1948.

———. *Nazi-Soviet Relations, 1939-1941.* Edited by R. J. Sontag and J. S. Beddie. Washington: Government Printing Office, 1948.

———. *Papers Relating to the Foreign Relations of the United States; Japan, 1931-1941.* 2 vols. Washington: Government Printing Office, 1943.

———. *Papers Relating to the Foreign Relations of the United States; The Soviet Union, 1933-1939.* Washington: Government Printing Office, 1952.

———. *Postwar Foreign Policy Preparation, 1939-1945.* Washington: Government Printing Office, 1949.

———. *The United States and Italy, 1936-1946.* Washington: Government Printing Office, 1946.

United States, Military Tribunal IV. "United States v. Ernst von Weizsäcker, *et alii,* Transcripts of Proceedings." Nuremberg, 1947-1948. Pp. 28000 (mimeographed).

United States, Military Tribunal V. "United States v. Wilhelm von Leeb, *et alii,* Transcript of Proceedings." Nuremberg, 1948. Pp. 11000 (mimeographed).

United States, National Archives, *Preliminary Inventory of the Records of the United States Counsel for the Prosecution of Axis Criminality.* Preliminary Inventory No. 21. Compiled by Fred. G. Halley. Washington, 1949.

United States, Office of Chief of Counsel for the Prosecution of Axis Criminality. *Nazi Conspiracy and Aggression.* 8 vols. and 2 supplements. Washington: Government Printing Office, 1946-1948.

United States, Office of Chief of Counsel for War Crimes. "Interrogation of Fritz Hesse (by R. M. W. Kempner)," 10 September 1947. NG - 2679. Translated by United States, OCCWC. Pp. 9 (mimeographed).

———. "Interrogation of Andor Hencke (by R. M. W. Kempner)," 2 October 1947. NG - 4080. Translated by United States, OCCWC. Pp. 10 (mimeographed).

———. "Interrogation of Ewald Loeser (by Mr. Thayer)," 21 April 1947. NIK - 11682. Pp. 17 (mimeographed).

———. "Interrogation of Legation Councillor Edwart von Selzam (by R. M. W. Kempner)," 18 July 1947. NG - 3703. Translated by United States, OCCWC. Pp. 3 (mimeographed).

United States, Office of Chief of Counsel for War Crimes, Subsequent Proceedings Division, Interrogation Branch. "Alfred Jodl," 6 September 1946. Interrogation Summary No. 87. Pp. 6 (mimeographed).[5]

———. "Wilhelm Keitel," 11 September 1946. Interrogation Summary No. 103. Pp. 3 (mimeographed).

———. "Wilhelm Keitel," 13 September 1946. Interrogation Summary No. 117. P. 1 (mimeographed).

———. "Wilhelm Scheidt," 4 October 1946. Interrogation Summary No. 215. Pp. 4 (mimeographed).

[5] The Interrogation Summaries are given in numerical order, the name of the witness interrogated being placed in quotation marks. The date is the date on which the interrogation took place.

——. "Walter Warlimont," 21 October 1946. Interrogation Summary No. 324. Pp. 3 (mimeographed).

——. "Erhard Milch," 18 October 1946. Interrogation Summary No. 327. Pp. 2 (mimeographed).

——. "Walter Warlimont," 4 November 1946. Interrogation Summary No. 409. P. 1 (mimeographed).

——. "Hermann von Stutterheim," 8 November 1946. Interrogation Summary No. 455. P. 1 (mimeographed).

——. "Werner von Tippelskirch," 27 December 1946. Interrogation Summary No. 804. Pp. 3 (mimeographed).

——. "Maximilian von Weichs," 31 January and 3 February 1947. Interrogation Summary No. 1147. Pp. 6 (mimeographed).

——. "Georg von Kuechler," 29 March 1947. Interrogation Summary No. 1650. Pp. 3 (mimeographed).

——. "Ewald Loeser," 29 March 1947. Interrogation Summary No. 1919. Pp. 2 (mimeographed).

——. "Hermann Hoelter," 19 June 1947. Interrogation Summary No. 2543. Pp. 4 (mimeographed).

——. "Werner von Schmieden," 26 June 1946. Interrogation Summary No. 2618. P. 1 (mimeographed).

——. "Alfred Hess," 13 August 1947. Interrogation Summary No. 3128. Pp. 3 (mimeographed).

——. "Wilhelm von Leeb," 25 September 1947. Interrogation Summary No. 3550. Pp. 3 (mimeographed).

——. "George Schild," 3 October 1947. Interrogation Summary No. 3670. Pp. 2 (mimeographed).

——. "Otto Schniewind," 21 November 1947. Interrogation Summary No. 4271. Pp. 4 (mimeographed).

——. "Bruno Peter Kleist," 8 January 1948. Interrogation Summary No. 4430. Pp. 4 (mimeographed).

Uthmann, Bruno von. "Uthmann to OKH, Gen. St. d. H., Att. Abt. (Mellenthin)," 27 February 1941. NG - 4310. P. 1 (photostat).

Warlimont, Walter. "Erklärung von Warlimont," 1 November 1946. NOKW - 152. Pp. 5 (photostat).

——. "Skizze der Abteilung Landesverteidigung nach dem Stande vom 1. 9. 1939 mit den bis 6. 9. 1944 eingetretenen Veraenderungen," 12 October 1946. NOKW - 121. P. 1 (photostat).

——. "Skizze der Organisation des Wehrmacht-Führungsstab (WFSt) nach dem Stande vom 1. 9. 1939," 12 October 1946. NOKW - 121. P. 1 (photostat).

Weizsäcker, Ernst von. "Marginal Note on Schulenburg to Ribbentrop," 8 January 1941. NG - 3263. P. 1 (photostat).

——. "Memorandum on a Conversation with the Chinese Ambassador," 26 August 1939. Pp. 2 (typescript). Original in the Library of Congress, Manuscripts Division: German Embassy in China, "Chinesische Botschaft in Berlin (Prot. 2A - 6)."

——. "Memorandum on a Conversation with Dekanozov," 10 January 1941. NG - 3999 and 4853. P. 1 (photostat).

——. "Memorandum on a Conversation with Dekanozov," 1 March 1941. NG - 3874. P. 1 (mimeographed).

——. "Memorandum on a Conversation with Dekanozov," 18 June 1941. NG - 4235. P. 1 (photostat).

——. "Memorandum on a Conversation with Sztojay," 16 June 1941. NG - 4236. P. 1 (photostat).

——. "Memorandum Regarding the Expulsion of a Swiss Journalist by the Reich," 2 July 1940. NG - 4994. P. 1 (mimeographed).

Weizsäcker, Ernst von. "Memorandum zur Sprachregelung für den 1. Juli 1940,"
30 June 1940. NG - 1718. P. 1. (photostat).
——. "Weizsäcker an Canaris; Entwurf einer Dienstanweisung für die Deutsche Mili-
tärmission in Rumänien," 14 September 1940. NG - 3824. Pp. 4 (photostat).
——. "Weizsäcker to Fabricius," 11 December 1940. NG - 2658. Pp. 2 (mimeographed).
——. "Weizsäcker to German Mission in Kabul," 2 February 1941. NG - 5465. Trans-
lated by United States, OCCWC. P. 1 (mimeographed).
——. "Weizsäcker an Lammers; Betrifft: Völkerrechtliche Bedeutung des Zerfalls des
Polnischen Staates," 15 May 1940. PS - 646. Pp. 2 (photostat).
——. "Weizsäcker to Mackensen," 31 May 1939. NG - 5366. P. 1 (mimeographed).
——. "Weizsäcker to Moltke," 31 May 1939. NG - 5366. P. 1 (mimeographed).
——. "Weizsäcker to Ribbentrop," 25 May 1939. NG - 5365. Pp. 2 (mimeographed).
——. "Weizsäcker to Ribbentrop," 19 August 1939. NG - 2172. Translated by United
States,, OCCWC. P. 1 (mimeographed).
——. "Weizsäcker to Ribbentrop," 3 October 1940. NG - 3823. Pp. 2 (photostat).
——. "Weizsäcker to Ribbentrop," 15 January 1941. NG - 5286. Pp. 2 (photostat).
——. "Weizsäcker to Ribbentrop," 22 February 1941. NG - 3827. Translated by United
States, OCCWC. Pp. 2 (mimeographed).
——. "Weizsäcker an Ribbentrop zu den Aufzeichnungen für den Matsuoka-Besuch,"
24 March 1941. NG - 3825. Pp. 2 (mimeographed).
——. "Weizsäcker to Ribbentrop," 4 April 1941. NG - 2693. Pp. 3 (mimeographed)
——. "Weizsäcker to Ribbentrop," 7 November 1942. NG - 4662. P. 1 (mimeographed).
——. "Weizsäcker to Richthofen," 15 January 1941. NG - 3144. Pp. 2 (photostat).
——. "Weizsäcker to Ritter," 24 January 1941. NG - 3144. P. 1 (photostat).
——. "Weizsäcker to Schulenburg," 22 July 1939. International Military Tribunal for
the Far East, Defense Document 1633, Exhibit 2726. Transcript of Proceedings, pp.
24185-86.
——. "Weizsäcker to Schulenburg," 14 August 1939. NG - 5367. P. 1 (mimeographed).
——. "Weizsäcker to Schulenburg," 26 August 1939. NG - 2371. P. 1 (mimeographed).
——. "Weizsäcker to Schulenburg," 29 August 1939. NG - 2406. Pp. 2 (mimeographed).
——. "Weizsäcker to Schulenburg," 1 September 1939. NG - 4849. SEA, United States,
OCCWC. P. 1 (mimeographed).
——. "Weizsäcker to Thomsen," 10 October 1939. NG - 1424. Translated by United
States, OCCWC. P. 1 (mimeographed).
Woermann, Ernst. "Memorandum on a Conversation with Attolico," 30 April 1940.
NG - 1773. SEA, United States, OCCWC. P. 1 (mimeographed).
——. "Memorandum on a Conversation with Sztojay," 26 June 1941. NG - 2975. P. 1
(photostat).
——. "Memorandum on a Conversation with the Rumanian Ambassador," 30 May
1941. NG - 4182. P. 1 (mimeographed).
——. "Memorandum of Woermann," 19 July 1939. International Military Tribunal for
the Far East, Defense Document 1632, Exhibit 2723. Transcript of Proceedings, pp.
24179-84.
——. "Woermann to Ribbentrop," 3 April 1941. NG - 3493. Pp. 3 (photostat).
——. "Woermann to Schulenburg," 9 February 1941. NG - 3868. SEA, United States,
OCCWC. P. 1 (mimeographed).
——. "Woermann to Schulenburg," 25 March 1941. NG - 3868. SEA, United States,
OCCWC. P. 1 (mimeographed).
——. "Woermann to Schulenburg," 16 April 1941. NG - 3831. Translated by United
States, OCCWC. P. 1 (mimeographed).
Wohlthat, Helmuth. "Wirtschaftsverhandlungen mit Japan und Mandschukuo. Be-
sprechung über eine Regelung mit China," 27 March 1941. International Military
Tribunal for the Far East, Document 4038.

B

B

I

Primary Sources: Diaries

Ciano, Galeazzo. *The Ciano Diaries, 1939-1943.* Edited by Hugh Gibson. Garden City, New York: Doubleday and Company, Inc., 1946.
———. *Tagebücher, 1937-1938.* Translated by Hans Mollier and Maximilian Wiesel. Hamburg: Wolfgang Krüger Verlag, 1949.
Goebbels, Josef. *The Goebbels Diaries, 1942-1943.* Translated and Edited by Louis P. Lochner. Garden City, New York: Doubleday and Company, Inc., 1948.
Halder, Franz. *The Halder Diaries.* Edited by Arnold Lissance. 7 vols. and notes. Washington: Infantry Journal, 1950 (mimeographed).
Hassell, Ulrich von. *Vom anderen Deutschland.* Zürich: Atlantis-Verlag, 1946.
Jodl, Alfred. "Tagebuch, 13. Oktober 1939—30. Januar 1940." PS - 1811. Pp. 100 (photostat).
Shirer, William L. *Berlin Diary.* New York: Alfred A. Knopf, 1941.
Simoni, Léonardo (pseud.). *Berlin, ambassade d'Italie.* Translated by C. D. Jonquières. Paris: Robert Laffont, 1947.
Szembek, Jan. *Journal, 1933-1939.* Paris: Plon, 1952.

Primary Sources: Memoirs

Ahrens, Adolf. *Die Siegesfahrt der "Bremen".* Berlin: Steiniger Verlag, 1940.
Alfieri, Dino. *Due dittatori di frente.* Milan: Rizzoli, 1948.
Blücher, Wipert von. *Gesandter zwischen Diktatur und Demokratie.* Wiesbaden: Limes Verlag, 1951.
Bor-Komorowski, Tadeusz. *The Secret Army.* New York: The Macmillan Co., 1951.
Bross, Werner. *Gespräche mit Hermann Göring während des Nürnberger Prozesses.* Flensburg: Verlagshaus Christian Wolff, 1950.
Bryans, James Lonsdale. *Blind Victory.* London: Skeffington and Son, Ltd., 1951.
Byrnes, James F. *Speaking Frankly.* New York: Harper and Brothers, Publishers, 1947.
Churchill, Winston S. *The Second World War.* Vol. I. *The Gathering Storm.* Boston: Houghton Mifflin Company, 1948. Vol. II. *Their Finest Hour.* Londen: Cassell and Co., Ltd., 1949. Vol. III. *The Grand Alliance.* Boston: Houghton Mifflin Company, 1950.
Coulondre, Robert. *Von Moskau nach Berlin, 1936-1939.* Translated by G. L. Sigwart. Bonn: Athenäum-Verlag, 1950.
Craigie, Robert. *Behind the Japanese Mask.* London: Hutchinson and Co., Ltd., 1946.
Dahlerus, Birger. *Der letzte Versuch.* Munich: Nymphenburger Verlagshandlung, 1948.
Davies, Joseph E. *Mission to Moscow.* New York: Simon and Shuster, 1941.
Davignon, Jacques. *Berlin, 1936-1940, souvenirs d'une mission.* Paris: Éditions Universitaires, 1951.
Dirksen, Herbert von. *Moskau Tokio London, 20 Jahre deutscher Aussenpolitik.* Stuttgart: W. Kohlhammer Verlag, 1950.
Erfurth, Waldemar. *Der finnische Krieg, 1941-1944.* Wiesbaden: Limes Verlag, 1950.
Foote, Alexander. *Handbook for Spies.* Garden City, New York: Doubleday and Company, Inc., 1949.
Gafencu, Grigore. *Last Days of Europe.* Translated by E. Fletcher-Allen. New Haven: Yale University Press, 1948.
———. *Vorspiel zum Krieg im Osten.* Zürich: Verlag Amstutz, Herdeg und Companie, 1944.
Geyr von Schweppenburg, Leo. *Erinnerungen eines Militärattachés, London, 1933-1937.* Stuttgart: Deutsche Verlags-Anstalt, 1949.
Gisevius, Hans Bernd. *Bis zum bittern Ende.* Vol. II. Zürich: Fretz und Wasmuth Verlag, A.G., 1946.

Greiner, Helmuth. *Die oberste Wehrmachtführung, 1939-1943*. Wiesbaden: Limes Verlag, 1951.

Grew, Joseph C. *Ten Years in Japan*. New York: Simon and Schuster, 1944.

Guderian, Heinz. *Erinnerungen eines Soldaten*. Heidelberg: Kurt Vowinckel, 1951.

Hagen, Walter (pseud. of Höttl, Wilhelm). *Die geheime Front*. Linz: Nibelungen-Verlag, 1950.

Henderson, Nevile. *Failure of a Mission, Berlin, 1937-1939*. New York: G. P. Putnam's Sons, 1940.

Heusinger, Adolf. *Befehl im Widerstreit*. Tübingen: Rainer Wunderlich Verlag, 1950.

Hilger, Gustav, and Meyer, Alfred G. *The Incompatible Allies, German-Soviet Relations 1918-1941*. New York: The Macmillan Co., 1953.

Horthy, Nikolaus von. *Ein Leben für Ungarn*. Bonn: Athenäum Verlag, 1953.

Hossbach, Friedrich. *Zwischen Wehrmacht und Hitler*. Wolfenbüttel: Wolfenbütteler Verlagsanstalt G.m.b.H., 1949.

Hull, Cordell. *The Memoirs of Cordell Hull*. 2 vols. New York: The Macmillan Company, 1948.

Kase, Toshikazu. *Journey to the Missouri*. Edited by David Nelson Rowe. New Haven: Yale University Press, 1950.

Kleist, Bruno Peter. *Zwischen Hitler und Stalin, 1939-1945*. Bonn: Athenäum-Verlag, 1950.

Knatchbull-Hugessen, Hugh M. *Diplomat in Peace and War*. London: John Murray, 1949.

Kordt, Erich. *Nicht aus den Akten*. Stuttgart: Union Deutsche Verlagsgesellschaft, 1950.

Kravchenko, Victor. *I Chose Freedom*. New York: Charles Scribner's Sons, 1946.

Lossberg, Bernhard von. *Im Wehrmachtführungsstab*. Hamburg: H. H. Nölke Verlag, 1950.

Mannerheim, Carl Gustav. *Erinnerungen*. Translated by H. von Born-Pilsach. Zürich: Atlantis Verlag, 1952.

Meissner, Otto. *Staatssekretär unter Ebert-Hindenburg-Hitler*. Hamburg: Hoffmann und Campe Verlag, 1950.

Messe, Giovanni. *Der Krieg im Osten*. Zürich: Thomas Verlag, 1948.

Noël, Léon. *L'agression allemande contre la Pologne*. Paris: Flammarion, 1946.

Papen, Franz von. *Der Wahrheit eine Gasse*. Munich: Paul List, 1952.

Rahn, Rudolf. *Ruheloses Leben*. Düsseldorf: Diederichs Verlag, 1949.

Rosenberg, Alfred. *Portrait eines Menschheitsverbrechers*. Edited by Serge Lang and Ernst von Schenck. St. Gallen: Verlag Zollikofer and Co., 1947.

Schacht, Hjalmar. *Abrechnung mit Hitler*. Hamburg: Rowohlt Verlag, 1948.

Schlabrendorff, Fabian von. *They Almost Killed Hitler*. Edited by Gero v. S. Gaevernitz. New York: The Macmillan Company, 1947.

Schmidt, Paul. *Statist auf diplomatischer Bühne, 1923-1945*. Bonn: Athenäum-Verlag, 1950.

Teske, Hermann. *Die silbernen Spiegel, Generalstabsdienst unter der Lupe*. Heidelberg: Kurt Vowinckel, 1952.

Thomas, Georg. "Gedanken und Ereignisse," *Schweizer Monatshefte*, XXV (December, 1945), 537-58.

Weizsäcker, Ernst von. *Erinnerungen*. Munich: Paul List Verlag, 1950.

Welles, Sumner. *The Time for Decision*. New York: Harper and Brothers, Publishers, 1944.

Secondary Sources

Abshagen, Karl Heinz. *Canaris, Patriot und Weltbürger*. Stuttgart: Union Deutsche Verlagsgesellschaft, 1950.

Assmann, Kurt. *Deutsche Schicksalsjahre.* Wiesbaden: Eberhard Brockhaus, 1950.
Becker, Hellmut. "Final Plea for Ernst von Weizsäcker," Nuremberg, 1948. Pp. 58 (mimeographed).
Beloff, Max. *The Foreign Policy of Soviet Russia.* Vol. II. *1936-1941.* Royal Institute of International Affairs. London: Oxford University Press, 1949.
——. "Soviet Foreign Policy, 1929-41: Some notes," *Soviet Studies,* II (1950), 123-37.
Bernstein, Victor H. *Final Judgement, the Story of Nuremberg.* New York: Boni and Gaer, 1947.
Bor, Peter. *Gespräche mit Halder.* Wiesbaden: Limes Verlag, 1950.
Borkenau, Franz. *European Communism.* New York: Harper and Brothers, Publishers, 1953.
Bullock, Alan L. C. *Hitler, A Study in Tyranny.* London: Odhams Press Ltd., 1952
Butler, Ewan, and Young, Gordon. *Marshal without Glory.* London: Hodder and Stoughton, 1953.
Carr, Edward H. *German-Soviet Relations between the two World Wars, 1919-1939* Baltimore: The Johns Hopkins Press, 1951.
——. "From Munich to Moscow," *Soviet Studies,* I (1949), 3-17, 93-105.
Colvin, Ian G. *Master Spy, the Incredible Story of Admiral Wilhelm Canaris.* New York: McGraw-Hill Book Company, Inc., 1951.
Craig, Gordon A. "High Tide of Appeasement: The Road to Munich, 1937-1938," *Political Science Quarterly,* LXVI (1950), 20-37.
Craig, Gordon A., and Gilbert, Felix (eds.). *The Diplomats, 1919-1939.* Princeton, New Jersey: Princeton University Press, 1953.
Dallin, Alexander. "The Month of Decision: German-Soviet Diplomacy, July 22-August 22, 1939," *Journal of Central European Affairs,* IX (1949), 1-31.
Dallin, David J. *Soviet Russia's Foreign Policy, 1939-1942.* Translated by Leon Dennen. New Haven: Yale University Press, 1942.
Dirksen, Herbert von. "Englisch-Deutsche Verhandlungen, Sommer 1939," *Die Neue Woche,* 27 September 1948, p. 5.
Dulles, Allen W. *Germany's Underground.* New York: The Macmillan Company, 1947.
Elliston, H. B. *Finland Fights.* Boston: Little, Brown and Company, 1940.
Estorick, Eric. *Stafford Cripps: Master Statesman.* New York: The John Day Company, 1949.
Feiling, Keith. *The Life of Neville Chamberlain.* London: Macmillan and Co., Ltd., 1946.
Feis, Herbert *The Road to Pearl Harbor.* Princeton, New Jersey: Princeton University Press, 1950.
Fischer, George. *Soviet Opposition to Stalin.* Cambridge: Harvard University Press, 1952.
Görlitz, Walter. *Der deutsche Generalstab.* Frankfurt am Main: Verlag der Frankfurter Hefte, 1950.
Grosse, Franz. "Die Bedeutung des deutsch-russischen Wirtschaftsabkommens," *Hamburger Monatshefte für Auswärtige Politik,* VI (November, 1939), 964-67.
Halder, Franz. *Hitler als Feldherr.* Munich: Münchener Dom-Verlag, 1949.
Harrison, Ernest John. *Lithuania's Fight for Freedom.* New York: The Lithuanian American Information Center, 1945.
Harrison, Gordon A. *United States Army in World War II, The European Theater of Operations: Cross-Channel Attack.* United States, Department of the Army, Office of Chief of Military History. Washington: Government Printing Office, 1951.
Hildebrandt, Rainer. *Wir sind die Letzten.* Neuwied, Berlin: Michael Verlag, [1949(?)].
Hinsley, Francis H. *Hitler's Strategy.* Cambridge: University Press, 1951.
Howard, Harry N. "Germany, the Soviet Union, and Turkey during World War II," *The Department of State Bulletin,* XIX (1948), 63-78.

Hubatsch, Walther. *Die deutsche Besetzung von Dänemark und Norwegen, 1940.* "Göttinger Beiträge für Gegenwartsfragen," Band 5. Göttingen: Musterschmidt, 1952.

Jackson, Robert H. *The Nürnberg Case.* New York: Alfred A. Knopf, 1947.

Jędrzejewicz, Wacław (ed.). *Poland in the British Parliament, 1939-1945.* Vol. I. *British Guarantees to Poland to the Atlantic Charter.* New York: Josef Pilsudski Institute of America for Research in the Modern History of Poland, 1946.

Keenan, Joseph B., and Brown, Brendon F. *Crimes against International Law.* Washington: Public Affairs Press, 1950.

Kohn, Isabelle. "British Diplomacy with Regard to the German-Polish Borderlands at Crucial Periods in the Era 1919-1939." Unpublished Master's Thesis, Department of International Relations, University of Chicago, 1948.

Kordt, Erich. *Wahn und Wirklichkeit.* 2d ed. revised. Stuttgart: Union Deutsche Verlagsgesellschaft, 1948.

Kosack, Hans-Peter. *Wörterverzeichnis für russische Karten.* Berlin: Verlag des Reichsamts für Landesaufnahme, 1943.

Krupinski, Kurt. *Die Komintern seit Kriegsausbruch.* Die Bücherei des Ostraumes. Berlin: Verlagsanstalt Otto Stollberg, [1941].

Langer, William L., and Gleason, S. Everett. *The Challenge to Isolation, 1937-1940.* Council on Foreign Relations. New York: Harper and Brothers, Publishers, 1952.

Lenczowski, George. *Russia and the West in Iran, 1918-1948.* Ithaca: Cornell University Press, 1949.

Leningrad, Geografo-ekonomicheskii nauchno-issledovatel'skii institut, Murmanskii filial [Economic-geography scientific research institute, Murmansk branch]. *Ekonomicheskii atlas Murmanskogo okrugay Leningradskoi oblasti* [Economic atlas of the okrug of Murmansk in Leningrad oblast]. Leningrad, 1935.

Liddell-Hart, B. H. *The German Generals Talk.* New York: William Morrow and Company, 1948.

Mansergh, Nicholas. *Survey of British Commonwealth Affairs, Problems of External Policy, 1931-1939.* Royal Institute of International Affairs. London: Oxford University Press, 1952.

McCallum, Ronald B. *England and France, 1939-1943.* London: Hamish Hamilton, 1944.

Makarov, Alexander N. "Die Eingliederung Bessarabiens und der Nordbukowina in die Sowjet-Union," *Zeitschrift für ausländisches öffentliches Recht und Völkerrecht,* X (October, 1940), 336-59.

——. "Der sowjetrussisch-finnische Konflikt," *Zeitschrift für ausländisches öffentliches Recht und Völkerrecht,* X (October, 1940), 294-336.

Martienssen, Anthony. *Hitler and his Admirals.* London: Secker and Warburg, 1948.

Mendelssohn, Peter de. *Design for Aggression.* New York: Harper and Brothers, Publishers, 1946.

Mlinarić, Bruno (pseud.). *Tito, der rote Rebell.* Translated by J. Edler. Zürich: Thomas-Verlag, 1948.

Morison, Samuel E. *History of United States Naval Operations in World War II.* Vol. III. *The Rising Sun in the Pacific, 1931—April, 1942.* Boston: Little, Brown and Company, 1950.

Moore, Harriet L. *Soviet Far Eastern Policy, 1931-1945.* Princeton, New Jersey: Princeton University Press, 1945.

Namier, Lewis B. *Diplomatic Prelude, 1938-1939.* New York: The Macmillan Company, 1948.

——. *Europe in Decay.* London: Macmillan and Co., Ltd., 1950.

——. *In the Nazi Era.* London: Macmillan and Co., Ltd., 1952.

Poland, Information Department. *Germano-Soviet Collusion against Poland and Europe.* Paris, Angers, 1940.

Poole, DeWitt C. "Light on Nazi Foreign Policy," *Foreign Affairs,* XXX (October, 1946), 130-54.

Pope, Arthur Upham. *Maxim Litvinoff.* New York: L. B. Fischer, 1943.

Potemkin, Vladimir P. (ed.). *Histoire de la Diplomatie.* Vol. III. *1919-1939.* Translated by I. Levin, J. Tarr, and B. Metzel. Paris: Librairie de Médicis, 1946.

Potemkin, Vladimir P. *Politika umirotvorenia agressorov i borba Sovetskogo Soyuza za mir* [The Appeasement Policy and the Struggle of the Soviet Union for Peace]. Moscow, 1946.

Pritt, D. N. *The State Department and the Cold War.* New York: International Publishers, 1948.

Rees, J. R. (ed.). *The Case of Rudolf Hess.* New York: W. W. Norton and Company, Inc., 1948.

Procopé, Hjalmar J. *Sowjetjustiz über Finnland.* Zürich: Thomas-Verlag, 1947.

Rein, Adolf. "England, Polen und Russland," *Hamburger Monatshefte für Auswärtige Politik,* VI (November, 1939), 959-63.

Rossi, Angelo (pseud. of Tasca, Angelo) (ed.). *Les Cahiers du Bolchevisme pendant la campagne 1939-1940.* Paris: Dominique Wapler, 1951.

Rossi, Angelo. *Les communistes français pendant la drôle de guerre; une page d'histoire.* Paris: Iles d'or, 1951.

——. *Deux ans d'alliance germano-soviétique, août 1939-juin 1941.* Paris: Librairie Arthème Fayard, 1949.

——. *Physiologie du parti communiste français.* Paris: Editions Self, 1948.

Rothfels, Hans. *The German Opposition to Hitler.* Hillsdale, Illinois: Henry Regnery Co., 1948.

Schlesinger, Rudolf. "Max Beloff, The Foreign Policy of Soviet Russia, Vol. II, 1936-1941," *Soviet Studies,* I (October, 1949), 140-50.

Schuman, Frederick L. *Europe on the Eve.* New York: Alfred A. Knopf, 1939.

——. *Soviet Politics at Home and Abroad.* New York: Alfred A. Knopf, 1946.

Seabury, Paul. "Ribbentrop and the German Foreign Office," *Political Science Quarterly,* LXVI (1951), 532-55.

Seraphim, Hans-Günther. *Die deutsch-russischen Beziehungen, 1939-1941.* Göttinger Beiträge für Gegenwartsfragen, Heft 1. Hamburg: H. H. Nölke Verlag, 1949.

Sokol, Anthony E. "The Cruise of 'Schiff 45'," *United States Naval Institute Proceedings,* LXXVII (1951), 476-89.

Sokolnicki, Michael. *The Turkish Straits.* Beirut: American Press, 1950.

Super, Margaret L. (pseud. of Cardwell, Ann Su). *Poland and Russia: the Last Quarter Century.* New York: Scheed and Ward, 1944.

Taylor, Telford, *Sword and Swastika.* New York: Simon and Schuster, 1952.

Thursfield, H. G. (ed.). *Brassey's Naval Annual, 1939, 1940.* London: William Clowes, 1940, 1941.

Toscano, Mario. *L'Italia e gli accordi tedesco-sovietici dell'agosto 1939.* Florence: G. C. Sansoni, 1952.

——. *Una mancata intesa italo-sovietica nel 1940 e 1941.* Florence: G. C. Sansoni, 1953.

——. *Le origini del patto d'acciaio.* Florence: G. C. Sansoni, 1948.

Trefousse, H. L. *Germany and American Neutrality, 1939-1941.* New York: Bookman Associates, 1951.

Trevor-Roper. H. R. *The Last Days of Hitler.* New York: The Macmillan Company, 1947.

United States, Office of Naval Intelligence. "German Naval Air, 1933 to 1945. A Report Based on German Naval Staff Documents," 15 January 1947. Washington, 37pp. (mimeographed).

United States, Office of Strategic Services, Research and Analysis Branch, Far Eastern

Division. "German-Japanese Blockade-Running," 25 July 1942. Washington, 10 pp. (typescript).

Umiastowski, R. *Russia and the Polish Republic, 1918-1941*. London: Aquafondata, 1945.

Watson, Mark S. *United States Army in World War II, The War Department*. Vol. I. *Chief of Staff: Prewar Plans and Preparations*. United States, Department of the Army, Office of Chief of Military History. Washington: Government Printing Office, 1950.

Weinberg, Gerhard L. "The Chapter on Russo-German Relations in Volume IV of *Documents on German Foreign Policy, 1918-1945," Journal of Central European Affairs*, XII (1952), 70-74.

——. "Der Deutsche Entschluss zum Angriff auf die Sowjet-Union," *Vierteljahrshefte für Zeitgeschichte*, I (1953), 301-18.

——. "Research Problems in German-Russian Relations, 1939-1941." Unpublished Master's Thesis, Department of History, University of Chicago, 1949.

Wheeler-Bennet, John W. *The Nemesis of Power, The German Army in Politics, 1918-1945*. London: Macmillan and Co., Ltd., 1953.

Willoughby, Charles A. *Shanghai Conspiracy, the Sorge Spy Ring*. New York: E. P. Dutton and Company, Inc., 1952.

Wilmot, Chester. *The Struggle for Europe*. New York: Harper and Brothers Publishers, 1952.

Wiskemann, Elizabeth. *The Rome-Berlin Axis*. New York: Oxford University Press, 1949.

Wuorinen, John H. (ed.) *Finland and World War II, 1939-1944*. New York: The Ronald Press Company, 1948.

ABBREVIATIONS AND TECHNICAL TERMS

A.A.: Auswärtiges Amt — the German Foreign Ministry.

Abt.: Abteilung — major division of a German government agency.

A.G.: Aktiengesellschaft — a corporation.

Ag. Ausl.: Amtsgruppe Ausland — section of the OKW concerned with Germany's relations with other governments.

A.G.K.: Ausfuhrgemeinschaft für Kriegsgerät — a representative committee of German industry concerned with the export of arms, under the control of the Reichsgruppe Industrie.

AK: Armeekorps — Army Corps.

AOK: Armeeoberkommando — headquarters of an army.

A.P.A.: Aussenpolitisches Amt — foreign policy office of the Nazi Party, headed by Rosenberg.

Att.Abt.: Attaché Abteilung — the section of the General Staff of the German Army which directed the work of German military attachés and received their reports.

Ausl/Abw.: Ausland Abwehr — the Intelligence and Counterintelligence Department in the OKW.

Büro RAM: Büro Reichsaussenminister — the official office of the German Foreign Minister.

C - . . .: The initial of one of the Nuremberg trials document series.

Dienststelle Rosenberg: Office established to prepare the civilian administration of the occupied U.S.S.R., later became the Reich Ministry for the Occupied Eastern Territories.

Gen.Kdos.: General Kommandos — headquarters of army corps.

Gen.St.d.H.: Generalstab des Heeres — the General Staff of the German Army.

H.Gr.: Heeresgruppe — an army group.

H.Gr.K.: Heeresgruppenkommando — headquarters of an army group.

L: Landesverteidigung — the National Defense Department, the most important section of the Operations Staff (WFSt) of the OKW.

Lw.Fü.St.: Luftwaffenführungsstab — the Operations Staff of the German Air Force.

NG - . . .: The initial of one of the Nuremberg trials document series.

NI - . . . (also NIK - and NID -): The initial of one of the Nuremberg trials document series.

NOKW - . . .: The initial of one of the Nuremberg trials document series.

Ob.d.H.: Oberbefehlshaber des Heeres — Commander in Chief of the German Army.

Ob.d.L.: Oberbefehlshaber der Luftwaffe — Commander in Chief of the German Air Force.

Ob.d.M.: Oberbefehlshaber der Marine — Commander in Chief of the German Navy.

Oberster Befehlshaber der Wehrmacht: Supreme Commander of the German Armed Forces.

OCCPAC: Office of Chief of Counsel for the Prosecution of Axis Criminality — the office which conducted the American part of the main trial at Nuremberg.

OCCWC: Office of Chief of Counsel for War Crimes — the office which conducted the twelve subsequent proceedings at Nuremberg.

OKH: Oberkommando des Heeres — High Command of the German Army.

OKM: Oberkommando der Marine — High Command of the German Navy.

OKW: Oberkommando der Wehrmacht — Higt Command of the German Armed Forces, Hitler's military staff as Supreme Commander of the Armed Forces.

Op.Abt.: Operationsabteilung — the Operations Section of the General Staff of the German Army, corresponds to the American G-3.

PB - . . .: The initial of the Publication Board reports on captured German documents released by the Office of Technical Services of the U.S. Department of Commerce. The originals are now in the Library of Congress and are serviced by the Newspaper Division.

Pol I M: The designation for the department of the Political Section of the German Foreign Ministry dealing with military affairs.

PS - . . .: The initial of one of the Nuremberg trials document series.

Pz.Gr.: Panzer Gruppe — a German panzer army.

R - . . .: The initial of one of the Nuremberg trials document series.

R.d.L.: Reichsminister der Luftfahrt — Reich Minister of Aviation.

Reichsgruppe Industrie: One of the major corporate organizations of economic enterprises in the Third Reich.

SEA: Staff Evidence Analysis — a legal form used in processing documents at the Nuremberg trials, gives some indication of the source and contents of the document.

Skl: Seekriegsleitung — naval war staff or operations staff of the German Navy.

St.S.: Staatssekretär — the file mark of State Secretary Weizsäcker of the German Foreign Ministry.

USSR - . . .: The initial of one of the Nuremberg trials document series.

WFA: Wehrmachtführungsamt — the operations staff of the OKW, name changed to Wehrmachtführungsstab on 8 August 1940.

WFSt: Wehrmachtführungsstab — the operations staff of the OKW, called Wehrmachtführungsamt before 8 August 1940.

Wi Rü Amt: Wehrwirtschaft- und Rüstungsamt — the War Economy and Armaments Office of the OKW.

z.b.V.: zur besonderen Verwendung — for special assignments.

z.Hd.: zur Hand — to the attention of.

For the military documents:

Ia: the operations officer of a German unit, approximately equivalent to the American G - 3.

Ic: the intelligence officer of a German military unit, approximately equivalent to the American G - 2.

File numbers: In general, German military commands number their documents consecutively and then add the last two figures of the year and an abbreviation for the classification, e.g., 621/41g. would be secret order number 621 issued in 1941.

INDEX

The identifications apply to the period referred to in the book. Diplomatic and other officials who appear as authors or recipients of documents cited or whose testimony is referred to in notes are merely identified; page references are given only for names which appear in the text and in textual material contained in the notes.

Alfieri, Dino, Italian Ambassador to Germany

Altenburg, Günther, Chief of Division IVb of the Political Section of the German Foreign Ministery

Altmark incident, 92

Anti-Comintern Pact, 11, 22, 51

Antonescu, Ion, Dictator of Rumania

Assmann, Kurt, Historical Officer of the German Navy

Astakhov, Georgei, Counselor of Embassy and Chargé d'Affaires of the Soviet Union in Germany, 23, 26, 27, 28, 30f., 33, 34f., 38, 39, 40, 169, 170

Attolico, Bernardo, Italian Ambassador to Germany, 30f., 96n

Aufbau Ost order, 112, 119, 124, 178f.

Babarin, Eugene, Deputy Soviet Trade Representative in Berlin, 37, 38, 43, 68

Batilc States: and Germany, 71; and the U.S.S.R., 16, 48, 85f., 99; *see also* Estonia, Latvia, Lithuania, Mariampol, and Memel

Barbarossa plan *see* Germany: plan to attack the U.S.S.R.

Basis Nord, German naval base in the Soviet Union, 79ff.

Baumbach, N. von, German Naval Attaché in the Soviet Union, 159

Beaverbrook, Lord, British Minister of Aircraft Production, 117

Beck, Józef, Foreign Minister of Poland, 5n, 10, 18f.

Belgium, 162

Belorussians in German-occupied Poland, 59

Bentivegni, Franz von, Head of Department III of the Intelligence and Counterintelligence Department of the High Command of the German Armed Forces (OKW, Ausl./Abw.)

Bessarabia, 48, 99-103

Biddle, Anthony J. Drexel, United States Minister to Poland

Bismarck, German warship, 76

Blank, Margarete, Ribbentrop's Secretary

Blücher, Wipert von, German Minister to Finland, 87

Bock, Fedor von, Commander in Chief of the German Army Group B, 126

Bodenschatz, Karl Heinrich, Hitler's air force adjutant, close friend of Göring, 25

Bohemia and Moravia, Protectorate of, 70

Bohle, Ernst Wilhelm, Head of the Foreign Section of the Nazi Party

Bonnet, Georges, Foreign Minister of France, 4, 6

Boris, King of Bulgaria, 17

Boryslaw-Drohobyyzc oil area in Poland, 56, 57, 60, 70, 144n

Bräutigam, Otto, German Foreign Ministry official detailed to work in the Ministery for the Occupied Eastern Territories

Brammer, Karl August, owner of a news service in Germany

Brauchitsch, Walter von, Commander in Chief of the German Army, 109, 111, 112, 113, 116n, 127

Braun von Stumm, Gustav, Deputy Chief of the Press Section of the German Foreign Ministry

Bremen, German liner, 78f

Bruckmann, Heinrich, German Military Attaché in Bulgaria

Bucharest Conference, *see* Danube

Bürkner, Leopold, Head of the Section *Ausland* in the High Command of the German Armed Forces (OKW, Ag.-Ausl.), 154

Bukovina, 101, 102, 103, 104, 117, 128, 130, 143

Bulgaria, 17, 34, 99f, 131, 139, 143, 144, 145, 147, 151-155

Buschenhagen, Erich, Chief of Staff of the German army in Norway

Byrnes, James F., Secretary of State of the United States, 139

Cadogan, Sir Alexander, British Permanent Under Secretary of State for Foreign Affairs

Canaris, Wilhelm, Chief of the Intelligence and Counterintelligence Department of the High Command of the German Armed Forces

Carpatho-Ukraine, 4, 8

Chamberlain, Neville, Prime Minister of Great Britain, 4f., 15, 19, 27, 46, 63

Chicherin, George V., People's Commissar for Foreign Affairs of the U.S.S.R., 24

Chilston, Lord A. Aken-Douglas, British Ambassador to the Soviet Union

Churchill, Winston, Prime Minister of Great Britain, 49, 117, 123, 139

Ciano, Galeazzo, Italian Minister of Foreign Affairs, 25, 29, 30, 36, 40n, 92, 93, 94, 95, 96, 102, 104, 105

City of Flint, American ship, 79

Communist parties outside the U.S.S.R., 65

Coulondre, Robert, French Ambassador to the Soviet Union, 1936-November, 1938: French Ambassador to Germany, November, 1938-September, 1939, 42

Crete, 163, 180-182

Cripps, Sir Stafford, British Ambassador to the Soviet Union, 116, 163

Curzon Line, 59, 62

Cvetković, Dragisa, Prime Minister of Yugoslavia, 154

Czechoslovakia: and Germany, 5, 6, 13, 44; proposed guarantee of, 4

Daily Mail, London newspaper, 10n

Daladier, Edouard, Prime Minister of France, 4

Danube River and Danube Conference, 122-134, 141

Danzig, 39, 44

Davies, Joseph E., United States Minister to Belgium

Dekanozov, Vladimir G., Deputy People's Commissar for Foreign Affairs of the U.S.S.R., Soviet Ambassador to Germany, 152, 153, 164n, 167

Denmark, 97

Dienststelle Ribbentrop, special office for foreign affairs of Ribbentrop, 22

Dirksen, Herbert von, German Ambassador to Great Britain

Dobrudja, 99

Dönitz, Karl, Commander of the German submarine fleet, 80

Draganov, Parvan, Bulgarian Minister to Germany, 34f.

Erdmannsdorff, Otto von, German Minister to Hungary

Erkko, Eljas, Foreign Minister of Finland, 87

Estonia: and Germany, 48; and the U.S.S.R., 48, 99; see also Baltic States

Etzdorf, Hasso von, Liaison official of the German Foreign Ministry to the High Command of the Army, 121

European Commission, see Danube

Fabricius, Wilhelm, German Minister to Rumania

Falkenstein, von, First Air Force Officer in the National Defense Section of the High Command of the German Armed Forces (OKW, WFSt, L)

Far East, transit of good to Germany from, 66, 70, 72 ff., 83, 93, 151, 156, 161

Fath, Hildegard, Secretary of Rudolf Hess

Finland: and Germany, 48, 126-28, 140-144, 149f.; and Italy, 91-93; and the U.S.S.R., 16, 48, 98, 126-128, 162; Russo-Finnish War, 1939-1940, 84, 85-90, 91-93; Russo-Finnish War, 1941-1944, 110n, 126-128, 139, 149f., 170

Forster, Albert, Gauleiter of Danzig, 44

France: foreign polity, 4, 62; and Poland, 14; and Rumania, 90; and the Russo-Finnish War, 1939-1940, 89; and the U.S.S.R., 31

Frank, Hans, Generalgouverneur of the Generalgouvernement (the part of Poland occupied but not annexed by Germany in 1939)

Gafencu, Grigore, Foreign Minister of Rumania, Rumanian Minister to the Soviet Union, 17

Gallagher, William, Communist member of Parliament, 19, 63

Gaus, Friedrich, Head of the Legal Section of the German Foreign Ministry, 22n, 30, 31

Germany: attack on the U.S.S.R., 110ff., 125f., 137-39, 148-50, 155, 158, 163, 164, 165, 171, 176-82; distribution of forces, 98f., 108, 109, 119, 176-79; opposition to the Nazi regime, 25n, 40n, 42, 64n, 123f., 156, 164n; planned invasion of England, 106ff., 171; planned reduction of armed forces, 104, 107, 118; press, 9n, 13, 23, 24, 147, 163; and the Russo-Finnish War, 1939-1940, 84, 85ff., 170, 174f.,; and the Baltic States, 47, 78; and Bulgaria, 151-53; and Czechoslovakia, 5, 13, 44; and Estonia, 47; and Finland, 47, 120, 126-28, 140, 142-44, 149f., 171, 172; and Great Britian, 5, 14, 23, 37f., 45f., 49f., 122f.; and Greece, 137, 140, 151-53, 157; and Hungary, 98, 116, 120, 166; and Italy, 6, 22, 88, 91-95, 97, 121, 135, 145; and Japan, 6, 22, 29, 51, 72, 73, 84, 135, 142 *see also* Matsuoka; and Latvia, 47; and Lithuania, 47, 121; and Norway, 78, 79, 80, 97; and Poland, 6, 10, 14, 21, 23, 25n, 27ff., 43, 44, 47f., 50, 58, 59; and Rumania, 98, 100n, 101ff., 116, 119, 121, 128-34, 149f., 153, 171, 172; and Spain, 22, 87, 137; and Turkey, 60, 151; and the U.S.S.R.,[1] economic, 8ff., 25ff., 33ff., 39n, 43f., 50f., 59f., 65-75, 76, 84f., 91, 93, 120, 145-47, 150f., 161, 165, 167, 170; and the U.S.S.R., military, 53-58; and the U.S.S.R., naval, 65, 75-85, 174f.; and Yugoslavia 154, 155, 157, 158

Gerstenberg, Alfred, Chief of the German Air Force Mission to Rumania

Goerdeler, Carl Friedrich, Civilain leader of the German opposition to Hitler, 25n

Göring, Hermann, Commander in Chief of the German Air Force; Delegate for the Four Year Plan; Chairman

of the Council of Ministers for National Defense, 25, 71n, 72, 120, 126n, 127, 142n, 146, 151, 158

Gorelkin, Nikolai, Soviet Ambassador to Italy, 91, 95

Great Britain: foreign policy, general, 4-5; and German-Soviet relations, 11f., 25n, 63; plans for the conduct of the war, 117, 147, 154; and the Russo-Finnish War, 1939-1940, 89; and Germany, 11, 14, 23, 37f., 45f., 49f., 63f.; and Japan, 72; and Poland, 5n, 14f., 41f., 45f., 49f.; and Rumania, 90, 110; and Turkey, 61; and the U.S.S.R., 14f., 19f., 27, 28, 31f., 41f., 49f., 84f., 89, 90, 100, 110-18, 132f., 156f.

Greece, 132, 137, 140, 147, 151-53, 157, 162

Greiffenberg, Hans von, Chief of the Operations Section of the High Command of the German Army, 111f.

Greiner, Helmuth, an officer who kept the war diary of the National Defense Section in the High Command of the German Armed Forces (OKW, WFSt, L), 113n

Grew, Joseph C., United States Ambassador to Japan

Grolman, Helmuth von, an officer in the Operations Section of the High Command of the German Army

Grosskopf, W., official of the German Foreign Ministry who worked with the office which later became the Ministry for the Occupied Eastern Territories

Grzybowski, Waclaw, Polish Ambassador to the Soviet Union

Halder, Franz, Chief of Staff of the German Army, 106, 108, 109, 111, 113, 114, 121, 126n, 127, 138, 139

Halifax, Viscount Edward, British Secretary of State for Foreign Affairs, 4f., 15, 20

Hamilton, Duke of, British peer, 122f.

Hassell, Ulrich von, former German Ambassador to Italy, member of the opposition, 96n

Haushofer, Albrecht, advisor of Rudolf Hess, 122f.

Hedler, an officer in the War Economy

---

[1] General political relations between Germany and the U.S.S.R. have not been indexed.

and Armaments Office in the High Command of the German Armed Forces (OKW, Wi Rü Amt)

Heeren, Viktor von, German Minister to Yugoslavia

Helfand, Leon, Soviet Chargé d'Affaires in Italy, 93, 94, 95

Hencke, Andor, German Chargé d'Affaires in Czechoslovakia

Henderson, Sir Nevile, British Ambassador to Germany, 42, 46

Hess, Alfred, deputy of Bohle, brother of Rudolf Hess

Hess, Rudolf, Hitler's Deputy as head of the Nazi Party, 116, 122f., 142n

Hewel, Walter, Representative of Ribbentrop on Hitler's staff

Hilger, Gustav, Counselor of Embassy in the German Embassy in Moscow, 25n, 29, 31, 33f., 36, 68, 141

Himmler, Heinrich, Head of the German Police

Hiranuma, Baron Kiichiro, Prime Minister of Japan, 51

Hitler, Adolf, dictator of Germany, 5, 11, 21, 23, 24, 27, 31, 36, 38, 39n, 40n, 45-49, 52, 63, 69, 71, 79-81, 83, 88, 92f., 98, 101, 104-07, 109-114, 116-21, 122f., 127-29, 137-40, 142-44, 147, 149, 151, 155, 158f., 162-65, 167, 171-172, 174

Hoare, Sir Reginald, British Minister to Hungary

Hoelter, Hermann, German general on the Finnish part of the Eastern front

Holland, 5

Horthy, Nikolaus von, Regent of Hungary

Hossbach, Friedrich, military adjutant of Hitler

Hudson, Robert S., British Secretary of the Department of Overseas Trade, 37f.

Huenermann, Rudolf, Chief of Staff of the War Economy and Armaments Office of the High Command of the German Armed Forces

Hull, Cordell, Secretary of State of the United States

Hungary: Tripartite Pact, 141; and Czechoslovakia, 4; and Germany, 11n, 98, 116, 166; and the U.S.S.R., 11n, 155n, 166; and Yugoslavia, 155n

Indo-China, French, 73n

International Commission, see Danube

Iran, 74

Iraq, 59

Italy: and the Russo-Finnish War, 1939-1940, 87, 90-92; and Finland, 90-92; and Germany, 6, 22, 51, 87, 90-94, 118, 128, 129, 132, 139, 142; and Great Britain, 4f.; and Greece, 129, 144; and Japan 6, 22, 132; and Rumania, 98, 100, 101, 128f.; and the U.S.S.R., 39n, 90-94, 96, 118, 141, 142

Jan Wellem, German supply ship, 80, 81n

Japan: and Germany, 6, 22, 29, 51, 71, 72, 83, 132, see also Matsuoka; and Great Britain, 22, 71; and Italy, 6, 22, 132; and the U.S.S.R., 30, 54, 140

Jodl, Alfred, Chief of the Operations Staff of the High Command of the German Armed Forces (OKW, WFSt), 55, 104, 110, 116n, 155

Junge, Wolfgang, First Naval Officer in the National Defense Section of the High Command of the German Armed Forces

Kamphoevener, von, Chief of Division I of the Political Section of the German Foreign Ministry

Kandelaki, Soviet Trade Delegate to Germany, 8

Keitel, Wilhelm, Chief of the High Command of the German Armed Forces, 21, 55, 67, 87, 104, 106, 110, 116, 148

Kennard, Sir Howard, British Ambassador to Poland

Kennedy, Joseph P., United States Ambassador to the United Kingdom

Keppler, Wilhelm, State Secretary for Special Assignments in the German Foreign Ministry

Kessel, Albrecht von, an official in the Political Section of the German Foreign Ministry

Killinger, Manfred von, German Minister to Rumania

Kinzel, Eberhard, Chief of the Eastern Intelligence Department of Command of the German Army (OKH, GenStdH, FHO), 109

Kirk, Alexander, United States Chargé d'Affaires in the Soviet Union

Kirkpatrick, Ivone, British Foreign Office official
Kitchman, German Military Attaché in Finland
Kleist, Bruno Peter, official for Eastern affairs in the *Dienststelle Ribbentrop,* 22f.
Knatchbull-Hugessen, Sir Hugh, British Ambassador to Turkey, 17n
Komet, see Schiff 45
Köstring, Ernst, German Military Attaché in the Soviet Union, 56, 57
Kordt, Erich, Chief of the Bureau of the German Foreign Minister (Büro RAM), 9, 27, 40n
Kramarz, Hans, Chief of the Department of the Political Section of the German Ministry dealing with military matters (Pol I M)
Krutikov, Aleksei D., First Deputy People's Commissar for Foreign Trade of the U.S.S.R., 161
Küchler, Georg von, Commander in Chief of the German Eighteenth Army, 108, 126

Lammers, Hans-Heinrich, Reich Minister and Chief of the Reich Chancellery
Latvia: and Germany, 47; and the U.S.S.R., 47, 99
League of Nations, 19, 20
Leeb, Wilhelm von, Commander in Chief of the German Army Group C, 98, 167
Leitgen, Alfred, Adjutant of Rudolf Hess
Likus, Rudolf, official in the German Foreign Ministry
Lipski, Jósef, Polish Ambassador to Germany
Lithuania: and Germany, 47, 58, 59, 99, 121; and the U.S.S.R., 47, 58, 59f., 99, 121; *see also* Mariampol
Little Entente, 4, 17
Litvinov, Maksim, People's Commissar for Foreign Affairs of the U.S.S.R., 6f., 18, 20, 23, 24, 25, 93
Loraine, Sir Percy, British Ambassador to Italy
Lossberg, Bernhard von, First Army Officer in the National Defense Section of the High Command of the German Armed Forces

Ludin, Hans, German Minister to Slovakia
Luetzow, German cruiser, 76-78

Mackensen, Hans-Georg von, German Ambassador to Italy, 30n, 94f., 102
Madagascar, 73n
Magistrati, Count Massimo, Counsellor of Embassy in the Italian Embassy in Berlin
Maisky, Ivan, Soviet Ambassador to Great Britain, 15, 20
Manchuria, 72, *see also* Far East
Mannerheim, Carl Gustav, Finnish Field Marshal, 124
Mannerheim Line, 90
Marcks, Werner, Chief of Staff of the German Eighteenth Army, 108, 112
Mariampol, 59, 121, 147
Martius, George, Head of the Transportation Department (W XII) of the Economic Policy Section of the German Foreign Ministry
Matsuoka, Yosuke, Foreign Minister of Japan, 151, 156-57, 159f.
Mellenthin, Horst von, Chief of the Attaché Section of the General Staff of the German Army
Memel, 99, 121
Merekalov, Aleksei, Soviet Ambassador to Germany, 10, 23, 25, 29
Meyer-Heydenhagen, Maximilian, official of the Political Section of the German Foreign Ministry
Middle East, transit of good to Germany, 65, 69, 72ff.
Mikoyan, Anastas, People's Commissar for Foreign Trade of the U.S.S.R.; Deputy Chairman of the Council of People's Commissars, 11, 33f., 36, 68, 69n
Molotov, Vyacheslav M., People's Commissar for Foreign Affairs of the U.S.S.R.; Chairman of the Council of People's Commissars, 1, 7, 18, 20n, 24, 26-28, 30-33, 35f., 38-43, 48, 52f., 55-57, 59-62, 63n, 64, 66, 80n, 87, 89, 94-97, 100n, 101f., 110n, 128, 130, 133, 135-45, 152f., 162, 167, 169, 172
Moltke, Hans Adolf von, German Ambassador to Poland, 58
Moraht, official in the Economic Policy Section of the German Foreign Ministry

Müller, Vinzenz, officer on the staff of the German Army Group C
Munich agreement, 4-7, 15
Murmansk, 78, 79, 80n, 82
Mussolini, Benito, dictator of Italy, 5, 92-95

Narvik, 81f.
Netherlands, *see* Holland
Noël, Léon, French Ambassador to Poland
Norem, Owen J. C., United States Minister to Lithuania
Northeast Passage, 82f.
Norway, 78-82, 92, 97, 107, 120, 162
Nuremberg Trials, 1f., 21n, 38n, 47, 100, 158

Ogilvie-Forbes, Sir George, British Chargé d'Affaires in Germany
Oshima, Hiroshi, Japanese Ambassador to Germany, 6, 30, 51
Ott, Eugen, German Ambassador to Japan, 157

Paasikivi, Juho K., Finnish negotiator in the conversations preceding the outbreak of the Russo-Finnish War of 1939-1940, 86
Papen, Franz von, German Ambassador to Turkey
Paulus, Friedrich, First Quartermaster General in the General Staff of the German Army, 126, 137-39
Petsamo, 124, 144n
Phipps, Sir Eric, British Ambassador to France
Pieckenbrock, Hans, Chief of Section I of the Intelligence and Counterintelligence Department of the High Command of the German Armed Forces
Poland: and Czechoslovakia, 4; and Germany, 4, 6, 10, 14f., 18f., 21, 23, 27, 43f., 47-49, 56-59, 62; and Great Britain, 5n, 14f., 45f., 49f.; and Rumania, 17f.; and the U.S.S.R., 7, 16, 18f., 47f., 50, 52-54, 56-59, 170
Potemkin, Vladimir P., Deputy People's Commissar for Foreign Affairs of the U.S.S.R., 16-20, 23f., 26, 30, 36, 47, 60
Prinz Eugen, German cruiser, 76
Puttkamer, Karl Jesko von, Hitler's naval adjutant, 114

Raczynski, Edward, Polish Ambassador to Great Britain, 15
Raeder, Erich, Commander in Chief of the German Navy, 76f., 79-83, 88, 107, 109, 112, 114, 120, 164
Rapallo Treaty, 24
Rashid Ali, Prime Minister of Iraq, 162
Raussendorff, Ernst von, an employee of the Friedrich Krupp A.G.
Rendel, George W., British Minister to Bulgaria
Ribbentrop, Joachim von, Foreign Minister of Germany, 9f., 12f., 22f., 25ff., 35f., 38-49, 53-61, 68, 70, 88f., 92-96, 101f., 104f., 121, 127f., 130, 133, 135f., 140-42, 143n., 144n., 146, 157f., 164, 167
Richthofen, Herbert von, German Minister to Bulgaria
Rintelen, Emil von, official of the German Foreign Ministry
Ristelhueber, René, French Minister to Bulgaria
Ritter, Karl, Ambassador for special Assignments in the German Foreign Ministry, negotiator in economic questions, 66, 68f., 76
Rössing, H., German Military Attaché in Finland, 127
Roosevelt, Franklin D., President of the United States, 156
Rosenberg, Alfred, Head of the Foreign Policy Office of the Nazi Party, Reich Minister for the Occupied Eastern Territories, 185n
Rosso, Augusto, Italian Ambassador to the Soviet Union, 29f., 35f., 92, 95, 101n
Rossoni, Edmondo, Italian Minister of Agriculture and Forestry
Rumania: and the Tripartite Pact, 141; and Bulgaria, 99f., and France, 88, and Germany, 66, 68, 98, 100n, 101ff., 116, 120, 128-33, 149f., 153, 172; and Great Britain, 90, 100; and Italy, 100, 103; and Poland, 17f.; and the U.S.S.R., 16f., 99ff., 128-33, 139, 141f., 149f., 162; *see also* Bessarabia; Bukovina; Dobrudja
Rundstedt, Gerd von, Commander of the German Army Group A, 98

Salmuth, Hans von, Chief of Staff of the German Army Group B

Saracoglu, Sükrü, Foreign Minister of Turkey, 16f., 61, 154

Schacht, Hjalmar, President of the German Reichsbank, 8

Scheidt, Wilhelm, an officer who helped keep the diary of the Operations Staff of the High Command of the German Armed Forces (OKW, WFSt)

Schiff 45, code name of German auxiliary cruiser, 83f.

Schild, Georg, official in charge of the export of war materials at the Krupp firm

Schindel, official of the Press Section of the German Foreign Ministry

Schliep, Martin, Head of the Eastern Department of the Political Section of the German Foreign Ministry

Schlotterer, Gustav, official in the Reich Ministry of Economics, 75n

Schmidt, Paul Otto, chief interpreter of the German Foreign Ministry, 157

Schmieden, Werner von, member of the liaison staff of the German Foreign Ministry to the High Command of the Army

Schmundt, Rudolf, military adjutant of Hitler

Schniewind, Otto, Chief of Staff of the German Naval War Staff (Seekriegsleitung)

Schnurre, Karl, Head of the East European Department of the Economic Policy Section of the German Foreign Ministry, 10f., 23, 26, 34, 37-40, 43, 66, 68, 69n., 70, 146, 161

Schulenburg, Count Friedrich Werner von der, German Ambassador to the Soviet Union, 8n, 9f., 26-30, 34-43, 45, 48, 50, 52f., 54n, 55-57, 68, 82, 89, 94, 97, 101f., 128, 130, 133, 135, 141, 145, 152f., 159, 162-64, 166, 169

Schulte-Möntig, Erich, Chief of Staff of Admiral Raeder

Schwarze Korps, newspaper published by the SS, 23

Schwerin-Krosigk, Count Lutz von, Reich Minister of Finance

Seeds, Sir William, British Ambassador to the Soviet Union

Seydlitz, German cruiser, 76

Shiratori, Toshio, Japanese Ambassador to Italy, 35n

Skvartsev, Aleksander, Soviet Ambassador to Germany, 53

Skoda works, 25

Skossyrev, Deputy Soviet Trade Representative in Berlin, 9

Slovakia, 141

Smuts, Jan Christian, Prime Minister of the Union of South Africa, 117

Sommer, Erich, official of the German Foreign Ministry

Soviet Union, see U.S.S.R.

Spain, 22, 85, 137

Stalin, Joseph V., dictator of the Soviet Union, 1, 7, 12f., 27, 45, 49, 55-57, 59, 63, 65, 69f., 110, 140-42, 162, 169

Steengracht von Moyland, Gustav Adolf, member of the personal staff of the German Foreign Minister

Steinhardt, Lawrence, United States Ambassador to the Soviet Union

Stohrer, Eberhard von, German Ambassador to Spain

Straits question, 143, 152

Strang, Sir William, Assistant Undersecretary of State and Head of the European Department in the British Foreign Office

Sudeten question, 5, 44

Suwalki, 57, 59

Sweden, 81, 87f.

Switzerland, 5

Tass, Soviet official news agency, 32, 87, 99, 152, 162

Teleki, Count Paul, Prime Minister of Hungary, 155n

Teriberka, 80n

Thomas, Georg, Head of the War Economy and Armaments Office in the High Command of the German Armed Forces (OKW, Wi Rü Amt), 68f., 118, 120, 127, 151, 165n, 189n, 190n

Thomsen, Hans, German Chargé d'Affaires in the United States

Tippelskirch, Kurt von, Quartermastergeneral IV in the General Staff of the German Army, 135f.

Todt, Fritz, German Minister for Defense Construction, 165n

Toussaint, Rudolf, German Military Attaché in Czechoslovakia

Transsiberian Railway, 72, 84, 156, 170, see also Far East; Germany, and the U.S.S.R., economic

Transylvania, 129
Tripartite Pact, 135f., 140-43, 145, 151,
   153, 158
Troutbeck, J. M., British Chargé d'Affaires in Czechoslovakia
Turkey: and France, 17, 60; and Germany, 60, 151; and Great Britain, 17,
   60; and the U.S.S.R., 16f., 60, 143,
   154
Twardowski, Fritz von, Deputy Director
   of the Cultural Policy Section of the
   German Foreign Ministry

Ukrainians in German-occupied Poland,
   59
Ukrainian nationalists, 98
U.S.S.R.: foreign policy, general, 6f.,
   12f., 15f., 18, 20, 34, 62, 87, 99f., 144,
   153f., 162f., see also Tass; intelligence
   network, 156n; navy, 76; press, 9n,
   153, see also Tass; Russo-Finnish
   War, 1939-1940, 85-90, 174f.; and the
   Batic States, 16, 47, 84f., 99; and
   Belgium, 162; and Bulgaria, 99f., 143-
   145, 151-54; and Estonia, 47, 99; and
   Finland, 16, 47, 99, 123-25, 139-41,
   162; and Germany, economic, 8ff.,
   25ff., 33ff., 39n, 43f., 50f., 59f., 64-75,
   83f., 90, 92, 120, 145-48, 151, 161, 165,
   169f.; and Germany, military coor-
   dination, 53-58; and Germany, naval,
   65, 75-85, 174f.; and Great Britain,
   14f., 19f., 27f., 31f., 84f., 90f., 109-17,
   132 f., 156; and Greece, 162; and Hungary, 11n, 155n; and Iraq, 162; and
   Italy, 39n, 92-96, 121, 144f.; and Japan, 30, 54, 143; and Latvia, 47, 99;
   and Lithuania, 47, 99, 121; and Norway, 162; and Poland, 7, 16, 18f., 47f.,
   50, 52-54, 56-59, 170; and Rumania,
   16, 99ff., 128-34, 143, 162, see also
   Bessarabia, Bukovina; and Turkey,
   16f., 61, 143, 154; and the United States, 64, 77n., 156; and Yugoslavia,
   154f., 157, 162
United States; general, 110, 115, 119,
   135, 147, 154; and German-Soviet relations, 40n; and the U.S.S.R., 63, 77n,
   156
Uthmann, Bruno von, German Military
   Attaché in Sweden.
Vansittart, Sir Robert, Permanent Secretary of the British Foreign Office, 40n

Veesenmayer, Edmund, special assistant
   to Wilhelm Keppler, 44
Veltjens, Theo, a German Air Force of-
   ficer who worked in the Office of the
   Four Year Plan, 127
Vereker, G., Counsellor in the British
   Embassy in Moscow
Vienna Award, 129f., 140
Vilna, 48
Volksdeutsche, people of German des-
   cent living outside Germany, 59, 103
Voroshilov, Klement, People's Commis-
   sar for Defense of the U.S.S.R., 58
Vyshinsky, Andrei, First Deputy Peo-
   ple's Commissar for Foreign Affairs of
   the U.S.S.R., 133

Wagner, Gerhard, Chief Operations Officer in the German Naval War Staff
Warlimont, Walter, Head of the Natio-
   nal Defense Department in the High
   Command of the German Armed For-
   ces; Deputy Chief of the Operations
   Staff of the High Command of the
   German Armed Forces, 55-57, 104,
   110
Weizsäcker, Ernst von, State Secretary
   in the German Foreign Ministry, 23,
   25, 27-31, 33, 38, 40n, 41f., 44f., 47,
   50f., 68, 86f., 136, 163f., 167, 168
Welles, Sumner, Under Secretary of State
   of the United States, 153
Western Litza Bay, see Basis Nord
Wiehl, Emil K., Head of the Economic
   Policy Section of the German For-
   eign Ministry, 9f., 31n
Wiley, John C., United States Minister
   to Latvia
Woermann, Ernst, Head of the Political
   Section of the German Foreign Ministry, 35
Wolhthat, Helmuth, Ministerial Director
   in the Office of the Four Year Plan,
   37f.

Yrjö-Koskinen, Aarno, Finnish Minister
   to the Soviet Union
Yugoslavia, 154f., 157, 162f.

Zapadnaya Litza Bay, see Basis Nord
Ziemke, Kurt, Representative of the Ger-
   man Foreign Ministry with the Reich
   Protector of Bohemia and Moravia

---

[2] General political relations between the U.S.S.R. and Germany have not been indexed.